Impacts of Artificial Intelligence on Educational Psychology and Cognitive Development

Bahaddin Demirdis
https://orcid.org/0000-0001-5843-5072
Çankırı Karatekin University, Turkey

IGI Global
Scientific Publishing
Publishing Tomorrow's Research Today

Vice President of Editorial Melissa Wagner
Director of Acquisitions Mikaela Felty
Director of Book Development Jocelynn Hessler
Production Manager Mike Brehm
Cover Design Jose Rosado

Published in the United States of America by
IGI Global Scientific Publishing
701 East Chocolate Avenue
Hershey, PA, 17033, USA
Tel: 717-533-8845 | Fax: 717-533-7115
Website: https://www.igi-global.com E-mail: cust@igi-global.com

Library of Congress Cataloging-in-Publication Data

LCCN: 2025038346 (CIP Data Pending)
ISBN13: 979-8-3373-6375-2
Isbn13Softcover: 979-8-3373-6376-9
EISBN13: 979-8-3373-6377-6

British Cataloguing in Publication Data
A Cataloguing in Publication record for this book is available from the British Library.

Table of Contents

Detailed Table of Contents

This chapter critically analyses the impact of artificial intelligence (AI) on contemporary education and considers the transformations imposed by the post-digital era. Starting with the observation that AI is reshaping the how we access, produce, and apply knowledge, the chapter discusses the emergence of smart learning as a new educational paradigm. It explores two main models. The first is the integration of AI into traditional educational systems, which are limited by inherited practices. The second is a transformative vision that proposes a profound restructuring of education. The study adopts an exploratory approach grounded in a narrative review of the literature. The analysis identifies three dimensions — organisational, pedagogical, and ethical — that describe how AI is shaping new learning ecosystems and redefining the teacher's role. The study concludes that AI should not be seen as a substitute, but as a catalyst for pedagogical practices centred on the student, creativity, and critical thinking.

This book chapter examines the growing role of artificial intelligence (AI) in improving mental health services for students and highlights both the opportunities and challenges associated with its use. AI applications are increasingly being integrated into learning and counseling processes, mitigating the limitations of traditional learning and counseling services. Significant benefits such as increased accessibility, faster decision-making, reduced stigma, and personalized psychological interventions are crucial for student mental health. However, each student is unique, and therefore, the symptoms of mental health disorders may vary from student to student. Furthermore, the similarity of symptoms across mental disorders and the lack of standardized measurement tools used in the diagnostic process can negatively impact the diagnostic and therapeutic capabilities of AI. Despite risks, AI holds promise for improving the effectiveness of mental health interventions in education when developed in collaboration with mental health professionals.

This study examines the intergenerational digital divide emerging during AI integration in educational environments and proposes balanced bridging strategies. The research analyzes differences between Generation Z's natural AI affinity and experienced educators' cautious attitudes, grounded in Prensky's digital native-immigrant theory and technology acceptance models. Generation Z's perception of AI as integral to learning processes contrasts sharply with educators' concerns about academic integrity, critical thinking, and pedagogical values, creating classroom tensions around assessment and academic standards. Critiquing polarized AI-maximalist and technology-opposition approaches, this study proposes a hybrid pedagogy model synthesizing traditional and technology-supported methods. The main contribution involves developing innovative strategies including reverse mentoring and intergenerational learning communities that leverage both generations' strengths for mutual learning.

This study aimed to examine how artificial intelligence supports teachers' classroom practices and school leadership practices. Using conceptual literature review approach, the study summarized the literature into three main thema, including "Educational benefits of AI," "School Leadership and AI," and "Using AI for School Leadership: Evidence from Research." Literature has demonstrated the impact of AI in the school environment in two main ways. First, from practical perspective, AI systems organize the time management of school leaders and teachers by doing routine tasks. It also notes that they can use it by providing individualized feedback to students and parents. Second, from theoretical perspective, social cognitive theory explains three dimensions: personal factors, including cognitive processes such as beliefs, skills, and self-efficacy. Behavioral factors refer to the actions that a person performs. Environmental factors include work settings, organizational support, and social norms. In conclusion, AI can support leadership efficiency but raises ethical challenges.

This chapter examines how transformational school leaders engage with artificial intelligence technologies and how teachers make sense of AI and its potential effects. Using a quantitative, cross-sectional design, the study focused on 34,222 public secondary and high school teachers in Şanlıurfa, with 648 selected through non-probability sampling from three central districts reflecting diverse socio-economic contexts. Data were gathered through scales measuring transformational leadership, AI, and sensemaking, with gender, education, and teaching experience as control variables. Ethical approval was obtained, and responses were collected via Google Forms through email and WhatsApp. Analyses with SPSS and Mplus revealed significant associations, showing a strong link between transformational leadership and AI, and AI's mediating role between leadership and sensemaking. Findings suggest that leaders should manage AI's complexities to enhance teachers' sensemaking and awareness. However, the cross-sectional design limits causal inference, and future longitudinal research is recommended

This study aims to present theoretical arguments regarding the potential of artificial intelligence as a supportive resource for teacher psychology. To this end, it constructs a comprehensive theoretical framework demonstrating how AI applications can strengthen key psychological resources crucial for teacher effectiveness and resilience: self-efficacy, optimism, trust, hope, and well-being. The analysis grounds the relationship between AI and each resource within established psychological theories. This theoretical examination concludes that the functions of AI, including reducing administrative burden, offering personalized data and objective feedback, and resource conservation, are posited to support these psychological resources. Consequently, the chapter argues for a paradigm shift in perceiving AI not as a threat but as a strategic partner that empowers teachers, and it offers practical implications for educational policy and school leadership.

This study examined AI literacy as a potential mediator in the relationship between technostress and cognitive load among students in ELT, ELL, and ETI programs in Türkiye. A total of 301 participants completed the AI Literacy Scale, the Technostress Scale, and a single-item Cognitive Load measure. Data were analyzed using descriptive statistics, reliability analysis, Pearson correlations, and mediation analysis via JASP's SEM module. Findings indicated a significant direct effect of technostress on cognitive load, suggesting higher technostress increases cognitive load. AI literacy significantly predicted cognitive load, but it did not mediate the technostress–cognitive load relationship. These results highlight a direct link between technostress and cognitive load and suggest that while AI literacy may influence cognitive load, it does not buffer the effects of technostress. Implications for curriculum design and digital pedagogical practices in language education are discussed.

Generative language models threaten the validity of text-based assessments through AI-enabled plagiarism. This chapter argues that integrity and deep learning can be preserved by replacing static essays with enactment-based performance tasks. Grounded in the enactment effect, ICAP theory and self-regulated learning research, it synthesizes experimental and meta-analytic studies showing that students who build and teach domain-specific chatbots exhibit higher engagement, stronger knowledge transfer and far lower plagiarism than peers writing essays. A quasi-experimental study illustrates how chatbot creation, oral defence and learning-analytics logs provide triangulated evidence of competence that AI cannot forge. The chapter distils design principles—multimodal evidence, synchronous questioning, transparent AI use—that give institutions a scalable blueprint for equitable, performance-oriented evaluation. It closes with a research and policy agenda for an ethically grounded, AI-resilient assessment ecosystem.

Preface

Artificial intelligence (AI) has emerged as one of the most transformative forces in education, reshaping how students think, learn, and engage with knowledge. It offers tools capable of analyzing vast amounts of learning data, adapting instructional content, and supporting personalized learning experiences that address the unique cognitive profiles of individual learners. The integration of AI into educational environments allows teachers and researchers to observe not only how knowledge is acquired but also how motivation, attention, and emotional regulation evolve throughout the learning process. By doing so, AI enables educators to bridge the gap between theory and practice, offering new insights into how cognitive processes unfold within technologically mediated environments. This intersection of technology and psychology positions AI as both a catalyst for innovation and a challenge for traditional conceptions of learning.

At the same time, the rise of AI invites deeper reflection on what it means to educate and to be human in a digital age. The automation of assessment, feedback, and instructional design raises critical philosophical and ethical questions regarding autonomy, empathy, and the role of the teacher. As intelligent systems increasingly support cognitive and affective learning tasks, they simultaneously redefine pedagogical relationships and learning agency. AI-driven environments encourage educators to reconsider foundational concepts such as creativity, curiosity, and critical reasoning within the context of machine-assisted cognition. Consequently, this field demands a balance between embracing technological advancement and safeguarding the humanistic dimensions of education.

Moreover, the psychological impact of AI on learners cannot be underestimated. Exposure to AI-mediated learning platforms influences not only students' performance but also their self-concept, sense of competence, and emotional well-being. Understanding how AI affects motivation, cognitive load, and self-regulation is essential to creating sustainable and equitable learning ecosystems. This book brings together diverse perspectives from educational psychology, cognitive science, and AI research to examine how these forces interact in shaping the future of education.

By situating AI within the framework of human development, it contributes to the ongoing dialogue about the ethical and cognitive implications of intelligent learning technologies.

In today's interconnected world, AI has moved beyond experimentation to become an integral component of educational systems worldwide. Schools and universities across the globe are implementing AI-based tutoring, automated grading, and data-driven decision-making to improve instructional efficiency and learning outcomes. These innovations mirror a global shift toward evidence-based education and adaptive learning models. However, this rapid adoption also reveals deep inequalities between regions, institutions, and generations, underscoring the importance of equitable access to AI tools and digital literacy. Within this context, the educational community must navigate how to leverage AI for inclusion while addressing the potential risks of bias and depersonalization in algorithmic systems.

The relevance of AI in education extends far beyond the classroom. Governments and international organizations now view AI literacy as a fundamental twenty-first-century skill, critical for future employability and civic engagement. As automation reshapes the labor market, education systems face pressure to cultivate cognitive flexibility, emotional intelligence, and lifelong learning capacities. AI not only enables but also necessitates these competencies, requiring students to understand the logic of intelligent systems and their broader social implications. In this regard, educational psychology plays a pivotal role in understanding how learners internalize and respond to technological transformation.

At the same time, AI's influence is not uniform, it manifests differently across cultural, economic, and disciplinary boundaries. Developing nations grapple with infrastructural and pedagogical challenges, while advanced economies face concerns over data privacy, surveillance, and ethical governance. The global conversation about AI in education thus involves both technological optimism and critical caution. This book situates itself at the heart of this conversation, offering empirical and theoretical insights that help reconcile innovation with humanity. By emphasizing the psychological and cognitive dimensions of AI integration, it encourages educators and researchers to move beyond technical efficiency and toward holistic human development.

This book is intended for a broad audience of scholars, practitioners, and policymakers who are committed to understanding and shaping the evolving relationship between artificial intelligence and human learning. Educational psychologists, teachers, school leaders, and instructional designers will find in these chapters frameworks for implementing AI-based solutions that enhance, not replace, pedagogical practice. For researchers, the book offers theoretical perspectives that link AI with established principles of motivation, cognition, and emotional development. Graduate students and academics in education, psychology, and computer science can use the text as a reference for exploring how technological systems interact with human intelligence and creativity.

In addition, this volume provides guidance for policymakers and educational technology developers seeking to build ethical, equitable, and psychologically sound AI systems. It encourages decision-makers to consider not only technological efficiency but also the human consequences of AI adoption. The book underscores that the future of education depends on collaborative efforts between technologists, educators, and psychologists to ensure that intelligent systems serve as partners in learning rather than as substitutes for human insight. Through this interdisciplinary focus, the book appeals to anyone invested in designing the future of education where technology and humanity coexist in harmony.

The Era of Smart Learning explores how artificial intelligence transforms education through adaptive, data-driven, and personalized learning environments. The chapter emphasizes the evolution from traditional pedagogy to AI-powered systems that enhance interactivity, engagement, and learner autonomy. It underscores the psychological and cognitive effects of smart learning, including increased motivation and metacognitive awareness. Ultimately, it defines the foundations of AI-driven education in the twenty-first century.

Artificial Intelligence and Student Mental Health; Risks and Opportunities examines how AI technologies impact students' psychological well-being. The chapter highlights both the benefits, such as early detection of mental health issues, and the risks, including privacy concerns and emotional dependency on AI systems. It presents a balanced discussion on ethical use, human empathy, and digital surveillance. By doing so, it offers insights into building psychologically supportive AI-based learning environments.

AI in Education: Intergenerational Digital Divide and Bridging Strategies investigates how generational differences shape the use and acceptance of AI in educational contexts. The chapter analyzes the digital gap between younger, tech-native learners and more experienced educators. It proposes collaborative mentoring and inclusive training approaches to promote shared digital literacy. Ultimately, it calls for bridging intergenerational divides to ensure equitable and sustainable AI integration in schools.

Artificial Intelligence in School Leadership: Artificial Intelligence focuses on how AI redefines leadership roles within educational institutions. The chapter discusses how school leaders utilize AI for data-driven decision-making, performance monitoring, and strategic innovation. It also examines the challenges of maintaining trust, ethics, and transparency in AI-supported leadership. By integrating human values with intelligent systems, it envisions a model of visionary and ethical digital leadership.

When Teachers Code Change, How AI and Strategic Intelligence Spark a Sensemaking Revolution in Organizations analyzes how teachers interpret and adapt to AI-driven organizational transformation. The chapter connects AI with sensemaking theory, explaining how educators make meaning from technological shifts. It highlights the role of strategic intelligence in fostering adaptability and innovation among teaching staff. This discussion provides a theoretical bridge between leadership, cognition, and digital transformation in schools.

The Impact of Artificial Intelligence on Teacher Psychology, Theoretical Connections to Its Potential Benefits explores the psychological dimensions of AI adoption among teachers. The chapter identifies changes in motivation, job satisfaction, and professional identity resulting from technological integration. It also discusses how AI can reduce cognitive load and enhance creative engagement in educational settings. The findings contribute to understanding how educators psychologically adapt to intelligent technologies.

The Mediating Role of AI Literacy in the Relationship Between Technostress and Cognitive Load in Higher Education investigates how AI literacy serves as a buffer against the negative effects of technostress. The chapter presents empirical findings showing that AI competence reduces cognitive strain and anxiety in academic environments. It underscores the importance of professional development programs focused on digital and AI literacy. This perspective highlights the psychological benefits of technological empowerment in higher education.

Beyond the Written Word: Chatbot-Enabled, Competency-Based Assessment Redesign examines how AI-driven chatbots revolutionize assessment practices in education. The chapter demonstrates how conversational AI tools support personalized feedback, formative evaluation, and competency-based learning models. It addresses concerns related to reliability, ethics, and student engagement. By emphasizing interactivity and reflection, it reimagines assessment as a dynamic, AI-supported learning process.

Digital Transformation in Education: School Principals' Attitudes Towards Artificial Intelligence explores how school leaders perceive and respond to AI integration within educational systems. The chapter highlights factors influencing principals' openness to innovation and their strategic approaches to implementing AI tools. It also examines organizational culture, resource readiness, and leadership competencies. The findings offer valuable insights into how leadership attitudes shape digital transformation in schools.

In the Age of AI, Effective Teaching and Learning Strategies for Students with SEND Involve Collaboration and Interactive Strategies addresses inclusive education in AI-supported environments. The chapter discusses how technology can assist students with special educational needs and disabilities through adaptive and interactive tools. It emphasizes collaboration between teachers, technologists, and support staff to create equitable learning opportunities. Ultimately, it presents AI as an enabler of accessibility, empathy, and personalized support in inclusive education.

The book Impacts of Artificial Intelligence on Educational Psychology and Cognitive Development makes a significant contribution to the intersection of technology, learning sciences, and psychology by offering an integrated understanding of how AI transforms human cognition and educational experience. It moves beyond surface-level discussions of digital tools to examine the psychological, emotional, and ethical dimensions of AI-driven learning environments. Through empirical evidence and theoretical reflection, the book highlights the dual nature of AI, as both a catalyst for educational innovation and a challenge to traditional pedagogical roles. This perspective encourages a redefinition of learning as a co-evolutionary process between human and machine intelligence. In doing so, the book advances the discourse on how education can remain deeply human while embracing the technological transformations of the 21st century.

Furthermore, this volume bridges multiple disciplines by bringing together insights from educational psychology, cognitive development, artificial intelligence, and organizational behavior. Each chapter demonstrates how AI reshapes learning processes, leadership practices, and emotional well-being across different educational contexts. The contributors collectively emphasize that the psychological readiness of educators and students is as vital as technological infrastructure in ensuring successful AI adoption. This multidimensional approach helps stakeholders understand that effective digital transformation requires not only technical literacy but also emotional intelligence and ethical awareness. As such, the book offers a holistic framework for fostering resilience, adaptability, and critical reflection in the era of intelligent education.

Finally, the book contributes to the global dialogue on equitable and sustainable education by promoting inclusive, ethical, and human-centered AI integration. It argues that the future of education depends on aligning technological innovation with principles of empathy, accessibility, and lifelong learning. By addressing issues such as mental health, teacher psychology, leadership, and digital divide, it provides actionable insights for researchers, practitioners, and policymakers. The book thus serves not only as a scholarly reference but also as a roadmap for designing educational systems that nurture both cognitive growth and human flourishing. In essence, it reimagines AI not as a replacement for human intelligence, but as a partner in expanding the possibilities of teaching, learning, and personal development.

Chapter 1
The Era of Smart Learning

Manuel Meirinhos
https://orcid.org/0000-0003-1756-709X
Polytechnic Institute of Bragança, Portugal

Ana Cláudia Loureiro
https://orcid.org/0000-0001-7919-6891
Polytechnic Institute of Viseu, Portugal

ABSTRACT

This chapter critically analyses the impact of artificial intelligence (AI) on contemporary education and considers the transformations imposed by the post-digital era. Starting with the observation that AI is reshaping the how we access, produce, and apply knowledge, the chapter discusses the emergence of smart learning as a new educational paradigm. It explores two main models. The first is the integration of AI into traditional educational systems, which are limited by inherited practices. The second is a transformative vision that proposes a profound restructuring of education. The study adopts an exploratory approach grounded in a narrative review of the literature. The analysis identifies three dimensions — organisational, pedagogical, and ethical — that describe how AI is shaping new learning ecosystems and redefining the teacher's role. The study concludes that AI should not be seen as a substitute, but as a catalyst for pedagogical practices centred on the student, creativity, and critical thinking.

INTRODUCTION

There is no doubt that Artificial Intelligence (AI) is transforming contemporary life. However, in both education and society at large, its rapid expansion has led to ambivalent and polarised discourses. Clear antagonistic perceptions about its impact

DOI: 10.4018/979-8-3373-6375-2.ch001

have emerged. On the one hand, some authors present a pedagogical utopia. They see AI as promising to personalise learning, promote inclusion by adapting education to each student, and optimise human capital through creative, collaborative, and student-centred approaches (Deckker & Sumanasekara, 2025; Leong et al., 2025; Sadiku et al., 2021). On the other hand, for others, AI in the classroom evokes a dystopian vision. Automation could dehumanise teacher-student relationships, diminish creativity and critical thinking, and raise concerns about privacy, authorship, and data control (Bulathwela et al., 2024; Sijing & Lan, 2018; Zhang & Deng, 2022). Between this pedagogical utopia and automated dystopia, a reflective space emerges. This space demands understanding both the fears that drive resistance and the hopes that motivate innovation. Recent trends indicate that AI has a profound impact not only on education but also on societies, economies, and the labour market. The central question is no longer whether to adopt AI, but how to shape its use so that it ethically benefits education as a whole without compromising the human essence (Holmes et al., 2023; Luckin, 2025).

The arrival of Generative Artificial Intelligence, now accessible to the general public, constitutes a disruptive milestone in the ways we work with information and knowledge. Generative AI is a branch of AI capable of imitating human logic, writing, and even creativity. It mirrors certain human thought processes and questions the relevance of some skills, principles, formulas, and processes taught in classrooms, including basics like writing, grammar, and even logic and discourse (Mishra, 2025; World Economic Forum, 2024). In education, this form of AI marks a new era. Educational environments are transformed, and new cognitive development scenarios based on intelligent technologies are emerging. In this paradigm, educational systems must readjust to a society that is more interconnected, automated, and dependent on AI—the so-called post-digital society (Cormier et al., 2019; Fawns, 2019). The concept of post-digital society indicates that the digital is no longer an external element but an intrinsic part of social, cultural, and educational practices. More than just introducing technologies, the post-digital era implies rethinking how we learn, teach, and produce knowledge (Fawns, 2019; Gourlay, 2023). For many teachers, accustomed to routines and incremental changes, this transition can generate resistance and anxiety. Skills acquired during professionalisation may be at risk as disruptive educational processes profoundly alter traditional dynamics (Holmes et al., 2023; Tang, 2024). The cognitive simulation capacity of Generative AI raises new epistemological questions about authorship, originality, and critical thinking. Education must now rethink the human role in the era of intelligent learning.

In this context, the present study is justified by the urgent need to reconfigure educational systems in response to rapid AI advances and the consolidation of the post-digital society. This effort is necessary to ensure the relevance of education in the era of intelligent learning. In this new model, intelligent learning is an adaptive, dynamic approach. The collaboration between humans and machines is essential to boost personalisation and educational equity (Chen et al., 2021; Mishra, 2025; Molina-Carmona & Villagrá-Arnedo, 2018; Rajkumar et al., 2025). This transition will mean overcoming the dominance of the Pedagogy of the Answer—the practice of reproducing and standardising correct answers. Instead, education should move toward a Pedagogy of the Question, where questions drive problem investigation and solution-finding. This promotes active, creative, and critical thinking in students (Freire, 1998).

In light of this paradigm shift and the challenges that arise from it, this chapter is organised to provide a clear, reflective exploration of AI's impact on contemporary education. Following this introduction, which proposes an overview of the impact of AI and the emergence of new educational ecosystems more consonant with the needs of the post-digital society, a brief methodological section is included, which describes the approach adopted for this study. Next, three main themes are discussed, organised into three interdependent sections. The first section, "The Emergence of the Post-Digital Era", contextualises the socio-technological and epistemological scenario in which Artificial Intelligence consolidates itself as a structuring force in contemporary society; the second, "Intelligent Learning", explores the dynamics of interaction between humans and machines, highlighting the potential of AI to personalise, adapt, and humanise learning processes; and the third, "Educational Trends in the Context of Intelligent Learning", presents a prospective synthesis of emerging educational trends, highlighting the ethical, pedagogical, and organisational challenges. With this structure, the study aims to contribute to a critical understanding of education in the post-digital era, articulating technological, cognitive, and human dimensions in a careful approach that points out both the potentials and risks of AI, including ethical concerns, and issues of privacy and equity.

METHODOLOGY

This study explores the field using a narrative literature review methodology (Ferrari, 2015; Mitchell & Egudo, 2003) as its main method. This approach critically, interpretively, and integratively examines the rapidly evolving presence of AI in education and the emergence of intelligent learning in the post-digital era. Snyder (2019) argues that a narrative review suits emergent, complex themes, enabling the mapping of trends, identification of gaps, and combination of different theoretical currents, while avoiding the methodological constraints of a systematic review. Paré et al. (2015) note that a narrative review generates new theoretical understandings and frameworks for emerging fields. Xiao and Watson (2019) emphasize that this method integrates various perspectives and suggests future research directions, encouraging conceptual advances in innovative areas. In this research, we analysed how AI affects teaching and learning, examining pedagogical, ethical, and socio-technological dimensions. We consulted diverse sources, including scientific articles, books, technical reports, and institutional documents published between 2018 and 2025, with a focus on materials from UNESCO, the European Education and Culture Executive Agency, and the World Economic Forum. We searched articles in the Scopus, ERIC, ScienceDirect, and Google Scholar databases and prioritized studies on educational innovation, digital ethics, and public policies for AI innovation. Our analysis used an interpretive and critical approach, drawing from qualitative review methodologies that prioritize contextualizing evidence and synthesizing concepts.

Therefore, the present study does not aim to quantify evidence or limit itself to describing trends. Instead, it seeks to critically interpret existing knowledge, promoting a broad reflection on the role of AI in transforming educational ecosystems and redefining the role of the teacher in the context of a post-digital society. This reflection serves as the basis for the analyses developed in the following sections, which progressively explore the emergence of the post-digital era, the dynamics of intelligent learning, and the educational trends associated with this new paradigm.

THE EMERGENCE OF THE POST-DIGITAL ERA

If we consider how technological evolution has influenced human societies over the past 30 years, we observe a remarkable acceleration in the process of social transformation. Those of us who have experienced these last three decades, witnessing an accelerated transformation towards digitalisation, might ask whether people are truly aware of this reality. Will all sectors of society and all professions be able to keep pace with this rate of change towards the full digitalisation of services, which has completely transformed the ways we access and disseminate information, engage in leisure activities, work, learn, and relate to one another? Institutions, too, need to readjust to survive in a fluid world, where everything is more volatile and nothing seems stable. They have had to digitalise, virtualise, and even globalise, based on a strategic management of constant adaptation to technological and social evolution. Institutions that fail to transform risk extinction, due to functional mismatch or the inadequacy of their offerings. In a prospective, yet plausible short-to-medium-term scenario, we can foresee the arrival of humanoid robots, quantum computing, and sentient AI—the latter an inevitability, as, according to Blum and Blum (2024), AI experiments involving psychological models of consciousness are already underway. The concept of sentient artificial intelligence refers to an advanced, still hypothetical, form of AI capable of feeling, understanding, and having subjective experiences, going beyond the mere simulation of cognitive responses (Bostrom,

2016; Kurzweil, 2005). Unlike current AIs, which simulate intelligent behaviour based on data patterns, Sentient AI would imply the capacity to 'feel' and 'understand' the world autonomously (Floridi, 2019). Leong et al. (2025) also argue that there is a realistic and non-negligible possibility that some AI systems may exhibit consciousness soon, which will necessarily raise profound epistemological and moral questions. Bryson (2019) and Coeckelbergh (2020) discuss future predictions of a sentient AI capable of equalling or even surpassing human consciousness, prompting ethical debates about the rights, moral responsibility, and the attribution of ontological status to a conscious AI. It is a fact that this technological evolution is occurring, but currently, there is no scientific evidence of any AI system endowed with consciousness. Nevertheless, all these technological transformations influence and shape contemporary society, giving rise to a new era, which some authors call the post-digital era (Aoun, 2024; Cormier et al., 2019; Escaño, 2019; Fawns, 2019; Gratani et al., 2023; Mishra, 2025; Ray & Ray, 2024; Sari et al., 2024).

In the post-digital era, decision-making must be faster and adapted to an increasingly complex world full of technologies and information. It can be characterised by the fusion of the digital with the physical and the biological, where digital technology is not merely a tool but an essential part of how we live and interact (Escaño, 2019; Leong et al., 2025). It is an era that probably precedes transhumanism. The relationship between transhumanism and the post-digital era is intrinsically linked to how technology redefines human experience and social interaction. Transhumanism seeks to enhance human capabilities through advanced technologies such as artificial intelligence and biotechnology. In this new era, the boundaries between the digital and the physical blur, challenging traditional notions of humanity and proposing a future where technology and human experience are inseparably connected (Sari et al., 2024). The post-digital can be defined as a critical reflection on the current condition of culture following the digital revolution (Gratani et al., 2023). According to Aoun (2024), Mishra (2025), and Ray & Ray (2024), the post-digital era refers to a stage of technological and social development where digital technologies are so profoundly integrated into daily life that they cease to be perceived as distinct or isolated innovations. Instead of being viewed as separate tools, digital technologies become an inherent part of social, educational, cultural, and economic processes, resulting in the fusion between the digital and the physical. Thus, the post-digital enters the sphere of critical reflection on the current condition of culture following the digital revolution, suggesting it can serve as a term to indicate a complex blend of relations between humans and technology, in a context where technology is increasingly omnipresent (Knox, 2019) and where AI will make many decisions for us. In this context, the relationship between humans and machines evolves into a state of symbiosis, where technology is not just a tool, but a direct extension of human capabilities. We can also associate this era with what Beck (2011) calls reflexive modernity, a phase of society where people and institutions begin to question the side effects of modern progress, and the advancement of science and technology is no longer blindly accepted. We begin to reflect on risks, consequences, ethical dilemmas, global uncertainties, and collective responsibility.

Based on these references, we can state that the post-digital era represents the definitive fusion between technology and daily life, characterised by a total integration between the physical and the digital, in which the digital constitutes an existential condition of contemporaneity (Escaño, 2019; Fawns, 2019). Human-machine interactions become increasingly natural, adaptive, and immersive, with ubiquitous AI, invisible interfaces, and cognitive automation shaping the human experience and transforming the modes of production, communication, and learning (Gratani et al., 2023; Mishra, 2025; Sari et al., 2024). In this scenario, the great challenge will be to ensure transparency, ethical regulation, and a balance between technological autonomy and human control, preventing the symbiosis with AI from compromising autonomy and privacy, reconfigured to respond to epistemological, social, and cognitive challenges, overcoming obsolete pedagogical models, and preparing citizens to live well and co-exist in a society increasingly mediated by technologies (Aoun, 2024; Cormier et al., 2019). Indeed, if the school were fully fulfilling its educational function, it should already be adapting to these transformations. To respond to the emerging challenges of the post-digital society, we need a new learning model – intelligent learning – as a paradigm capable of integrating AI ethically, responsibly, creatively, and humanely (Gratani et al., 2023; Mishra, 2025).

SMART LEARNING

In the future, human-machine interaction could be significantly enhanced by the increasing use of AI (Grinschgl & Neubauer, 2022). Distributed cognition theory offers a pertinent perspective for understanding this new social and educational landscape. This theory posits that intelligence does not reside exclusively within the human mind but also within machines constructed to perform specific mental processes (Furniss et al., 2019; Hollan et al., 2000; Hutchins, 1996). The human mind has limitations in terms of storage capacity and information processing speed. In this context, we develop machines capable of storing and processing data with significantly greater efficiency than the human mind. Through collaboration with these machines, we extend our cognitive capabilities and competences. In this collaborative scenario, the human mind, in synergy with technological devices, enables us to anticipate situations and solve problems more swiftly and effectively.

Generative AI tools are a paradigmatic example of this dynamic. This new model of cognition paves the way for the emergence of a new learning ecosystem.

Emergent learning ecosystems are based on environments that integrate Artificial Intelligence with the aim of creating more personalised and adaptive opportunities for students (Deckker & Sumanasekara, 2025; Imran et al., 2024). These ecosystems utilise large volumes of data and machine learning algorithms to analyse student behaviours and preference patterns, enabling the creation of learning trajectories tailored to the individual needs of each student (Sadiku et al., 2021). In this context, the concept of hybrid intelligence emerges, understood as the synergistic collaboration between human intelligence and AI, where both complement each other to enhance learning, creativity, and decision-making (Akata et al., 2020; Bredeweg & Kragten, 2022). Thus, hybrid intelligence results from the convergence between human cognitive abilities and the analytical competencies of AI. This approach integrates with the post-digital paradigm, in which technology becomes an extension of human reasoning (Leong et al., 2025; Sari et al., 2024). The articulation between human intelligence and AI not only optimises performance in complex tasks but also provides new approaches to rethinking current models of information and knowledge acquisition and management. It is fundamental to underline that AI should not be seen as a replacement for human intelligence, but rather as an extension of it — a tool intended to augment our cognitive capacities.

Reflecting on the emerging learning models in the AI era, two distinct paradigms can be identified: (i) an integrative vision, centred on the inclusion of AI in traditional educational systems, where intelligent tools complement the teacher's role and optimise the teaching and learning process, and (ii) a transformative vision, which proposes the restructuring of pedagogical methods, aiming to prepare students for a future profoundly influenced by advanced technologies, emphasising dynamic, inclusive, and adaptive educational environments, in which AI plays a central role in learning personalisation.

The paradigm of the integrative vision of AI in traditional education is valid but limited. By attempting to integrate AI into existing educational ecosystems without undertaking a deep reconfiguration, it prevents the full exploitation of its transformative pedagogical potential. In this scenario, AI runs the risk of becoming merely another technology serving an outdated pedagogy. It is in this context that topics such as "improving learning with AI," "integrating AI into the classroom," or "using AI in assessments" are frequently discussed (Chen et al., 2021; Deckker & Sumanasekara, 2025; Imran et al., 2024; Molina-Carmona & Villagrá-Arnedo, 2018; Sadiku et al., 2021). Although these approaches may generate some incremental innovations in the teaching and learning process, they also raise serious challenges. Among the main ones, we can highlight problems related to copying and plagiarism, due to easy access to information, and the potential reduction in human cognitive capacity by transferring information processing to the machine, often without a critical or reflective approach by the student (Zhang & Deng, 2022). Such issues pose substantial ethical challenges, raising doubts about the suitability of AI within a traditional view of education. These doubts fuel simplistic and polarised debates, such as the recurring question: "Artificial Intelligence in school, yes or no?"

The second vision, which presents a transformative perspective, proposes a deeper and more structural paradigm shift. This approach highlights the urgent need to prepare students for a post-digital world, promoting the development of skills such as computational thinking, critical thinking, creativity, and ethics associated with emerging technologies, among other essential skills, in an increasingly technological, volatile, and uncertain future. This is a vision that demands disruptive innovations, with a direct impact on the reconfiguration of the entire traditional educational ecosystem (Aoun, 2024; Gratani et al., 2023; Lampou, 2023; Mishra, 2025).

In this paradigm, AI should be seen as a starting point for new ways of teaching and learning and not as a finish line or a mere instrumental resource. Some international institutions, such as UNESCO, recognise the need for transition to this new paradigm, as evidenced in the Beijing Consensus on artificial intelligence and education (UNESCO, 2019), as well as in the digital publication Artificial Intelligence: Do we need a new education? (UNESCO, 2023). The UNESCO report (2025) introduces the concept of shared human intelligence, also known as human-machine collective intelligence, as a fundamental paradigm of intelligent learning. This notion goes beyond the instrumental use of artificial intelligence and emphasises the collaborative integration of human and non-human intelligences in the collective construction of knowledge. As stated in the report, "Harnessing this opportunity would result in a new form of human-machine collective intelligence. Such intelligence would interweave human and non-human intelligence, rather than merely replacing human intelligence, leading to triadic learning experiences among learners, teachers, and AI" (UNESCO, 2025, p. 63). In this view, learning is no longer an individual cognitive process but a distributed and interconnected phenomenon, supported by hybrid cognitive networks that combine human competencies (creativity, empathy, and critical thinking) with the analytical and predictive capabilities of AI. This model foresees an educational ecosystem where knowledge is constructed collaboratively and where students, teachers, and intelligent systems engage in reciprocal cognitive relationships, promoting a more collaborative, ethical, and human-centred educational approach.

In this educational ecosystem, the concept of intelligent learning refers to a scenario where digital technology is so integrated and widespread that it becomes an essential and organic part of the educational environment. This significant change in the educational environment signals the beginning of a new era, characterised by personalised, inclusive, and dynamic learning environments that lead to a profound transition in the design and implementation of learning experiences where AI ceases to be just a technical tool and is instead understood as an extension of human mental capacities — a complement that challenges the status quo of contemporary education (Deckker & Sumanasekara, 2025; Gratani et al., 2023; Leong et al., 2025; Rajkumar et al., 2025).

As de Kerckhove (2024) points out, the arrival of Generative AI is causing an epistemological crisis. This form of intelligence is transforming the traditional system of written production and, consequently, knowledge itself. The introduction of algorithms, coupled with the growing automation of processes, as well as the traditional structure of literacy, is being challenged, bringing a fundamental shift in how society understands, organises, and shares knowledge (Mishra, 2025; Tang, 2024; World Economic Forum, 2024). The emphasis on exclusive content, previously predominant in schools, made sense in the context of the 20th-century industrial society era, when access to relevant information was limited. However, in the post-digital era, where information circulates at great speed and is accessible anytime and anywhere, the relevance of acquired knowledge becomes more ephemeral. The volatility of contemporary knowledge imposes a new dynamic: it is imperative to continuously learn, unlearn, and relearn. This continuous process applies both to mastering knowledge and to developing new competencies, respecting the individual difficulties, interests, and talents of each student (Fawns, 2019; Gratani et al., 2023; Rajkumar et al., 2025). Along this line of thought, intelligent learning also implies the adaptation of content and skills, continuous assessment of student progress, the identification of learning patterns, and the provision of personalised feedback. Thus, this approach is closely associated with learning personalisation, educational innovation, and pedagogical effectiveness, aiming to use technology strategically to improve the quality of learning and promote cognitive development (Deckker et al., 2025; Lampou, 2023; Luckin, 2025). AI also allows for presenting materials in various formats to meet different visual, auditory, and physical needs. Customisable interfaces and adaptive technologies prove particularly valuable for neurodiverse students, as well as for those with varying physical abilities (World Economic Forum, 2024). Hybrid pedagogical practices characterise this new era, as they promote the fluid integration of technologies such as Artificial Intelligence (AI), Augmented Reality (AR), and Virtual Reality (VR), among others, enabling an integrated and strategic approach between the digital and the face-to-face (Bushuyev et al., 2024; Mishra, 2025).

This profound reconfiguration of the educational ecosystem dictates the emergence of pedagogical trends with more dynamic, personalised, and advanced technology-driven approaches (Zohuri, 2024; Mishra, 2025) that will shape the future of education, and which will be explored next in the context of intelligent learning.

EDUCATIONAL TRENDS IN THE CONTEXT OF SMART LEARNING

The new educational trends necessitate a metamorphosis in educational systems and in how we learn, teach, and organise knowledge. In the context of smart learning, fundamental educational trends emerge, such as the smart management of educational institutions, the need for a new educational and teacher training ecosystem, the pedagogy of the question, adaptive learning, attention to neurodiversity, and the focus on the human factor. Based on the analysis of the theoretical framework of this study, we group these trends into three dimensions: (i) the organisational, (ii) the pedagogical, and (iii) the ethical, which together shape the new paradigm of smart learning.

I. Organisational and Educational Management

The smart management of educational institutions will be based on advanced AI platforms for optimising processes such as curriculum administration, enrolment, distribution of educational resources, and academic performance prediction based on predictive analytics (Pawar & Khose, 2024). Predictive analytics can rely on large amounts of data and enable the anticipation of situations, such as school dropout. AI amplifies the pressure that educational systems have been under to transform. Rethinking schools and their organisation is an urgent and pressing necessity. This task is not easy, as while society is entering a post-digital era, schools have not yet fully entered the digital era, despite attempts and guidelines from international organisations and investment by Western countries. The integration of AI management systems in education can profoundly alter the strategic management of schools, particularly in monitoring students' educational progress through real-time analysis, verification of trends, and the possibility of anticipating actions and facilitating decision-making (Aoun, 2024; Gratani et al., 2023; Mishra, 2025; Tang, 2024). A crucial area where these institutional management systems can also be useful is in institutional self-assessment, through the analysis of large amounts of data, forecasting and future trends, and accurate and personalised reports, facilitating both the identification of problems and opportunities for improvement, while also promoting a culture of transparency, efficiency, and continuous innovation within schools (Chen et al., 2021).

In parallel, the development of a new educational and training ecosystem is observed, where human interaction with AI will create a complete new disruption of educational processes and methods (Deckker & Sumanasekara, 2025; Imran et al., 2024; Mishra, 2025). Intelligent tutoring and real-time feedback using AI-based tutoring systems offer students continuous support without necessarily relying on a full-time teacher. These virtual assistants can aid in clarifying doubts, recommending complementary materials, and assessing individual difficulties (Imran et al., 2024). Traditional continuous assessment, based on standardised tests, will give way to dynamic and interactive assessment models, where algorithms analyse student progress over time. AI tools adapt quizzes, activities, and challenges according to the student's level of understanding, ensuring a more accurate measurement of what has been learned (Mishra, 2025) or the competencies developed. The integration of Augmented Reality (AR) and Virtual Reality (VR) technologies creates immersive environments that make learning more engaging and interactive. As a result, abstract concepts and simulated experiences can be explored in a more intuitive and experimental manner (Grinschgl & Neubauer, 2022; Taufikin et al., 2024). Lifelong learning will be viewed naturally, as smart learning is not limited to formal education. According to Aldossemani (2024), with AI, learning becomes a continuous process, accessible anytime and anywhere, adapting to individuals' professional and personal development needs in a context of information superabundance. Teachers will also have to enter this dynamic of constant learning and adaptation. It becomes necessary to think about a reconfiguration of teacher training and role to empower teachers to become mentors and facilitators of smart learning (Cormier et al., 2019; Fawns, 2019; Escaño, 2019). With AI, educators and teachers will be able to focus their efforts on methodological innovation, learning personalisation (Ray & Ray, 2024), and the development of skills for future life.

II. Emerging Pedagogical Methodologies and Processes

From a pedagogical standpoint, smart learning trends privilege models focused on autonomy, adaptability, and critical reflection. The Pedagogy of the Question is central in this context, as it replaces the traditional paradigm of the "correct answer" with a pedagogical approach that encourages students to formulate questions, thus awakening curiosity, intellectual autonomy, and reflection on knowledge, promoting the development of cognitive and metacognitive competencies (Freire, 1998). To formulate good questions, students need to develop competencies such as the ability to synthesise, creative thinking, clear and articulate reasoning, the capacity to visualise different scenarios, and grounded decision-making. With the development of Generative AI, knowing how to dialogue with and question the AI is fundamental. A pedagogy based on questions and human-machine dialogue can be seen as an educational approach that responds to the changes in how information is transmitted and received in the post-digital era. This approach creates dynamic interactions and exchanges that reflect the impact of AI on students' learning, much more aligned with their personal interests and specific needs, guided by personalised learning.

Education for the answer does not stimulate curiosity, which is indispensable for the creative process. According to UNESCO:

> *Schools should teach how to formulate higher-level questions, which begin with a 'what', 'where', 'when', and 'who'. These are the questions that – as we've seen – start with a 'why', implying what changes are presupposed, and what consequences are generated. In other words, these are the questions that require students to develop capacities for reflection, curiosity, investigation, analysis, inference, anticipation, argumentation, communication, collaboration, evaluation, imagination, creativity, and participation (2023, p. 42)*

One of the main pedagogical challenges of the AI era is the strengthening of students' intellectual and emotional autonomy. Successful integrations, such as the "Socratic learning" model mediated by chatbots and intelligent tutors, have shown potential for stimulating critical thinking and problem-solving through guided questions and adaptive feedback (Zhang & Deng, 2022). However, for these tools to be effectively disruptive, it is essential that students are educated to challenge the "standard answers" provided by AI, questioning the validity of the information and the contexts in which decisions are generated (Moustaghfir & Brigui, 2024). Also, based on the work of Walter (2024), we can infer that prompt elaboration can be seen as a pedagogical use of AI capable of reinforcing the pedagogy of the question, empowering students to formulate questions that promote deep understanding, critical analysis, and active content investigation.

Associated with this trend is the growth of adaptive learning, which allows for the creation of personalised development paths, adapting strategies, content, competencies, and methodologies to the pace, knowledge level, and learning style of each student (Bulathwela et al., 2024). There is no shortage of current experiences where intelligent systems monitor student performance, suggesting real-time interventions to optimise learning and skills development. Adaptive learning gained popularity with the emergence of AI in the 1970s. The basic principle was to adapt learning to the weaknesses or potential of each student. Success was not possible because it was based on the behaviourist theory of learning, at the high price of digital technology, and the limited processing and multimedia capabilities of computers. Personalised and adaptive learning is a dynamic process that recognises the uniqueness of each learner. Morris and Rohs (2023) emphasise that students are increasingly involved in self-directed learning processes, leading to the need to involve their context in educational processes mediated by new digital ecosystems. In this regard, there is a greater appreciation for personalised and self-regulated learning, with strong potential to improve learner engagement and motivation (Molina-Carmona & Villagrá-Arnedo, 2018; Sadiku et al., 2021). We are increasingly aware of human neurodiversity and that each individual is unique in their interests, capacities, and talents. This AI-driven educational personalisation celebrates the uniqueness of each person, equipping them with the necessary skills and knowledge to succeed in this flexible, diverse, and rapidly evolving global environment of the post-digital society (Aldossemani, 2024).

III. Neurodiversity, Inclusion, and Ethics

The educational focus on human neurodiversity, inclusive education, and ethical responsibility points towards a more human and social dimension of education. In this context, the accessibility, teaching personalisation, and adaptive support offered by AI can mitigate inequalities and provide a truly inclusive education for all students, regardless of their needs or socioeconomic conditions (Coeckelbergh, 2020; Deckker et al., 2025). AI-based tools offer a proactive approach, enabling teachers and managers to make more informed and personalised decisions (Adeleye et al., 2024; Ray & Ray, 2024) based on problem diagnostics conducted by AI. The appreciation of neurodiversity emerges as a central dimension: it is recognised that each individual possesses different cognitive styles, talents, and ways of learning, requiring flexible and personalised pedagogical approaches (Bulathwela et al., 2024; Gratani et al., 2023; World Economic Forum, 2024). Personalised learning requires continuous diagnostics and the collection of big data to tailor the next learning step; it also requires personalised assessment, and therefore, non-comparative assessment with other students. Personalised learning implies pedagogical differentiation, where neuropedagogy and AI, when combined (Camargo & Fernández, 2024; Vovk et al., 2022), can facilitate the development of individual educational development plans, based on each student's learning difficulties and talents, allowing them to advance at differentiated paces, according to their personal development potential (Ray & Ray, 2024; World Economic Forum, 2024).

The diversity of tools for inclusion is varied (Filatro & Loureiro, 2020). AI-based translation and interpretation tools can help students who do not speak the language of instruction to better understand the content to be learned or the processes for task completion. This facilitates the integration of students from different cultural and linguistic backgrounds, promoting a more inclusive learning environment. AI can be used to develop assistive technologies that help students with specific needs access information. For example, text-to-speech software, automatic captions, and adaptive interfaces can facilitate learning, as can text or spoken language translators to sign language, which is important for students with hearing difficulties. Inclusion only happens if the person feels respected, valued, and recognised for their competencies. AI can be the springboard for this recognition. In terms of problem detection, AI can analyse student performance data to identify those who may need additional support. Various systems can scrutinise human neurodiversity and identify problems such as ASD (Autism Spectrum Disorder), dyslexia, dyscalculia, among others. This allows educators to intervene early and offer personalised attention, ensuring that all students have the opportunity to achieve school success.

However, the dissemination of AI also raises ethical issues. Concerns about algorithmic transparency, data security, and equity of access will be the major challenges of this new era (Aoun, 2024; OECD, 2024; Ray & Ray, 2024). Education will need to assign relevance to ethical training, helping students understand the implications of using artificial intelligence, making responsible decisions, and considering the social impacts of technology. According to UNESCO (2022), ethics must guide the responsible development of AI, ensuring that technologies advance without compromising human dignity and fundamental rights. This implies the creation of transparent, fair, and explicable systems that respect privacy and avoid exclusion. The European Education and Culture Executive Agency (2023, p. 87) also supports these ideas: "An adequate ethical framework for AI in education needs to be built using learning and human development as a starting point, so it can be used as the core for regulation of AI-based systems used in education". Regarding equity, UNESCO (2025) emphasizes that technology alone does not guarantee equity: an ethical, pedagogical, and culturally sensitive approach is needed to transform the way we conceive of diversity. Thus, inclusive education and neurodiversity become pillars of expanded human intelligence, where learning is also an act of recognising and respecting the plurality of human minds. Socio-emotional skills, critical thinking, and creativity will become preponderant as artificial intelligence takes over repetitive functions. The need to focus education on human value, interpersonal relationships, empathy, collaboration, and resilience is growing. Creativity and complex problem-solving will be indispensable in an AI-driven world (Imran et al., 2024). We need education to be more holistic and for the school to become an institution of well-being. Digital ethics, algorithmic literacy, and critical thinking will therefore be essential competencies that should integrate 21st-century curricula, empowering students and teachers to act in an informed and responsible manner in emerging digital ecosystems.

In this context, Holmes et al. (2023) guide that, to avoid the potential risks of AI, it is necessary to educate not only with AI, but also about AI and for AI, to ensure that students and teachers develop a critical and ethical understanding of its implications. In an era where AI will play an ever-increasing role, investing in education is vital to ensuring that the future is guided by human values, creativity, critical thinking, and social skills. While AI can augment and automate, only human beings can interpret, create meaning, and make grounded decisions with a positive and ethical impact on society. On this matter, the European Education and Culture Executive Agency (2023) warns of the extreme necessity of AI ethics in education:

> *The issues related to AI ethics, the right to privacy, data protection, gender inequality, or human rights are also present in the education sector, where the*

population is often more vulnerable, particularly due to their young age and lack of understanding. Therefore, it is extremely important to put in place and implement legal safeguards and technical norms for the ethical use of AI in education, to ensure that its use does not violate the rights of students, teachers, and other people in the educational sphere (p. 3).

These trends, by articulating the organisational, pedagogical, and ethical dimensions, reveal that education in the post-digital era goes far beyond technological integration. It must be a space for critique, reflection, and action, empowering students to understand and shape its impact on the world (Knox, 2019). The INTEF (2024) highlights a necessary responsible approach to the implementation of AI, emphasising the importance of considering ethical issues such as algorithmic bias, data privacy and security, equity and inclusion, as well as technological dependence. Furthermore, this era of smart learning implies a profound cultural, cognitive, and institutional reconfiguration, in which learning becomes a continuous, adaptive, and ethical process. It is from this understanding that the conclusions of the present study are grounded, focusing on the potential of AI to humanise knowledge and promote intelligent and inclusive education.

CONCLUSIONS

From the last decade of the 20th century to the present day, the human relationship with information and knowledge has undergone an accelerated transformation. We have moved from a scenario of scarcity to an era of informational superabundance, where Artificial Intelligence (AI) asserts itself as a new cognitive agent, capable of significantly amplifying our ability to access, process, and produce knowledge (Deckker & Sumanasekara, 2025). In this context, AI has the potential to revolutionise learning processes, challenging traditional methodologies and promoting more dynamic, inclusive, and adaptive experiences (Deckker et al., 2025; Lampou, 2023; Sadiku et al., 2021).

The school, as a structuring institution of knowledge, no longer adequately responds to the demands of a world shaped by AI and continuous technological innovation. The transition to the era of smart learning has become an educational urgency, as it allows for the offering of personalised pathways, meaningful assessments, and training aligned with 21st-century competencies (Grinschgl & Neubauer, 2022; Imran et al., 2024). Educational systems that fail to adapt to this new reality risk perpetuating obsolete models, disconnected from the real needs of students and contemporary society.

This paradigm shift does not only benefit learners: it also redefines the role of the teacher, who moves on to act as a mentor, facilitator, and designer of learning experiences. The deep integration of AI and immersive technologies, when supported by a student-centred pedagogy, allows education to truly fulfil its formative role: preparing critical, creative, and time-aware citizens. However, it is important to underline that no technology, no matter how sophisticated, will transform education unless it is preceded by a clear and ethical definition of the type of education one wishes to build. Without this reflection, AI runs the risk of being absorbed or neutralised by the pre-digital models still dominant in schools (Selwyn, 2024; Tang, 2024; Zhang & Deng, 2022).

The era of smart learning and the post-digital era intertwine in the transformation of how knowledge is acquired and applied. AI, by integrating into educational processes, ceases to be an external tool and becomes an extension of human experience itself, promoting collaborative, distributed, and interactive learning that reflects the complexity of the contemporary world (Aoun, 2024; Knox, 2019). In this constantly evolving scenario, it is important to remember that human uniqueness lies in the capacity to question, feel, create, and act ethically. AI can amplify our competencies, but it is up to humanity to define the values that guide its use. As Holmes et al. (2023) and the European Education and Culture Executive Agency (2023) warn, it is fundamental to educate not only with AI but also about AI, ensuring a critical, ethical, and responsible appropriation of these technologies in the educational context.

Recommendations and Future Perspectives

In light of the conclusions of this study, several strategic guidelines emerge, directed at the main stakeholders in the educational ecosystem, aiming for an ethical, effective, and humanising integration of Artificial Intelligence: (i) in the political sphere, it is imperative to develop educational policies that articulate digital innovation with equity and ethics. Investments in smart infrastructures, continuous teacher training, and AI regulation mechanisms that ensure algorithmic transparency, data protection, and universal accessibility must be part of governmental agendas (OECD, 2023, 2024; UNESCO, 2024). The creation of national and international projects and observatories can ensure monitoring of the social and pedagogical impacts of these technologies; (ii) in the research field, the scientific community should expand and deepen studies on the cognitive, pedagogical, and social impacts of AI on learning, moving beyond purely instrumental approaches (Bredeweg & Kragten, 2022; Chen et al., 2021); (iii) in the educational area, teachers and school managers must adopt a reflective and experimental stance, learning with and about AI in order to promote pedagogical models based on questioning, adaptability, and collaborative learning, adopting AI as a partner in designing personalised and meaningful learning experiences (Freire, 1998; Luckin, 2025; Mishra, 2025; Sadiku et al., 2021; World Economic Forum, 2024); (iv) in the family sphere, the role of the family is crucial in mediating the use of technologies by children and adolescents. The development of a “family digital intelligence” (Holmes et al., 2023) can mitigate risks such as misinformation, technological dependence, and the erosion of human interactions.

AI should not be seen as a threat, but rather as an opportunity to rethink education and the role of the learner as a knowledge builder. For its use to be effective and useful, it is necessary to balance technological innovation and ethics, as well as disruptive and incremental strategies, to ensure the configuration of a new educational ecosystem that translates into learning that is more adaptive, personalised, self-regulated, smart, inclusive, and truly human.

REFERENCES

Adeleye, O. O., Eden, C. A., & Adeniyi, I. S. (2024). Innovative teaching methodologies in the era of artificial intelligence: A review of inclusive educational practices. World Journal of Advanced Engineering Technology and Sciences, 11(2), 069–079. DOI: 10.30574/wjaets.2024.11.2.0091

Akata, Z., Balliet, D., De Rijke, M., Dignum, F., Dignum, V., Eiben, G., Fokkens, A., Grossi, D., Hindriks, K., Hoos, H., Hung, H., Jonker, C., Monz, C., Neerincx, M., Oliehoek, F., Prakken, H., Schlobach, S., Van Der Gaag, L., Van Harmelen, F., & Welling, M. (2020). A Research Agenda for Hybrid Intelligence: Augmenting Human Intellect With Collaborative, Adaptive, Responsible, and Explainable Artificial Intelligence. *Computer*, *53*(8), 18–28. DOI: 10.1109/MC.2020.2996587

Aldossemani, T. I. (2024). Dar forma al futuro del aprendizaje: El papel fundamental de la inteligencia artificial en la microeducación. In J. M. Muñoz, N. Lorenzo, & X. Suñé (Coords.), Inteligencia Artificial en la Microeducación: Transformando el Aula del Futuro (pp. 33–41). Observatorio de Innovación Educativa y Cultura Digital (ODITE).

Aoun, J. E. (2024). Robot-Proof: Higher Education in the Age of Artificial Intelligence (2.a ed.). MIT Press.

Beck, U. (2011). Sociedade de risco: Rumo a uma Outra Modernidade. Editora 34.

Blum, L., & Blum, M. (2024). AI Consciousness is Inevitable: A Theoretical Computer Science Perspective (Versão 12). arXiv. DOI: 10.48550/ARXIV.2403.17101

Bostrom, N. (2016). *Superintelligence: Paths, Dangers, Strategies*. Oxford University Press.

Bredeweg, B., & Kragten, M. (2022). Requirements and challenges for hybrid intelligence: A case-study in education. *Frontiers in Artificial Intelligence*, *5*, 891630. DOI: 10.3389/frai.2022.891630 PMID: 36003066

Bryson, J. J. (2019). The Artificial Intelligence of the Ethics of Artificial Intelligence: An Introductory Overview for Law and Regulation. In Dubber, M., Pasquale, F., & Das, S. (Eds.), *The Oxford Handbook of Ethics of Artificial Intelligence Oxford University Press*.

Bulathwela, S., Pérez-Ortiz, M., Holloway, C., Cukurova, M., & Shawe-Taylor, J. (2024). Artificial Intelligence Alone Will Not Democratise Education: On Educational Inequality, Techno-Solutionism and Inclusive Tools. *Sustainability (Basel)*, *16*(2), 781. DOI: 10.3390/su16020781

Bushuyev, S., & Saidullayev, R., & Others. (2024). Transformation of the education landscape in an AI environment. In Proceedings of the 12th IPMA Research Conference: Project Management in the Age of Artificial Intelligence DOI: 10.56889/strd5315

Camargo, C. D. B., & Fernández, A. H. (2024). Neuropedagogy and Neuroimaging of Artificial Intelligence and Deep Learning. *Educational Process International Journal, 13*(3). Advance online publication. DOI: 10.22521/edupij.2024.133.6

Chen, X., Zou, D., Xie, H., & Wang, F. L. (2021). Past, present, and future of smart learning: A topic-based bibliometric analysis. *International Journal of Educational Technology in Higher Education, 18*(1), 2. DOI: 10.1186/s41239-020-00239-6

Coeckelbergh, M. (2020). *AI Ethics*. MIT Press. DOI: 10.7551/mitpress/12549.001.0001

Cormier, D., Jandrić, P., Childs, M., Hall, R., White, D., Phipps, L., Truelove, I., Hayes, S., & Fawns, T. (2019). Ten Years of the Postdigital in the 52group: Reflections and Developments 2009–2019. *Postdigital Science and Education, 1*(2), 475–506. DOI: 10.1007/s42438-019-00049-8

de Kerckhove, D. (2024). Preguntas, no respuestas. In J. M. Muñoz, N. Lorenzo, & X. Suñé (Coords.), Inteligencia Artificial en la Microeducación: Transformando el Aula del Futuro (pp. 18–32). Observatorio de Innovación Educativa e Cultura Digital (ODITE).

Deckker, D., & Sumanasekara, S. (2025). The role of Artificial Intelligence in education: Transforming learning and teaching. EPRA International Journal of Research & Development (IJRD), 5–15. DOI: 10.36713/epra20429

Deckker, D., Sumanasekara, S., & Fakhrou, A. (2025). AI-Powered Personalised Learning: Promise and Pitfalls. *World Journal of Advanced Research and Reviews, 26*(3), 2081–2095. DOI: 10.30574/wjarr.2025.26.3.2425

Escaño, C. (2019). Sociedad postdigital (ontología de la remezcla). Iberoamérica Social: Revista-red de estudios sociales, 7(12), 51–53. https://dialnet.unirioja.es/servlet/articulo?codigo=6992796

European Education and Culture Executive Agency. (2023). AI report: By the European Digital Education Hub's Squad on artificial intelligence in education. Publications Office. https://data.europa.eu/doi/10.2797/828281

Fawns, T. (2019). Postdigital Education in Design and Practice. *Postdigital Science and Education, 1*(1), 132–145. DOI: 10.1007/s42438-018-0021-8

Ferrari, R. (2015). Writing narrative style literature reviews. *Medical Writing, 24*(4), 230–235. DOI: 10.1179/2047480615Z.000000000329

Filatro, A., & Loureiro, A. C. (2020). *Novos produtos e serviços na Educação 5.0 (1st edição).* Artesanato Educacional.

Floridi, L. (2019). *The Logic of Information: A Theory of Philosophy as Conceptual Design.* Oxford University Press. DOI: 10.1093/oso/9780198833635.001.0001

Freire, P. (1998). *Por uma Pedagogia da Pergunta.* Paz e Terra.

Furniss, D., Garfield, S., Husson, F., Blandford, A., & Franklin, B. (2019). Distributed Cognition: Understanding Complex Sociotechnical Informatics. In *Studies in Health Technology and Informatics.* IOS Press., DOI: 10.3233/SHTI190113

Gourlay, L. (2023). Postdigital/More-Than-Digital: Ephemerality, Seclusion, and Copresence in the University. In Jandrić, P., MacKenzie, A., & Knox, J. (Eds.), *Postdigital Research* (pp. 51–68). Springer Nature Switzerland., DOI: 10.1007/978-3-031-31299-1_4

Gratani, F., Giannandrea, L., & Rossi, P. G. (2023). Learning in the post-digital era. Transforming education through the Maker approach. *Research on Education and Media, 15*(1), 111–119. DOI: 10.2478/rem-2023-0015

Grinschgl, S., & Neubauer, A. C. (2022). Supporting Cognition With Modern Technology: Distributed Cognition Today and in an AI-Enhanced Future. *Frontiers in Artificial Intelligence, 5*, 908261. DOI: 10.3389/frai.2022.908261 PMID: 35910191

Hollan, J., Hutchins, E., & Kirsh, D. (2000). Distributed cognition: Toward a new foundation for human-computer interaction research. *ACM Transactions on Computer-Human Interaction, 7*(2), 174–196. DOI: 10.1145/353485.353487

Holmes, W., Bialik, M., & Fadel, C. (2023). Artificial intelligence in education. In Stückelberger, C., & Duggal, P. (Eds.), *Data ethics: Building trust: How digital technologies can serve humanity* (pp. 621–653). Globethics Publications., DOI: 10.58863/20.500.12424/4276068

Hutchins, E. (1996). *Cognition in the Wild.* MIT Press.

Imran, M., Almusharraf, N., Abdellatif, M. S., & Abbasova, M. Y. (2024). Artificial Intelligence in Higher Education: Enhancing Learning Systems and Transforming Educational Paradigms. [iJIM]. *International Journal of Interactive Mobile Technologies, 18*(18), 34–48. DOI: 10.3991/ijim.v18i18.49143

INTEF. (2024, julho 4). Guía sobre el uso de la inteligencia artificial en el ámbito educativo. INTEF. https://intef.es/Noticias/guia-sobre-el-uso-de-la-inteligencia-artificial-en-el-ambito-educativo/

Knox, J. (2019). What Does the 'Postdigital' Mean for Education? Three Critical Perspectives on the Digital, with Implications for Educational Research and Practice. *Postdigital Science and Education, 1*(2), 357–370. DOI: 10.1007/s42438-019-00045-y

Kurzweil, R. (2005). *The Singularity Is Near: When Humans Transcend Biology.* The Viking Press.

Lampou, R. (2023). The Integration of Artificial Intelligence in Education: Opportunities and Challenges. *Review of Artificial Intelligence in Education, 4*(00), e015. DOI: 10.37497/rev.artif.intell.educ.v4i00.15

Leong, W. Y., Leong, Y. Z., & Leong, W. S. (2025). Artificial Intelligence in education. *IET Conference Proceedings*, 2024(22), 183–184. DOI: 10.1049/icp.2024.4341

Luckin, R. (2025). Nurturing human intelligence in the age of AI: Rethinking education for the future. *Development and Learning in Organizations, 39*(1), 1–4. DOI: 10.1108/DLO-04-2024-0108

Mishra, D. (2025). Artificial Intelligence as a Mediator between Educator and Learner: The New Paradigm Shift. *International Journal of Research and Innovation in Applied Science, X*(VII), 91–95. DOI: 10.51584/IJRIAS.2025.100700008

Mishra, S. (2025). Artificial Intelligence as a Mediator between Educator and Learner: The New Paradigm Shift. *International Journal of Research and Innovation in Applied Science, X*(VII), 91–95. DOI: 10.51584/IJRIAS.2025.100700008

Mitchell, M., & Egudo, M. (2003). A Review of Narrative Methodology [Dataset]. DOI: 10.1037/e426492005-001

Molina-Carmona, R., & Villagrá-Arnedo, C. (2018). Smart Learning. *Proceedings of the Sixth International Conference on Technological Ecosystems for Enhancing Multiculturality*, 645–647. DOI: 10.1145/3284179.3284288

Morris, T. H., & Rohs, M. (2023). The potential for digital technology to support self-directed learning in formal education of children: A scoping review. *Interactive Learning Environments, 31*(4), 1974–1987. DOI: 10.1080/10494820.2020.1870501

Moustaghfir, S., & Brigui, H. (2024). Navigating Critical Thinking in the Digital Era: An Informative Exploration. International Journal of Linguistics. *Literature and Translation, 7*(1), 137–143. DOI: 10.32996/ijllt.2024.7.1.11x

OECD. (2023). *OECD Digital Education Outlook 2023: Towards an Effective Digital Education Ecosystem*. OECD., DOI: 10.1787/c74f03de-

OECD. (2024). *Education Policy Outlook 2024: Reshaping Teaching into a Thriving Profession from ABCs to AI*. OECD., DOI: 10.1787/dd5140e4-

Paré, G., Trudel, M.-C., Jaana, M., & Kitsiou, S. (2015). Synthesizing information systems knowledge: A typology of literature reviews. *Information & Management*, *52*(2), 183–199. DOI: 10.1016/j.im.2014.08.008

Pawar, G., & Khose, J. (2024). *Exploring the role of artificial intelligence in enhancing equity and inclusion in education. International Journal of Innovative Science and Research Technology*. IJISRT.

Rajkumar, S., Kishore, R., Lavanya, N., Prashanth Kumar, M., Naveen, B., Prathap Raju, S., & Swathi, P. (2025). The Role of Artificial Intelligence Tools in Teaching and Learning Process of Education. [IRJAEM]. *International Research Journal on Advanced Engineering and Management*, *3*(05), 1774–1783. DOI: 10.47392/IRJAEM.2025.0280

Ray, S., & Ray, D. P. (2024). Artificial Intelligence in Education: Navigating the nexus of innovation and ethics for future learning landscapes. International Journal of Research -GRANTHAALAYAH, 11(12). DOI: 10.29121/granthaalayah.v11.i12.2023.5464

Sadiku, M. N. O., Ashaolu, T. J., Ajayi-Majebi, A., & Musa, S. M. (2021). Artificial Intelligence in Education. *International Journal Of Scientific Advances*, *2*(1). Advance online publication. DOI: 10.51542/ijscia.v2i1.2

Sari, T., Nayi̇, R. F., & Bozkurt, A. (2024). Reimagining education: Bridging artificial intelligence, transhumanism, and critical pedagogy. *Journal of Educational Technology and Online Learning*, *7*(1), 102–115. DOI: 10.31681/jetol.1308022

Selwyn, N. (2024). On the Limits of Artificial Intelligence (AI) in Education. Nordisk tidsskrift for pedagogikk og kritikk, 10(1). DOI: 10.23865/ntpk.v10.6062

Sijing, L., & Lan, W. (2018). Artificial Intelligence Education Ethical Problems and Solutions. 2018 13th International Conference on Computer Science & Education (ICCSE), 1–5. DOI: 10.1109/ICCSE.2018.8468773

Snyder, H. (2019). Literature review as a research methodology: An overview and guidelines. *Journal of Business Research*, *104*, 333–339. DOI: 10.1016/j.jbusres.2019.07.039

Tang, K. H. D. (2024). Implications of Artificial Intelligence for Teaching and Learning. *Acta Pedagogia Asiana, 3*(2), 65–79. DOI: 10.53623/apga.v3i2.404

Taufikin, M. S. I., Parminder, & Others. (2024). The impact of AI on teacher roles and pedagogy in the 21st-century classroom. In 2024 International Conference on Knowledge Engineering and Communication Systems (ICKECS). DOI: 10.1109/ICKECS61492.2024.10617236

UNESCO. (2019). Beijing Consensus on Artificial Intelligence and Education. United Nations Educational, Scientific and Cultural Organization. https://unesdoc.unesco.org/ark:/48223/pf0000368303

UNESCO. (2022). Recomendação sobre a ética da inteligência artificial. Organização das Nações Unidas para a Educação, a Ciência e a Cultura. https://unesdoc.unesco.org/ark:/48223/pf0000380455

UNESCO. (2023). La inteligencia artificial: ¿Necesitamos una nueva educación? UNESCO Publishing. https://unesdoc.unesco.org/ark:/48223/pf0000386262

UNESCO. (2024). Guia para a IA generativa na educação e na pesquisa. https://unesdoc.unesco.org/ark:/48223/pf0000390241

UNESCO. (2025). *AI and the future of education: Disruptions, dilemmas and directions – AI pedagogies, assessment and emerging educational futures*. UNESCO Publishing.

Vovk, O., Zenya, L., Brovarska, I., & Bohdan Khmelnitsky. (2022). Neuropedagogy: A Concept of Brain Compatible Teaching a Foreign Language. Cherkasy University Bulletin: Pedagogical Sciences, 2, 64–73. DOI: 10.31651/2524-2660-2022-2-64-73

Walter, Y. (2024). Embracing the future of Artificial Intelligence in the classroom: The relevance of AI literacy, prompt engineering, and critical thinking in modern education. *International Journal of Educational Technology in Higher Education, 21*(1), 15. DOI: 10.1186/s41239-024-00448-3

World Economic Forum. (2024). Shaping the Future of Learning: The Role of AI in Education 4.0. World Economic Forum. https://www.weforum.org/publications/shaping-the-future-of-learning-the-role-of-ai-in-education-4-0/

Xiao, Y., & Watson, M. (2019). Guidance on Conducting a Systematic Literature Review. *Journal of Planning Education and Research, 39*(1), 93–112. DOI: 10.1177/0739456X17723971

Zhang, K., & Deng, P. (2022). Exploring the Technology and Problems of Artificial Intelligence Education Applications. 2022 4th International Conference on Computer Science and Technologies in Education (CSTE), 265–268. DOI: 10.1109/CSTE55932.2022.00056

Zohuri, B. (2024). Revolutionizing education: The dynamic synergy of personalized learning and artificial intelligence. International Journal of Advanced Engineering and Management Research.

Chapter 2
Artificial Intelligence and Student Mental Health:
Risks and Opportunities

Muhammed Akat
https://orcid.org/0000-0002-8543-8022
Karamanoglu Mehmetbey University, Turkey

ABSTRACT

This book chapter examines the growing role of artificial intelligence (AI) in improving mental health services for students and highlights both the opportunities and challenges associated with its use. AI applications are increasingly being integrated into learning and counseling processes, mitigating the limitations of traditional learning and counseling services. Significant benefits such as increased accessibility, faster decision-making, reduced stigma, and personalized psychological interventions are crucial for student mental health. However, each student is unique, and therefore, the symptoms of mental health disorders may vary from student to student. Furthermore, the similarity of symptoms across mental disorders and the lack of standardized measurement tools used in the diagnostic process can negatively impact the diagnostic and therapeutic capabilities of AI. Despite risks, AI holds promise for improving the effectiveness of mental health interventions in education when developed in collaboration with mental health professionals.

INTRODUCTION

Education aims to promote students' development in academic, social, emotional, behavioral, and cognitive domains (Li & Ding, 2023). In the academic domain, students are expected to acquire skills such as critical thinking, conducting research,

DOI: 10.4018/979-8-3373-6375-2.ch002

problem-solving, and oral presentation (Balleisen et al., 2024). In the social domain, students are expected to develop abilities such as adhering to school rules, establishing healthy communication with peers, resolving interpersonal conflicts, participating in group activities, and demonstrating prosocial behaviors. In the emotional domain, students need to develop skills such as recognizing, expressing, and regulating their own emotions, perceiving the feelings of others, coping with stress and anxiety, and managing anger (Francis et al., 2019). In the behavioral domain, another area of development, students are expected to acquire abilities such as utilizing gross and fine motor skills, coordinating hand-eye movements, and participating in sports activities. Finally, in the cognitive domain, developing effective decision-making, critical and creative thinking, and planning skills constitutes a central aim of education (Kök et al., 2005; Yeşilyaprak, 2024). In addition to these core developmental domains, schools also aim to support students' growth in technological literacy dimensions (Berkowitz, 2011). It should be noted that each developmental area supported by education is interconnected (Yeşilyaprak, 2024). Although education primarily aims to facilitate students' development, each educational level entails inherent challenges. Students who are unable to cope effectively with these challenges may experience psychological problems. Currently, among the tools used to support students' development and help them address problems adversely affecting their mental health are artificial intelligence-based applications (Chen et al., 2024).

Each educational stage has its own specific developmental tasks. For example, during the preschool period, children begin to intensify their interactions with social environments outside the family for the first time. During this stage, children may experience separation anxiety as they are away from their parents (Pepito & Montalbo, 2019). Additionally, adaptation problems such as insufficient communication skills, difficulties in peer relationships, challenges in adhering to school rules, and aggression may occur. In the primary school period, the concept of academic achievement gains importance, marking a phase in which students' self-efficacy perceptions begin to develop. Adaptation problems in primary school may include school refusal, attention deficit and hyperactivity symptoms, learning difficulties, school phobia, peer relationship problems, and low self-efficacy (Wang & Liu, 2021). Considering that the middle school period coincides with the onset of adolescence, students may experience adaptation difficulties related to identity formation, coping with physical and emotional changes, substance and behavioral addictions, academic failure, involvement in negative peer groups, and bullying. The high school period represents a stage in which students begin transitioning from childhood to adulthood, with increasing independence from their families (Savi Cakar, 2024). During this period, various adaptation problems may occur, including academic failure, exam anxiety, uncertainty about the future, role confusion, loneliness, romantic relationship problems, family conflicts, negative peer influence, bullying, behavioral and substance addictions, conflicts with authority figures, and engagement in risky behaviors (Akat, 2024). Finally, in the university period, students live more independently from their families, which brings additional responsibilities. Towards the end of this stage, students may face multiple developmental challenges, such as marriage and entering the workforce, as well as adaptation problems, including substance and behavioral addictions, risky behaviors, romantic relationship issues, and economic difficulties (Shek & Wong, 2025).

Adaptation and developmental problems are seen at different educational levels. Students belong to a psychologically vulnerable group when confronted with stressful life events. Research has shown that students experience a wide range of psychological disorders, including anxiety, depression, stress, sleep disorders, behavioral and substance addictions, aggression, and eating disorders (Kapus et al., 2021; Kumar & Akoijam, 2017). Therefore, students must have access to mental health services that can protect or treat their mental well-being. In schools, psychological counselors or other mental health professionals carry out preventive work to safeguard students' mental health. Additionally, they provide psychological treatment for students who are experiencing psychological problems. In recent years, parallel to technological advancements, artificial intelligence has begun to play a role in protecting students' mental health within educational environments (Gao, 2024). Artificial intelligence tools also function as a psychotherapist, assisting in the treatment of students' psychological disorders.

With technological advancements, mental health services have transitioned from face-to-face interactions to online engagement (Amichai-Hamburger et al., 2014). The use of artificial intelligence has become widespread in the fields of education and psychology in recent years. One of the main uses of artificial intelligence in the field of mental health is the diagnosis and treatment of psychological disorders. During the diagnostic phase of psychological disorders, AI tools gather data about the individual and the illness from various sources and perform matching. AI tools have been developed to use different therapeutic approaches, such as cognitive-behavioral therapy and behavioral therapy (Chen et al., 2025; Naor et al., 2022). These AI tools integrate with various therapeutic approaches to provide personalized professional psychological services for clients (D'Alfonso, 2020).

In recent years, the increasing prevalence of student mental health issues has highlighted the need for the development of new psychological approaches in this field. In this context, artificial intelligence applications stand out as a contemporary approach that provides students with more accessible and personalized mental health support. The first application demonstrating that artificial intelligence can be used to treat individuals' mental health is the ELIZA chatbot. ELIZA was developed in the 1960s at the Massachusetts Institute of Technology by Joseph Weizenbaum (Weizenbaum, 1966). ELIZA functioned as a psychotherapist, analyzing users' input sentences and generating responses based on pre-determined patterns. The most significant limitation of ELIZA was its lack of learning ability, meaning it could only provide responses that had been pre-programmed. However, it is an important early example of artificial intelligence-based mental health applications (Bassett, 2019; Hatch et al., 2025; Moons, 2024).

Over time, artificial intelligence-based mental health applications have evolved into forms capable of performing more complex tasks. For example, with the recent use of AI-based mental health applications, students' data can be analyzed to early detect risk groups related to mental health. Moreover, AI applications can also be used to provide personalized treatments for individuals in need of psychological counseling services (Lee et al., 2021). The increasing number of studies showing the success of AI in mental health has led to the integration of AI-based applications into educational environments. The implementation of AI-based applications in schools offers students the opportunity for early and effective intervention (Tian & Yi, 2024). AI can be used to prevent mental health disorders in students, predict the onset of these disorders, personalize treatment, and support students' participation in the treatment process and self-management. The rapid adoption of AI in education and mental health has brought certain risks. For instance, there are risks to student privacy, informed consent, parental approval, and data privacy. Therefore, the use of AI in protecting students' mental health and treating their psychological problems must be thoroughly addressed from psychological, pedagogical, legal, and ethical perspectives (Li & Gu, 2023; Olawade et al., 2024).

LITERATURE REVIEW

Artificial intelligence in Education

Artificial intelligence has basic features such as learning, problem solving, effective decision making, and adapting to changing conditions. With these features, artificial intelligence contributes to various stages of educational processes such as planning, execution, and evaluation of teaching processes. In addition, artificial intelligence-based applications are also used in other processes of education such as personalized teaching, Smart Tutoring Systems, language teaching, measurement and evaluation, special education, teaching material development, and psychological counseling and guidance (Urmeneta & Romero, 2024). The use of artificial intelligence in nearly all stages of education has facilitated the restructuring of teaching and learning processes and the provision of comprehensive psychological counseling services. For example, AI-based chatbots and humanoid robots have begun to participate in the interaction between students and teachers during the teaching process. Similarly, they are also integrated as an assisting tool in the relationship between students and psychological counselors (Canpolat, 2021). Therefore, it is believed that artificial intelligence is closely related to education and will become an indispensable part of contemporary educational practices in the coming years (Huang et al., 2021). The use of AI in education is increasing every day. Technological developments have always been adapted to educational environments. Indeed, there are many examples where technological advancements have been adapted to learning, teaching, and psychological counseling. Today, however, discussions are ongoing about the opportunities and risks associated with the integration of AI applications into education (Chen et al., 2022).

One of the main contributions of artificial intelligence in education is the benefits it provides to the teaching process. In traditional education, learning processes took place in face-to-face classroom environments where teachers and students interacted. This situation limited teachers' ability to collect data on students' learning levels outside the classroom environment. Another limitation of traditional education was that the learning process in crowded classes could not be adapted to the learning level of each student. In such classes, teachers were limited to using a single teaching method due to temporal and spatial constraints. This situation underwent significant changes with the COVID-19 pandemic. During the pandemic, the transition of teaching and learning processes to online environments required adjustments in teaching methods and techniques to be suitable for online settings (Sari & Nayır, 2020).

In today's world, the transfer of teaching and learning processes to online environments is undoubtedly a positive development. However, distance education has its own set of limitations. These limitations include a lack of interaction (teacher-student, student-student, etc.), motivational issues, lack of social interactions, technological infrastructure problems, challenges in assessment and evaluation processes, and deficiencies in practical courses (Öğdem & Sönmez, 2022). With the integration of artificial intelligence-based applications into education, the limitations of both traditional and online education have started to decrease (Tosunoğlu et al., 2021).

One of the artificial intelligence-based applications in education is machine learning. Machine learning, a subfield of artificial intelligence, involves programming computers to learn from large datasets and adapt to new situations (Korkmaz & Correia, 2019). In other words, machine learning is the process through which computers learn from datasets, solve problems, make decisions, or complete tasks. Machine learning is used actively in various fields, including finance, healthcare, social media, security, and education. One use of machine learning in education is to predict student performance. Through machine learning, various data such as the time students spend on course materials, their exam scores, their level of completion of assignments, and their participation in class can be processed to predict their academic success. Additionally, by analyzing similar data, the subjects in which students face difficulties can be identified (Alkan, 2024).

Once the areas where students struggle are identified, another function of machine learning, which is personalized learning, can be initiated. In this process, machine learning can be used to design learning methods tailored to each student in order to address the deficiencies in areas where they struggle. Furthermore, additional lessons or supplementary topic studies can be planned to help students overcome their deficiencies in a specific course or subject. Throughout these processes, a teaching method and content are determined based on each student's individual characteristics, knowledge, and the areas where they face difficulties, ultimately enhancing the student's performance (Essa et al., 2023). In this way, students' educational achievements can be supported through machine learning.

Another area where machine learning is applied in teaching processes is the supportive role it provides to teachers. Through machine learning, teachers can identify topics that students are struggling to learn. Thus, in crowded classrooms where it isn't easy to track each student individually, machine learning facilitates the monitoring of students both individually and in groups. Machine learning can also help teachers identify the personalized learning needs of their students. (Tiwari, 2023). Through machine learning, it is possible to determine the level at which students meet the learning outcomes of a lesson. In addition, machine learning allows teachers to evaluate exams and assignments more easily and in more detail (Minn, 2022; Tiwari, 2023). All of this shows that machine learning is also used in evaluation processes in educational environments (Alenezi & Faisal, 2020).

Machine learning facilitates the process of recommending additional teaching methods to students identified with deficiencies in exams and assignments. Therefore, artificial intelligence improves the quality of assessment and evaluation processes in education, providing teachers with continuous and detailed feedback on students' progress (El-Alfy & Abdel-Aal, 2008; Zhai et al., 2020). It is well-known that teachers have many responsibilities in educational environments. Therefore, the time teachers must dedicate to teaching processes can sometimes be insufficient. However, with AI-based applications, tasks can be completed quickly and efficiently, which is thought to enhance teachers' performance in teaching processes.

Another area of artificial intelligence application in education is mental health services. In schools, mental health services involve the prevention of psychological problems among students, treatment, and referring them to relevant institutions. Additionally, guidance services are provided in the areas of educational, vocational, and social development (Akat, 2025). In the process of delivering mental health services in schools, school psychological counselors collect and analyze data from students and offer appropriate treatment methods (Emre et al., 2021). However, in situations where there are a large number of students, delivering effective mental health services becomes challenging. The development that eliminates the limitations of traditional mental health services is the integration of artificial intelligence into mental health services in schools (Tian & Yi, 2024). The rapid adoption of artificial intelligence in the education system and the development of its various forms require a careful consideration of both its potential benefits and risks. Therefore, this section of the book will focus on the use of artificial intelligence in the context of mental health.

Use of Artificial Intelligence in Mental Health

Psychological disorders are widely prevalent worldwide. For example, anxiety disorders affected 301 million individuals in 2019, and the symptoms of anxiety disorders often begin during childhood or adolescence (WHO, 2025). This indicates the need to focus on the prevalence of anxiety disorders among students. Like anxiety, depression is also a common issue among adolescents. A meta-analysis study found that 34% of adolescents aged 10-19 worldwide are at risk of developing clinical depression (Shorey et al., 2022). This meta-analysis highlights the widespread nature of psychological problems among students. In recent years, there has been a noted increase in psychological problems among students, which raises concerns (Storrie et al., 2011). Mental health disorders negatively impact students' academic, social, emotional, and cognitive development. Therefore, it is important to provide necessary mental health services, including preventive measures, in schools for community mental health.

To address the psychological problems students face, the school's mental health professional typically intervenes. However, in some severe cases, the student may need to be referred to other institutions for treatment. In such cases requiring referral, collaboration between the school mental health professional and the parents is essential for the effectiveness of the treatment. The psychological help process can be disrupted due to factors such as the cost of psychological treatment, parents not allocating the required time, the student's school hours, and the unavailability of a suitable mental health professional (Balamurugan et al., 2024). However, in today's world, AI-based mental health applications can be utilized to overcome such limitations.

The use of artificial intelligence applications in the field of mental health has the potential to bring about a significant transformation and change in this area (Straw & Callison-Burch, 2020). Today, human-based mental health services undoubtedly provide successful outcomes, benefiting students. However, the traditional method also has limitations stemming from time and space constraints, therapist burnout, and the difficulty in achieving rapport between the therapist and the client. For instance, a student in need of mental health services may have to wait for an appropriate time when the school counselors are available, or the school psychologist must schedule the service during a time when the student does not have classes. In some cases, the large number of students that school counselors need to serve leads to burnout among them, preventing students from effectively utilizing mental health services. The use of AI-based applications in providing mental health services to students will eliminate these limitations faced by both students and school counselors. At this point, artificial intelligence is increasingly being used for diagnostic, treatment, and prevention purposes. In the next section, the benefits and potential risks of artificial intelligence-based applications in diagnosis, treatment, and prevention processes will be examined.

Diagnosis and Decision Making

Artificial intelligence plays a significant role in the diagnostic processes within the field of mental health. The diagnostic process is a fundamental building block for an effective treatment plan. If this building block is incorrect, it can lead to the failure of the treatment. Therefore, it is essential to evaluate data obtained from various sources to correctly diagnose individuals' psychological problems (Hackney & Cormier, 2005). In this context, machine learning can be used as an assisting tool for mental health professionals. Through machine learning, students' sleep and eating patterns, speech patterns, online interactions, individual counseling data, and self-report data can be analyzed to determine their psychological conditions (Andrew et al., 2023). In this way, machine learning simplifies the process of school counselors identifying students' psychological problems. Big data analytics contributes to the diagnostic process for mental health professionals. Big data analytics involves the collection, analysis, and interpretation of large amounts of data obtained from different sources (Pramanik et al., 2021).

In the diagnostic processes within the field of mental health, it is necessary to collect data from multiple sources. For instance, data is collected from numerous sources such as students' peer relationships, school attendance rates, academic performance, communication with teachers, and physical measurements (e.g., blood values, various imaging results). The analysis of symptoms using machine learning algorithms, based on massive symptom clusters collected from individuals who have previously experienced psychological problems, increases the chances of early and accurate diagnosis. As a result, by using big data analytics and machine learning algorithms, students' cognitive, emotional, behavioral, and social symptoms are comprehensively identified. In this regard, big data analytics plays a crucial role in diagnosing mental health disorders and identifying individuals in at-risk groups (Rosenfeld et al., 2021).

Mental health professionals may face challenges in determining which disorder best matches the data collected from clients during traditional diagnostic processes.

This is because some mental health problems share common symptoms, which can create difficulties for mental health professionals during the diagnosis (Forbes et al., 2024). At this point, big data analytics can facilitate a faster and more objective identification of accurate diagnoses and individuals in at-risk groups. Considering the increasing prevalence of psychological disorders among students, the use of big data analytics, machine learning, and various AI-based applications in the diagnostic and risk group identification processes is important for public mental health.

Treatment

Students may require professional psychological guidance for various reasons. Issues such as personal development, academic failures, family problems, sleep disturbances, problematic peer relationships, depression, and exam anxiety are among the psychological disorders that may drive students to seek psychological counseling (El-Hachem et al., 2023; Le et al., 2024). Additionally, students may seek psychological counseling for development-oriented reasons, such as the desire for self-actualization, identity development, and career planning. Psychological counseling is an effective method used to address students' problems as well as to support their personal development. However, students may experience difficulties in receiving professional counseling in schools or various private psychological counseling centers. One of these challenges is the cost of psychological counseling services. Although school counselors offer psychological counseling services for free, the high fees at private psychological counseling centers make it difficult for students to access professional counseling. Another factor that hinders students' access to psychological support is the insufficient number of school counselors. In schools, counselors provide counseling and guidance services to a large number of students. In some cases, there may even be only one school counselor in an entire school. This situation makes it difficult for students to find psychological counseling services at appropriate times. Another issue that complicates students' access to effective psychological counseling services is finding qualified mental health professionals outside of school. Due to their location, students may face difficulties in reaching mental health specialists in the field they require. As a result, traditional mental health services have human-based limitations (Kuhail et al., 2024). These limitations can be overcome or minimized through artificial intelligence-based mental health applications (Rosenfeld et al., 2021).

In recent years, artificial intelligence applications have increasingly been used in psychological counseling processes. The effective use of artificial intelligence in various stages of psychological counseling is undoubtedly a revolutionary development in the field of mental health. Applications such as chatbots and virtual therapists hold promise in the treatment of psychological problems. Below, each stage of the psychological counseling process is explained, and how artificial intelligence can be utilized at each stage is discussed. Generally, the stages of the psychological counseling process are as follows (Hackney & Cormier, 2008):

(1) Integrating and establishing a relationship with the client
(2) Identifying the problem presented by the client
(3) Defining and establishing goals
(4) Selecting and implementing counseling interventions
(5) Termination and Follow-Up

In the first stage of the psychological counseling process, the initial relationship is established between the counselor and the client (in this book chapter, the clients are students). For the successful completion of the first stage, the counselor must create therapeutic conditions such as empathy, unconditional positive regard, presence in the here and now, and transparency. During this stage of counseling, it is crucial for students to feel comfortable and safe, as this will significantly impact the subsequent stages of the counseling process (Voltan Acar, 2020). At this point, the question remains whether artificial intelligence can provide the therapeutic conditions that the counselor is expected to establish in the first stage. However, there are situations where AI-based chatbots and virtual therapists could be beneficial during the first stage of psychological counseling. For example, during the process of providing information about the purpose of the counseling process, the methods to be used, confidentiality and its limits, the rights and responsibilities of the client, and the counselor's role and boundaries, AI-based applications may be helpful. Additionally, AI-based applications can help students feel more comfortable due to the anonymity they provide. While receiving psychological counseling in a school setting may carry concerns about stigma, AI-based applications minimize this issue (Manole et al., 2025).

In the second stage of psychological counseling, the aim is to identify the problems that led the student to seek counseling. During this stage, the student's life and the problems they are experiencing are examined comprehensively. A wide range of information is collected, including the underlying causes of the client's problems, cognitive, emotional, and behavioral symptoms, relationship patterns, triggering situations, and family dynamics. The information gathered from the client is assessed holistically to define the problem (Akat, 2025). At this point, AI-based applications can assist psychological counselors. Data collected from the client can be analyzed with previously acquired large datasets to help identify the client's problem. For example, at this stage of the counseling process, the student's level of exam anxiety can be determined through AI algorithms. Therefore, using AI, counselors can identify the client's problem with larger data sets.

The third stage of the psychological counseling process is goal setting. For the successful completion of the counseling process, the goals must be realistic and achievable (Hackney & Cormier, 2008). During the goal-setting stage, AI-based applications can provide realistic and achievable suggestions for goals by analyzing data from similar cases based on the problems identified in previous sessions. Although the goals proposed by AI are derived from analyses of large datasets of cases, the final goals must be determined through collaboration between the counselor and the client. Therefore, the psychological counselor can use AI as an assisting tool during the goal-setting stage.

The fourth stage of the psychological counseling process is the selection and implementation of interventions. At this stage, interventions are determined to achieve the goals identified in previous sessions. Following this, the client is expected to develop the skills to apply these interventions. AI-based applications can suggest interventions based on different psychotherapeutic theories (Hackney & Cormier, 2008). For example, AI applications programmed based on cognitive behavioral therapy can propose interventions such as cognitive restructuring, behavioral experiments, exposure exercises, and relaxation techniques (Farzan et al., 2025). In this way, AI provides the counselor with intervention suggestions from different therapeutic approaches, promoting a holistic approach to the counseling process.

The final stage of the psychological counseling process is termination and follow-up. One of the main objectives of this stage is to maintain the gains achieved during the counseling process. After the sessions are concluded, follow-up sessions are planned to determine whether the client continues to apply the skills acquired and to support the client's ongoing development. Follow-up sessions also provide information regarding the potential recurrence of the client's problems. At this point, AI-based applications can assist psychological counselors. Through AI applications, reminders related to the skills the client has gained during the counseling process can be sent, mood assessments can be conducted at regular intervals, and clients' psychological states can be assessed using self-report measurement tools. All these applications can help detect the risk of relapse early and facilitate necessary interventions.

In conclusion, artificial intelligence can be used in nearly every stage of the psychological counseling process. However, when it comes to students, it should be noted that families will also be part of the treatment process. This situation requires collaboration between the counselor, the student, and the family. Studies need to be conducted regarding the role of AI in this collaboration. The important point to be considered is to obtain the necessary permissions from the students' parents and to ensure the confidentiality of the student data uploaded to the artificial intelligence systems. Furthermore, the question of whether AI serves as a helpful tool in the process of treating students' mental health or whether it can independently conduct the treatment should be carefully examined. As the use of AI-based applications in therapeutic processes increases in the coming years, the potential benefits and risks of AI in the field of mental health will become clearer.

Prevention

Programs that aim to protect students' mental health include supporting their psychological resilience and reducing risk factors. This section will first explain the use of artificial intelligence in practices aimed at enhancing students' psychological resilience. Subsequently, the use of AI in reducing risk factors that make students vulnerable to psychological problems will be discussed. Psychological resilience refers to students' potential to effectively cope with stressful life events, maintain their functionality, and continue their daily lives (Doğan, 2015). Students with low levels of psychological resilience are more vulnerable to stressful life events and have a higher risk of experiencing psychological problems. As a result, their mental well-being can easily decline when they face challenging life events. On the other hand, students with high psychological resilience effectively cope with stressful situations, and this helps maintain their mental well-being (Mesman et al., 2021; Şahin & Hepsöğütlü, 2018).

Increasing psychological resilience supports students in coping with academic challenges (test anxiety, parental pressure, academic performance anxiety, etc.), educational problems (study methods and time, course preparation, in-class performance, etc.), and interpersonal problems. In this context, artificial intelligence can be utilized to enhance students' psychological resilience. For example, AI-based applications can help students develop coping skills for exam anxiety before it becomes a serious issue. Additionally, personalized problem-solving skills can be provided through AI to address school-related problems that students may encounter at different educational stages. Considering that students may also experience emotional problems, personalized emotional regulation psychoeducation programs can be implemented using AI-based applications. In prevention efforts, identifying students in at-risk groups is crucial. Big data analytics can be used to identify students in these at-risk groups. For example, students at high risk of being bullied can be identified through big data analytics, and AI-based applications can help these students develop coping skills to deal with bullying in a safe environment.

Another type of use of artificial intelligence in prevention studies is the identification of risk factors related to students' mental health. In the development of preventive interventions aimed at protecting students' mental health, it is essential to identify risk factors and detect students in at-risk groups at an early stage. School counselors use a variety of resources, including self-report instruments, observations, and individual or group counseling sessions, to identify at-risk groups. For example, during the initial weeks of the academic year, problem screening inventories are used to identify the problems students are facing and the issues that school counselors need to focus on. Additionally, collaboration between classroom guidance teachers and school psychological counselors is an effective method for identifying students in at-risk groups. In some cases, discussions between school psychological counselors and parents facilitate the identification of students in at-risk groups. Traditional methods for identifying students in at-risk groups have limitations in terms of time and resources. The use of artificial intelligence in identifying at-risk students can overcome the limitations of traditional methods. Due to its capacity to quickly process a large amount of data (personal, familial, social, academic, emotional, etc.), AI can categorize students based on their mental well-being. In this way, preventive efforts can be delivered in a more cost-effective, reliable, valid, and practical manner.

Preventive interventions are fundamentally divided into three groups, and artificial intelligence is used in different ways at each level of prevention. Table 1 provides examples of AI applications for each level of prevention.

Table 1. Prevention Levels and Use of Artificial Intelligence

Prevention Level	Definition	How to Use Artificial Intelligence
Primary Prevention	This level of prevention focuses on all individuals in the community, aiming to reduce the likelihood of mental problems emerging. Reducing risk factors and enhancing protective factors are among the objectives at this level of prevention (Caplan, 1964; Korkut Owen, 2017).	Artificial intelligence-based psychoeducation programs Artificial intelligence-based awareness programs Personalized learning experiences Skill-building with artificial intelligence-based applications
Secondary Prevention	This level of prevention is aimed at individuals who are at risk or showing early signs of mental problems. The focus is on early diagnosis and the implementation of rapid interventions to reduce the prevalence of the problem (Caplan, 1964; Korkut Owen, 2017).	Identifying risk factors and groups using big data analytics Monitoring students in at-risk groups Providing personalized intervention or referral options to students in at-risk groups
Tertiary Prevention	The aim of this level of prevention is to provide the necessary support for students experiencing psychological problems to cope with the difficulties caused by these problems. In this regard, tertiary prevention efforts are conducted to support psychological treatment (Caplan, 1964; Korkut Owen, 2017).	Using AI chatbots to support therapy Monitoring students during or after treatment

In conclusion, artificial intelligence enhances the effectiveness of preventive interventions aimed at increasing students' psychological resilience and reducing risk factors. The use of AI in preventive efforts offers advantages such as identifying at-risk groups, enabling early interventions, implementing personalized preventive programs, and providing easy accessibility to these programs (Basile et al., 2024).

BENEFITS OF ARTIFICIAL INTELLIGENCE FOR MENTAL HEALTH

Accessibility

One of the significant benefits of using artificial intelligence to protect students' mental health is accessibility. In terms of accessibility, AI tools have several advantages over human-based mental health professionals (Babu & Joseph, 2024). First, AI tools do not possess performance-decreasing characteristics such as fatigue and burnout, which are commonly experienced by mental health professionals. Additionally, AI tools can complete complex tasks with high reliability and efficiency. Another advantage of AI tools is their lack of personal biases. In some cases, students' meetings with psychological counselors in schools may lead to stigma. However, psychological help provided through AI tools eliminates this issue. Individuals can receive psychological assistance from AI tools in environments and at times where they feel comfortable (Spytska, 2025). Furthermore, obtaining assistance from a mental health professional requires making an appointment. AI tools, however, are capable of providing mental health services at any time of the day (Luxton, 2016). All these advantages provided by AI make it easier for students to access professional mental health services when faced with their problems. The ability of AI tools to minimize human-related negative factors, such as location, time, and stigma, increases students' motivation to seek mental health services.

Inclusion and Equity

UNESCO has set the goal of providing "inclusive, equitable, and quality education for all" by 2030. It is thought that the integration of artificial intelligence (AI) into learning-teaching and psychological counseling processes in education will promote equal opportunities in education by helping to achieve UNESCO's 2030 goal. Undoubtedly, the important contribution of AI is to improve the quality of students' learning. AI enhances students' learning levels by detecting learning gaps, monitoring student performance, and offering adaptive content. At this point, it can be said that AI will also contribute to the educational guidance services provided by school psychological counselors. Additionally, AI supports teaching processes by strengthening teachers' pedagogical skills and enabling them to use various teaching methods in their instructional practices. UNESCO (2025) highlights that one of AI's most significant contributions is providing educational equality of opportunity for disadvantaged groups. This can contribute to the development of students both in teaching processes and in psychological counseling and guidance services. For example, providing personalized learning environments based on the needs of disadvantaged students can improve their learning outcomes. Similarly, facilitating access to the psychological counseling and guidance services required by students in disadvantaged groups can be made easier through AI tools.

As a result, UNESCO emphasizes that AI applications can achieve goals related to educational equality, enhancing the quality of learning processes, and supporting teachers in their teaching practices (Miao & Holmes, 2023; UNESCO, 2025a). If these goals are achieved, AI is expected to also contribute to the effectiveness of school psychological counseling and guidance services. Throughout these processes, it should be remembered that adhering to human values in the use of AI will ensure that this technology is used for the benefit of humanity in education (UNESCO, 2025b).

Artificial Intelligence-Assisted Chatbots and Virtual Therapists

The use of AI-powered chatbots and virtual therapists in mental health services is revolutionary. These AI tools aim to eliminate the economic, spatial, and temporal limitations of human-based mental health services as much as possible. One of the advantages of chatbots is their ability to provide mental health services to a large number of clients simultaneously, which offers a clear advantage over traditional mental health services. These advantages are particularly beneficial in crises. In moments of crisis, the psychological support required by clients can be provided through chatbots.

AI-powered tools facilitate therapist-client interactions through natural language processing, big data analytics, and machine learning. Through the algorithms they use, chatbots can offer empathetic responses, transfer skills, and help customers effectively solve their problems (Olawade et al., 2024). One of the most significant advantages of chatbots and virtual therapists is their ability to minimize clients' fears of stigma. Particularly in environments such as schools, where there are many individuals, students may fear being stigmatized by their peers. This fear can reduce students' motivation to seek face-to-face mental health services. However, mental health services provided through chatbots can increase confidentiality and, in turn, enhance students' motivation to engage in therapy (Shankar & Venkateswaramurthy, 2025).

The use of AI-powered robots in mental health has led researchers to investigate the effectiveness of AI-based applications through experimental methods. These studies are undoubtedly essential in reducing doubts about the future use of AI in mental health. In one such study, Heinz and colleagues (2025) conducted a randomized controlled trial. Adults exhibiting symptoms of major depressive disorder and generalized anxiety disorder received intervention through Therabot. As a result, the group that received the Therabot intervention showed significantly lower symptoms in both disorders compared to the control group. One important finding from this study was that participants evaluated Therabot's therapeutic alliance similarly to human therapists. This finding challenges the claim that AI-powered therapists cannot establish therapeutic alliances similar to those of human-based therapists.

In another study, Zhong and colleagues analyzed 18 studies to determine whether AI-powered chatbots are effective in reducing symptoms of depression and anxiety. The study concluded that interventions using AI-powered chatbots were effective in reducing depression and anxiety symptoms. However, it was also found that this effect did not persist in follow-up assessments. Therefore, the long-term effects of AI-powered chatbots should be evaluated in different studies. While there are studies showing the effectiveness of AI robots, there are also studies indicating their ineffectiveness. In one such study, the effectiveness of a chatbot-based intervention was examined in adults with moderate to high levels of stress. The intervention lasted for 3 weeks. The results showed that the intervention did not have a significant effect on perceived stress (Schillings et al., 2024). An important consideration in this study is that the intervention was conducted over a short period of time. Given the difficulty of reducing stress levels in such a short time, the effect of AI chatbots on stress should be investigated in longer-term studies. Furthermore, the effectiveness of AI-based applications is generally studied for issues such as depression (Lim et al., 2022) and anxiety (Klos et al., 2021). For this reason, the effectiveness of chatbots should also be examined for problems like school phobia, parent-child conflict, bullying, and burnout. These problems are frequently encountered in schools, and school counselors need supportive tools to assist in the treatment of these issues.

POSSIBLE MENTAL HEALTH RISKS OF ARTIFICIAL INTELLIGENCE

The contribution of artificial intelligence to the processes of protecting and treating students' mental health creates hope for the future. However, as with other technological developments, there are important considerations to be aware of when using AI. This section of the book focuses on the potential risks associated with the use of AI in the field of mental health. It is particularly important to thoroughly examine the potential risks of AI when working with vulnerable groups, such as students. This section first addresses ethical issues, followed by reliability, usage habits, the complex nature of mental disorders, and individual differences.

Reliability Problems in Artificial Intelligence-Enhanced Mental Health Applications

It is a fact that AI-based mental health applications will continue to play an increasingly significant role in our lives. Millions of people spend a considerable portion of their day navigating online environments through their smartphones. Accessing AI applications has become as easy as posting on social media. Therefore, with the integration of AI-based applications, accessing mental health services will become more convenient. However, it is known that institutions and organizations that determine how effectively and safely AI applications meet people's psychological help-seeking needs are either insufficiently identified or not involved. Additionally, most AI-based mental health applications currently serve adults. As accessibility increases, younger individuals will also start using these applications more frequently. Therefore, it is essential to update informed consent forms and parental consent forms regarding the use of AI for children and adolescents. It is crucial for researchers working in the field of mental health to empirically examine the effectiveness of AI-based applications among individuals with different developmental characteristics (such as students, workers, children, adolescents, and the elderly). Finally, how AI-based mental health applications protect the confidentiality of clients' personal information remains a significant concern. For this reason, legal regulations need to be developed to ensure the privacy of clients' personal data.

The Problem of Usage Practice

While artificial intelligence is used in almost every field, its application in certain areas takes time. One of these areas is mental health. For many years, medication and psychotherapy have been the treatment methods used for the psychological needs of individuals. In recent years, online psychotherapy methods have gained popularity, and ethical and legal frameworks regarding online psychotherapy have been established. Despite this, debates continue today about whether face-to-face psychotherapy or online therapy is more effective. Moreover, for individuals accustomed to face-to-face psychotherapy, online therapy may introduce differences and uncertainties. Considering that AI-based mental health services are currently more up-to-date and contain more uncertainties than online therapy, it may take time for clients to adapt to this very new form of therapy. However, students who are more familiar with artificial intelligence applications than older individuals may adapt more easily to artificial intelligence-based psychological help applications.

Ethical Considerations

Artificial intelligence, with the opportunities it provides in both education and mental health, is making the work of students, teachers, and mental health professionals easier. However, the use of AI in mental health has made it necessary to establish an ethical framework. Additionally, legal regulations must also be implemented to protect the rights of students and clients in the use of AI in both education and mental health fields. Errors made by AI in mental health could lead to serious negative consequences for clients. In such cases, the issue of responsibility needs to be discussed from a legal standpoint (Luxton, 2014; Riva et al., 2025).

Mental health services in education are a process where confidentiality is of utmost importance. One of the concerns is how well AI will protect the confidentiality and privacy of the information it collects. At this point, it is crucial to ensure that clients' data remains confidential and is prevented from misuse. Specifically, the risk of individuals' images and voices being used without consent in generative AI must be addressed within an ethical and legal framework. To address this, ethical and legal frameworks should be established to ensure the confidentiality of information obtained through AI in education and mental health. Additionally, the risk of cultural and political biases in the use of AI in education poses one of the ethical challenges related to AI (Akgun & Greenhow, 2022; Chen et al., 2024).

It is a fundamental assumption that there are individual differences among individuals in the fields of education and mental health. For example, a teaching method that helps one student learn more easily may not be effective for another student. In the field of mental health, an example would be a student who exhibits social anxiety through cognitive symptoms, while another may express it through emotional symptoms. Due to AI's data-driven approach, its tendency to attempt to codify clients' problems undermines the "each individual is unique" approach (Akgun & Greenhow, 2022). This situation can lead to ethical issues, as it may cause harm to students or clients in the diagnosis and treatment processes. As a result, AI is increasingly used in education and mental health. However, as with any emerging technology, the ethical and legal issues surrounding its use in these fields should be regulated in collaboration with educators and mental health professionals.

Risks Arising from the Complexity of Mental Disorders

For the use of artificial intelligence in the field of mental health to be valid and reliable, collaboration with mental health professionals is essential. Psychological problems can manifest with varying severity, symptoms, complexity, and duration in each individual. This indicates that psychological problems have a complex nature. Moreover, some mental health disorders have subtypes that share similar symptoms. For example, anxiety disorders are commonly seen in students and have different subtypes. This can particularly pose a challenge for newly graduated mental health professionals in the diagnostic process. Additionally, psychological problems often share the common feature of impairing functionality in different areas of an individual's life. Therefore, for a mental disorder classification to be made, the symptoms experienced by individuals must reduce functionality in various aspects of life (DSM-5, 2013). Mental health professionals take these complex situations into account during the diagnostic process.

The complex nature of mental health disorders requires collaboration between the student, mental health professional, and parents in the diagnosis and treatment process. However, there is an ongoing debate about how accurately AI-based applications can analyze the complexity of mental disorders. For instance, collecting information about a student with an anxiety disorder solely from the student could lead to misdiagnosis and ineffective treatment. In some cases, cooperation with teachers and parents is necessary to accurately determine the nature of the problem. The extent to which AI-based applications can successfully facilitate this collaboration has not been sufficiently researched to date.

One of the risks related to the use of artificial intelligence in mental health is the lack of standardized criteria to be used in the diagnostic process of mental health disorders. Currently, sources such as the DSM-5 and ICD-11, along with self-report data collection tools, are prominent as valid and reliable resources in the diagnostic process. However, over time, it has been observed that the diagnostic criteria for certain psychological disorders have changed. This is due to the inherently more difficult-to-measure nature of psychological disorders compared to physical health problems (Rosenfeld et al., 2021). Another issue where AI applications may face challenges in valid and reliable diagnostic processes related to mental health disorders is the comorbidity of psychological disorders. For example, a student may exhibit not only an anxiety disorder but also attention deficit and hyperactivity disorder. This situation can complicate the diagnostic process even further. As a result, mental disorders have a complex nature, which may lead to AI generating false positive or false negative results.

Risks Due to Individual Differences

The use of artificial intelligence in relation to students' mental health is undoubtedly important; however, there are also some challenges. At the heart of these challenges is the fact that the causes of mental health disorders are not as concretely measurable as those of physical illnesses. The causes of a student's physical health deterioration can be identified through methods such as measuring blood values, various imaging techniques, and monitoring with devices. However, when it comes to identifying the underlying causes of a student's exam anxiety, it is not possible to measure these causes concretely. The causes of a student's exam anxiety may involve a complex combination of factors such as parental attitudes, childhood abuse, teacher behavior, personality traits, cultural influence, and the education system of the country. Therefore, it is thought that artificial intelligence-based applications that analyze the symptoms experienced by students with big data will have difficulty incorporating individual differences into the diagnosis and treatment process.

CONCLUSION

In conclusion, the use of AI in student mental health services presents both significant opportunities and risks. AI offers significant benefits by increasing the accessibility, efficiency, and personalization of mental health services. Thus, it mitigates the limitations and risks inherent in traditional mental health services. However, the use of AI also carries risks that must be addressed. Potential risks that should be addressed with AI-based applications include the security of student information, ensuring accurate diagnosis and treatment, obtaining necessary parental consent, and various ethical considerations. As AI-based applications continue to be used in student mental health services, increased collaboration with mental health professionals is necessary to effectively and reliably meet students' mental health needs. Collaboration between educators, mental health professionals, and AI researchers will be crucial to addressing these challenges and increasing the effectiveness of AI in improving student mental health.

ACKNOWLEDGEMENT

I declare that I used artificial intelligence-supported applications, including ChatGPT and DeepL, to assist in translating expressions from Turkish into English during the writing of the research paper. Firstly, I translated the Turkish text into English using DeepL's academic translation setting. Then, I sought to enhance the academic tone and fluency of the output by requesting ChatGPT to rewrite the text ib British English, employing a fluent and scholarly style.

REFERENCES

Akat, M. (2024). *Intergenerational transmission of family conflict and trait anxiety: Serial mediation of adolescent positive youth development and aggression* (Unpublished doctoral dissertation). Necmettin Erbakan University.

Akat, M. (2025). Psychological counseling. In Günlü, A., & Oral, T. (Eds.), *Psychological counseling and guidance* (pp. 169–190). Eğiten Publishing.

Akgun, S., & Greenhow, C. (2022). Artificial intelligence in education: Addressing ethical challenges in K-12 settings. *AI and Ethics*, *2*(3), 431–440. DOI: 10.1007/s43681-021-00096-7 PMID: 34790956

Alenezi, H. S., & Faisal, M. H. (2020). Utilizing crowdsourcing and machine learning in education: Literature review. *Education and Information Technologies*, *25*(4), 2971–2986. DOI: 10.1007/s10639-020-10102-w

Alkan, A. (2024). Öğrencilerin sınavlardaki performansının makine öğrenmesi teknikleriyle tahminlenmesi. *Osmaniye Korkut Ata Üniversitesi Fen Bilimleri Enstitüsü Dergisi*, *7*(3), 1116–1128. DOI: 10.47495/okufbed.1420959

Amichai-Hamburger, Y., Klomek, A. B., Friedman, D., Zuckerman, O., & Shani-Sherman, T. (2014). The future of online therapy. *Computers in Human Behavior*, *41*, 288–294. DOI: 10.1016/j.chb.2014.09.016

Andrew, J., Rudra, M., Eunice, J., & Belfin, R. V. (2023). Artificial intelligence in adolescents mental health disorder diagnosis, prognosis, and treatment. *Frontiers in Public Health*, *11*, 1110088. Advance online publication. DOI: 10.3389/fpubh.2023.1110088 PMID: 37064712

Babu, A., & Joseph, A. P. (2024). Artificial intelligence in mental healthcare: Transformative potential vs. the necessity of human interaction. *Frontiers in Psychology, 15*, 1378904. Advance online publication. DOI: 10.3389/fpsyg.2024.1378904 PMID: 39742049

Balamurugan, G., Sevak, S., Gurung, K., & Vijayarani, M. (2024). Mental Health Issues Among School Children and Adolescents in India: A Systematic Review. *Cureus, 16*(5), e61035. DOI: 10.7759/cureus.61035 PMID: 38916009

Balleisen, E. J., Howes, L., & Wibbels, E. (2024). The impact of applied project-based learning on undergraduate student development. *Higher Education, 87*(4), 1141–1156. DOI: 10.1007/s10734-023-01057-1

Basile, J. L., Carbonara, N., Panniello, U., & Pellegrino, R. (2024). The role of big data analytics in improving the quality of healthcare services in the Italian context: The mediating role of risk management. *Technovation, 133*, 103010. Advance online publication. DOI: 10.1016/j.technovation.2024.103010

Bassett, C. (2019). The computational therapeutic: Exploring Weizenbaum's ELIZA as a history of the present. *AI & Society, 34*(4), 803–812. DOI: 10.1007/s00146-018-0825-9

Berkowitz, M. W. (2011). What works in values education. *International Journal of Educational Research, 50*(3), 153–158. DOI: 10.1016/j.ijer.2011.07.003

Canpolat, M. (2021). Psikolojik danışmanlık ve rehberlikte yapay zekâ kullanılabilirliği üzerine bir araştırma. *Milli Eğitim Özel Eğitim Ve Rehberlik Dergisi, 1*(1), 1–25.

Caplan, G. (1964). *Principles of preventive psychiatry*. Basic Books.

Chen, D., Liu, Y., Guo, Y., & Zhang, Y. (2024). The revolution of generative artificial intelligence in psychology: The interweaving of behavior, consciousness, and ethics. *Acta Psychologica, 251*, 104593. Advance online publication. DOI: 10.1016/j.actpsy.2024.104593 PMID: 39522296

Chen, J., Yuan, D., Dong, R., Cai, J., Ai, Z., & Zhou, S. (2024). Artificial intelligence significantly facilitates development in the mental health of college students: A bibliometric analysis. *Frontiers in Psychology, 15*, 1375294. Advance online publication. DOI: 10.3389/fpsyg.2024.1375294 PMID: 38515973

Chen, L. T., Yang, L. C., Lin, F. Y., & Lin, Y. H. (2025). Systematic review: The integration of artificial intelligence-powered cognitive-behavioural therapy for autonomous mental health management. *Archives of Psychiatric Nursing, 57*, 151916. DOI: 10.1016/j.apnu.2025.151916 PMID: 40816782

Chen, X., Zou, D., Xie, H., Cheng, G., & Liu, C. (2022). Two Decades of Artificial Intelligence in Education: Contributors, Collaborations, Research Topics, Challenges, and Future Directions. *Journal of Educational Technology & Society*, *25*(1), 28–47.

D'Alfonso, S. (2020). AI in mental health. *Current Opinion in Psychology*, *36*, 112–117. DOI: 10.1016/j.copsyc.2020.04.005 PMID: 32604065

Doğan, T. (2015). Adaptation of the Brief Resilience Scale into Turkish: A validity and reliability study. *The Journal of Happiness & Well-Being*, *3*(1), 93–102.

El-Alfy, E., & Abdel-Aal, R. E. (2008). Construction and analysis of educational tests using abductive machine learning. *Computers & Education*, *51*(1), 1–16. DOI: 10.1016/j.compedu.2007.03.003

El-Hachem, S. S., Lakkis, N. A., Osman, M. H., Issa, H. G., & Beshara, R. Y. (2023). University students' intentions to seek psychological counseling, attitudes toward seeking psychological help, and stigma. *Social Psychiatry and Psychiatric Epidemiology*, *58*(11), 1661–1674. DOI: 10.1007/s00127-023-02470-8 PMID: 37037916

Emre, İ. E., Taş, C., & Erol, Ç. (2021). Use of Machine Learning Methods in Psychiatry. *Psikiyatride Güncel Yaklasimlar*, *13*(2), 332–353. DOI: 10.18863/pgy.779987

Essa, S. G., Celik, T., & Human-Hendricks, N. E. (2023). Personalized Adaptive Learning Technologies Based on Machine Learning Techniques to Identify Learning Styles: A Systematic Literature Review. *IEEE Access : Practical Innovations, Open Solutions*, *11*, 48392–48409. DOI: 10.1109/ACCESS.2023.3276439

Farzan, M., Ebrahimi, H., Pourali, M., & Sabeti, F. (2025). Artificial Intelligence-Powered Cognitive Behavioral Therapy Chatbots, a Systematic Review. *Iranian Journal of Psychiatry*, *20*(1), 102–110. DOI: 10.18502/ijps.v20i1.17395 PMID: 40093525

Forbes, M. K., Neo, B., Nezami, O. M., Fried, E. I., Faure, K., Michelsen, B., Twose, M., & Dras, M. (2024). Elemental psychopathology: Distilling constituent symptoms and patterns of repetition in the diagnostic criteria of the DSM-5. *Psychological Medicine*, *54*(5), 886–894. DOI: 10.1017/S0033291723002544 PMID: 37665038

Francis, D. C., Liu, J., Bharaj, P. K., & Eker, A. (2019). Integrating social-emotional and academic development in teachers' approaches to educating students. *Policy Insights from the Behavioral and Brain Sciences*, *6*(2), 138–146. DOI: 10.1177/2372732219864375

Gao, Y. (2024). The impact and application of artificial intelligence technology on mental health counseling services for college students. *Journal of Computational Methods in Sciences and Engineering*, *25*(2), 1686–1701. DOI: 10.1177/14727978241302641

Hackney, H., & Cormier, L. S. (2005). *The professional counselor: A process guide to helping*. Pearson.

Hackney, H., & Cormier, S. (2008). *Psikolojik danışma ilke ve teknikleri: Psikolojik yardım süreci el kitabı* (Çev. T. Ergene, S. Aydemir Sevim). Mentis Yayıncılık. (Orijinal eser 2005'te yayımlandı)

Hatch, S. G., Goodman, Z. T., Vowels, L. M., Hatch, H. D., Brown, A. L., Guttman, S., Le, Y., Bailey, B., Bailey, R. J., Esplin, C. R., Harris, S. M., Holt, D. P., McLaughlin, M., O'Connell, P., Rothman, K., Ritchie, L., Top, D. N., & Braithwaite, S. R. (2025). When ELIZA meets therapists: A Turing test for the heart and mind. *PLOS Mental Health, 2*(2), e0000145. DOI: 10.1371/journal.pmen.0000145

Heinz, M. V., Mackin, D. M., Trudeau, B. M., Bhattacharya, S., Wang, Y., Banta, H. A., Jewett, A. D., Salzhauer, A. J., Griffin, T. Z., & Jacobson, N. C. (2025). Randomized trial of a generative AI chatbot for mental health treatment. *NEJM AI, 2*(4). Advance online publication. DOI: 10.1056/AIoa2400802

Huang, J., Saleh, S., & Liu, Y. (2021). A Review on Artificial Intelligence in Education. *Academic Journal of Interdisciplinary Studies, 10*(3), 206–217. DOI: 10.36941/ajis-2021-0077

Kapus, K., Nyulas, R., Nemeskeri, Z., Zadori, I., Muity, G., Kiss, J., Feher, A., Fejes, E., Tibold, A., & Feher, G. (2021). Prevalence and risk factors of internet addiction among Hungarian high school students. *International Journal of Environmental Research and Public Health, 18*(13), 6989. DOI: 10.3390/ijerph18136989 PMID: 34208800

Klos, M. C., Escoredo, M., Joerin, A., Lemos, V. N., Rauws, M., & Bunge, E. L. (2021). Artificial intelligence–based chatbot for anxiety and depression in university students: Pilot randomized controlled trial. *JMIR Formative Research, 5*(8), e20678. Advance online publication. DOI: 10.2196/20678 PMID: 34092548

Kök, M., Tuğluk, M. N., & Bay, E. (2005). Okul öncesi eğitimin öğrencilerin gelişim özellikleri üzerindeki etkisinin incelenmesi. *Journal of Kazım Karabekir Education Faculty*, (11), 294–303.

Korkmaz, C., & Correia, A. P. (2019). A review of research on machine learning in educational technology. *Educational Media International, 56*(3), 250–267. DOI: 10.1080/09523987.2019.1669875

Korkut Owen, F. (2017). *Okul temelli önleyici rehberlik ve psikolojik danışma* (4. baskı). Anı Yayıncılık.

Kuhail, M. A., Alturki, N., Thomas, J., Alkhalifa, A. K., & Alshardan, A. (2024). Human-human vs human-aı therapy: An empirical study. *International Journal of Human-Computer Interaction*, *41*(11), 6841–6852. DOI: 10.1080/10447318.2024.2385001

Kumar, K. S., & Akoijam, B. S. (2017). Depression, anxiety and stress among higher secondary school students of Imphal, Manipur. *Indian Journal of Community Medicine : Official Publication of Indian Association of Preventive & Social Medicine*, *42*(2), 94–96. DOI: 10.4103/ijcm.IJCM_266_15 PMID: 28553025

Le, C. M., Huynh, S. V., Nguyen, V. H. A., Le, V. T., Luu-Thi, H. T., & Tran-Chi, V. L. (2024). Psychological difficulties and the needs for psychological services for high school students. *Discover Mental Health*, *4*(1), 50. DOI: 10.1007/s44192-024-00101-5 PMID: 39495430

Lee, E. E., Torous, J., De Choudhury, M., Depp, C. A., Graham, S. A., Kim, H. C., Paulus, M. P., Krystal, J. H., & Jeste, D. V. (2021). Artificial Intelligence for mental health care: Clinical applications, Barriers, facilitators, and artificial wisdom. *Biological Psychiatry: Cognitive Neuroscience and Neuroimaging*, *6*(9), 856–864. DOI: 10.1016/j.bpsc.2021.02.001 PMID: 33571718

Li, S., & Gu, X. (2023). A risk framework for human-centered artificial ıntelligence in education: Based on literature review and Delphi–AHP Method. *Journal of Educational Technology & Society*, *26*(1), 187–202.

Li, Y.-D., & Ding, G.-H. (2023). Student-centered education: A meta-analysis of ıts effects on non-academic achievements. *SAGE Open*, *13*(2), 21582440231168792. Advance online publication. DOI: 10.1177/21582440231168792

Lim, S. M., Shiau, C. W. C., Cheng, L. J., & Lau, Y. (2022). Chatbot-delivered psychotherapy for adults with depressive and anxiety symptoms: A systematic review and meta-regression. Behav Ther. *Behavior Therapy*, *53*(2), 334–347. DOI: 10.1016/j.beth.2021.09.007 PMID: 35227408

Luxton, D. D. (2014). Artificial intelligence in psychological practice: Current and future applications and implications. *Professional Psychology, Research and Practice*, *45*(5), 332–339. DOI: 10.1037/a0034559

Luxton, D. D. (2016). An Introduction to Artificial Intelligence in Behavioral and Mental Health Care. In Luxton, D. D. (Ed.), *Artificial Intelligence in behavıoral and mental health care* (pp. 1–25). Academic Press. DOI: 10.1016/B978-0-12-420248-1.00001-5

Manole, A., Cârciumaru, R., Brînza , R., & Manole, F. (2025). An exploratory investigation of chatbot applications in anxiety management: A focus on personalized interventions. *Information (Basel)*, *16*(1), 11. DOI: 10.3390/info16010011

Mesman, E., Vreeker, A., & Hillegers, M. (2021). Resilience and mental health in children and adolescents: An update of the recent literature and future directions. *Current Opinion in Psychiatry*, *34*(6), 586–592. DOI: 10.1097/YCO.0000000000000741 PMID: 34433193

Miao, F., & Holmes, W. (2023). *Guidance for generative ai in education and research (UNESCO publication)*. United Nations Educational, Scientific and Cultural Organization. https://unesdoc.unesco.org/ark:/48223/pf0000386693

Minn, S. (2022). AI-assisted knowledge assessment techniques for adaptive learning environments. *Computers and Education: Artificial Intelligence*, *3*, 100050. Advance online publication. DOI: 10.1016/j.caeai.2022.100050

Moons, P. (2024). For better or for worse: When chatbots influence human emotions and behaviours. *European Journal of Cardiovascular Nursing*, *23*(5), e49–e51. DOI: 10.1093/eurjcn/zvad098 PMID: 37791604

Naor, N., Frenkel, A., & Winsberg, M. (2022). Improving well-being with a mobile artificial intelligence–powered acceptance commitment therapy tool: Pragmatic Retrospective Study. *JMIR Formative Research*, *6*(7), e36018. Advance online publication. DOI: 10.2196/36018 PMID: 35598216

Öğdem, Z., & Sönmez, E. (2022). Evaluation of the Distance Education Process based on Teachers' Opinions during the Covıd-19 Pandemic. *Malaysian Online Journal of Educational Technology*, *10*(1), 61–75. DOI: 10.52380/mojet.2022.10.1.351

Olawade, D. B., Wada, O. Z., Odetayo, A., David-Olawade, A. C., Asaolu, F., & Eberhardt, J. (2024). Enhancing mental health with Artificial Intelligence: Current trends and future prospects. *Journal of Medicine, Surgery, and Public Health*, *3*, 100099. Advance online publication. DOI: 10.1016/j.glmedi.2024.100099

Pepito, G. M., & Montalbo, I. C. (2019). Separation anxiety on preschoolers' development. *International Journal of Engineering Education*, *8*(1), 229–239.

Pramanik, P. K. D., Pal, S., Mukhopadhyay, M., & Singh, S. P. (2021). Big Data classification: techniques and tools. In Khanna, A., Gupta, D., & Dey, N. (Eds.), *Applications of big data in healthcare* (pp. 137–171). Academic Press. DOI: 10.1016/B978-0-12-820203-6.00002-3

Riva, G., Wiederhold, B. K., & Cipresso, P. (2025). Humane Artificial Intelligence: Psychological, Social, and Ethical Dimensions. *Cyberpsychology, Behavior, and Social Networking, 28*(7), 457–461. DOI: 10.1089/cyber.2025.0202 PMID: 40501330

Rosenfeld, A., Benrimoh, D., Armstrong, C., Mirchi, N., Langlois-Therrien, T., Rollins, C., Tanguay-Sela, M., Mehltretter, J., Fratila, R., Israel, S., Snook, E., Perlman, K., Kleinerman, A., Saab, B., Thoburn, M., Gabbay, C., & Yaniv-Rosenfeld, A. (2021). Big Data analytics and artificial intelligence in mental healthcare. In Khanna, A., Gupta, D., & Dey, N. (Eds.), *Applications of big data in healthcare* (pp. 137–171). Academic Press. DOI: 10.1016/B978-0-12-820203-6.00001-1

Şahin, S., & Hepsöğütlü, Z. B. (2018). Psychological Resilience and Coping Strategies of High School Students Based on Certain Variables. *Journal of Educational and Social Research, 8*(2), 49–64. DOI: 10.22521/jesr.2018.82.2

Sari, T., & Nayır, F. (2020). Challenges in distance education during the (Covid-19) pandemic period. *Qualitative Research in Education, 9*(3), 328–360. DOI: 10.17583/qre.2020.5872

Savi Cakar, F. (2024). *Yaşam dönemleri ve uyum sorunları* (10th ed.). Pegem.

Schillings, C., Meißner, E., Erb, B., Bendig, E., Schultchen, D., & Pollatos, O. (2024). Effects of a chatbot-based ıntervention on stress and health-related parameters in a stressed sample: Randomized controlled trial. *JMIR Mental Health, 11*, e50454. DOI: 10.2196/50454 PMID: 38805259

Shankar, G. M., & Venkateswaramurthy, N. (2025). Artificial intelligence (AI) generated health counseling for mental illness patients. *Current Psychiatry Research and Reviews, 21*(3), 269–283. DOI: 10.2174/0126660822277500240109050359

Shek, D. T., & Wong, T. T. Y. (2025). Developmental Issues of University Stud Shek, D.T., Wong, T.T.Y. (2025). Developmental Issues of University Students in Hong Kong. In: Promoting holistic development in university students. Quality of Life in Asia, vol 17. Springer, Singapore. https://doi.org/DOI: 10.1007/978-981-96-0251-3_3

Shorey, S., Ng, E. D., & Wong, C. H. J. (2022). Global prevalence of depression and elevated depressive symptoms among adolescents: A systematic review and meta-analysis. *British Journal of Clinical Psychology, 61*(2), 287–305. DOI: 10.1111/bjc.12333 PMID: 34569066

Spytska, L. (2025). The use of artificial intelligence in psychotherapy: Development of intelligent therapeutic systems. *BMC Psychology, 13*(1), 175. DOI: 10.1186/s40359-025-02491-9 PMID: 40022267

Storrie, K., Ahern, K., & Tuckett, A. (2011). A systematic review: Students with mental health problems—a growing problem. *International Journal of Nursing Practice*, *16*(1), 1–6. DOI: 10.1111/j.1440-172X.2009.01813.x PMID: 20158541

Straw, I., & Callison-Burch, C. (2020). Artificial Intelligence in mental health and the biases of language based models. *PLoS One*, *15*(12), e0240376. Advance online publication. DOI: 10.1371/journal.pone.0240376 PMID: 33332380

Tian, Z., & Yi, D. (2024). Application of artificial intelligence based on sensor networks in student mental health support system and crisis prediction. *Measurement. Sensors*, *32*, 101056. Advance online publication. DOI: 10.1016/j.measen.2024.101056

Tiwari, R. (2023). The Integration of AI and Machine Learning in Education and its Potential to Personalize and Improve Student Learning Experiences. [IJSREM]. *International Journal of Scientific Research in Engineering and Management*, *7*(2), 1–11. DOI: 10.55041/IJSREM17645

Tosunoğlu, E., Yılmaz, R., Özeren, E., & Sağlam, Z. (2021). Machine Learning in Education: A Study on Current Trends in Researchs. *Journal of Ahmet Kelesoglu Education Faculty*, *3*(2), 178–199.

UNESCO. (2025a). *Digital learning Week 2025.* Retrieved August 29, 2025, from https://www.unesco.org/en/weeks/digital-learning?hub=32618

UNESCO. (2025b). *What you need to know about UNESCO's new AI competency frameworks for students and teachers.* Retrieved August 29, 2025, from https://www.unesco.org/en/articles/what-you-need-know-about-unescos-new-ai-competency-frameworks-students-and-teachers?hub=32618

Urmeneta, A., & Romero, M. (2024). Creative Application of Artificial Intelligence in Education. In Urmeneta, A., & Romero, M. (Eds.), *Creative applications of artificial ıntelligence in education* (pp. 3–16). Palgrave Macmillan. DOI: 10.1007/978-3-031-55272-4_1

Voltan Acar, N. (2020). *Yeniden terapötik iletişim kişiler arası ilişkiler (tamamı bizim toplumdan örnekler).* Nobel.

Wang, Y., & Liu, Y. (2021). The development of internalizing and externalizing problems in primary school: Contributions of executive function and social competence. *Child Development*, *92*(3), 889–903. DOI: 10.1111/cdev.13462 PMID: 32857446

Weizenbaum, J. (1966). ELIZA—A computer program for the study of natural language communication between man and machine. *Communications of the ACM*, *9*(1), 36–45. DOI: 10.1145/365153.365168

WHO. (2025). *Anxiety disorders*. From https://www.who.int/news-room/factsheets/detail/anxiety-disorders

Yeşilyaprak, B. (2024). *Eğitim psikolojisi gelişim-öğrenme-öğretim*. Pegem Akademi.

Zhai, X., Haudek, K. C., Shi, L., Nehm, R. H., & Urban-Lurain, M. (2020). From substitution to redefinition: A framework of machine learning-based science assessment. *Journal of Research in Science Teaching*, *57*(9), 1430–1459. DOI: 10.1002/tea.21658

Zhong, W., Luo, J., & Zhang, H. (2024). The therapeutic effectiveness of artificial intelligence-based chatbots in alleviation of depressive and anxiety symptoms in short-course treatments: A systematic review and meta-analysis. *Journal of Affective Disorders*, *356*, 459–469. DOI: 10.1016/j.jad.2024.04.057 PMID: 38631422

Chapter 3
AI in Education:
Intergenerational Digital Divide and Bridging Strategies

Abdullah Yasin Gunduz
https://orcid.org/0000-0003-2370-6199
Usak University, Turkey

ABSTRACT

This study examines the intergenerational digital divide emerging during AI integration in educational environments and proposes balanced bridging strategies. The research analyzes differences between Generation Z's natural AI affinity and experienced educators' cautious attitudes, grounded in Prensky's digital native-immigrant theory and technology acceptance models. Generation Z's perception of AI as integral to learning processes contrasts sharply with educators' concerns about academic integrity, critical thinking, and pedagogical values, creating classroom tensions around assessment and academic standards. Critiquing polarized AI-maximalist and technology-opposition approaches, this study proposes a hybrid pedagogy model synthesizing traditional and technology-supported methods. The main contribution involves developing innovative strategies including reverse mentoring and intergenerational learning communities that leverage both generations' strengths for mutual learning.

INTRODUCTION

The rapid proliferation of artificial intelligence technologies in the education sector brings about fundamental transformations in pedagogical paradigms. In recent years, the development of machine learning algorithms and the beginning of the use of large language models as educational tools have created a situation that requires

DOI: 10.4018/979-8-3373-6375-2.ch003

re-questioning traditional teaching methods (Luckin et al., 2016). This technological evolution has created an urgent need for adaptation in educational institutions, especially with the widespread access to generative artificial intelligence tools such as ChatGPT after 2022. Recent empirical evidence confirms the rapid acceleration of this transformation. According to IDC's 2024 study, education organizations now report the highest rate of generative AI adoption among all industries, with 86% currently utilizing these technologies (Microsoft Education, 2025). The EDUCAUSE 2025 AI Landscape Study reveals that 86% of higher education participants use AI for at least one work-related task, with the most common applications being content summarization (74%), brainstorming and ideation (71%), and presentation creation (51%) (EDUCAUSE, 2025). These findings indicate that artificial intelligence integration has moved beyond experimental phases to become embedded in daily educational practices.

The entry of multimodal artificial intelligence tools into educational environments in 2024 has further deepened this transformation. These tools, which can simultaneously process visual, auditory, and textual content, have begun to be used at every level of education with examples such as Khan Academy's Khanmigo platform and Carnegie Learning's MATHia system (Russell & Norvig, 2021). These developments have created a new field called "pedagogical AI" in educational technology literature, signaling sectoral transformation.

The most striking phenomenon in this technological revolution process is the attitudinal differences that different generations exhibit toward artificial intelligence tools. Prensky's (2001) distinction between digital natives and digital immigrants gains new dimensions in the context of artificial intelligence. The natural affinity that Generation Z students show toward these tools creates a sharp contrast with the cautious stance of experienced educators. This situation points to fundamental differences in pedagogical philosophy and academic value systems beyond a technical adaptation problem.

Current research reveals the dimensions of this intergenerational divide with concrete data. While results show that students largely use artificial intelligence tools in their academic work, teaching staff do not show the same level of interest in these tools (Bollmann, 2024; EDUCAUSE, 2023). However, the findings primarily belong to research in North American and European contexts. Given the determining effect of cultural context on technology acceptance processes, the universal validity of these findings appears limited. Particularly in societies where traditional educational structures are strong, resistance to questioning teacher authority affects artificial intelligence integration processes in different ways (Hofstede, 2001). This situation reveals the complex nature of technology acceptance intertwined with cultural values.

When examining the current literature, it is observed that two extreme approaches dominate the role of artificial intelligence in education. The technology-focused approach sees artificial intelligence as the future of education and advocates for the complete transformation of traditional methods (Zawacki-Richter et al., 2019). The opposing approach emphasizes the need to preserve traditional pedagogy due to concerns that artificial intelligence will undermine academic integrity and may dull critical thinking skills. Both approaches do not adequately address intergenerational differences and ignore the complexity of the educational ecosystem.

The main purpose of this study is to systematically analyze the intergenerational digital divide in educational environments and develop balanced approaches in the artificial intelligence integration process. The research goes beyond the polarized perspectives in the existing literature by examining the theoretical foundations of hybrid pedagogy models and proposing practical applications.

The original contribution of the study is the reconceptualization of the hybrid pedagogy concept in the context of artificial intelligence and the systematization of the reverse mentoring model as an intergenerational bridging tool in education. While the existing hybrid pedagogy literature mainly focuses on blending online and face-to-face teaching (Graham et al., 2013), this study presents a new framework for the pedagogical integration of artificial intelligence technologies. Similarly, while the reverse mentoring literature generally concentrates on applications in the business world (Murphy, 2012), this research systematically analyzes the specific dynamics and risks of the model in educational environments.

The main research questions are formulated as follows:

RQ1. What perception and attitude differences exist between different generations during the integration of artificial intelligence into educational environments?

RQ2. How do these differences affect educational processes and which bridging strategies yield effective results?

RQ3. How can hybrid pedagogy models support intergenerational cooperation and which approaches should be adopted for sustainable educational transformation?

The methodological approach is based on critical literature analysis and theoretical synthesis methods. Due to the newly developing nature of the subject and the not-yet-crystallized character of intergenerational dynamics, empirical data collection processes are not included. In constructing the theoretical framework, the synthesis of Prensky's digital native-immigrant theory with technology acceptance models was taken as the basis. Through the analysis of findings from existing empirical research, a conceptual map of intergenerational dynamics was created and a hybrid pedagogy model was proposed.

THEORETICAL FRAMEWORK

This section addresses the theoretical foundations necessary to understand the intergenerational dynamics in the artificial intelligence integration process in education. The development of the digital divide concept, technology acceptance processes, and the reflections of these processes on artificial intelligence applications in educational environments are systematically examined.

Digital Native and Digital Immigrant Distinction

Marc Prensky's distinction between digital natives and digital immigrants, introduced in 2001, constitutes a critical theoretical ground for understanding current artificial intelligence debates. While Prensky defined the generation born after 1980 as “digital natives,” he evaluated previous generations in the “digital immigrants” category. This theoretical distinction provides an important framework for explaining fundamental differences in forms of relationship with technology.

The basic characteristics of digital natives are shaped around the capacity to establish a natural and intuitive relationship with technology. This group shows superiority in skills such as processing information in parallel, performing multiple tasks simultaneously, and rapidly comprehending visual-auditory content (Prensky, 2001). When evaluated in the context of artificial intelligence, digital natives' open attitude toward these technologies and speed of adaptation align with theoretical predictions.

Digital immigrants, on the other hand, develop their relationships with technology more cautiously and gradually. The behavioral patterns defined as “accent” observed in this group's technology use also manifest in their approaches to artificial intelligence tools. For example, digital immigrants' tendency to evaluate alternative methods before using technology explains their cautious stance toward artificial intelligence tools (Helsper & Eynon, 2010).

However, Prensky's theory has been subject to various criticisms over time. Bennett and colleagues (2008) argued that the digital native concept is overly generalizing and that age-based categorization ignores individual differences in technology use skills. These criticisms reveal that intergenerational approaches in the artificial intelligence integration process need to be more nuanced.

Recent research shows that the digital native-immigrant distinction is not absolute and that technology experience is related to frequency and quality of exposure rather than age (Corrin et al., 2010). Helsper and Eynon (2010) deepened this criticism by empirically proving that technology use shows stronger relationships with socio-economic status, education level, and cultural capital. Similarly, Livingstone and Helsper (2007) emphasized that age-based categorization creates misleading generalizations and masks individual differences. In line with these findings, adopting approaches based on technology use profiles rather than generation-based analysis appears more appropriate. Behavioral factors such as technology competency, motivation for use, and pedagogical orientation emerge as more explanatory variables than age categories.

This approach is particularly valuable in explaining "gray area" situations where generational categories are not absolute. For example, groups such as educators who are in the digital immigrant category by age but show high adaptation to technology, or students from Generation Z who approach technology with distance, demonstrate the inadequacy of traditional age-based classifications. Kohlbacher and Herstatt (2011) define this situation as "technological hybrid identities." The existence of these groups reveals the necessity of flexible and multi-dimensional approaches rather than uniform strategies in educational institutions.

Technology Acceptance Models

Understanding technology acceptance processes is fundamentally important for explaining the resistance and acceptance encountered in the integration of artificial intelligence into educational environments. In this context, theoretical frameworks such as the Technology Acceptance Model (TAM) and the Unified Theory of Acceptance and Use of Technology (UTAUT) enable us to understand different generations' attitudes toward artificial intelligence.

The Technology Acceptance Model, developed by Davis (1989), systematically explains the factors affecting individuals' intentions to use technology. The main components of the model, perceived usefulness and perceived ease of use, constitute critical variables for understanding the adoption processes of artificial intelligence tools in educational environments.

Perceived usefulness refers to individuals' belief that technology use will improve their performance. In the educational context, students' beliefs that artificial intelligence tools will accelerate their learning processes or improve their quality directly affect their tendency to adopt these tools. Research shows that Generation Z students' perceptions of the usefulness of artificial intelligence tools are significantly higher than previous generations.

Perceived ease of use encompasses the belief that technology use does not require mental and physical effort. Digital natives' natural relationship with technology leads them to evaluate artificial intelligence tools more positively in terms of ease of use. In contrast, the difficulties that digital immigrants experience in learning these tools negatively affect their acceptance tendencies.

The UTAUT model was created by Venkatesh and colleagues (2003) by developing TAM and addresses the factors affecting technology acceptance more comprehensively. Basic constructs such as performance expectancy, effort expectancy, social influence, and facilitating conditions offer valuable perspectives in explaining the acceptance of artificial intelligence technologies in educational environments.

The social influence factor is critically important in terms of intergenerational dynamics. While students' observation of artificial intelligence use from their peers strengthens their tendency to adopt these technologies, negative opinions from educators' colleagues can slow down the acceptance process (Tamilmani et al., 2019).

Facilitating conditions emphasize the importance of institutional-level support systems. Educational institutions' infrastructure support, training programs, and political approaches toward artificial intelligence tools create determining effects on different generations' adoption of these technologies.

Theoretical Implications for AI Integration in Education

The combination of digital native-immigrant theory and technology acceptance models creates a powerful theoretical framework for explaining the dynamics that emerge during the integration of artificial intelligence into educational environments. This theoretical synthesis offers valuable perspectives for understanding the current situation and developing future predictions.

In line with the theoretical framework's predictions, digital natives are expected to rapidly adopt artificial intelligence tools and actively use them in educational processes. Indeed, current research confirms this prediction and shows that students widely use artificial intelligence tools in homework preparation, research, and creative project development processes (Rudolph et al., 2023).

The more cautious approach of educators in the digital immigrant category toward artificial intelligence integration is consistent with theoretical expectations. This group questions the pedagogical value of technology and emphasizes the priority of preserving the effectiveness of traditional teaching methods. However, this situation does not mean absolute rejection; a longer-term and gradual acceptance process is predicted.

The application of technology acceptance models in the artificial intelligence context reveals that the factors playing a role in different generations' acceptance processes differ. While perceived usefulness and social influence factors are more determining for younger generations, facilitating conditions and effort expectancy are critically important for experienced educators (Al-Rahmi et al., 2019).

The theoretical framework's predictions regarding educational strategies to be followed emphasize the necessity of differentiated approaches. Developing flexible strategies that consider intergenerational differences rather than uniform training programs is seen as critical for successful integration. The long-term predictions of theoretical models indicate that the intergenerational divide will close over time, but this process should not be limited to natural development. Active bridging strategies and hybrid approaches are seen as necessary for accelerating this process and preserving educational quality.

In conclusion, the theoretical framework reveals that the integration of artificial intelligence into education is not a linear process and that intergenerational dynamics need to be carefully managed. In the direction indicated by theoretical foundations, developing balanced and inclusive approaches will create beneficial results for all stakeholders in the educational ecosystem. In light of theoretical foundations, different generations' perceptions and attitudes toward artificial intelligence technologies will be analyzed in light of empirical findings in the next section.

INTERGENERATIONAL AI PERCEPTION IN EDUCATIONAL ENVIRONMENTS

The entry of artificial intelligence technologies into educational environments has brought to light the deep differences in different generations' approaches to these technologies. This section addresses the contrasts between Generation Z's open attitude toward artificial intelligence and experienced educators' cautious approaches, examining the dynamics these differences create in classroom environments. The reflections of intergenerational perception differences on pedagogical processes, academic integrity debates, and uncertainties in assessment systems are systematically analyzed.

Generation Z's AI-Friendly Approach

Generation Z, born between 1997-2012, as the first generation to grow up with digital technologies, exhibits a natural affinity toward artificial intelligence tools. This generation's perception of artificial intelligence technologies has become one of the fundamental factors shaping their learning experiences. Research shows that Generation Z students view artificial intelligence tools as a natural part of their learning processes and do not hesitate to use these technologies (Seemiller & Grace, 2018).

Generation Z's basic motivations in artificial intelligence use are shaped around efficiency enhancement and personalization of the learning experience. This group evaluates artificial intelligence tools as technologies that save time, simplify complex topics, and support creative processes. They particularly prefer artificial intelligence-supported approaches in research, content production, and problem-solving processes (García-Peñalvo, 2023).

The behavioral patterns observed in this generation's artificial intelligence use reflect their intuitive relationship with technology. Generation Z students prefer learning through trial and error when using artificial intelligence tools and discover the possibilities of these technologies without formal training. This approach explains their speed in technology adaptation while also bringing some risks.

Empirical data strongly supports these theoretical observations about Generation Z's AI adoption patterns. Carnegie Learning's 2025 national survey of over 650 respondents across 49 states found that the percentage of educators who use AI "often" and "always" nearly doubled from the previous year, with administrators showing even higher usage rates than teachers (Carnegie Learning, 2025). More significantly, the study revealed that 68% of participants believe students use AI "somewhat more" or "much more" than faculty members, confirming the intergenerational usage gap. In the United States specifically, students using AI "often" for school-related purposes increased by 26 percentage points year-over-year, while the portion who never used AI dropped by 20 points (Microsoft Education, 2025). A particularly striking finding from Cengage Group's research indicates that by January 2023, nearly 90% of college students were already using ChatGPT for homework assistance, with 65% believing they know more about AI than their instructors and 45% wishing their professors would incorporate AI skills into relevant coursework (Cengage Group, 2025).

The opportunities that Generation Z gains from using artificial intelligence technologies can be evaluated multidimensionally. These technologies accelerate learning processes, making it easier to understand complex topics and providing personalized learning experiences. AI-supported tools provide content production suitable for different learning styles while also offering significant support in creative projects. This situation improves students' multitasking skills and saves time in routine tasks, allowing them to focus on more complex analytical thinking activities. It also supports the acquisition of digital skills that will be critically important in their future professional lives (Kasneci et al., 2023).

However, this intensive use can bring dangers such as excessive dependence on artificial intelligence tools, weakening of critical thinking and independent problem-solving capacities. Research reveals that students who constantly resort to these tools experience performance decline when technological support is not available (Borenstein & Howard, 2021). The lack of critical approach regarding information accuracy and source reliability can increase the risk of including misinformation in academic work. The paradox between originality and creativity and the weakening of social learning skills are other critical problem areas. Generation Z's pragmatic approach to artificial intelligence use relegates ethical dimensions to the background and creates significant differences in value systems with educators.

Experienced Educators' AI Concerns

The approaches of educators with decades of experience in the field of education toward artificial intelligence technologies show fundamental differences from Generation Z's attitudes. Experienced educators' concerns about these technologies concentrate around pedagogical values, ethical standards, and educational quality concerns. These concerns are not merely technology fears but reflect deep evaluations regarding educational philosophy and the nature of learning processes (Chan & Hu, 2023).

The primary concern areas of experienced AIED researchers focus on fairness and algorithmic bias. In research conducted by Holmes and colleagues (2022) with 17 leading AIED researchers, participants expressed significant concerns about AI systems showing bias against certain demographic groups and the need for greater transparency in educational AI decision-making processes. The study revealed that most AIED researchers are not trained to tackle emerging ethical questions, and found a notable lack of critical reflection on ethical implications in the field. Zawacki-Richter et al.'s (2019) systematic review of 146 studies on AI in higher education revealed that only 8.9% of first authors came from Education departments, with the vast majority (62%) from Computer Science and STEM fields. Most concerning, only 1.4% of the reviewed studies critically reflected on ethical implications, challenges, and risks of applying AI in education. Educators who have worked with traditional homework and exam systems for many years have concerns that artificial intelligence tools could fundamentally shake these systems. The thought that students could hide their real abilities by producing artificial intelligence-supported solutions leads to questioning assessment processes in terms of fairness and reliability.

The fundamental problem in assessment systems is the difficulty of accurately measuring student performance and the traditional grading system losing its meaning. The inability to detect artificial intelligence use in written assignments and research projects creates deep mistrust among educators, leading to the adoption of skeptical approaches (Rudolph et al., 2023).

Contemporary survey data validates these theoretical concerns about educator resistance. The Carnegie Learning study found that 61% of educators have experienced students using AI for cheating, representing an increase from 53% in the previous year (Carnegie Learning, 2025). Despite this increase in observed cheating behaviors, educators' worry levels about cheating remained relatively stable, suggesting a complex relationship between experience and concern. Privacy issues have emerged as another significant barrier, with 27% of educators reporting privacy-related challenges, up from 24% previously. The EDUCAUSE study confirms that only 22% of institutions have developed comprehensive AI strategies, while 55% report that AI initiatives remain isolated within individual departments rather than being institutionally coordinated (EDUCAUSE, 2025). This fragmentation reflects the cautious, department-by-department approach that characterizes educator adoption patterns.

Concerns about the nature of learning processes stem from the understanding that education is not only a result-oriented but also a process-oriented activity. The quick solutions offered by artificial intelligence tools can hinder the development of higher-order cognitive processes such as critical thinking and analytical evaluation. The disappearance of experiences that students gain by struggling with difficulties, which are considered critically important for the development of personality traits such as resilience and perseverance, creates concern.

In the ethical dimension, there is concern about the weakening of education's character-building and value-imparting function. The uncertainty created by artificial intelligence use in copying, plagiarism, and academic fraud causes educators to experience indecision in guidance. The transformation of pedagogical authority and the teacher role brings the concern that years of acquired experience and expertise will become worthless. The possibility that students will find artificial intelligence sources more reliable than teacher explanations leads to questioning classroom authority.

The concern about erosion of educational quality and standards encompasses the risk of weakening basic academic skills such as language skills, writing abilities, and research methodology. Regarding technology dependence and digital divide, there is the thought that inequality among students will be created and the concern that a situation where learning cannot be done without technology will emerge. Finally, experienced educators having to redefine their professional identities and feeling inadequate in the face of the speed of technological change are among the factors that increase resistance in the adaptation process.

Examples of Classroom Tensions

Intergenerational artificial intelligence perception differences create concrete tensions in classroom environments and directly affect educational processes. These tensions crystallize most around homework preparation, assessment systems, and academic integrity standards. These problems experienced in classroom dynamics have become issues that educational institutions urgently seek solutions for.

The tensions experienced in homework preparation processes are one of the areas where intergenerational differences are most prominently observed. Generation Z students view artificial intelligence tools as a natural part of the homework preparation process. For them, ChatGPT, Grok, Claude, or similar tools are no different from Google used for research. In this perspective, artificial intelligence tools are positioned as auxiliary technologies that support access to information and thought development processes (Cotton et al., 2024).

However, experienced educators view the homework preparation process as the fundamental arena where learning takes place. For them, homework is a critical process where students synthesize information through individual efforts, develop critical thought, and reinforce written expression skills. The use of artificial intelligence bypassing these processes and focusing on results means losing the essence of learning.

These different perspectives create concrete problems in classrooms. While students prepare artificial intelligence-supported homework, educators have difficulty determining which part of these assignments belongs to the student and which part belongs to artificial intelligence. This uncertainty creates unfairness in assessment processes and undermines the student-teacher trust relationship.

A concrete example is a character analysis assignment requested from students in a literature class. A Generation Z student asks ChatGPT about the character's traits to create a basic framework, then completes the assignment by adding their own interpretations. From the student's perspective, this approach is a legitimate method that accelerates the research process and helps organize thoughts. However, from the educator's perspective, it becomes impossible to measure the student's real level of text analysis, critical reading, and written expression skills.

Tensions in assessment systems gain even more complex dimensions. While traditional assessment approaches focus on measuring students' individual performances, there are uncertainties about how this measurement will be made in the artificial intelligence age. Students can produce much higher quality texts with artificial intelligence tools, but whether these texts reflect their real competencies becomes problematic.

An example situation experienced in an engineering faculty concretizes this tension. In a project design assignment requested from students, many students used artificial intelligence tools to make technical calculations and prepare detailed reports. The results appear much more professional and technically sophisticated compared to previous years. However, it was revealed in oral exams that students had difficulty explaining these projects and could not adequately grasp basic engineering concepts. This situation led to serious inconsistencies between written assessment and real competency.

Tensions regarding academic integrity constitute the most sensitive area. Traditional academic integrity rules are based on students clearly indicating the sources they use in their work and not presenting others' ideas as their own. However, artificial intelligence tools make these boundaries blurred.

While the concept of "thinking together with artificial intelligence" is becoming widespread among students, educators interpret this situation as "being thought by artificial intelligence." This perspective difference leads to uncertainties in defining behaviors that are considered academic integrity violations.

To exemplify this problem with a case experienced in the psychology department: In a case analysis assignment requested from students, a student told ChatGPT about the patient's symptoms and asked for possible diagnoses, then wrote their own evaluation based on these diagnoses. The student stated that they used artificial intelligence as a consultant and made the final decisions themselves. However, the educator thinks that the diagnosis process should be based on the student's own knowledge and experience, and that artificial intelligence support invalidates this process.

Tensions experienced in classroom discussions also reach notable dimensions. Generation Z students come to class prepared by obtaining information about topics from artificial intelligence tools before discussions. This situation can improve the quality of discussions but also affects students' processes of developing their own opinions. When educators notice that students are presenting artificial intelligence-supported views, they doubt the authenticity of the discussion.

Problems experienced in group projects constitute another source of tension. While some students use artificial intelligence tools intensively, others prefer traditional methods. This situation leads to unfair distribution of workload within groups and different quality standards. Students using artificial intelligence produce faster and more comprehensive content while students adopting traditional methods fall into a disadvantaged position in terms of time.

Similar tensions are experienced in exam systems. The possibility for students to use artificial intelligence tools in online exams threatens exam reliability. Institutions returning to face-to-face exams observe performance decline in students accustomed to technology-supported learning.

These tensions are not limited to academic dimensions but are also reflected in social dynamics. Performance differences between students who use and do not use artificial intelligence change the classroom competitive environment and affect inter-student relationships. While some students view using artificial intelligence as an unfair advantage, others evaluate it as a natural skill required by the age. These approach differences actually reflect symptoms of a broader generational divide.

The scope of these tensions has expanded significantly as AI usage has become more widespread. Recent data from Carnegie Learning reveals that concerns about academic integrity have intensified, with educators reporting a 15% increase in students using AI for potential academic misconduct (Carnegie Learning, 2025). However, the response strategies have also evolved. The study found that 64% of teachers now discuss proper and improper uses of AI with students, compared to 42% in the previous year, indicating growing awareness of the need for explicit guidance. Policy development has accelerated, with 40% of schools and districts now having AI policies compared to 20% the previous year, yet this still leaves the majority of educational institutions without formal guidelines (Carnegie Learning, 2025). The

Microsoft study confirms that institutional responses vary significantly, with Title I schools and rural districts significantly less likely to have developed AI policies compared to their non-Title I and urban counterparts (Microsoft Education, 2025).

These fundamental perception differences between Generation Z and experienced educators constitute the root of conflicts in educational environments. Systematically examining these differences is critically important for understanding the dimensions of the problem.

Table 1. Comparison of Intergenerational AI Perception

Dimension	Generation Z Approach	Experienced Educator Approach
AI Perception	Natural tool, "digital assistant"	Potential threat, "academic risk"
Usage Motivation	Efficiency, creativity	Concern, reluctance
Academic Integrity	Flexible interpretation	Strict standards
Learning Process	Result-oriented	Process-oriented
Approach to Change	Rapid adaptation	Cautious evaluation

This comparative analysis summarizes the fundamental dynamics of tension in educational environments. The sharp difference between Generation Z's approach to artificial intelligence as a "natural tool" and experienced educators' perception of it as a "potential threat" creates continuous conflict in daily educational practices. Particularly, Generation Z's flexible interpretation of academic integrity and educators' rigid standard understanding lead to serious difficulties in assessment systems.

These findings show the necessity of reorganizing current educational systems to meet the needs of both groups. Adopting hybrid pedagogy approaches and developing bridging strategies are seen as indispensable for overcoming this generational divide. The synthesis of both groups' strengths constitutes the fundamental condition for successful artificial intelligence integration.

In conclusion, classroom tensions affect all dimensions of educational processes and create situations requiring urgent solutions. These tensions reveal the need for developing intergenerational bridging strategies and adopting hybrid pedagogical approaches.

HYBRID PEDAGOGY AND BALANCED APPROACHES

The intergenerational tensions that emerge during the integration of artificial intelligence into educational environments reveal the inadequacy of current approaches and the necessity of new pedagogical models. This section provides a critique of the polarized perspectives dominant in the literature and examines the theoretical foundations of the hybrid pedagogy concept. Additionally, practical applications of intergenerational bridging strategies and the potential of the reverse mentoring model in educational environments are evaluated.

Critique of Polarized Approaches in Literature: AI-Maximalism and Technology Opposition

Two extreme approaches that have become prominent in the literature regarding the role of artificial intelligence in education negatively affect educational policies and pedagogical practices. These polarized perspectives manifest as approaches that either completely embrace or categorically reject artificial intelligence technologies. Both approaches ignore the complexity of educational processes and the nuances of intergenerational dynamics.

The AI-maximalism approach positions artificial intelligence technologies as the future of education and advocates for the complete transformation of traditional pedagogical methods. Researchers who adopt this perspective argue that artificial intelligence can solve all problems in educational processes and can revolutionarily improve learning experiences (Luckin et al., 2022). The maximalist approach is shaped within the technological determinism paradigm and is based on the assumption that technology is the driving force of social change.

Advocates of this approach emphasize the advantages of artificial intelligence such as personalized learning, instant feedback, and unlimited access to information, while characterizing traditional educational methods as inefficient and outdated. According to them, teachers' role as information transmitters should end and AI-supported systems should be placed at the center of learning processes. This perspective emphasizes the inevitability of digital transformation in education while interpreting factors that delay technology integration as resistance.

However, the AI-maximalism approach has significant limitations. First, this approach ignores the human factor and the emotional dimensions of pedagogical relationships. The fact that educational processes are not just information transfer but also include social, emotional, and ethical development processes is not sufficiently considered. The current limitations and potential risks of artificial intelligence technologies are also minimized. Critical issues such as algorithmic bias, data security, and technology dependence are not adequately addressed (Holmes et al., 2022).

The maximalist approach also ignores intergenerational differences and educators' accumulated experience. The assumption that experienced educators' pedagogical expertise is worthless increases resistance in educational institutions and makes change processes more difficult. Another weakness of this approach is that it does not sufficiently consider the fact that technology use in education can increase socio-economic inequalities. These limitations show that the AI-maximalism approach cannot be a sustainable and inclusive solution for the education system.

At the other extreme, the technology-opposed approach views artificial intelligence technologies as threats to educational processes and categorically opposes the use of these technologies. Educators and researchers who adopt this perspective argue that traditional pedagogical values should be preserved and that technological integration will deteriorate educational quality (Watters, 2023).

The basic arguments of the technology-opposed approach are shaped around the importance of human-centered education and the potential harms of technology in learning processes. This approach argues that the development of critical thinking, creativity, and social skills is only possible through traditional methods. Additionally, the thought that artificial intelligence use violates academic integrity and prevents students from developing basic skills is dominant.

Advocates of this approach think that technology integration will increase standardization in education and restrict teachers' pedagogical autonomy. According to them, educational processes should be based on human relationships and technology inevitably creates damaging effects on these relationships. This perspective adopts the strategy of preserving current practices rather than adapting to technological developments.

The technology-opposed approach also has significant limitations. This approach ignores changing world conditions and student needs. Generation Z's natural relationship with technology and the necessity of digital skills they will need in their future professional lives are not sufficiently considered. The positive contributions that artificial intelligence technologies can make to educational processes are also systematically rejected. This attitude carries the risk of isolating educational institutions from changing social dynamics. Educational systems that completely exclude technological developments may be insufficient in preparing students for real-world conditions.

The technology-opposed approach can also create innovation-inhibiting effects in education and limit pedagogical development. These limitations reveal that the technology-opposed stance cannot provide a comprehensive response to the needs of the educational system. Both polarized approaches prevent the development of pragmatic solutions in educational policies. AI-maximalism forces technology integration and increases resistance. Technology opposition, on the other hand, exhibits a closed attitude to change, weakening the adaptation capacity of educational institutions. This situation reveals the need to develop balanced and inclusive approaches.

Theoretical Foundations of Hybrid Pedagogy as a Balanced Path

In the face of the inadequacies of polarized approaches, the hybrid pedagogy model offers a balanced alternative for artificial intelligence integration in education. The concept of "hybrid pedagogy" used in this study refers to the systematic integration of AI-supported teaching approaches with traditional pedagogical methods. This model adopts neither technological determinism nor technology resistance; instead, it offers a balanced approach that supports technology use in line with pedagogical purposes. Hybrid pedagogy is built on the principles of student-centered flexibility, pedagogical continuity, and critical technology literacy. This concept, unlike "blended learning," encompasses not only the combination of online and face-to-face teaching but also the integration of artificial intelligence technologies into pedagogical processes. This model creates a framework that supports technology use in educational processes while preserving the central role of the human factor (Graham et al., 2019).

The theoretical foundations of hybrid pedagogy consist of a synthesis of socio-cultural learning theory, constructivist learning approach, and technology-supported pedagogy research. Vygotsky's socio-cultural theory emphasizes that learning occurs through social interactions and highlights the importance of the zone of proximal development. Hybrid pedagogy expands this perspective by positioning artificial intelligence tools as elements that support and enrich social interaction in the learning process.

The constructivist learning approach is based on the principle of students' active participation and structuring knowledge through their own experiences. Hybrid pedagogy, while adopting this approach, evaluates artificial intelligence tools as scaffolding tools that support students' knowledge structuring processes. From this perspective, technology ceases to be a passive information source and becomes a component of active learning processes.

One of the fundamental principles at the center of hybrid pedagogy is the mutual compatibility of technology and pedagogy. This approach argues that technological tools should serve pedagogical purposes while emphasizing that pedagogical approaches should also be adapted to benefit from technological possibilities. This balance creates a middle way that adopts neither technological determinism nor technology resistance.

The principle of student-centered flexibility advocates developing flexible approaches by recognizing that different students have different learning preferences and technology use levels. This principle is particularly important in classroom environments where students from both digital native and digital immigrant categories coexist. Offering students options in technology use meets the needs of both technology-friendly and traditional approach-preferring students.

The principle of pedagogical continuity adopts a gradual transformation strategy rather than radical changes in education. This principle aims to integrate new technological possibilities while preserving experienced educators' pedagogical accumulations. Thus, minimizing resistance during the change process and ensuring sustainable transformation are targeted.

The principle of critical technology literacy aims to teach students and educators not only the technical dimensions of technology use but also its ethical, social, and epistemological dimensions. This approach supports conscious and responsible use of artificial intelligence tools, reducing the risks of technology dependence.

The principle of intergenerational cooperation supports mutual learning processes by synthesizing different generations' technology experiences and pedagogical perspectives. This principle encourages Generation Z, experienced in technology, and educators experienced in pedagogical matters to learn from each other. The complex relationship network and dynamic interaction of these principles are visualized in the following model.

Figure 1. Hybrid Pedagogy Model Flow Chart

The model presented in Figure 1 reveals that hybrid pedagogy is not a linear process but a multidimensional and interactive system. The teacher-centered and process-oriented approach of traditional pedagogy and the speed and personalization advantages of artificial intelligence tools create a balanced synthesis in the hybrid integration phase. The success of this integration depends on the simultaneous application of the principles of student-centered flexibility, pedagogical continuity, and critical technology literacy. The model's output, intergenerational cooperation, aims for sustainable transformation through reverse mentoring and learning communities.

One of the fundamental strategies adopted in implementing hybrid pedagogy is gradual integration. This strategy envisages the gradual and controlled integration of artificial intelligence tools into educational processes rather than sudden and radical inclusion. In the first stage, awareness programs are implemented to help educators and students become familiar with these tools. In the second stage, limited and controlled usage experiences are provided. In the third stage, the skills and ethical standards necessary for widespread use are developed.

The contextual adaptation strategy aims to adapt technology integration to these contexts by recognizing that different disciplines, educational levels, and institutional cultures have unique needs. For example, artificial intelligence use in STEM fields may require different approaches than use in social sciences fields.

The continuous evaluation and improvement strategy envisages systematically monitoring the effects of technology integration and improving processes based on feedback. This approach requires evaluations in terms of both learning outcomes and process quality.

The theoretical framework of hybrid pedagogy establishes strong connections with social learning theory. From Bandura's social learning theory perspective, role modeling strategies are used in intergenerational learning processes through observation, imitation, and modeling. Generation Z students serve as role models in technology use, while experienced educators provide guidance on pedagogical skills. In epistemological foundations, in alignment with pragmatist philosophy, the practical value of knowledge and the validity of multiple perspectives are emphasized, accepting the simultaneous existence of different learning styles, technology preferences, and pedagogical perspectives.

A Practical Model: Reverse Mentoring and Intergenerational Learning Communities

One of the most striking practical applications of hybrid pedagogy is the reverse mentoring model. This model is based on the principle of reversing traditional mentoring relationships, where technologically experienced young individuals guide experienced but technology-development-open adults. In the educational context, reverse mentoring is implemented through Generation Z students introducing artificial intelligence tools to educators and sharing usage skills (Murphy, 2012).

The theoretical foundations of the reverse mentoring model are built on social exchange theory and mutual interdependence principles. This model recognizes that different generations' different areas of expertise are of equal value and supports mutual learning processes. In educational environments, this approach flexes the student-teacher hierarchy while enabling both sides to assume both learner and teacher roles. In the reverse mentoring process, Generation Z students guide educators on the technical features, usage strategies, and creative applications of artificial intelligence tools. This process is effective not only in terms of technical knowledge transfer but also attitude change toward technology. Experienced educators reduce their concerns about artificial intelligence technologies through this interaction with students and find opportunities to discover the pedagogical potential of these tools.

Reciprocally, experienced educators transfer their pedagogical expertise, academic standards, and ethical values to Generation Z students in the reverse mentoring process. This interaction helps students develop more conscious approaches to artificial intelligence use and gain awareness about academic integrity. Thus, a bidirectional learning process takes place and the intergenerational divide is bridged.

Various practical strategies can be adopted in implementing the reverse mentoring model. The first strategy is structured pairing programs. In this approach, students with advanced experience in technology are systematically paired with educators who want to learn artificial intelligence tools. In the pairing process, optimal pairs are formed by considering the needs, expectations, and compatibility of both parties. The second strategy is the workshop-based approach. In this model, Generation Z students organize workshops introducing artificial intelligence tools and provide hands-on experiences to educators. Workshops help students develop teaching skills while enabling educators to experience technology in a comfortable environment.

Establishing clear ethical boundaries in reverse mentoring applications is critically important. Students' technical guidance role should not be transformed into a pedagogical decision-maker position. The design of instructional processes, determination of evaluation criteria, and preservation of academic standards should remain entirely under educators' responsibility (Murphy, 2012). Additionally, professional boundaries of the mentoring relationship should be maintained and transformation into personal relationships should be prevented. Establishing institutional oversight mechanisms will ensure that the process is conducted within ethical principles.

On the other hand, there are risks to be considered in implementing the reverse mentoring model. The first risk is the possibility of pedagogical depth becoming superficial. Although students may be experts in the technical use of artificial intelligence tools, they have limited experience in how to integrate these tools for pedagogical purposes (Murphy, 2012). This situation can lead to technology's instrumental use in educational processes not going beyond. The second risk includes emotional difficulties arising from the disruption of the traditional teacher-student hierarchy. Experienced educators receiving guidance from students can create tension in professional identity and authority perception (Chaudhuri & Ghosh, 2011). The third risk emerges as organizational difficulties at the institutional level. Conducting effective pairing processes, ensuring program sustainability, and performing quality control require significant resources.

Intergenerational learning communities represent a larger-scale application of the reverse mentoring model. These communities can be defined as structures where individuals from different age groups, experience levels, and technology skills come together to collaborate toward common learning goals. In educational institutions, these communities function as platforms for knowledge sharing, experience transfer, and collective problem-solving in the artificial intelligence integration process (Kaplan & Haenlein, 2020).

Among the basic characteristics of intergenerational learning communities are non-hierarchical structure, mutual respect principle, and acceptance of diversity as a value. These communities create flexible structures where everyone can be in both learner and teacher positions while flexing traditional teacher-student roles. This situation provides advantages especially in rapidly developing and multidimensionally expertise-requiring topics like artificial intelligence.

The organizational structure of learning communities can be shaped through various models. The centrally coordinated model refers to communities organized by an educational institution or department and directed toward specific goals. In this model, systematic solutions are developed for problems encountered in the artificial intelligence integration process and institutional policies are formed.

The autonomous organization model encompasses communities formed and managed by members through their own initiatives. These communities have more flexible and dynamic structures and are shaped according to members' immediate needs and interests. The hybrid organization model aims to balance both institutional support and member autonomy by combining the strengths of both approaches. The basic activities adopted in the functioning of intergenerational learning communities show diversity. Knowledge sharing sessions refer to regular meetings where members share their different areas of expertise and support mutual learning. In these sessions, Generation Z members introduce innovations in artificial intelligence tools while experienced educators share their pedagogical perspectives and ethical evaluations.

Problem-solving workshops are activities where specific problems related to artificial intelligence integration in educational processes are collectively addressed. In these workshops, different generations' perspectives are synthesized to develop solutions that are applicable both technologically and pedagogically. For example, in designing AI-supported homework evaluation systems, balanced approaches are created by combining students' usage experiences with educators' pedagogical concerns.

Research and development projects are an important activity area for learning communities to create long-term impact. These projects aim to systematically examine the effects of artificial intelligence integration and develop new approaches. Intergenerational cooperation provides methodological diversity and perspective richness in these projects.

Social activities and informal interactions are also critically important for learning communities to create cohesion. These activities enable the development of trust relationships between different generations and the reduction of prejudices. Thus, discussions on technology and pedagogy can take place in a more open and constructive atmosphere. In conclusion, reverse mentoring and intergenerational learning community models offer powerful frameworks for practical applications of hybrid pedagogy. These models create mutual learning and development opportunities while reducing intergenerational tension in the technology integration process.

DISCUSSION AND CONCLUSION

The findings of this study reveal that intergenerational dynamics in the artificial intelligence integration process in educational environments exhibit a complex and multidimensional structure. The theoretical frameworks and empirical findings examined within the scope of the research show the inadequacy of current approaches and the necessity of balanced strategies. In this section, the main findings of the study are evaluated and recommendations for educational policies and practices are developed.

Findings regarding research questions systematically reveal the effects of intergenerational dynamics on educational processes. When examining intergenerational perception and attitude differences, Generation Z approaches artificial intelligence with a pragmatic and opportunity-focused attitude, evaluating technological tools as natural learning support. In contrast, experienced educators' cautious and value-oriented attitude stems from concerns about the integrity of educational processes and preservation of academic standards. This divide manifests itself particularly in assessment systems and learning process perceptions.

Findings regarding effects on educational processes and bridging strategies reveal that intergenerational differences create multidimensional effects. These differences can negatively affect educational quality, create classroom tensions, and lead to reliability problems in assessment systems. Findings regarding the effectiveness of bridging strategies show that reverse mentoring and learning communities are particularly effective. These approaches support mutual learning and development processes by leveraging the strengths of both generations. Additionally, it is observed that institutional culture and leadership support play critical roles in the implementation process of these strategies.

Findings regarding hybrid pedagogy models and sustainable transformation show that these approaches have long-term success potential. Hybrid models have the potential to create synergistic effects by supporting intergenerational cooperation. These models support gradual and controlled transformation processes rather than sudden and radical changes, minimizing resistance and facilitating adaptation. It was found that the principles of student-centered flexibility, pedagogical continuity, and critical technology literacy need to be adopted for sustainable educational transformation. The adoption of these approaches in educational policies increases the sector's capacity to adapt to technological developments.

These theoretical findings align with emerging empirical evidence about successful integration strategies. The Carnegie Learning study identified six distinct types of AI users in educational environments, ranging from "AI Enthusiasts" (21%) to "Traditionalists" (4%), with the largest group being "Cautious Observers" (40%) who represent the target population for hybrid approaches (Carnegie Learning, 2025). Microsoft's research supports the effectiveness of collaborative models, showing that institutions implementing structured AI literacy programs report higher satisfaction rates and more sustainable adoption patterns. Significantly, the study found that 82% of students believe knowing how to use AI effectively and responsibly is important for their future, indicating strong motivation for balanced approaches that combine technical skills with ethical considerations (Microsoft Education, 2025).

Equity, Inclusion, and Collaboration Dimensions in Education

One of the most critical issues in the artificial intelligence integration process in educational environments is the impact of these technologies on equity and inclusion in education. The intergenerational digital divide is not limited to technology usage skills but also creates deep effects on access to educational opportunities and academic success. This situation creates significant challenges for educational institutions' missions to ensure social justice.

Technology access inequalities carry the risk of deepening existing socio-economic differences in the artificial intelligence integration process. From an algorithmic justice perspective, bias problems in artificial intelligence tools create critical risks for educational equity. The concept of "algorithms of oppression" emphasized by Noble (2018) gains validity in the educational context as well. Particularly, demographic biases in the training data of language models can negatively affect the level of benefit that students from minority groups derive from artificial intelligence tools. The "fairness through awareness" approach developed by Barocas and Selbst (2016) should be adopted in educational institutions' artificial intelligence policies.

Similarly, the difficulties experienced by experienced educators in their adaptation process to artificial intelligence tools are issues that need to be addressed in terms of equity. The disadvantage these educators experience in technology use can affect the quality of education they can provide to their students. Particularly, experienced teachers working in rural areas or disadvantaged schools being unable to receive technology support causes students in these schools to be unable to benefit from AI-supported educational opportunities.

From an inclusion perspective, it is seen that the artificial intelligence integration process requires approaches that consider different learning styles, special education needs, and cultural differences. The use of dominant cultural and linguistic codes in the design of artificial intelligence tools can prevent students from minority groups from effectively benefiting from these technologies. Additionally, additional arrangements are needed regarding the access of students with visual, hearing, or motor skill deficiencies to artificial intelligence tools.

From a gender perspective, gender biases observed in language models in artificial intelligence tools can negatively affect especially female students' experiences in STEM fields (Bolukbasi et al., 2016). Similarly, developing AI interfaces compatible with screen reader technologies for visually impaired students and providing visual-based interaction options for hearing-impaired students is critically important. Considering these dimensions is one of the basic requirements of inclusive artificial intelligence integration policies.

The intergenerational cooperation approach can offer effective solutions for equity and inclusion problems. Combining Generation Z's technology experience with experienced educators' pedagogical expertise enables the development of balanced approaches that will meet all students' needs. This cooperation model provides peer support to students who are disadvantaged in technology use while also offering pedagogical guidance to students at risk of technology dependency.

The collaboration dimension constitutes the key to reducing intergenerational tension and creating synergistic effects. The study findings show that when collaborative models are adopted instead of competitive approaches, both student and educator satisfaction increases. Developing a collaboration culture enables different generations to benefit from each other's strengths and support each other's weaknesses.

In the Turkish context, intergenerational dynamics show different characteristics within the framework of Hofstede's (2001) cultural dimensions theory. As a characteristic of high power distance culture, traditional respect for teacher authority can affect artificial intelligence integration processes. This situation requires additional attention in implementing reverse mentoring models. Additionally, the centralized structure and national curriculum standards in Turkey's education system can create structural limitations in flexible application of hybrid pedagogy models. Social attitudes toward technology also shape intergenerational differences; there is dynamic tension between young generations' rapid adaptation to global technology trends and tendencies to maintain traditional values. Considering these factors is critically important for increasing the effectiveness of proposed strategies in local contexts.

Differentiated Approaches by Educational Levels

Differentiating artificial intelligence integration strategies according to educational levels is critically important for successful implementation. Each educational level has its own pedagogical needs, student development characteristics, and teacher profiles. These differences require adopting different approaches in integrating artificial intelligence technologies.

Artificial intelligence integration at the elementary school level requires cautious approaches that support children's healthy relationship with technology. At this level, since students' critical thinking skills have not yet developed, it is important to use artificial intelligence tools with pedagogical guidance. Since the majority of elementary school teachers consist of experienced educators, reverse mentoring models can be applied more limitedly at this level. Instead, comprehensive training programs and continuous support systems for teachers' technology use gain importance.

The main purposes of artificial intelligence use in elementary school should be to develop students' basic skills and support their creativity. AI-supported applications in reading-writing instruction can offer personalized learning experiences, while visual and interactive tools in mathematics instruction can support concept development. However, the principle that these applications should support, not substitute, children's basic skill acquisition process should be adopted.

Middle school level is one of the levels where intergenerational dynamics are most intensely experienced. During this period, students become more active in technology use while also experiencing identity search and social development processes. Since middle school teachers' age distribution generally shows a mixed structure, there are environments where both young and experienced educators work together. This situation creates opportunities for developing intergenerational learning communities.

The focus of artificial intelligence integration in middle school should be developing students' technology literacy and gaining responsible usage habits. At this level, basic information about how artificial intelligence tools work should be provided and ethical usage principles should be taught. Additionally, through group projects and collaborative learning activities, the social dimensions of technology use should be experienced.

High school level is the period when Generation Z is most active in technology use. At this level, students can be considered mature enough to freely use artificial intelligence tools in creative projects, research studies, and problem-solving activities. However, reinforcing academic integrity and ethical values is critically important during this period. Since high school teachers' attitudes toward artificial intelligence show diversity, consistent school-based policies need to be developed.

Among the goals of artificial intelligence integration in high school should be preparing students for their future professional lives and supporting them in their transition to university education. In this context, experiences should be provided on how artificial intelligence tools are used in professional environments and students' skills to develop creative and ethical solutions with these technologies should be supported.

Higher education level is the level where intergenerational dynamics reach the most complex dimensions. While universities have both young and experienced academics, the student profile consisting almost entirely of Generation Z creates a special situation. At this level, reverse mentoring models can be most effectively applied and intergenerational learning communities can develop.

The focus of artificial intelligence integration in higher education is to ensure the ethical and effective use of these technologies in academic research and knowledge production processes. Students' ability to receive artificial intelligence support in academic tasks such as dissertation writing, data analysis, and literature review, while maintaining academic integrity standards in these processes, is critically important. At this level, clear and detailed guidelines for artificial intelligence use should be developed and continuously updated.

Vocational education and lifelong learning programs constitute a special area that brings together participants from different age groups. Since participants' technology experiences and educational backgrounds show great differences in these programs, flexible and personalized approaches need to be adopted. Artificial intelligence integration in vocational education should focus on meeting sectoral needs while aiming to develop participants' existing skills.

Developing strategies that consider each level's unique needs rather than uniform policies positively affects both student and educator satisfaction. Additionally, ensuring continuity in inter-level transition processes provides significant benefits for educational quality.

Limitations

This study has various limitations and acknowledging these limitations is important for interpreting the findings. First, the study is based on theoretical analysis and literature review methods and does not include empirical data collection processes. This situation limits testing the validity of theoretical predictions in real-world applications. Supporting future research with empirical methods will increase the reliability of findings.

The second limitation is that the generational categories focused on in the study are defined through general characteristics. Intra-generational differences, individual experiences, and the effects of cultural factors are not sufficiently detailed in this study. In reality, individuals within the same generation can show significant differences in terms of technology use and educational approaches. This situation needs to be examined in more detail in future research.

Future Research Recommendations

Based on the study findings, various recommendations can be developed for future research. First, comprehensive empirical research on intergenerational artificial intelligence perception and use needs to be conducted. These studies should adopt mixed-method approaches, collecting both quantitative and qualitative data, and conducting comparative analyses in different educational contexts.

The second recommendation is adopting longitudinal research designs. Changes in intergenerational dynamics over time, long-term effects of hybrid pedagogy models, and processual effects of artificial intelligence integration on educational quality should be examined in multi-year research projects. Such research will provide valuable evidence for developing educational policies.

The third recommendation is conducting scale development studies to measure the effectiveness of hybrid pedagogy models. In the existing literature, standardized tools for evaluating the success of hybrid approaches are limited. Developing these tools will enable comparing different applications and identifying best practice examples.

This study emphasizes the necessity of balanced and inclusive approaches by revealing the complexity of intergenerational dynamics created by artificial intelligence in educational environments. Synthesizing Generation Z's technology-friendly approach with experienced educators' pedagogical experience is critically important for improving educational quality and ensuring sustainable technology integration.

Hybrid pedagogy models and intergenerational cooperation strategies offer practical and effective solutions as alternatives to polarized approaches in existing literature. The success of these approaches is directly related to institutional culture, leadership support, and participation of all stakeholders. Educational institutions taking proactive roles in this transformation process and developing balanced policies will be the determinant of future educational quality.

In conclusion, the future of education in the artificial intelligence age will be shaped by strengthening intergenerational cooperation and mutual learning processes. In this process, not ignoring any generation's knowledge and experience, but rather benefiting from each one's strengths, will create beneficial results for all stakeholders in the educational ecosystem. Future research contributing in this direction and developing practical solutions is vitally important for the success of technology integration in education.

REFERENCES

Al-Rahmi, W. M., Yahaya, N., Aldraiweesh, A. A., Alamri, M. M., Aljarboa, N. A., Alturki, U., & Aljeraiwi, A. A. (2019). Integrating technology acceptance model with innovation diffusion theory: An empirical investigation on students' intention to use E-learning systems. *IEEE Access : Practical Innovations, Open Solutions, 7*, 26797–26809. DOI: 10.1109/ACCESS.2019.2899368

Barocas, S., & Selbst, A. D. (2016). Big data's disparate impact. *California Law Review, 104*, 671.

Bennett, S., Maton, K., & Kervin, L. (2008). The 'digital natives' debate: A critical review of the evidence. *British Journal of Educational Technology, 39*(5), 775–786. DOI: 10.1111/j.1467-8535.2007.00793.x

Bollmann, U. (2024). Artificial intelligence and education: A teacher-centred approach to safety and health.

Bolukbasi, T., Chang, K. W., Zou, J. Y., Saligrama, V., & Kalai, A. T. (2016). Man is to computer programmer as woman is to homemaker? debiasing word embeddings. *Advances in Neural Information Processing Systems*, •••, 29.

Borenstein, J., & Howard, A. (2021). Emerging challenges in AI and the need for AI ethics education. *AI and Ethics, 1*(1), 61–65. DOI: 10.1007/s43681-020-00002-7 PMID: 38624388

Carnegie Learning. (2025). *The State of AI in Education 2025: Key Findings from a National Survey*. Carnegie Learning.

Cengage Group. (2025). 4 Ways AI Is Transforming Education. Cengage Group Research Report.

Chan, C. K. Y., & Hu, W. (2023). Students' voices on generative AI: Perceptions, benefits, and challenges in higher education. *International Journal of Educational Technology in Higher Education, 20*(1), 43. DOI: 10.1186/s41239-023-00411-8

Chaudhuri, S., & Ghosh, R. (2011). Reverse Mentoring: A Social Exchange Tool for Keeping the Boomers Engaged and Millennials Committed. *Human Resource Development Review, 11*(1), 55–76. DOI: 10.1177/1534484311417562

Corrin, L., Lockyer, L., & Bennett, S. (2010). Technological diversity: An investigation of students' technology use in everyday life and academic study. *Learning, Media and Technology, 35*(4), 387–401. DOI: 10.1080/17439884.2010.531024

Cotton, D. R., Cotton, P. A., & Shipway, J. R. (2024). Chatting and cheating: Ensuring academic integrity in the era of ChatGPT. *Innovations in Education and Teaching International, 61*(2), 228–239. DOI: 10.1080/14703297.2023.2190148

Davis, F. D. (1989). Perceived usefulness, perceived ease of use, and user acceptance of information technology. *Management Information Systems Quarterly, 13*(3), 319–340. DOI: 10.2307/249008

EDUCAUSE. (2023). *2023 EDUCAUSE Horizon Report: Teaching and Learning Edition*. EDUCAUSE Publications.

EDUCAUSE. (2025). *EDUCAUSE 2025 AI Landscape Study: Into the Digital AI Divide*. EDUCAUSE Publications.

García-Peñalvo, F. J. (2023). The perception of Artificial Intelligence in educational contexts after the launch of ChatGPT: Disruption or Panic?. *Education in the knowledge society.*

Graham, C. R., Borup, J., Short, C. R., & Archambault, L. (2019). K-12 blended teaching: A guide to personalized learning and online integration. *Provo, UT: EdTechBooks.*

Graham, C. R., Woodfield, W., & Harrison, J. B. (2013). A framework for institutional adoption and implementation of blended learning in higher education. *The Internet and Higher Education, 18*, 4–14. DOI: 10.1016/j.iheduc.2012.09.003

Helsper, E. J., & Eynon, R. (2010). Digital natives: Where is the evidence? *British Educational Research Journal, 36*(3), 503–520. DOI: 10.1080/01411920902989227

Hofstede, G. (2001). *Culture's consequences: Comparing values, behaviors, institutions and organizations across nations*. Sage Publications.

Holmes, W., Porayska-Pomsta, K., Holstein, K., Sutherland, E., Baker, T., Shum, S. B., Santos, O. C., Rodrigo, M. T., Cukurova, M., Bittencourt, I. I., & Koedinger, K. R. (2022). Ethics of AI in education: Towards a community-wide framework. *International Journal of Artificial Intelligence in Education, 32*(3), 504–526. DOI: 10.1007/s40593-021-00239-1

Kaplan, A., & Haenlein, M. (2020). Rulers of the world, unite! The challenges and opportunities of artificial intelligence. *Business Horizons, 63*(1), 37–50. DOI: 10.1016/j.bushor.2019.09.003

Kasneci, E., Seßler, K., Küchemann, S., Bannert, M., Dementieva, D., Fischer, F., Gasser, U., Groh, G., Günnemann, S., Hüllermeier, E., Krusche, S., Kutyniok, G., Michaeli, T., Nerdel, C., Pfeffer, J., Poquet, O., Sailer, M., Schmidt, A., Seidel, T., & Kasneci, G. (2023). ChatGPT for good? On opportunities and challenges of large language models for education. *Learning and Individual Differences*, *103*, 102274. DOI: 10.1016/j.lindif.2023.102274

Kohlbacher, F., & Herstatt, C. (Eds.). (2011). *The silver market phenomenon: Marketing and innovation in the aging society*. Springer Science & Business Media.

Livingstone, S., & Helsper, E. (2007). Gradations in digital inclusion: Children, young people and the digital divide. *New Media & Society*, *9*(4), 671–696. DOI: 10.1177/1461444807080335

Luckin, R., Cukurova, M., Kent, C., & Du Boulay, B. (2022). Empowering educators to be AI-ready. Computers and Education. *Artificial Intelligence*, *3*, 100076.

Luckin, R., Holmes, W., Griffiths, M., & Forcier, L. B. (2016). *Intelligence Unleashed: An argument for AI in Education*. Open Ideas; Pearson Education, London.

Microsoft Education. (2025). *2025 AI in Education: A Microsoft Special Report*. Microsoft Corporation.

Murphy, W. M. (2012). Reverse mentoring at work: Fostering cross-generational learning and developing millennial leaders. *Human Resource Management*, *51*(4), 549–573. DOI: 10.1002/hrm.21489

Noble, S. U. (2018). *Algorithms of Oppression: How Search Engines Reinforce Racism*. NYU Press., DOI: 10.18574/nyu/9781479833641.001.0001

Prensky, M. (2001). Digital natives, digital immigrants part 2: Do they really think differently? *On the Horizon*, *9*(6), 1–6. DOI: 10.1108/10748120110424843

Rudolph, J., Tan, S., & Tan, S. (2023). War of the chatbots: Bard, Bing Chat, ChatGPT, Ernie and beyond. The new AI gold rush and its impact on higher education. *Journal of Applied Learning and Teaching*, *6*(1), 364–389.

Russell, S., & Norvig, P. (2021). Artificial intelligence: a modern approach, global edition 4th. *Foundations, 19*(23), 44-85.

Seemiller, C., & Grace, M. (2018). *Generation Z: A century in the making*. Routledge. DOI: 10.4324/9780429442476

Tamilmani, K., Rana, N. P., Prakasam, N., & Dwivedi, Y. K. (2019). The battle of Brain vs. Heart: A literature review and meta-analysis of "hedonic motivation" use in UTAUT2. *International Journal of Information Management*, *46*, 222–235. DOI: 10.1016/j.ijinfomgt.2019.01.008

Venkatesh, V., Morris, M. G., Davis, G. B., & Davis, F. D. (2003). User Acceptance of Information Technology: Toward a Unified View. *Management Information Systems Quarterly*, *27*(3), 425–478. DOI: 10.2307/30036540

Watters, A. (2023). *Teaching machines: The history of personalized learning*. MIT Press.

Zawacki-Richter, O., Marín, V. I., Bond, M., & Gouverneur, F. (2019). Systematic review of research on artificial intelligence applications in higher education–where are the educators? *International Journal of Educational Technology in Higher Education*, *16*(1), 1–27. DOI: 10.1186/s41239-019-0171-0

Chapter 4
Artificial Intelligence in School Leadership

Nedim Özdemir
https://orcid.org/0000-0002-3054-926X
Ege University, Turkey

ABSTRACT

This study aimed to examine how artificial intelligence supports teachers' classroom practices and school leadership practices. Using conceptual literature review approach, the study summarized the literature into three main thema, including "Educational benefits of AI," "School Leadership and AI," and "Using AI for School Leadership: Evidence from Research." Literature has demonstrated the impact of AI in the school environment in two main ways. First, from practical perspective, AI systems organize the time management of school leaders and teachers by doing routine tasks. It also notes that they can use it by providing individualized feedback to students and parents. Second, from theoretical perspective, social cognitive theory explains three dimensions: personal factors, including cognitive processes such as beliefs, skills, and self-efficacy. Behavioral factors refer to the actions that a person performs. Environmental factors include work settings, organizational support, and social norms. In conclusion, AI can support leadership efficiency but raises ethical challenges.

INTRODUCTION

OECD has monitored recent trends every two or three years due to their potential to shape education (James et al., 2025). In this context, the faster growth of digital trade compared to traditional trade, the increasing use of industrial robots and the programming of these robots to work collaboratively with humans, and the increasing

DOI: 10.4018/979-8-3373-6375-2.ch004

demand for jobs based on artificial intelligence (AI) skills are gaining a significant place on the agenda of education systems. This is due to the need to ensure that digital skills find a place in the workplace, to develop individuals who can work in harmony with robots, and to reduce inequalities stemming from digitalization. Disparities in internet access between low- and high-income countries, inequalities in broadband access, and the fact that some people only consume digital content while others produce it, lead education systems to focus on developing active digital users. Furthermore, mental health has become one of the most significant problem areas in recent years. The intense penetration of digital content into our lives and the increasing stress factors of modern life have begun to negatively impact individuals' well-being. Therefore, it is possible to speak of two fundamental dimensions of transformation in 21st-century education: The first is to educate students as individuals with digital skills; the second is to develop them into individuals with strong human resilience, creativity, and emotional well-being. Therefore, the roles of schools, teachers, and school principals in the digital transformation process have become an increasingly debated important topic today.

The concept of AI was introduced in the 1950s with the question of whether machines could think (Arar et al., 2024). It refers to machine learning systems that replicate human intelligence (Aljemely, 2024). AI is used to develop machines that can replicate human thought processes and problem-solving abilities. For example, they can automatically learn from previously provided data and perform tasks such as visual perception, decision-making, and language processing (Cheung et al., 2024). Although the concept of AI is relatively new, it is the rise of generative artificial intelligence (GenAI) technologies that has made it popular (Arriola-Mendoza and Valerio-Ureña, 2024). Chatbots such as ChatGPT, Copilot, Claude, and Gemini have made AI accessible to everyone through natural language interfaces (Cheung et al., 2024). A study by Herold (2019) revealed that 40% of teachers' tasks could be automated by AI. This study highlights the need for teachers to develop new skills and become more comfortable collaborating with algorithmic systems. According to Microsoft's 2024 Business Trend Index report, 75% of global knowledge workers regularly use AI tools, and 46% of them have started using these tools within the last six months. In this context, many researchers believe that AI and AI-gen have the potential to fundamentally change teaching and learning processes in educational settings (Ng et al., 2023; Adams and Chuah, 2022). Furthermore, most studies on AI and leadership discuss scenarios where AI could completely take over organizational leadership roles in the future or work symbiotically with leadership (e.g., Van Quaquebeke and Gerpott, 2023). Although previous studies have explored the use of AI in education, few studies have systematically reviewed its practical implications for school leadership (e.g. Abdallah & Musah, 2025).

METHODOLOGY

This book chapter adopts a conceptual literature review approach following the guidelines outlined by Snyder (2019) and presented in four stages, including design, conduct, data abstraction and analysis, and structuring and writing the review. The first stage, the "Design" phase, determined the need for this study. In this era of rapid digital transformation and artificial intelligence, the roles expected of teachers and school principals have begun to change. An increasing number of studies have been conducted in this area in recent years. Therefore, the purpose of this chapter is to examine how artificial intelligence shapes teachers' classroom practices and school leadership behaviors through a conceptual literature review and to present a theoretical synthesis and applied perspectives on this topic. In the second stage, "conduct", the search was conducted using the SCOPUS and Web of Science databases, using these keywords: TITLE-ABS-KEY ("artificial intelligence*" OR "digital transform*") AND ("school leadership" OR "teacher"). As a result of this search, only the type of articles was examined, and others such as conference papers were excluded. In this context, this chapter examined 4,569 studies. Initially, the abstracts of the studies were reviewed, and due to the limitations of this study, the decision was made to read the full text. In the "data abstraction and analysis" phase, this study follows social cognitive theory for the framework, and self-efficacy and ethical dilemma for conceptual framework. After reading abstracts, 63 studies were included for full-text review. Data were collected using Excel spreadsheets under three themes: "Educational benefits of AI," "School Leadership and AI," and "Using AI for School Leadership: Evidence from Research." In the last phase, structuring and writing the review, the findings and synthesis combined both the applications and the transformation in the leadership role of AI.

EDUCATIONAL BENEFITS OF AI AND 21ST CENTURY EDUCATION

The use of AI in education is gaining increasing attention with the aim of improving student learning outcomes. Acknowledging its pivotal role, researchers have suggested that the use of AI could remove barriers to student learning such as a lack of qualified teachers and resources and increase educational capacity (Zawacki-Richter et al, 2019). Recent studies have examined the impact of AI on education, revealing how it shapes students' academic performance. For example, Hwang (2022) examined the effect of AI on primary school pupils' mathematics achievement using a meta-analysis of 21 empirical studies published between 2000 and 2022 and 30 independent samples, finding that AI had a small effect on primary school pupils' mathematics achievement Similarly, Martínez et al. (2023), in their systematic review and meta-analysis of 25 articles, revealed that AI and computational sciences positively affect student performance, showing that students' attitudes towards learning and motivation increase, particularly in STEM fields. These findings highlight the potential benefits of AI on academic achievement and motivation to learn. Thus, teachers are increasingly compelled to move away from traditional teaching and learning approaches, focusing instead on developing their knowledge and expertise to deliver AI-assisted instruction to students. As improving achievement is one of the primary goals of schools, it is becoming increasingly important for school leaders to strengthen their AI literacy and effectively integrate AI into their leadership practices. Because school leadership has direct (Hou et al., 2019) and indirect (Gao et al., 2024) links on student learning.

The World Economic Forum has highlighted that the professions of the future will differ from those of today. Indeed, it is predicted that 40% of current skills will change by 2030. This means that the roles of teachers and school principals will evolve. Teachers are no longer expected to simply provide information, but to design and mentor learning. In the past, simply possessing knowledge was considered sufficient. Now, students are expected to think with knowledge, solve problems related to daily life, and address social issues such as environmental pollution. For example, some paper cups and plastic bottles contain BPA, which can potentially leach into our beverages. The amount of BPA leaching can vary depending on the type of beverage, the time it remains in the glass, and the temperature, such as hot or acidic beverages. In addition to understanding the rationale for using BPA, students should also understand the potential problems it poses in daily use, including health concerns. Furthermore, the design of disposable cups and their subsequent release into the environment constitutes a separate issue. Alternatively, students should infer that using glass cups would be more appropriate. In this context, acquiring 21st-century skills—creativity, critical thinking, communication, collaboration, and digital well-being—becomes crucial. Acquiring these skills will contribute to students' success in school and life.

To foster these skills, AI can be used as a creative learning partner in classroom practices. For example, students can generate multiple solutions to solve a problem through AI. They can then discuss and choose which of these solutions is more practical and creative. Similarly, in writing classes, students can ask AI to generate different story beginnings and complement these stories with their own original ideas. The teacher's role here is not to have AI "think for students", but to support students in "thinking beyond AI". In other words, the goal is for students to build upon AI-generated texts and create new, original, and creative content.

AI can also be used to develop critical thinking in students. A teacher can show students content generated through AI and ask them the following questions: Is this information accurate? Is there any bias? What sources do you think the AI relies on to answer this question? This way, we teach students not only how to use AI content but also how to conduct research based on it.

Another example highlights AI's potential to simulate real-world problems. Such applications require students to develop teamwork, problem-solving, and innovative thinking skills. Starting with a problem posed by AI, students can work together, even collaborating with peers in different countries, to develop solutions to global challenges. These challenges could include designing sustainable cities, reducing waste, or raising mental health awareness through digital campaigns. In this process, AI can significantly support students in analyzing data, testing ideas, and visually designing solutions.

ALGORITHMIC LEADERSHIP: A NEW APPROACH IN THE AI ERA

School leaders experience time constraints due to the large number of administrative tasks, which has become one of the main sources of stress. Some recent studies have reported that this administrative burden has increased over the years (Green, 2021). Some administrative duties require conducting meetings outside the school, adding another dimension to the overall workload. In this context, a study by Reid and Creed (2023) involving ten school leaders found that these administrators worked approximately 16 hours per week outside regular school hours. Similarly, Sebastian et al. (2018) reported that principals engaged in work-related activities for about 7.4 hours per day. Moreover, it has been estimated that principals work at least 50 hours per week on average. The growing workload has been found to have negative effects, such as increased stress and burnout. This intense workload has led school leaders to seek technological solutions. This is where AI-powered management approaches have come to the fore.

The concept of *algorithmic leadership* emerged in the late 2010s with the integration of digital management, data analytics, and artificial intelligence into decision-making process. It refers to use of AI algorithms to influence employees to achieve organizational goals (Chang et al., 2025). This leadership approach is a new concept that involves artificial intelligence algorithms replacing human leaders, directing tasks and managing relationships (Harms & Han, 2019). In other words, algorithms guide employees to achieve goals and provide feedback. In many organizations, such as food delivery companies, technology has begun to partially take over the role of leaders. This process automates the planning of tasks and monitors employee behavior. This makes work faster and more efficient. However, this also creates some negative psychological experiences. Employees can feel monitored, insecure, and isolated (Griesbach et al., 2019). Furthermore, algorithms cannot provide the empathy and support that human leaders provide.

But algorithmic leadership is not just a technical innovation; it also demands new roles and skills from school leaders. Because school leaders play a critical role in communicating the potential benefits of AI in education to stakeholders such as teachers, parents, and the community. In this approach, algorithms don't replace leaders. They support them by providing data-based insights into their decision-making processes. For example, AI systems can analyse student performance, monitor absenteeism patterns, and offer recommendations. In this context, first, they are expected to take the lead in showing how AI can be used effectively and how teachers can integrate it into their lessons. Therefore, school leaders should address the need for *technical knowledge* about the use of AI (See Figure 1). They should first learn about the topic, explore effective tools, and then support teachers and students in using technology effectively in their learning progress. Second, it is necessary to enrich classroom learning environments with AI. To achieve this, it would be beneficial to start by developing a *clear vision*. School leaders should create an inspiring and shared vision of how technology can transform teaching and learning processes. Then, through a *strategic plan*, technology should be used with a clear educational purpose. In other words, instead of simply purchasing tablets or software and using them without direction, or for non-educational purposes, it is important to determine how and for what goals technology will be applied in the learning process. For example, a goal such as "Students will improve their creative thinking skills by 30% through AI-supported learning" can be established. In this context, AI can provide students with personalized feedback, and AI-based assessment tools can be integrated into this feedback process. Moreover, instead of being passive listeners, students will learn by actively engaging in the lessons. Another important issue addressed here is the provision of *personalized learning* opportunities. In traditional education, all students are expected to learn the same material at the same pace. However, in personalized learning, the educational content is designed based on each student's current knowledge level, learning speed, interests, and strengths and weaknesses. The main goal is to ensure that no student is left behind and to enhance the learning experience so that every student can reach their full potential. One of the aims in this context is also to develop students' soft skills. In addition to academic achievement, it is important to equip students with *21st-century skills* such as critical thinking, collaboration, and problem-solving. For example, critical thinking skills can be supported by asking students to analyze AI-generated content in terms of accuracy, bias, and source reliability. Furthermore, students can be given complex problems, such as climate change or traffic congestion, and be asked to develop hypotheses for solutions and test them through simulations in a virtual environment. In another example, students work on a joint project with groups from different geographical locations or other classes within the school, sharing tasks and exchanging feedback, thereby supporting collaboration skills. School leaders should lead the examination of student progress data provided by AI, including data from adaptive assessments, across the school, enabling teachers to make more informed decisions about curriculum and instructional strategies (Adams & Thompson, 2025).

Figure 1. New responsibilities for school leaders

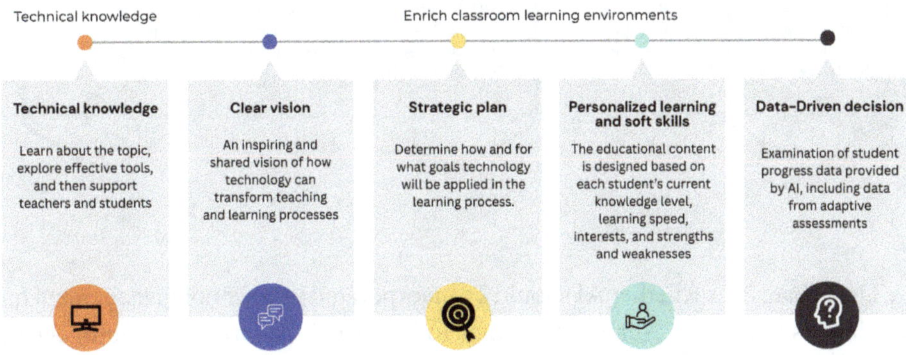

Effective communication demonstrates how AI can support student learning and reduce teachers' workload. Leaders must be able to manage risks associated with AI use, such as data privacy, security, and algorithmic bias (Fullan et al., 2024). Implementing technology leadership enhances the effectiveness of school management. Effective technology leaders demonstrate five essential characteristics (see Figure 2). First, they collaborate with teachers, students, and other stakeholders. Second, they set high expectations to ensure that the entire team raises its standards of quality and achievement. Third, having a clear vision for technology and learning enables leaders to define and guide educational and technological goals. Fourth, taking risks supports the testing of innovative practices and the adoption of new technologies. Finally, personally using and applying technology allows leaders to set an example through their own behaviour, encouraging the team to engage more readily with technology (Richardson et al., 2015).

Figure 2. Five Essential Characteristics of Effective Technology Leaders (Richardson et al., 2015).

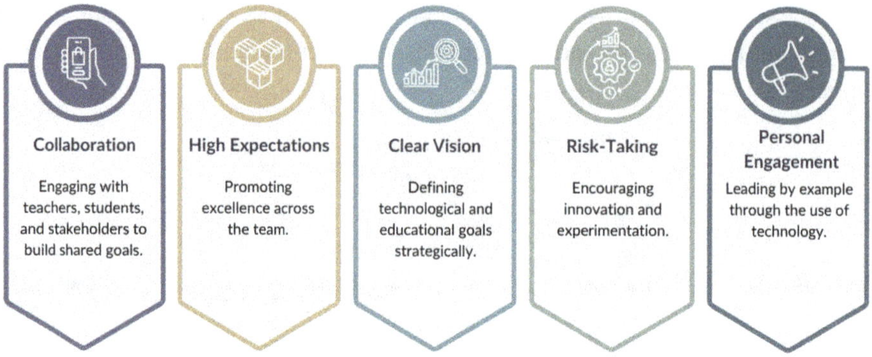

The debate over whether AI should be incorporated into school management has now lost its relevance. Numerous studies today reveal that artificial intelligence is increasingly being integrated into school management processes. Many leadership functions, such as decision-making, data analysis, planning, performance monitoring, and resource management, are now supported by algorithms and intelligent systems. Adams and Thompson (2025) reviewed the literature on the use of AI in the context of school leadership and highlighted some key benefits of models such as ChatGPT: AI can streamline administrative tasks, facilitate leader-teacher-student-parent communication, increase leaders' efficiency, and provide personalized support. The findings indicate that leaders' perceptions and decision-making processes are critical for the effective integration of AI into school systems, with leaders' perspectives directly influencing the applicability and success of AI in education. Specifically, qualitative interviews conducted with 11 school leaders in Australia examined their attitudes, beliefs, and concerns regarding AI integration (Marrone et al., 2025). The results reveal that the adoption of AI presents both significant opportunities and various challenges. Crucially, how school leaders perceive this technology and the factors they consider in their decision-making processes are paramount for the effective integration of AI into school systems. Leaders' viewpoints thus emerged as a fundamental element directly impacting the feasibility and ultimate success of AI in educational settings. In a study, Pietsch & Mah (2025) found that leaders with a proactive and empathetic digital mindset, encouraging change and focusing on teaching were increasing AI integration.

AI can alleviate the heavy administrative and managerial burdens on school leaders and teachers. In this regard, AI facilitates the administrative and managerial tasks of school leaders, allowing them to focus more on instructional leadership and student outcomes (Coccoli et al., 2016; Fullan et al., 2024). Some research even suggests that AI could partially take over traditional human leadership tasks, including building relationships, mentoring, monitoring, and inspiring (Van Quaquebeke & Gerpott, 2023). In this context, AI has the potential to transform the nature of leadership roles, rather than remaining merely a technical tool. This situation demonstrates that a fundamental transformation is taking place in school leadership. Van Quaquebeke and Gerpott (2023) pose a compelling question at this point: The issue is no longer "Will AI play a role in school leadership?" but rather "What role will we still play?" This emphasis indicates that the roles of human leaders need to be redefined in the age of AI. Indeed, as artificial intelligence takes on routine and technical tasks, the true value of school leaders will emerge in their abilities to provide human guidance, ethical responsibility, empathy, vision development, and the ability to motivate teams around a common purpose. Therefore, future school leadership will require not only technological competence but also a strong ethical awareness and human leadership dimension.

According to Arar et al. (2024), this transformation fundamentally reshapes the role of the educational leader along three "Frontiers of Learning": Curriculum, Pedagogy, and the Time-Space of Learning (see, Figure 3). From a curriculum perspective, leadership is required to determine how the curriculum will be updated with AI, for example data literacy, critical thinking and human-specific skills. From a pedagogical perspective, the introduction of AI-based tools such as Intelligent Teaching Systems into classrooms means that the way teachers teach and the way leaders support these new teaching approaches must be reconsidered. From the time-space of Learning, in an environment where learning is not limited to traditional school hours and physical classrooms, leaders undergo a transformation in how they manage and organize learning processes and experiences.

Figure 3. Frontiers of Learning.

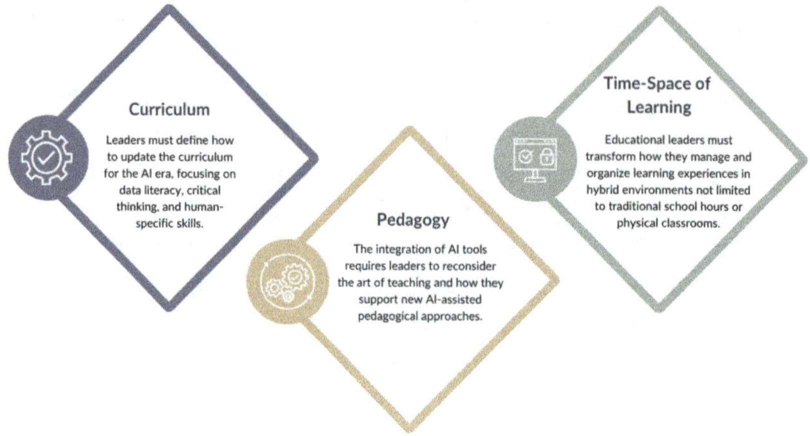

Indeed, as artificial intelligence takes over routine and technical tasks, the true value of school leaders will emerge in their abilities for human guidance, ethical responsibility, empathy, vision development, and motivating teams around a common purpose. Therefore, future school leadership will require not only technological competence but also a strong ethical awareness and human leadership dimension.

USING AI FOR SCHOOL LEADERSHIP: EVIDENCE FROM RESEARCH

The growing workload of school leaders has increasingly led to the adoption of AI tools, particularly for routine administrative tasks. Despite this emerging trend, research suggests that empirical studies examining AI use in schools remain limited (Berkovich, 2025). Figure 4 provides a summary of the main tasks where AI is currently being applied.

Figure 4. Using AI for School Leadership

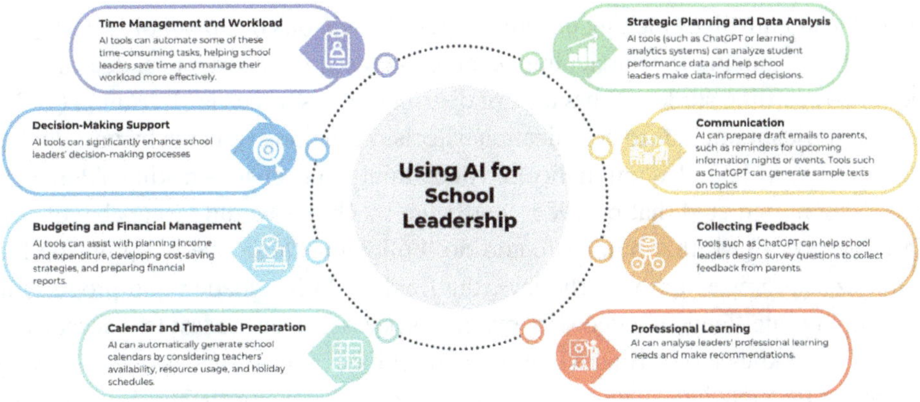

Time Management and Workload: Research indicates that school leaders' administrative tasks are increasing and that they are often forced to work outside of regular working hours (Reid & Creed, 2023). Artificial intelligence (AI) tools increase managers' efficiency by automating some of these time-consuming tasks, allowing them to devote more time to strategic tasks. Calendar planners, meeting management, and document editing systems are prominent examples of applications in this context. For example, ChatGPT can integrate with Google Calendar by analysing specific dates and events specified by the user. This means important days, meetings or tasks throughout the year are automatically added to the calendar. As a result, school leaders and administrators can plan their time more efficiently and speed up the planning process without having to manually enter dates. *Otter.ai* automatically transcribes what is said during meetings and summarises key action points. This allows school leaders or administrators to quickly review meeting notes and easily identify tasks that require follow-up. In a study examining the extent to which school leaders use artificial intelligence in different task areas, Berkovich (2025) found that AI is mostly used occasionally and for support purposes in administrative tasks such as calendar planning, document editing, and meeting organisation. While a significant benefit of AI usage is increased efficiency, an important potential risk is excessive dependence on technology. For example, a school leader could use the following prompt in any AI tool:

"I am a school principal. I want help to plan my administrative work more efficiently. Below are the dates of my works. 1-List important dates, meetings, and tasks in Google Calendar format and suggest reminders. 2-Create a weekly or daily plan in order of priority.3-Add a description and duration suggestion for each task when adding it to the calendar."

Decision-Making Support: Griffiths (1959) argued that decision-making theory plays a central role in understanding educational leadership. Because the role of a school leader involves making different types of decisions on an ongoing basis. For example, organizing the curriculum, evaluating teacher performance, determining policies regarding student behaviors, or distributing resources fairly. Simon (1972) gave significant impetus to organizational decision-making research by introducing the concepts of bounded rationality and uncertainty in decision-making. Alongside this, Simon predicted that by 1985, intelligent machines would be capable of performing every task that humans could do. Following these overly optimistic but unrealized promises in the early days, the field of AI has made rapid progress in developing intelligence in decision-making processes over the last few decades.

Recent studies showed that AI significantly enhances managers' decision-making processes through data analysis and predictive models (Wang, 2021). AI-supported systems enable more informed and evidence-based decisions in school management by analyzing large data sets. For example, AI applications that analyze indicators such as declines in student grades and absenteeism rates can identify in advance which classes or student groups require additional support. However, most leaders view AI not as a final decision-making mechanism, but as a tool that improves and facilitates decision-making processes. This emphasis demonstrates that human judgement still plays a central role in educational leadership. Indeed, findings reveal that school administrators effectively use AI tools to support decision-making processes and shape school policies (Göçen & Döğer, 2025). The use of AI-based tools such as ChatGPT, Power BI, and learning analytics systems is particularly prevalent among young leaders (Berkovich, 2025). However, AI-based decision-making is not always compatible with value-based ethical decision-making. Therefore, leaders must use both AI-supported decisions and human judgement-based ethical decisions in their individual and organizational decisions (Wang, 2021). Indeed, Renta-Davids et al. (2025) stated in their scoping review that AI should be used as a complementary tool rather than completely replacing leadership. The human element should retain its central role in leadership, with AI merely supporting decision-making processes. For example, a school leader could use the following prompt in any AI tool:

"I'm a school principal. I want to increase student achievement. Some class data is below. Can you develop strategies based on class-by-class analysis?"

Communication: School leaders give speeches to pupils, teachers or parents; preparing these speeches is very time-consuming. Sebastian et al. (2018) found that a significant portion of principals' workweeks is spent on such tasks. AI-based tools can generate sample texts for them. This allows leaders to save time by simply editing the text and maintain a work-life balance. Göçen and Döğer (2025) found that most participants used AI to edit texts, correct grammar and spelling mistakes, translate, and summarise. For example, a school leader could use the following prompt in any AI tool:

"My school serves students aged 10-14. I will be addressing our students and parents at the ceremony as part of our Republic Day celebrations. Could you prepare a speech for me?"

AI can also create email templates for parents, such as reminders for informational special day invitations, making communication more professional and efficient.

Budgeting and Financial Management: Another duty of school principals is to use their existing resources in the most effective manner. In this regard, AI tools can help create savings measures by analyzing the distribution of expenditures. Similarly, they can assist in preparing the school's end-of-term financial report. This both increases accuracy and saves time. For example, a school leader could use the following prompt in any AI tool:

"Can you analyze school's income and expenses and list savings suggestions? I'll also be preparing a budget report. Could you provide me with a professional summary?"

Calendar and Timetable Preparation: Designing school celebration and commemoration programmes or preparing lesson plans is very time-consuming. AI can automatically generate a school calendar, considering teachers' availability, resource usage and holiday dates. However, the plans must be reviewed by school principal or teachers. For example, a school leader could use the following prompt in any AI tool:

"I've attached the teachers' availability schedule. Create a weekly lesson plan accordingly."

"Prepare an event calendar for the April 23rd ceremony, including poems and speeches."

"There are four locations in our school: the 1st floor, 2nd floor, 3rd floor, and the garden. Considering the teachers' class schedules, create a schedule that rotates the positions each week based on the days they have the fewest classes."

Strategic Planning and Data Analysis: Schools typically develop 3–5-year strategic plans. AI tools analyze student performance data to help school leaders make data-driven decisions. This contributes an evidence-based management approach.

"Analyze the exam scores of the following students and determine which courses will be needed."

"The school's teacher's board meeting minutes are attached. Write me three main strategic goals for the 2025-2028 period."

"Analyze student absence data and its causes and write possible solutions."

"Summarize the school's strengths, areas for development, opportunities, and threats in a SWOT analysis."

Collecting Feedback: Strong relationships with parents are crucial for effective school management. Tools like ChatGPT can also be used to develop questions to collect parent or student feedback. For example, open-ended questions about the school uniform policy can be generated. Also, school leaders can ask questions regarding school activities, such as school clubs, or sports. This allows schools to better understand students' interests and parents' perspectives. This can help to plan activities that engage the school community and improve satisfaction.

> *"Generate five open-ended questions for students and parents to get their feedback for school activities. For example, ask which sports, clubs, or extracurricular activities they would like to join. Also ask why these activities are important to them."*

Supporting the use of AI in schools increases managers' confidence in using this technology. However, support alone is not sufficient; managers' belief that "I can do this" (self-efficacy) is critical. Managers' perception of AI as valuable does not, by itself, increase its use. Berkovich and Eyal (2025) examined how an environment that supports the use of artificial intelligence technologies in schools affects middle school administrators' desire to integrate this technology into their leadership work. The results showed that as support for artificial intelligence in schools increased, administrators' confidence in using this technology also increased. However, this relationship is not direct: managers' trust in artificial intelligence (their self-efficacy) has been the key factor enabling support to translate into practice. In other words, providing support for artificial intelligence in schools is not sufficient on its own; managers must believe they can use this technology. Conversely, managers' perception of artificial intelligence as valuable has not played a significant role in increasing its use. Similarly, Erdoğan et al. (2025) found a direct relationship between school principals' self-efficacy and their attitudes towards artificial intelligence. This indicates that principals with high self-efficacy have a more positive attitude towards artificial intelligence.

THEORETICAL BACKGROUND OF USING AI IN LEADERSHIP

This section presents the main theoretical frameworks and related concepts that explain the integration of AI and GenAI into school leadership processes.

Social Cognitive Theory

AI technologies are examined within the framework of Social Cognitive Theory (SCT) (Bandura, 1986). This theory views individuals not as passive recipients, but as active agents who regulate their behavior through self-reflection, self-regulation, and self-direction (Otaye-Ebede et al., 2020). According to the theory, human behavior emerges from the reciprocal interaction of three factors: personal factors, including cognitive processes such as beliefs, skills, and self-efficacy. For example, if a teacher believes that AI can generate project ideas or lesson plans, this belief influences their behavior in using the AI tool. Behavioral factors, on the other hand, refer to the actions that a person performs. They are observable outcomes that result from personal and environmental factors. For example, a teacher taking attendance through an AI tool or submitting a project on time represents a behavioral factor. Environmental factors include work settings, organizational support, and social norms. If there are old computers and slow internet in the classroom, the teacher's intention to use this technology may weaken, and their behavior may be hindered. This principle of reciprocal determinism plays a central role in explaining AI integration in schools. This theory suggests that the success or failure of AI use does not depend solely on the teacher's willingness or the school's resources, but rather on the continuous interaction among these three elements.

Self-Efficacy

Within the SCT framework, self-efficacy has a critical role influencing individuals' adoption and use of AI technology. This concept refers to an individual's belief in their capability to plan and execute the behaviors necessary to achieve specific goals (Bandura, 1997). At the core of this concept lie an individual's forward-looking beliefs about what they can do. For example, questions such as "Can I do this?" or "How well can I do it?" reflect these beliefs. Individuals with high self-efficacy tend to think optimistically, whereas those with low self-efficacy are more likely to dwell on their shortcomings. For example, High self-efficacy leads principals to perceive challenges as less threatening and resources as more abundant, which in turn reduces burnout and increases satisfaction and motivation to remain in their jobs (Skaalvik, 2020).

Ethical dilemma

We can't see how AI creates information. Leaders want to ensure that decisions made by these "black box" model are fair and accurate (Kosztelnik, 2019). Because we enter an input into the box, an operation occurs within the box and ultimately produces an output. You look at the result, but we can't clearly understand why the AI came to that conclusion, which data it considers important, or the underlying logic. From an educational leadership perspective, when an AI system decides about a student, for example, that they need additional support, it means leaders struggle to ensure that the decision is fair and accurate. In addition, training AI systems on faulty datasets may lead to the production of wrong decisions (Wang, 2023).

The integration of AI systems into education has potential to both increase and decrease existing inequalities. This potential must be carefully considered, particularly in contexts where the "digital divide" exists (Sezgin & Fırat, 2020). Digital inequality begins with fundamental challenges, such as disparities in internet access and inequities in broadband internet access between low- and high-income countries (Akhmad, 2025). AI applications are heavily dependent on high-speed internet access. Rural schools, therefore, face significant challenges, such as high-speed internet access. These technological barriers complicate the efforts of leaders and teachers in these schools to integrate AI. Furthermore, some principals or teachers may not have received the necessary training to integrate AI into their classrooms. This means that AI can only succeed in schools with well-resourced and trained teachers. This can lead to a widening of achievement gap of students. When AI systems are trained on inaccurate datasets, they can produce inaccurate or biased decisions. This can lead to unfair decisions being made about already disadvantaged student groups. In other words, AI may serve the opposite of its intended purpose of being fair.

The following measures can be taken to mitigate these limitations. AI provides personalized learning opportunities by delivering educational content specifically tailored to student's current knowledge level. This aims to ensure that students who need additional support do not fall behind. AI systems have the potential to increase educational capacity by removing barriers to learning, such as a lack of resources. They can reduce the workload on teachers by taking routine tasks, allowing them to focus more on student learning needs. AI can predict which classes or groups of students need additional support, by using student grade declines or absence rates. This data-driven management approach promotes equity by directing resources where they are needed most.

CONCLUSION

Digitalisation and thereby artificial intelligence are main concepts in today's labour markets. Although the automation of routine tasks is causing some professions to lose their jobs, new professions are emerging in areas such as artificial intelligence applications, cyber security, renewable energy, and environmental technologies. This transformation requires new soft skills such as creativity and adaptability. Therefore, education systems must strengthen social-emotional skills such as creativity, critical thinking, communication and collaboration to prepare them for the future. Therefore, educational systems enable students to continuously develop themselves during their school years and through lifelong learning. They have stated that leadership and teaching teams need to rethink their roles and ways of working due to practices that have become obsolete in the emerging new educational paradigm (Azorin & Fullan, 2022).

Within this framework, digital well-being is a crucial issue. Instilling digital skills in students is not enough in the digital transformation process. However, students also need to learn how to protect their mental health. Education today is no longer merely a system for providing knowledge. It has also become a process that allows students to develop 21st-century skills, analyse daily and societal problems, and develop solutions. This book chapter has demonstrated the potential of AI to transform school leadership and teacher practices. However, in this rapidly changing environment, we need further empirical study to understand and support the integration of AI in education. In this context, it is critical for future research to focus on the following areas: First, research should focus on examining the effect of AI-integrated leadership strategies and learning tools on student achievement at different educational levels, such as elementary, middle, and high school. While existing literature indicates a small impact of AI on mathematics achievement, we should investigate differences across disciplines (e.g., science, reading) and age groups. Second, we need to focus on examining the cultural and regional differences (e.g. power distance, individualism, motivation towards achievement and success, uncertainty, avoidance, long term, orientation, and indulgence) that facilitate or hinder AI adoption. Moreover, leaders' attitudes toward AI and their decision-making processes are critical factors for its effective integration in schools. Therefore, we need to compare the impact of different education systems (decentralized vs. hierarchical) on AI policies and practices. Third, studies should be conducted to describe the practical implications of classroom practices, such as how teachers use AI to enhance students' critical thinking skills. Fourth, school principals' confidence in AI technology (e.g., self-efficacy) has been found to be a key factor in their willingness to use it. Future research should empirically examine the impact of antecedents and boundary conditions on self-efficacy and the fostering of a positive attitude towards AI. Fifth, when school principals used AI for their routine tasks, the other leader roles such as strategic thinking, guidance, empathy, and ethical responsibility need to be redefined. Qualitative studies should be conducted on how to balance human reasoning and value-based ethical decisions in AI-supported decision-making processes. Sixth, we need to develop concrete communication strategies to demonstrate how leaders can effectively communicate to teachers, parents, and students for the potential benefits of AI (e.g., workload reduction, student learning support). This communication should also focus on how to manage risks such as data privacy and algorithmic bias. Lastly, it is important to explore what strategies (e.g., establishing a clear vision, taking risks) school leaders should use to manage the transformation

REFERENCES

Abdallah, A. K., & Musah, M. B. (2025). Artificial intelligence in school leadership. In Abdallah, A. K., & Musah, M. B. (Eds.), *AI in learning, educational leadership, and special education: Innovations and ethical dilemmas* (pp. 79–102). IGI Global., DOI: 10.4018/979-8-3373-0573-8.ch003

Adams, D., & Chuah, K.-M. (2022). Artificial intelligence-based tools in research writing: Current trends and future potentials. In Churi, P. P., Joshi, S., Elhoseny, M., & Omrane, A. (Eds.), *Artificial intelligence in higher education: A practical approach* (pp. 169–184). CRC Press. DOI: 10.1201/9781003184157-9

Adams, D., & Thompson, P. (2025). Transforming school leadership with artificial intelligence: Applications, implications, and future directions. *Journal of Educational Administration, 63*(1), 77–89. DOI: 10.1108/JEA-01-2025-0007

Akhmad, A. (2025). Digital leadership practices in educational management: A narrative literature review on trends and challenges. *International Journal of Learning. Teaching and Educational Research, 24*(8), 112–135. DOI: 10.26803/ijlter.24.8.6

Aljemely, Y. (2024). Challenges and best practices in training teachers to utilize artificial intelligence: A systematic review. *Frontiers in Education, 9*, 1470853. DOI: 10.3389/feduc.2024.1470853

Arar, K., Tlili, A., & Salha, S. (2024). Human-Machine symbiosis in educational leadership in the era of artificial intelligence (AI): Where are we heading? *Educational Management Administration & Leadership*, 17411432241292295. Advance online publication. DOI: 10.1177/17411432241292295

Arriola-Mendoza, J., & Valerio-Ureña, G. (2024). Essential elements for implementing AI tools in elementary school: A systematic literature review. *Education Sciences, 14*(1292), 1–15. DOI: 10.3390/educsci14121292

Azorin, C., & Fullan, M. (2022). Leading new, deeper forms of collaborative cultures: Questions and pathways. *Journal of Educational Change, 23*(1), 131–143. DOI: 10.1007/s10833-021-09448-w PMID: 38624840

Bandura, A. (1986). *Social foundations of thought and action: A social cognitive theory*. Prentice-Hall.

Bandura, A. (1997). *Self-efficacy: The exercise of control*. W. H. Freeman.

Berkovich, I. (2025). The rise of AI-assisted instructional leadership: Empirical survey of generative AI integration in school leadership and management work. *Frontiers in Education, 10*, 1643023. DOI: 10.3389/feduc.2025.1643023

Berkovich, I., & Eyal, O. (2025). Support for generative artificial intelligence as a predictor of middle leaders' generative artificial intelligence self-efficacy, valuing, and integration in school leadership work. *Educational Management Administration & Leadership*, 17411432251361251. Advance online publication. DOI: 10.1177/17411432251361251

Chang, Q., Zhang, J., & Xiao, X. (2025). Leading Like Human: Clarifying the Connotation and Validating the Structure of Algorithmic Leadership. *International Journal of Human-Computer Interaction*, 1–28. DOI: 10.1080/10447318.2025.2543991

Cheung, K. K. C., Long, Y., Liu, Q., & Chan, H. Y. (2024). Unpacking epistemic insights of artificial intelligence (AI) in science education: A systematic review. *Science & Education, 34*(2), 747–777. DOI: 10.1007/s11191-024-00511-5

Coccoli, M., Maresca, P., & Stanganelli, L. (2016). Cognitive computing in education. *Journal of E-Learning and Knowledge Society, 12*(2), 55–69. DOI: 10.20368/1971-8829/1185

Erdoğan, O., Kaymak, M. N., Çoban, Ö., & Bora, H. T. (2025). Exploring the links between school principals' self-efficacy, open innovation mindset, transformational leadership, and artificial intelligence (AI) attitudes in Türkiye. *Educational Management Administration & Leadership*, 17411432251351830. Advance online publication. DOI: 10.1177/17411432251351830

Fullan, M., Azorín, C., Harris, A., & Jones, M. (2024). Artificial intelligence and school leadership: Challenges, opportunities and implications. *School Leadership & Management, 44*(4), 339–346. DOI: 10.1080/13632434.2023.2246856

Gao, C., Khalid, S., Lianyu, C., & Tadesse, E. (2024). Integrated leadership for coherent school improvement in Ethiopia: The moderating role of transformational leadership on the relationship between instructional leadership and student academic achievement mediated by school improvement process. *Psychology in the Schools, 61*(2), 455–474. DOI: 10.1002/pits.23065

Göçen, A., & Döğer, M. F. (2025). A global perspective on artificial intelligence in educational leadership. *The Journal of Educational Research, 118*(6), 1–19. DOI: 10.1080/00220671.2025.2510397

Green, F. (2021). British teachers' declining job quality: Evidence from the skills and employment survey. *Oxford Review of Education*, *47*(3), 386–403. DOI: 10.1080/03054985.2020.1847719

Griesbach, K., Reich, A., Elliott-Negri, L., & Milkman, R. (2019). Algorithmic control in platform food delivery work. *Socius: Sociological Research for a Dynamic World*, *5*, 1–15. DOI: 10.1177/2378023119870041

Griffiths, W. (1959). The principle of participation: Some points to consider. *Health Education Journal*, *17*(4), 222–229. Advance online publication. DOI: 10.1177/001789695901700403

Harms, P. D., & Han, G. (2019). Algorithmic leadership: The future is now. *Journal of Leadership Studies*, *12*(4), 74–75. DOI: 10.1002/jls.21615

Herold, B. (2019). Forty percent of elementary school teachers' work could be automated by 2030, McKinsey Global Institute predicts. *EducationWeek*. https://www.edweek.org/education/forty-percent-of-elementary-school-teachers-work-could-be-automated-by-2030-mckinsey-global-institute-predicts/2019/06

Hou, Y., Cui, Y., & Zhang, D. (2019). Impact of instructional leadership on high school student academic achievement in China. *Asia Pacific Education Review*, *20*(4), 543–558. DOI: 10.1007/s12564-019-09574-4

Hwang, S. (2022). Examining the effects of artificial intelligence on elementary students' mathematics achievement: A meta-analysis. *Sustainability (Basel)*, *14*(20), 13185. DOI: 10.3390/su142013185

James, J., Malkin, T., & Nusche, D. (2025). *Trends Shaping Education 2025*. OECD Publishing.

Kosztelnik, K. (2019). Black box thinking: Navigating ethical AI in educational leadership. *Journal of Educational Ethics*, *5*(2), 123–135. DOI: 10.1109/ICIME.2018.00075

Marrone, R., Fowler, S., Bathakur, A., Dawson, S., Siemens, G., & Singh, C. (2025). Perceptions and perspectives of Australian school leaders on the integration of artificial intelligence in schools. *School Leadership & Management*, *45*(1), 30–52. DOI: 10.1080/13632434.2024.2425019

Martínez, I. G., Fernández Batanero, J. M., Fernández Cerero, J., & León, S. P. (2023). Analysing the impact of artificial intelligence and computational sciences on student performance: Systematic review and meta-analysis. *NAER: Journal of New Approaches in Educational Research*, *12*(1), 171–197. DOI: 10.7821/naer.2023.1.1240

Ng, D. T. K., Leung, J. K. L., Su, J., Ng, R. C. W., & Chu, S. K. W. (2023). Teachers' AI digital competencies and twenty-first century skills in the post-pandemic world. *Educational Technology Research and Development*, *71*(1), 137–161. DOI: 10.1007/s11423-023-10203-6 PMID: 36844361

Otaye-Ebede, L., Shaffakat, S., & Foster, S. (2020). A multilevel model examining the relationships between workplace spirituality, ethical climate and outcomes: A social cognitive theory perspective. *Journal of Business Ethics*, *166*(3), 611–626. DOI: 10.1007/s10551-019-04133-8

Pietsch, M., & Mah, D. K. (2025). Leading the AI transformation in schools: It starts with a digital mindset. *Educational Technology Research and Development*, *73*(2), 1043–1069. DOI: 10.1007/s11423-024-10439-w

Reid, D. B., & Creed, B. M. (2023). Visible at night: US school principal nontraditional work-hour activities and job satisfaction. *Educational Management Administration & Leadership*, *51*(5), 1123–1140. DOI: 10.1177/17411432211027645

Renta-Davids, A. I., Camarero-Figuerola, M., & Camacho, M. (2025). Navigating the challenges and opportunities of artificial intelligence in educational leadership: A scoping review. *Review of Education*, *13*(2), e70101. DOI: 10.1002/rev3.70101

Sebastian, J., Camburn, E. M., & Spillane, J. P. (2018). Portraits of principal practice: Time allocation and school principal work. *Educational Administration Quarterly*, *54*(1), 47–84. DOI: 10.1177/0013161X17720978

Sezgin, S., & Fırat, M. (2020). Covid-19 pandemisinde uzaktan eğitime geçiş ve dijital uçurum tehlikesi. *Açıköğretim Uygulamaları ve Araştırmaları Dergisi*, *6*(4), 37–54.

Simon, H. A. (1972). Theories of bounded rationality. In McGuire, C. B., & Radner, R. (Eds.), *Decision and organization* (pp. 161–176). North-Holland.

Skaalvik, C. (2020). Self-efficacy for instructional leadership: Relations with perceived job demands and job resources, emotional exhaustion, job satisfaction, and motivation to quit. *Social Psychology of Education*, *23*(5), 1343–1366. DOI: 10.1007/s11218-020-09585-9

Snyder, H. (2019). Literature review as a research methodology: An overview and guidelines. *Journal of Business Research*, *104*, 333–339. DOI: 10.1016/j.jbusres.2019.07.039

Van Quaquebeke, N., & Gerpott, F. H. (2023). The now, new, and next of digital leadership: How artificial intelligence (AI) will take over and change leadership as we know it. *Journal of Leadership & Organizational Studies*, *30*(2), 265–275. DOI: 10.1177/15480518231181731

Wang, Y. (2021). Artificial intelligence in educational leadership: A symbiotic role of human–artificial intelligence decision-making. *Journal of Educational Administration, 59*(3), 256–270. DOI: 10.1108/JEA-10-2020-0216

Wang, Y. (2023). Addressing data biases in AI: Challenges and solutions for educational leaders. *Journal of AI and Society, 38*(1), 100–115.

Zawacki-Richter, O., Marín, V. I., Bond, M., & Gouverneur, F. (2019). Systematic review of research on artificial intelligence applications in higher education: Where are the educators? *International Journal of Educational Technology in Higher Education, 16*(1), 1–27. DOI: 10.1186/s41239-019-0171-0

Chapter 5
When Teachers Code Change:
How AI and Strategic Intelligence Spark a Sensemaking Revolution in Organizations

Ramazan Atasoy
https://orcid.org/0000-0002-9198-074X
Harran University, Turkey

Ramazan Özkul
http://orcid.org/0000-0001-9757-6062
Harran University, Turkey

ABSTRACT

This chapter examines how transformational school leaders engage with artificial intelligence technologies and how teachers make sense of AI and its potential effects. Using a quantitative, cross-sectional design, the study focused on 34,222 public secondary and high school teachers in Şanlıurfa, with 648 selected through non-probability sampling from three central districts reflecting diverse socio-economic contexts. Data were gathered through scales measuring transformational leadership, AI, and sensemaking, with gender, education, and teaching experience as control variables. Ethical approval was obtained, and responses were collected via Google Forms through email and WhatsApp. Analyses with SPSS and Mplus revealed significant associations, showing a strong link between transformational leadership and AI, and AI's mediating role between leadership and sensemaking. Findings suggest that leaders should manage AI's complexities to enhance teachers' sensemaking and awareness. However, the cross-sectional design limits causal inference, and future longitudinal research is recommended

DOI: 10.4018/979-8-3373-6375-2.ch005

INTRODUCTION

The rapid advancement of digitalization and artificial intelligence (AI) has raised a critical question for organizations and professional service firms: how can they construct their perceptions of technology and shape their future visions in order to ensure survival (Goto, 2022). Anticipating these dynamics at an early stage can significantly influence the trajectory of digital transformation processes and their outcomes (Armour & Sako, 2020). AI is commonly defined as computer systems capable of performing functions such as imitating human intelligence, learning, interacting, and solving problems (Glikson & Woolley, 2020; Raisch & Krakowski, 2021). Unlike traditional computer systems, AI possesses a rapidly expanding capacity, particularly in managing knowledge-intensive tasks (Glikson & Woolley, 2020). In this context, organizational leadership paradigms have undergone notable shifts, with technology introducing new challenges in managing the synergy between organizational processes and behaviors (Bednar & Welch, 2020; Wiesböck & Hess, 2020).

In such complex and uncertain environments, sensemaking (SM)—the process through which individuals and organizations interpret and assign meaning to their circumstances—offers a critical theoretical lens for understanding how employees engage with technology and seek to interpret its implications (Sandberg & Tsoukas, 2020; Weick et al., 2005). SM emphasizes how people in ambiguous contexts attempt to forecast the future while being shaped by social and cognitive factors (Beckert, 2021; Dwyer et al., 2021). As AI becomes increasingly integrated into work environments, the ways in which employees—particularly teachers—perceive and construct the future of their professions and institutions will be pivotal for effective technological adaptation (Fleming, 2019; Weick, 1990).

This study aims to examine the influence of transformational leadership (TL) on SM and to explore the mediating role of AI within this relationship. Prior research highlights transformational leadership's impact on organizational change and teaching–learning processes (Mumford et al., 2002), while also underscoring AI's transformative potential in decision-making and learning environments (Abositta et al., 2024). The proposed model investigates how transformational school leaders approach AI technologies and how teachers make sense of AI and its future implications. By doing so, this study seeks to offer fresh insights into the complex interplay between leadership and organizational adaptation in an era increasingly defined by AI. Consequently, the study investigates the following research questions (RQ):

RQ1. What are the direct associations between TL and AI; between TL and SM; and between AI and SM?

RQ2. Does AI have a mediating effect on the relationship between TL and SM?

Conceptual Framework

Figure 1 illustrates our hypothesised model, while the following section provides theoretical explanations for our constructs and the rationale behind our hypotheses.

Figure 1. Conceptual model

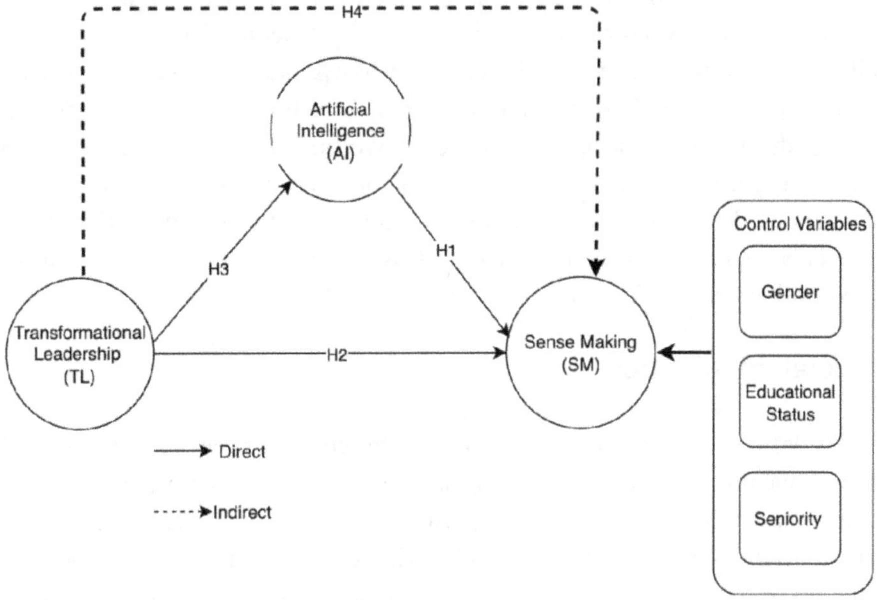

LITERATURE REVIEW AND HYPOTHESES

Transformational leadership

TL has been systematically developed by Bass (1995) as a theoretical framework that explains how leaders reshape institutional capacities (Abositta et al., 2024; Avolio & Bass, 1995; Smith & Green, 2018). This leadership style is characterized by four core dimensions: idealized influence, inspirational motivation, intellectual stimulation, and individualized consideration (Estherita & Shanmugam, 2024). These dimensions are particularly critical in processes of technological adaptation during organizational transformation (Abositta et al., 2024). Transformational leaders can be effective in guiding schools through technology integration by cultivating a culture that embraces innovation and strategic change. Moreover, the cognitive flexibility fostered by TL reduces resistance to technological transformations and facilitates knowledge exploration (Abositta et al., 2024).

TL has several positive effects, such as fostering teachers' openness to innovation in the workplace (Odugbesan et al., 2023) and enhancing their creative capacities (Jeong & Jeong, 2025). With the rise of AI, it has been argued that the skills required for leadership are evolving, and that leaders should increasingly utilize AI to inspire and motivate their employees (Abdeldayem & Aldulaimi, 2020). TL plays a crucial role in aligning AI with organizational goals (Jeong & Jeong, 2025). In educational institutions in particular, TL practices are seen as essential for supporting teachers' adoption of new technologies and digital tools, as well as for facilitating their SM processes during these transitions (Laursen & Weiss, 2025). TL can also encourage sense-making in the face of uncertainty and promote teachers' exploratory engagement (Goto, 2022). This highlights the multifaceted nature of leadership, showing how individuals interpret their cultural and professional values in ways that contribute to the development of TL qualities (Obmerga, 2024).

Artificial intelligence

AI is defined as an advanced computer technology that seeks to solve complex decision-making problems by emulating human intelligence (Berente et al., 2021). AI encompasses automation systems that perform cognitive functions such as learning, interaction, and problem-solving (Raisch & Krakowski, 2021). Its applications span a wide range of domains, including decision-making, prediction, natural language processing, and robotics (Engström et al., 2024).

AI technologies can enhance organizational efficiency by automating routine and repetitive tasks (Engström et al., 2024). Furthermore, AI contributes to improving decision-making processes by analyzing large datasets to produce more accurate predictions (Wang & Liu, 2019). On the other hand, the more abstract aspects of AI—such as algorithmic complexity and ethical considerations—may create uncertainty among employees, potentially leading to passivity and a reliance on top-down hierarchical instructions (Engström et al., 2024). Difficulties in understanding how AI reaches decisions may give rise to issues of trust and control (Goto, 2022). Nevertheless, AI can also contribute to social contexts by exposing existing biases within society (Coeckelbergh, 2023). Considering these insights, it can be argued that AI possesses the capacity to shape how individuals make sense of both their environments and themselves.

Sensemaking

SM has been defined as a process through which individuals attempt to interpret situations of uncertainty or disrupted expectations (Weick, 1995). In this process, people strive to generate plausible explanations to understand complex and ambiguous circumstances. It is a dynamic activity that unfolds over time and occurs through interaction with others (Dwyer et al., 2021; Sandberg & Tsoukas, 2020). SM is often categorized as retrospective, focusing on the interpretation of past events (Kaplan & Orlikowski, 2013; Weick, 1995), or as prospective, involving deliberate and conscious assessments oriented toward the future (Goto, 2022; Kaplan & Orlikowski, 2013).

The SM process is shaped by influences from the individual, the social environment, and the organizational context (Kaur et al., 2022). Weick identified seven key properties of SM: identity construction, which emphasizes who the sensemaker is (Kaur et al., 2022); social context, which highlights the role of others' expectations in SM (Levine et al., 1993); retrospectivity, which draws on past experiences (Kaur et al., 2022); enactment, which underscores how actions shape the environment (Weick, 1995); ongoing SM, which stresses its continuous nature (Kaur et al., 2022); extracted cues, which focus on filling in gaps using limited pieces of information (James, 2007); and plausibility over accuracy, which prioritizes satisfactory rather than strictly rational explanations (Weick, 1995).

In situations where the risk of uncertainty is high, forming a clear vision for the future can be challenging, often requiring continuous reassessment and revision (Goto, 2022). At this point, SM provides a cognitive framework that guides organizational members in determining which types of information to pay attention to and how to interpret them (Engström et al., 2024; Konlechner et al., 2019). Experts in their fields, such as teachers, monitor environmental changes, adjust their future plans in light of new practices, and come to accept the idea that the future may remain in a constant state of flux under uncertain conditions (Goto, 2022).

Mediating Role

In the model proposed in our research, artificial intelligence plays a mediating role between TL and SM. This illustrates how TL influences the way AI is perceived and integrated within schools, and how, in turn, this process shapes teachers' sensemaking. In this context, the relationships among the variables are supported by the existing literature.

First, in the relationship between TL and artificial intelligence technologies, transformational leaders facilitate employees' adaptation to technology by fostering an organizational environment that is open to innovation (Erdoğan et al., 2025) and strategic change (Abositta et al., 2024). Leaders also play a role in enhancing employees' trust in AI and in supporting its use as a tool to develop their capabilities (Bass & Riggio, 2006). Moreover, transformational leaders inspire and motivate their employees, thereby strengthening their engagement (Abdeldayem & Aldulaimi, 2020). This leadership style enhances confidence in AI applications and places data-driven decision-making at the center of organizational practice (Abositta et al., 2024).

Second, AI integrates into human life by shaping actions and structuring interpretations, thereby influencing sensemaking (Coeckelbergh, 2023). For instance, an AI tool can co-write an individual's daily narrative, which in turn shapes how that person makes sense of themselves (Coeckelbergh, 2023). AI's ability to analyze data and generate predictions directly contributes to individuals' sensemaking of events and expectations about the future by providing cues and outlining broader frameworks (Weick, 1995). However, the rational provision of statistical and probabilistic information by AI may at times conflict with how individuals construct causal and moral responsibility (Coeckelbergh, 2023). Yet, this challenge can be mitigated through AI's capacity to reveal social biases and assist individuals in gaining greater awareness of their social contexts, thereby fostering a more collective sensemaking process (Coeckelbergh, 2023).

In understanding the mediating role of AI, the practices of transformational leaders—such as fostering open communication, articulating a clear vision, and providing individualized support to employees—facilitate the adoption of AI within organizations. A positive orientation toward AI (e.g., perceiving it as an opportunity to enhance creative capacities rather than as a threat) influences the sensemaking process through which employees and organizations interpret the impact of technology on their professions and future trajectories (Jeong & Jeong, 2025; Shneiderman, 2020). Employees' interactions with AI may further shape how they interpret and make sense of new knowledge generated by AI systems (Engström et al., 2024). In this way, TL mediates how AI is perceived and utilized in the workplace, thereby influencing how employees construct meaning in the face of an uncertain future. The literature provides empirical evidence supporting the critical role of TL in strategic decision-making and decision processes involving AI (Abositta et al., 2024). Within this theoretical framework, TLemerges as a key mechanism that explicates the impact of AI on SM at both the individual and collective levels, thereby reinforcing the proposition that AI adoption and utilization in the workplace can be enhanced through effective leadership.

METHOD

Research Design

This quantitative study employs a cross-sectional survey design to examine the relationships between the variables. The quantitative cross-sectional design enables the collection of data from a large number of participants within the population, thereby allowing for statistical analyses and facilitating broader generalizations (Creswell, 2014).

Sampling

The population of the study consists of 34222 teachers working in public lower secondary and upper secondary schools in the province of Şanlıurfa. The sample was drawn from 648 teachers, selected to reflect the diversity of school contexts in Şanlıurfa. To this end, three central districts with differing socioeconomic characteristics—Karaköprü, Haliliye, and Eyyübiye—were included. Due to practical considerations such as time and accessibility, a convenience sampling method, specifically simple random sampling, was employed. Demographic information regarding the participants is presented in Table 1.

Table 1. Demographic Characteristics of the Participants (n = 648)

Variable	Category	n	%
Gender	Female	317	48.9
	Male	331	51.1
Educational Status	Bachelor's Degree	563	86.9
	Graduate Degree	85	13.1
Seniority	1–5 years	242	37.5
	6–10 years	172	26.6
	11 years and above	234	35.9
School Type	Primary School	316	48.8
	Lower Secondary School	165	25.5
	Upper Secondary School	167	25.7

Data Collection Tools

During the data collection process, a two-part instrument was employed. The first section gathered demographic information about the participants, including gender, educational status, years of professional experience, and the level of school at which they were employed (primary, lower secondary, or upper secondary.

Sensemaking. The seven-item scale developed by Cantarero et al. (2022) and translated into Turkish by the researchers was used to measure teachers' level of sensemaking. The original scale demonstrated strong internal consistency with a Cronbach's alpha of 0.88. Results of the confirmatory factor analysis (CFA) indicated an excellent model fit (χ^2/df = 2.51, RMSEA = 0.06, RMR = 0.01, CFI = 0.99, GFI = 0.97).

Artificial Intelligence. The four-item scale developed by Grassini (2023) and translated into Turkish by the researchers was employed to assess teachers' perceptions of artificial intelligence. The original scale demonstrated satisfactory internal consistency, with a Cronbach's alpha of 0.83. Confirmatory factor analysis (CFA) further indicated an excellent model fit (χ^2/df = 2.51, RMSEA = 0.06, RMR = 0.01, CFI = 0.99, GFI = 0.97).

Transformational Leadership. A 8-item scale developed by Berger et al. (2012) and translated into Turkish by Okan and Okan (2021) measured principals' transformational practices. The original scale had a Cronbach's alpha of 0.97. Confirmatory factor analysis (CFA) indicated an excellent fit (χ^2/sd= 2.51, RMSEA = 0.06, RMR = 0.01, CFI = 0.99, GFI = 0.97).

Control variables. Previous studies have suggested that demographic and institutional factors may shape TL and their willingness to adopt sensemaking in educational contexts (Obmerga, 2024). To account for potential confounding effects, this study included gender, educational attainment, and total teaching experience as control variables in examining teachers' SM perceptions.

Data Collection Process

During the data collection process, prior permission to use the scales was first obtained from the original authors. Subsequently, ethical approval for the study was granted by the ethics committee of a university in Türkiye on 18.09.2025 (Approval No: 2025/265). Following the permissions regarding the use of the instruments in the field, school principals were contacted via email and telephone to request their support in encouraging teachers to participate. Teachers who agreed to participate, on the basis of informed consent and adherence to the principles of voluntariness and anonymity, received the Google Form link containing the study instruments through email and/or WhatsApp communication channels. The data collection process lasted one week.

Analytical Strategy

The dataset was initially gathered through an online survey created via Google Forms. Once data collection was completed, responses were exported to SPSS version 27 for preliminary examination. In this phase, univariate outliers were detected and excluded to improve the quality and distributional assumptions of the data. After these initial adjustments, the refined dataset was imported into Mplus version 8.3 to conduct advanced statistical analyses. To evaluate the adequacy of the measurement model, a confirmatory factor analysis (CFA) was performed using Mplus version 8.1. The model fit was evaluated based on widely accepted criteria, including a chi-square to degrees of freedom ratio below 5, Standardized Root Mean Square Residual (SRMR) and Root Mean Square Error of Approximation (RMSEA) values less than .08, and Comparative Fit Index (CFI) and Tucker–Lewis Index (TLI) values exceeding .90, as suggested by Hu and Bentler (1999). Before testing the hypothesized mediation framework, the distributional properties of all study variables were examined. Skewness and kurtosis values were checked to verify univariate normality, and all estimates fell within the acceptable ±1.5 range, indicating normal distribution of the data (Tabachnick & Fidell, 2007). Furthermore, multicollinearity diagnostics were conducted to assess the independence of predictor variables. Variance Inflation Factor (VIF) values below 3 and Tolerance values above .10 indicated no violation of multicollinearity assumptions (Hair et al., 2022). In addition, Pearson correlation analyses were carried out to explore the bivariate relationships among the primary variables of interest. These associations provided initial empirical support for the conceptual links between the independent variable (TL), the mediator (AI), and the outcome variable (SM). Following the preliminary diagnostics, the mediation model was tested using the Maximum Likelihood estimation method. To assess the significance of both direct and indirect effects, a bias-corrected bootstrapping procedure with 5,000 resamples and a 95% confidence interval was applied (Preacher & Hayes, 2013).

FINDINGS

Preliminary Analysis

As part of the preliminary analyses, descriptive statistics and Pearson correlations among the study variables were examined. The results, presented in Table 2.

Table 2. Descriptive Statistics and Pearson Correlations

Variable	M (SD)	1	2	3	4	5	6
1. TL	4.15 (0.67)	-					
2. AI	4.02 (0.74)	.726**	-				
3. SM	4.32 (0.50)	.476**	.486**	-			
4. Gender	0.49 (0.50)	-.098*	-.108**	-.079*	-		
5. EdSta	0.87 (0.34)	-.046	-.071	-.028	.124**	-	
6. Seniority	9.88 (7.91)	-.111**	-.159**	-.055	-.223**	-.056	-
Skewness	-	-0.814	-0.747	-0.184	-	--	-
Kurtosis	-	0.818	0.740	-0.629	--	-	-

Notes: M = Mean; SD = Standard Deviation. * $p < .05$, ** $p < .01$ (two-tailed).

Table 2 shows that the mean score for TL was 4.15 (SD = 0.67), while AI and SM had mean values of 4.02 (SD = 0.74) and 4.32 (SD = 0.50), respectively. These results suggest generally high levels across all three constructs. Pearson correlation coefficients revealed statistically significant positive associations between TL and AI ($r = .726$, $p < .01$), TL and SM ($r = .476$, $p < .01$), and AI and SM ($r = .486$, $p < .01$), providing preliminary support for the hypothesized relationships. These findings indicate that both TL and AI are positively related to teachers' SM perceptions.

With regard to demographic variables, gender was negatively correlated with TL ($r = –.098$, $p < .05$), AI ($r = –.108$, $p < .01$), and SM ($r = –.079$, $p < .05$), suggesting minor gender-related differences in perceptions or engagement. Educational status exhibited a small positive correlation with gender ($r = .124$, $p < .01$), but no significant associations with the core constructs. Seniority was negatively associated with TL ($r = –.111$, $p < .01$) and AI ($r = –.159$, $p < .01$), suggesting that more experienced individuals may perceive lower levels of leadership and AI orientation in their institutions.

The distributional properties of the core variables were also examined. Skewness values for TL (–0.814), AI (–0.747), and SM (–0.184) indicated moderate to low left skewness. Kurtosis values remained within acceptable thresholds, ranging from –0.629 for SM to 0.818 for TL. These statistics supported the assumption of univariate normality and justified the use of parametric tests in subsequent analyses.

Measurement Model

To evaluate the adequacy of the latent constructs, a confirmatory factor analysis (CFA) (Table 3) was conducted using Mplus version 8.1. The analysis aimed to verify whether the observed variables adequately represented the underlying theoretical constructs. Model fit was assessed using multiple fit indices, including the chi-square to degrees of freedom ratio (χ^2/df), Comparative Fit Index (CFI), Tucker–Lewis Index (TLI), Root Mean Square Error of Approximation (RMSEA), and Standardized Root Mean Square Residual (SRMR). The results demonstrated a satisfactory model fit: $\chi^2(149) = 553.70$, yielding a χ^2/df ratio of 3.72, which falls within the acceptable range of 1.0 to 5.0. Additionally, the CFI (.936) and TLI (.927) both exceeded the recommended threshold of .90, indicating strong comparative fit. The RMSEA value of .065 and SRMR value of .038 were both well below the .08 cut-off, further supporting the model's fit to the data (Hu & Bentler, 1999). Collectively, these fit indices suggest that the measurement model adequately captures the structure of the latent constructs, justifying the use of the factor scores in subsequent structural analyse

Table 3. Confirmatory Factor Analysis Model Fit Indices (Baseline Model)

Model	χ^2/df	CFI	TLI	RMSEA	SRMR
CFA model	553.70 (149)	.936	.927	.065	.038
Cut-off Criteria	1.0 -5.0	≥0.90	≥0.90	<0.080	<0.080

Reliability and Validity Analysis

The reliability and validity of the latent constructs were evaluated in Table 4 through confirmatory factor analysis, and the results indicated robust psychometric properties for all three variables. Internal consistency was assessed using Cronbach's alpha (α) and McDonald's omega (ω), both of which demonstrated high reliability across constructs. Specifically, the SM factor, composed of seven items with standardized loadings ranging from .762 to .852, yielded $\alpha = .916$ and $\omega = .914$. The AI factor, consisting of four items with loadings between .821 and .874, showed $\alpha = .880$ and $\omega = .874$. The TL factor, represented by eight items with strong factor loadings (.826–.913), displayed excellent internal consistency ($\alpha = .923$; $\omega = .921$). Convergent validity was examined also through Average Variance Extracted (AVE) and Composite Reliability (CR) indices. All three constructs surpassed the commonly accepted thresholds, with AVE values above .50 and CR values exceeding .70 (Fornell & Larcker, 1981). The AVE scores were .681 for SM, .753 for AI, and .743 for TL, indicating that a substantial portion of variance was captured by the latent variables. Taken together, these results confirm that the measurement model exhibits both strong internal reliability and adequate construct validity, supporting its suitability for use in subsequent structural modeling analyses.

Table 4. Reliability and Validity Analysis of the Single-Factor Structure

Factor	Items	Factor Loadings (λ)	α	ω	AVE	CR
SM	7	.819, .838, .837, .829, .777,.852, .762	.916	.914	.681	.923
AI	4	.874, .866, .870, .821	.880	.874	.753	.923
TL	8	.828, .883, .858, .826, .848, .913, .898, .888	.923	.921	.743	.958

Hypothesis Testing

Direct, Indirect and Total Effect

The hypothesized mediation model was tested using maximum likelihood estimation, and the results supported the proposed relationships among the variables. As shown in Table 5, TL had a significant direct effect on SM ($\beta = .224$, SE = .080, $t = 2.81$, 95% CI [.062, .354], $p < .001$). Furthermore, TL was strongly predictive of AI ($\beta = .803$, SE = .023, $t = 34.89$, 95% CI [.754, .838], $p < .001$). In turn, AI significantly predicted SM ($\beta = .350$, SE = .080, $t = 4.23$, 95% CI [.192, .485], $p < .001$).

In addition to these direct effects, the model revealed a significant indirect effect of TL on SM through AI ($\beta = .281$, SE = .068, $t = 4.14$, 95% CI [.152, .394], $p < .001$), suggesting a mediating role of AI in the relationship between TL and SM. The total effect of TL on SM, combining both direct and indirect paths, was also significant ($\beta = .505$, SE = .036, $t = 14.18$, 95% CI [.432, .562], $p < .001$), indicating that AI accounts for a substantial portion of the overall relationship.

The influence of control variables (gender, educational status, and seniority) on SM was also examined. None of the covariates demonstrated statistically significant effects: gender ($\beta = -.026$, $p > .05$), educational status ($\beta = .000$, $p > .05$), and seniority ($\beta = .022$, $p > .05$), suggesting that the primary model relationships were not confounded by these background factors.

The findings provide strong empirical support for the mediating role of AI orientation in the link between TL and SM, reinforcing the theoretical assumption that AI-oriented environments facilitate employees' cognitive engagement in meaning-making processes.

Table 5. The results for the standardized effects of variables

Construct	Product of coefficients			95% bootstrap CI		Two-tailed (p)
	Estimate	SE	t	Lower	Upper	
Direct Effects						
TL → SM	.224	.080	2.81	.062	.354	.001
TL → AI	.803	.023	34.89	.754	.838	.001
AI → SM	.350	.080	4.23	.192	.485	.001
Standardized Indirect Effect						
TL → AI→SM	.281	.068	4.136	.152	.394	.001
Standardized Total Effect						
TL → AI→SM	.505	.036	14.183	.432	.562	.001
Covariants						
Gender	-.026	.037	-.716	-.098	.035	-
EdStatus	.000	.033	.013	-.063	.057	-
Seniority	.022	.038	.578	-.053	.084	-

Notes: TL = Transformational leadership; SM = sense making; AI = Artificial Intelligence. Based on 5,000 bootstrapped samples. Standardized indirect effects = 95% confidence interval *p < 0.05, ***p < .001

Figure 2. The results for the standardized effects

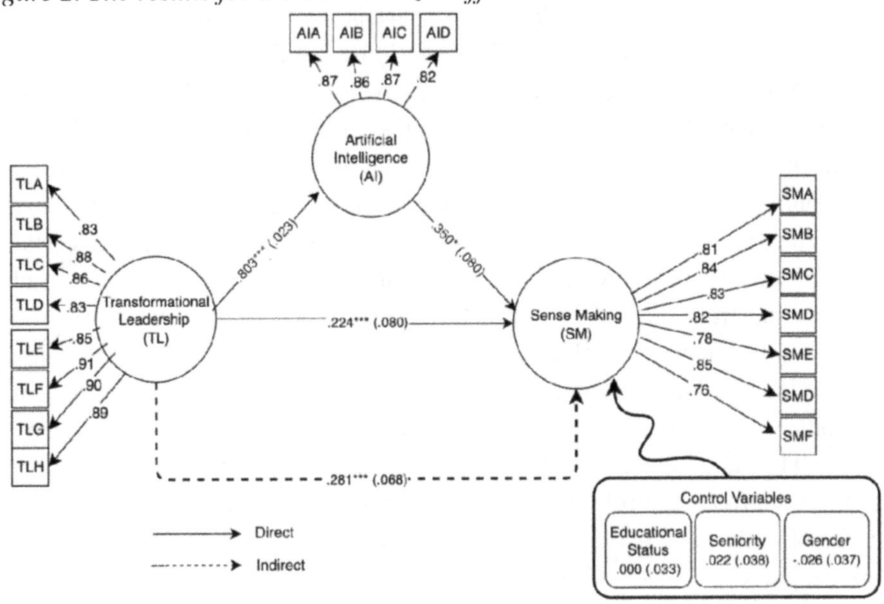

DISCUSSION

In this chapter, we focused the interactions among TL, the integration of artificial intelligence into schools, and SM processes. The findings revealed significant relationships among all three variables, with a particularly strong association identified between TL and AI. This result underscores the role of TL in fostering technological adaptation and innovation (Erdoğan et al., 2025; Laursen & Weiss, 2025), while also highlighting the capacity of AI to update decision-making processes and work practices in line with contemporary demands (Abositta et al., 2024).

With the increasing use of AI, organizations are increasingly confronted with uncertainty (Beckert, 2021), which elevates the role of leaders as guides in helping employees make sense of AI-enabled technologies and their future implications (Goto, 2022). The findings of our study suggest that the inspirational motivation and individualized consideration dimensions of TL (Laursen & Weiss, 2025) can contribute to teachers' positive perceptions and adoption of AI. This is closely related to teachers' tendency to view AI as a tool that can enhance or support their creative capacities (Shneiderman, 2020). By fostering positive attitudes toward AI, TL enables teachers to perceive uncertainty not as a threat, but as a pathway to learning and innovation (Engström et al., 2024). This view is consistent with evidence that technology-rich learning environments support not only technical proficiency but also social and emotional development, particularly when educators actively frame technology as part of a holistic learning experience (Demirdis, 2025).

The strong association between TL and AI also entails the risk that the abstract nature of AI may lead employees to adopt a passive "wait-and-see" attitude (Engström et al., 2024). By "abstractness," we refer to the complex algorithms and the often-insufficient data infrastructures underlying AI (Engström et al., 2024), which may cause employees to act solely on top-down directives (Ellstrøm, 2006). This situation clearly illustrates that TL is a critical form of leadership in reducing uncertainty arising from the abstract features of AI and in providing employees with a clear roadmap (Engström et al., 2024). Transformational leaders are therefore valuable in demonstrating that human influence and leadership competencies remain essential in sensemaking of AI and aligning it with organizational goals (Abositta et al., 2024).

Another key finding of our study is the mediating role of AI in the relationship between TL and SM. This result indicates that the adoption of AI within organizations strengthens the role of TL. Transformational leaders can enhance SM by transforming AI-generated data into vision, facilitating knowledge exchange, and supporting new practices (Yang et al., 2025). However, the inherent opacity of AI often generates uncertainty in interpretation. Transformational leaders, however, can address this challenge by anchoring technological results in the school's mission and value framework. In doing so, AI shifts from being an abstract phenomenon to becoming a concrete asset that supports organizational culture and vision. By fostering an environment in which humans and AI collaborate, TL elevates AI's participation in sensemaking processes to optimal levels (Coeckelbergh, 2023). In conclusion, this chapter provides both theoretical and empirical support for the view that leaders must integrate human-centered and technology-oriented approaches to successfully manage AI-driven change (Al Naqbi et al., 2024; Jeong & Jeong, 2025). While the growing role of AI appears inevitable, humans will continue to remain the primary creators of meaning (Coeckelbergh, 2023).

CONCLUSION AND IMPLICATIONS

This research demonstrates the significance of the interaction between TL and AI in shaping SM processes within organizational contexts. The findings of our study reveal that TL plays a pivotal role in fostering SM through the adoption of AI. Transformational leaders appear to act as mediators in decision-making processes, facilitating employees' constructive interpretation and engagement with this technology (Abositta et al., 2024). This indicates that leaders can create an environment that mitigates the uncertainty stemming from the abstract nature of artificial intelligence while enabling the exploration of its tangible potentials (Engström et al., 2024).

From a theoretical perspective, this study contributes to the literature by integrating TL and SM with AI. It is particularly important to elucidate how leaders' perceptions of AI influence their SM processes. We argue that AI should not be regarded merely as a tool but also as an active participant in SM processes, akin to a human collaborator.

From an empirical standpoint, the study offers tangible implications for leaders. It highlights the role of leaders in providing a vision regarding the benefits and potential of AI, thereby fostering more positive employee attitudes toward its adoption (Laursen & Weiss, 2025). This approach helps employees perceive AI not as a threat but as a resource to enhance their own capabilities and creativity (Jeong & Jeong, 2025). By managing the complexity of AI, leaders are expected to enhance employees' SM processes, thereby increasing their receptivity and responsiveness to this technology (Kaur et al., 2022).

LIMITATIONS AND FURTHER RESEARCH

While this study provides valuable insights into the relationships among AI, TL, and SM, it is important to acknowledge certain limitations. First, due to the cross-sectional nature of our research, we are constrained in making definitive claims about causal relationships among the variables. In this context, longitudinal studies could better support the examination of processual dynamics. Second, data collection could be expanded to include other key educational stakeholders, such as school administrators, students, parents, and academics, to enhance the diversity and generalizability of the findings.

For future research, it is crucial to increase the frequency of studies across different variables and contexts to achieve a clearer understanding of whether artificial intelligence should be conceptualized primarily as a technological tool or as a social agent. Additionally, qualitative or mixed-method studies based on classroom and school observations could provide a nuanced understanding of how leadership practices and SM processes influence the daily routines of teachers and other stakeholders.

REFERENCES

Abdeldayem, M. M., & Aldulaimi, S. H. (2020). Trends and opportunities of artificial intelligence in human resource management: Aspirations for public sector in Bahrain. *International Journal of Science and Technology Research*, *9*, 3867–3871.

Abositta, A., Adedokun, M. W., & Berberoğlu, A. (2024). Influence of artificial intelligence on engineering management decision-making with mediating role of transformational leadership. *Systems*, *12*(12), 570. Advance online publication. DOI: 10.3390/systems12120570

Al Naqbi, H., Bahroun, Z., & Ahmed, V. (2024). Enhancing work productivity through generative artificial intelligence: A comprehensive literature review. *Sustainability (Basel)*, *16*(3), 1166. DOI: 10.3390/su16031166

Armour, J., & Sako, M. (2020). AI-enabled business models in legal services: From traditional law firms to next-generation law companies? *Journal of Professions and Organization*, *7*(1), 27–46. DOI: 10.1093/jpo/joaa001

Avolio, B. J., & Bass, B. M. (1995). Individual consideration viewed at multiple levels of analysis: A multi-level framework for examining the diffusion of transformational leadership. *The Leadership Quarterly*, *6*(2), 199–218. DOI: 10.1016/1048-9843(95)90035-7

Bass, B. M., & Riggio, R. E. (2006). *Transformational leadership* (2nd ed.). Psychology Press. DOI: 10.4324/9781410617095

Beckert, J. (2021). The firm as an engine of imagination: Organizational prospection and the making of economic futures. *Organization Theory*, *2*(2), 1–20. DOI: 10.1177/26317877211005773

Bednar, P. M., & Welch, C. (2020). Socio-technical perspectives on smart working: Creating meaningful and sustainable systems. *Information Systems Frontiers*, *22*(2), 281–298. DOI: 10.1007/s10796-019-09921-1

Berente, N., Gu, B., Recker, J., & Santhanam, R. (2021). Managing artificial intelligence. *Management Information Systems Quarterly*, *45*(3), 1433–1450. DOI: 10.25300/MISQ/2021/16274

Berger, R., Romeo, M., Guardia, J., Yepes, M., & Soria, M. A. (2012). Psychometric properties of the Spanish human system audit short-scale of transformational leadership. *The Spanish Journal of Psychology*, *15*(1), 367–376. DOI: 10.5209/rev_SJOP.2012.v15.n1.37343

Cantarero, K., van Tilburg, W. A. P., Gasiorowska, A., & Igou, E. R. (2022). The efficient measurement of individual differences in meaning motivation: The need for sense-making short form. *Frontiers in Psychology*, *13*, 945692. DOI: 10.3389/fpsyg.2022.945692

Coeckelbergh, M. (2023). Narrative responsibility and artificial intelligence: How AI challenges human responsibility and sense-making. *AI & Society*, *38*(2), 2437–2450. DOI: 10.1007/s00146-021-01375-x

Creswell, J. W. (2014). *Research design: Qualitative, quantitative, and mixed methods approaches* (4th ed.). Sage Publications.

Demirdis, B. (2025). Integrating digital literacy to enhance emotional and social skills in education. In *Innovative Educational Frameworks for Future Skills and Competencies* (pp. 1–38). IGI Global Scientific Publishing., DOI: 10.4018/979-8-3693-7555-6.ch001

Dwyer, G., Hardy, C., & Maguire, S. (2021). Post-inquiry sensemaking: The case of the 'Black Saturday' bushfires. *Organization Studies*, *42*(4), 637–661. DOI: 10.1177/0170840619896271

Ellström, P.-E. (2006). Two logics of learning. In Antaqnacopoulou, H. (Ed.), *Learning, working and living: Mapping the terrain of working life learning* (pp. 33–49). Palgrave Macmillan.

Engström, A., Pittino, D., Mohlin, A., Johansson, A., & Edh Mirzaei, N. (2024). Artificial intelligence and work transformations: Integrating sensemaking and workplace learning perspectives. *Information Technology & People*, *37*(7), 2441–2461. DOI: 10.1108/ITP-01-2023-0048

Erdoğan, O., Kaymak, M. N., Çoban, Ö., & Bora, H. T. (2025). Exploring the links between school principals' self-efficacy, open innovation mindset, transformational leadership, and artificial intelligence (AI) attitudes in Türkiye. *Educational Management Administration & Leadership*, •••, 17411432251351830. DOI: 10.1177/17411432251351830

Estherita, A., & Shanmugam, V. (2024). Influence of artificial intelligence on transformational leadership. *AIP Conference Proceedings*, *3112*, 020013. DOI: 10.1063/5.0211330

Fleming, P. (2019). Robots and organization studies: Why robots might not want to steal your job. *Organization Studies*, *40*(1), 23–37. DOI: 10.1177/0170840618765568

Glikson, E., & Woolley, A. W. (2020). Human trust in artificial intelligence: Review of empirical research. *The Academy of Management Annals*, *14*(2), 627–660. DOI: 10.5465/annals.2018.0057

Goto, M. (2022). Accepting the future as ever-changing: Professionals' sensemaking about artificial intelligence. *Journal of Professions and Organization*, *9*(1), 77–99. DOI: 10.1093/jpo/joab022

Grassini, S. (2023). Development and validation of the AI Attitude Scale (AIAS-4): A brief measure of general attitude toward artificial intelligence. *Frontiers in Psychology*, *14*, 1191628. DOI: 10.3389/fpsyg.2023.1191628

James, W. (2007). *The principles of psychology* (Vol. 1). Cosimo, Inc.

Jeong, J., & Jeong, I. (2025). Driving creativity in the AI-enhanced workplace: Roles of self-efficacy and transformational leadership. *Current Psychology (New Brunswick, N.J.)*, *44*(9), 8001–8014. DOI: 10.1007/s12144-024-07135-6

Kaplan, S., & Orlikowski, W. J. (2013). Temporal work in strategy making. *Organization Science*, *24*(4), 965–995. DOI: 10.1287/orsc.1120.0792

Kaur, H., Adar, E., Gilbert, E., & Lampe, C. (2022). Sensible AI: Re-imagining interpretability and explainability using sensemaking theory. In *Proceedings of the 2022 ACM Conference on Fairness, Accountability, and Transparency (FAccT '22)* (pp. 702–714). https://doi.org/DOI: 10.1145/3531146.3533135

Konlechner, S., Latzke, M., Güttel, W. H., & Höfferer, E. (2019). Prospective sensemaking, frames and planned change interventions: A comparison of change trajectories in two hospital units. *Human Relations*, *72*(4), 706–732. DOI: 10.1177/0018726718773157

Laursen, R., & Weiss, F. (2025). The role of school leaders' transformational leadership practices and sense-making during the implementation of new technology: The case of the mandatory introduction of a learning management system in Danish schools. *Leadership and Policy in Schools*, 1–15. Advance online publication. DOI: 10.1080/15700763.2025.2482160

Levine, J. M., Resnick, L. B., & Higgins, E. T. (1993). Social foundations of cognition. *Annual Review of Psychology*, *44*(1), 585–612. DOI: 10.1146/annurev.ps.44.020193.003101

Mumford, M. D., Scott, G. M., Gaddis, B., & Strange, J. M. (2002). Leading creative people: Orchestrating expertise and competitive innovation. *The Leadership Quarterly*, *13*(6), 705–750. DOI: 10.1016/S1048-9843(02)00158-3

Obmerga, M. E. (2024). For whom the bell (really) tolls: A grounded theory of millennial academic supervisors' sensemaking of communitarian values as a springboard to enrich their transformational leadership attributes. *International Journal of Leadership in Education*, *27*(2), 283–315. DOI: 10.1080/13603124.2020.1862919

Odugbesan, J. A., Aghazadeh, S., Al Qaralleh, R. E., & Sogeke, O. S. (2023). Green talent management and employees' innovative work behavior: The roles of artificial intelligence and transformational leadership. *Journal of Knowledge Management, 27*(3), 696–716. DOI: 10.1108/JKM-08-2021-0601

Okan, N., & Okan, Y. T. (2021). Turkish adaptation and psychometric analysis of the short transformational leadership scale. *Turkish Studies - Social, 16*(2), 687–700. https://dx.doi.org/DOI: 10.47356/TurkishStudies.48329

Raisch, S., & Krakowski, S. (2021). Artificial intelligence and management: The automation-augmentation paradox. *Academy of Management Review, 46*(1), 192–210. DOI: 10.5465/amr.2018.0072

Sandberg, J., & Tsoukas, H. (2020). Sensemaking reconsidered: Towards a broader understanding through phenomenology. *Organization Theory, 1*(1), 1–34. DOI: 10.1177/2631787719879937

Shneiderman, B. (2020). Human-centered artificial intelligence: Reliable, safe & trustworthy. *International Journal of Human-Computer Interaction, 36*(6), 495–504. DOI: 10.1080/10447318.2020.1741118

Smith, A. M., & Green, M. (2018). Artificial intelligence and the role of leadership. *Journal of Leadership Studies, 12*(1), 85–87. DOI: 10.1002/jls.21605

Wang, R., & Liu, T. (2019). Human-AI collaboration in engineering management decision-making: A mixed-methods study. *Engineering Management Journal, 31*(4), 278–291.

Weick, K. E. (1990). Technology as equivoque: Sensemaking in new technologies. In Goodman, P. S., & Sproull, L. S. (Eds.), *Technology and organizations* (pp. 1–44). Jossey-Bass.

Weick, K. E. (1995). *Sensemaking in organizations*. Sage Publications.

Weick, K. E., Sutcliffe, K. M., & Obstfeld, D. (2005). Organizing and the process of sensemaking. *Organization Science, 16*(4), 409–421. DOI: 10.1287/orsc.1050.0133

Wiesböck, F., & Hess, T. (2020). Digital innovations: Embedding in organizations. *Electronic Markets, 30*(1), 75–86. DOI: 10.1007/s12525-019-00364-9

Yang, H., Chen, L., Wang, Z., Du, J., Zhang, C., & Cai, Y. (2025). Transformational leadership and sensemaking in sustainable strategic change aligned with the SDGs: A case study of a higher education institution pursuing university status. *Journal of Lifestyle and SDGs Review, 5*(5), e6123. DOI: 10.47172/2965-730X.SDGsReview.v5.n05.pe06123

Chapter 6
The Impact of Artificial Intelligence on Teacher Psychology:
Theoretical Connections to Its Potential Benefits

Alper Uslukaya
https://orcid.org/0000-0003-1455-8438
Faculty of Humanities and Social Sciences, Department of Educational Sciences, Turkey

ABSTRACT

This study aims to present theoretical arguments regarding the potential of artificial intelligence as a supportive resource for teacher psychology. To this end, it constructs a comprehensive theoretical framework demonstrating how AI applications can strengthen key psychological resources crucial for teacher effectiveness and resilience: self-efficacy, optimism, trust, hope, and well-being. The analysis grounds the relationship between AI and each resource within established psychological theories. This theoretical examination concludes that the functions of AI, including reducing administrative burden, offering personalized data and objective feedback, and resource conservation, are posited to support these psychological resources. Consequently, the chapter argues for a paradigm shift in perceiving AI not as a threat but as a strategic partner that empowers teachers, and it offers practical implications for educational policy and school leadership.

DOI: 10.4018/979-8-3373-6375-2.ch006

1. INTRODUCTION

Educational psychology literature has extensively examined the numerous transformations and challenges that have shaped the teaching profession throughout history. Many factors, from curriculum changes and examination systems to social dynamics and technological advancements, and from increasing workloads to diminishing resources, have profoundly affected teachers' professional identities, motivation, and psychological resilience. However, in this quarter of the 21st century, we are facing a revolution that is qualitatively different from others in its impact: artificial intelligence (AI). Particularly in recent years, the widespread adoption of AI applications among education stakeholders, while bringing certain conveniences, has also led to growing concerns about a potential dark side to this technology. The possibility of it moving beyond an assistive technology, coupled with the spreading perception that it could eventually replace teachers, is creating a natural environment of anxiety and pressure among colleagues. Nevertheless, AI also holds the potential to offer significant advantages, such as creating personalized learning pathways, alleviating administrative workload, and enhancing data-driven decision-making processes.

Within this framework, AI presents a dual role for teachers: on one hand, it is an innovative tool that enhances the quality of professional processes and supports teachers; on the other, it is a threat that triggers concerns about professional identity and the future. However, just as humanity is unlikely to reject AI entirely due to potential threats, it is neither feasible nor a response to the demands of the era or increasing job requirements for teachers to avoid these applications. Therefore, it is of great importance to focus on the positive aspects of AI, explore its supportive role in teacher psychology, and establish the theoretical foundation for this support. Furthermore, understanding the impact of AI on teacher psychology is critical not only in terms of the educational outcomes of technological innovations but also for the sustainability of educational organizations and the professional well-being of teachers. In this chapter, the implications of AI for teachers' psychology will be discussed within the context of potential opportunities; it will also provide a theoretical explanation of how teachers can adapt to this transformation and how educational systems can play a supportive role in this process.

Approach and Scope

This section constitutes a conceptual synthesis examining the potential positive impacts of artificial AI on teacher psychology. The scope of the study is to establish a theoretical foundation for the relationship between AI applications in education and teachers' core psychological resources (self-efficacy, optimism, trust, hope, and well-being). For this purpose, specific theoretical frameworks that are well-established in the literature have been selected to explain this relationship: Social Cognitive Theory, Expectancy-Value Models, Conservation of Resources Theory, the Job Demands-Resources Model, Hope Theory, and Self-Determination Theory. The rationale for selecting these theories stems from each one's potential to systematically explain how AI could function as a "psycho-social resource" for teacher motivation, resilience, and well-being. The review aims to systematize the existing literature at the intersection of teacher psychology and AI and to propose a theoretical groundwork for reframing AI not as a threat, but as a supportive role.

2. ARTIFICIAL INTELLIGENCE IN EDUCATION

AI is defined as the ability of machines to adapt to new situations, cope with emerging circumstances, solve problems, answer questions, develop plans, and perform various other functions that typically require a level of intelligence seen in humans (Coppin, 2004). However, AI can also be considered an ongoing process of development rather than a completed one. Indeed, Whitby (2008) defined AI as the study of intelligent behavior in humans, animals, and machines, and the effort to engineer this behavior into a product, such as computers and computer-related technologies. Given that this effort is expected to continue, it is quite difficult to predict the qualitative and quantitative dimensions that the current, relatively primitive AI applications (when considered in light of future developments) might reach in the future. As noted by Chen et al. (2020), the evolution of computer and information communication technologies over the years has paved the way for the emergence of AI. However, it is also a plausible possibility that these two now-integrated systems could trigger changes in each other and potentially escape the control of their creators. Therefore, considering the future potential of AI and charting a roadmap accordingly will be a significant responsibility for humanity.

Setting aside the debate on where AI will evolve, this technology is being widely used in various fields and is constantly being updated (Pannu, 2015). The Artificial Intelligence in Education (AIED) community has set its ultimate goal as creating effective educational experiences by developing AI-supported intelligent tutoring systems. This not only paves the way for making teaching-learning processes more personalized, flexible, and data-driven but has also facilitated the integration of AI into education. Indeed, AI currently finds broad application in the field of education, offering significant advantages for the instructional process and classroom management, and in these respects, it reveals profound impacts (Chassignol et al., 2018; Roll & Wylie, 2016). This is because AI optimizes educational experiences, thereby promoting student motivation and creativity (Yang & Bai, 2020). For teachers, AI applications provide significant advantages by facilitating classroom management and also offering the opportunity to monitor student performance more closely, develop teaching strategies tailored to individual needs, and make more efficient decisions in the instructional process (Wang, 2021).

Huang et al. (2021), evaluating the integration of AI into education and its impact on educational systems, detailed this under five different headings: adaptive learning, assessment of instruction, creation of virtual classrooms, transition to smart education campuses, and intelligent tutoring robots. Adaptive learning aims to create personalized learning pathways by considering students' individual differences (Cui et al., 2018; Goel & Polepeddi, 2018). The assessment of instruction allows for more objective and continuous monitoring of student achievement through AI-supported assessment tools (Li et al., 2018; Rahim et al., 2018). The creation of virtual classrooms offers students online and interactive learning environments by eliminating spatial limitations (Lakhal et al., 2017). Smart education campuses enable educational institutions to become safer, more efficient, and more functional through AI-based automation and data management (Dong et al., 2020; Liu et al., 2018). Finally, intelligent tutoring robots support students' learning processes even outside class hours by providing guidance according to their individual needs (Huang et al., 2021).

These five headings directly or indirectly profoundly affect teachers and cause teachers to reconsider their roles and responsibilities in light of AI applications. The organizational behavior literature often assumes that the outcomes of creative and innovative practices in the educational context are achieved by deeply influencing teachers' emotions, attitudes, and well-being. Therefore, evaluations made without considering the impact of AI on teacher psychology may lead to limited or even incorrect inferences. This study attempts to explain the positive effects of AI, particularly on teachers, by referring to specific theoretical frameworks.

3. TEACHER PSYCHOLOGY AND ARTIFICIAL INTELLIGENCE APPLICATIONS

Teaching is a profession characterized by high levels of stress, emotional labor, and constant change. In these challenging conditions, teachers' ability not only to endure but also to thrive is closely related to their psychological resources. Psychological resources are defined as positive and measurable attributes that individuals use to achieve their goals and that facilitate their coping with stress (Luthans, 2002). In the context of teaching, these resources are fundamental elements that support professional efficacy, motivation, and subjective well-being. The literature highlights a set of key psychological resources that play a critical role in teachers' professional resilience. In this study, we focus on personal resources (such as self-efficacy, optimism, hope, and well-being) that may be directly associated with AI applications.

3.1. Teacher Self-Efficacy

The concept of self-efficacy can be defined as individuals' beliefs and thoughts about how well they can execute the required behaviours and efforts to cope with the situations they encounter. From the perspective of social cognitive theory, self-efficacy is seen not merely as individuals giving simple responses to stimuli, but as a fundamental competence that enables them to influence and shape their environment (Bandura, 1977). Consequently, employees with high self-efficacy, in particular, can exhibit value-adding behaviours and make positive contributions to their surroundings through high levels of effort. In the workplace context, self-efficacy, which corresponds to employees' confidence in their ability to cope with the challenging conditions of the work environment (Luthans et al., 2007), is considered a significant personal resource in organisational behaviour and occupational health literature (Bakker and Demerouti, 2018). Self-efficacy is regarded by organisations as an important characteristic for employees to possess because, in increasingly difficult, complex, and demanding work environments, it can act as a shield for teachers in preserving their well-being and emotional states. From a psychoanalytic perspective, although personality traits like self-efficacy are largely acquired during childhood, recent research indicates that self-efficacy can be influenced by environmental conditions even in adulthood (Carter et al., 2018; Simbula et al., 2011; Vera et al., 2012).

From this viewpoint, it is conceivable that AI applications could enhance teachers' self-efficacy. Indeed, many studies have empirically demonstrated a relationship between AI applications and self-efficacy (Montag et al., 2023; Rodríguez-Ruiz et al., 2025; Wang et al., 2023). Even if direct theoretical links between AI and teacher self-efficacy have not yet been firmly established, this connection can be grounded in Bandura's (1977) social cognitive theory. Bandura (1997) proposed that self-efficacy is primarily nurtured by four main sources:

3.1.1 Mastery Experiences

According to Albert Bandura's Social Cognitive Theory, the experiences individuals gain directly from their own successes are the most powerful and critical source in the formation of self-efficacy beliefs. In this process, successfully completing a task or overcoming a challenge instils the belief in the person that "I did this; therefore I can handle similar challenges." The more repeatable and stable these successes are, the more rooted the sense of self-efficacy becomes, generalising and spreading to different areas. Especially in a dynamic and multi-faceted profession like teaching, these "small victories" are of great importance. AI technologies can play a significant role in increasing self-efficacy by providing teachers with these small-scale, manageable experiences where they can achieve success.

For example, in time-consuming and sometimes draining processes like lesson planning and material development, AI tools that offer teachers quick, concrete, applicable, and personalised solutions (e.g., tools that suggest an activity, adapt a text to different levels, or generate an assessment question) reinforce the teacher's confidence in both their technological and pedagogical capacity. This aligns directly with what Bandura (1997) emphasised as the strongest determinant of self-efficacy beliefs: "mastery experiences." By increasing opportunities to have these experiences, AI boosts teacher motivation, reduces the risk of professional burnout, and encourages them to try more innovative practices. Consequently, these tools are not just time-saving assistants but can also function as catalysts that nourish the teacher's professional identity and sense of competence.

3.1.2 Vicarious Experiences

According to Social Cognitive Theory, the development of self-efficacy is not based solely on an individual's direct experiences; vicarious experiences gained by observing others' performances are an equally effective source. When an individual observes a model, particularly one perceived to share similar characteristics (professional experience, student profile, resource constraints, etc.), successfully performing a task, they conclude, "If they can do it, so can I." This process enhances the individual's perception of their own competence through observational learning and social comparison. AI-supported platforms can offer teachers unprecedented access and personalisation opportunities for acquiring these indirect experiences. Unlike traditional peer observation, by eliminating geographical and time constraints, teachers can examine successful teaching strategies applied by colleagues worldwide in different contexts.

For instance, a mathematics teacher could watch a lesson on "fractions" from their curriculum, taught by a colleague in a school with a similar socio-economic background, on an AI-based video platform. Thanks to the platform's recommendation algorithm, they can discover more targeted examples of success in areas they need. This is fully consistent with social cognitive theory, as underlined by Schunk & DiBenedetto (2020), where individuals strengthen their beliefs about their own capabilities by observing the successes of others in similar situations. Furthermore, AI can not only present examples of success but also analyse and present the underlying strategies and techniques of the model's success, deepening the impact of the vicarious experience. Thus, the teacher gains more confidence in transferring the learning to their own practice by seeing not just *what* was achieved but *how* it was achieved.

3.1.3. Verbal Persuasion

In Social Cognitive Theory, verbal persuasion consists of verbal confidence, encouragement, constructive feedback, and motivating words about a person's abilities provided by important references in their environment (colleagues, administrators, mentors, even students). Positive and confident statements like "You can do this," "Your approach in the last lesson worked very well," or "I'm curious about your opinion on this matter" help the person overcome doubts about their capacity, take risks, and exert more effort in challenging tasks. The basic psychological mechanism here is the thought, "If someone thinks positively of me and believes in me, perhaps I should believe in myself too." AI systems have the potential to go beyond this traditional human interaction by offering a continuous, consistent, impartial, and data-driven mechanism for "verbal persuasion" and feedback.

For example, an AI tool analysing a teacher's lesson draft might not only suggest corrections but also provide positive and specific feedback such as, "You've added a great activity to increase student engagement," or "This open-ended question will encourage critical thinking." Similarly, AI analysing real-time progress data from a student learning platform could report to the teacher, "85% of your class has mastered this concept; you are making excellent progress." As noted by Panadero et al. (2018), effective feedback plays a critical role in enhancing motivation and self-efficacy perception. The objective, instant, and personalised confirmation provided by AI applications nurtures the teacher's confidence in standing behind their pedagogical decisions and practices. Specific language based on concrete data and appreciating the teacher's effort makes the effect of verbal persuasion meaningful.

3.1.4. Physiological and Affective States

According to Bandura, the fourth fundamental source of self-efficacy is directly related to how a person interprets their current emotional state (stress, anxiety, excitement, happiness, burnout) and physiological responses (palpitations, sweating, fatigue, energy level) as inferences about their own competence. The individual interprets these internal signals as performance indicators. For example, if heart palpitations and tension before a difficult parent-teacher meeting are interpreted as "I'm very anxious, which means I can't handle this situation," self-efficacy decreases. However, if the same physiological arousal is perceived as excitement and readiness (My body is preparing for this important meeting; I need to focus) self-efficacy increases. In short, the meaning we assign to our body's signals plays a critical role in shaping our self-efficacy beliefs. AI technologies can positively influence these emotional and physiological states of teachers, thereby indirectly strengthening their self-efficacy.

AI tools that automate administrative workload (grading, attendance tracking, reporting) and suggest personalised lesson plans and materials contribute to reducing the cognitive load and time pressure on teachers, leading to lower chronic stress levels. As Bandura (1997) pointed out, low levels of stress and anxiety make it easier for the individual to focus on their skills and create a positive emotional foundation. This positive emotional state, in turn, fosters the teacher's resilience against professional challenges and nurtures the belief that "I can handle this." Going a step further, some advanced AI applications even have the potential to analyse indicators of teacher fatigue or stress levels (e.g., through indirect indicators like changes in typing speed or voice tone) and intervene with suggestions like, "You've dealt with many emails today; I recommend a 10-minute break," or "This exam you prepared looks very comprehensive; would you like some help?" This could assist teachers in managing negative physiological states and interpreting them more positively.

In conclusion, it can be argued that AI has the potential for a positive and transformative impact on teacher self-efficacy. This effect has been explained through the framework of Albert Bandura's Social Cognitive Theory, specifically the four main sources that nurture self-efficacy: mastery experiences, vicarious experiences, verbal persuasion, and physiological/affective states. AI tools can strengthen teachers' beliefs in their professional capacity by providing opportunities for success, offering platforms to observe colleagues' successes, giving objective and data-based positive feedback, and reducing administrative burden to alleviate stress. Therefore, AI holds the potential to be not just an operationally supportive tool for teachers but also a strategic partner that enhances their psychological well-being and professional self-confidence.

3.2. Teacher Optimism

Optimism is a concept whose origins extend back to philosophical thought. Ancient Greek philosophers, in their discussions on the "good life," argued that positive expectations for the future played a central role in human happiness and virtuous living. With the Enlightenment period, optimism was also considered alongside the belief that human reason would bring progress and societal development. Following these philosophical foundations, the concept began to be addressed within a more scientific framework in the 20th century. Anthropologist Lionel Tiger (1979) defined optimism as a mood or attitude related to an individual's expectations for a future they perceive as socially valuable, conducive to their own benefit, or personally pleasurable (cited in Eagleton, 2015). Therefore, this approach shows that optimism is not merely an individual tendency but is also nourished by the social context.

In psychology literature, optimism has been defined over time as a multifaceted personality trait with cognitive, affective, and motivational dimensions (Peterson, 2000). This approach reveals that optimistic individuals develop positive expectations for the future, experience emotions consistent with these expectations, and tend to direct their behavior accordingly. Psychological theories regarding optimism took shape particularly around two important models in the 1980s. The dispositional optimism model developed by Scheier and Carver (1985) defines optimism as individuals having a general and enduring expectation that good things will happen in the future. In contrast, the explanatory style approach put forward by Gillham et al. (2001) emphasizes that optimism is related to how individuals explain negative events. Optimists tend to explain negative events with temporary, specific, and external causes, while pessimists tend to attribute these events to permanent, comprehensive, and internal causes. Today, optimism is addressed especially within the context of the positive psychology movement and is considered a fundamental personal resource that enhances an individual's psychological resilience, facilitates coping with stress, and supports both mental and physical health (Csikszentmihalyi & Seligman, 2000). Within this framework, optimism not only contributes to individual well-being but also plays a functional role in terms of social relationships and societal harmony.

However, optimism is shaped within a framework of understanding that focuses on expectations for the future (Carver et al., 2010). The quality of this expectation leads to the individual being assessed as optimistic or pessimistic. For example, the general belief that good things will happen in the future is called optimism, whereas the chronic belief that bad things will happen is called pessimism. Although the academic literature accepts that optimism or pessimism is a temperamental trait and therefore these traits are resistant to change, it has recently been argued that optimism or pessimism is influenced by environmental factors and experiences (Carver et al., 2010). In the workplace context, it is an expected situation for positive experiences to nurture employees' optimism. Particularly, the expectancy-value models of motivation are theoretical models frequently used to explain how optimism is nurtured. The most commonly referenced fundamental expectancy-value models are Atkinson's (1957) Model of Achievement Motivation, Vroom's (1964) Expectancy Theory, and Eccles and Wigfield's (2002) Expectancy-Value Model.

3.2.1. Atkinson's Model of Achievement Motivation

Atkinson (1957), in his model developed to explain achievement behavior, based motivation on two fundamental elements: the expectation of success and the value attributed to success. According to the model, when individuals believe the probability of success is high and perceive success as an important value, they engage more with the task and become more optimistic about the future. The model also explains the driving and inhibiting forces behind emotional states and motivation. The model focuses on the dynamic interaction between two fundamental personality traits: the Need for Achievement (N-Ach) and the Fear of Failure (FOF).

- ***Individuals with a High Need for Achievement (N-Ach)*:** These individuals derive intrinsic pleasure from achieving excellence, overcoming challenging tasks, and striving for success. For them, the primary source of motivation is success itself. Therefore, they are more inclined towards tasks with a moderate probability of success. Very easy tasks are meaningless and unexciting for them, while very difficult tasks lose their appeal due to the risk of failure. Tasks of moderate difficulty provide them with an opportunity to prove their abilities and satisfy their sense of accomplishment.
- ***Individuals with a High Fear of Failure (FOF)*:** For these individuals, the primary motivation is not to achieve success but to prevent the shame, disappointment, and negative evaluation that failure would create. Therefore, their task choices differ. They either choose extremely easy tasks (because the risk of failure here is almost zero) or extremely difficult tasks (because almost everyone will fail here, so no personal sense of failure is experienced). Tasks of moderate difficulty create anxiety in these individuals because the possibility of failure is evident and are seen as situations to be avoided.

Consequently, according to Atkinson's model, the ultimate motivation towards a task (Tendency to Achieve - T-Ach) can be expressed as a mathematical function of these opposing forces (need for achievement and fear of failure). The individual evaluates the attractiveness (need for achievement) and the threat (fear of failure) that a task holds for them simultaneously and shapes their behavior based on the outcome of this evaluation.

3.2.2. Vroom's Expectancy Theory

Vroom (1964) adapted the expectancy-value approach to the work environment and explained motivation through three basic and interconnected components:

- ***Expectancy:*** The individual's belief that "If I put in enough effort, I can be successful at this task." This refers to the perception of the relationship between effort and performance. This belief depends on the person's self-efficacy perception, past experiences, task difficulty, available resources, and support.

- ***Instrumentality:*** The individual's belief that "If I am successful at this task, I will receive a specific outcome (reward)." This expresses the perceived connection between performance and reward. For example, the thought "If I exceed my sales target, I will get a promotion" reflects a high instrumentality belief. This belief is directly related to the transparency and information flow in the work environment.
- ***Valence:*** Refers to how attractive or aversive the reward obtained as a result of performance is for the individual. This is a completely subjective evaluation. While extra pay may have high value for one employee (positive valence), avoiding overtime might be more valuable for another (negative valence). Valence depends on how much the reward aligns with the person's needs, desires, and values.

The theory acknowledges the importance of these components individually but particularly sees the simultaneous presence of all three as a necessity for employees' emotions, attitudes, and behaviors. The absence of any component neutralizes the effect of the others and assumes that desired work outcomes cannot be achieved. For example, if a teacher believes they can do the job (Expectancy is high) and knows they will get a bonus if they do it (Instrumentality is high), but does not care about the money (Valence is low), that employee's motivation for that task will be low. This approach revealed that motivation depends not only on the expectation of success but also on the value of the outcomes associated with success and the strength of the link between the two.

3.2.3. Eccles and Wigfield's Expectancy-Value Model

Eccles and Wigfield (2002) brought the expectancy-value approach into the educational context and explained achievement motivation with four value dimensions. This model proposes that an individual's motivation for a task is determined by a combination of not only the answer to "Can I do this?" (expectancy) but also "Why should I do this?" (value). The four value dimensions forming the basis of the model are:

The first value dimension is *Attainment Value*. This dimension is the personal meaning a task holds for an individual's identity and self-esteem. The more a task aligns with how an individual sees themselves or the person they want to be, the higher its attainment value. For example, for someone who sees themselves as a "good teacher," professional development means not just a professional qualification but also validating their identity.

The second value dimension is *Utility Value*. It concerns how much a task serves the individual's current or future goals (e.g., a career, preparing for an exam). Unlike attainment value, the task does not need to have a direct alignment with personal identity; it is sufficient for it to be useful as a means to a future end. For example, a teacher's participation in digital report card software training has high utility value because this training provides a practical benefit that will lighten their workload and save time.

The third value dimension is *Intrinsic Value*. It is related to the interest, curiosity, or enjoyment the task itself arouses in the individual. This is the entertainment or sense of satisfaction inherent in the nature of the task. Intrinsic value comes into play when a teacher derives pure pleasure from learning something new or when solving a problem is exciting for them. This is a source of motivation that exists without the expectation of an extrinsic reward.

The final value dimension is *Cost*. It refers to the perceived negative aspects associated with performing the task. Cost is a factor that balances or can outweigh the other three positive value components. It can be examined under four subheadings:

- ***Effort Cost:*** The time and energy required to complete the task.
- ***Psychological Cost:*** The anxiety, stress, or fear of failure associated with the task.
- ***Opportunity Cost:*** The alternative activities forgone while doing this task (e.g., spending time with friends, engaging in another hobby).
- ***Cost of Failure:*** The perceived negative impact that failure in the task would have on social reputation or self-esteem.

This model explains individuals' task choices and motivations in more detail. According to the model, a teacher's motivation to prepare for a challenging lesson emerges as a result of the comparison between their expectation of how well they can teach that lesson (expectancy belief) and the four value components above (especially cost). Within this framework, expectancy-value models provide a functional theoretical ground for understanding how teachers approach their professional duties. Teachers' professional optimism, that is, their belief that positive outcomes related to their profession will emerge in the future, can be explained through these models.

AI applications are increasingly playing a role in teachers' professional experiences. Within the framework of expectancy-value models, several ways can be suggested in which AI can enhance teachers' optimism. Firstly, the conveniences provided by AI tools in tasks such as lesson preparation, student monitoring, and assessment can strengthen teachers' beliefs that they can perform their duties more effectively. For example, a learning management system can automatically analyze students' learning levels and suggest appropriate materials for each student. This can increase the teacher's expectation of successfully implementing individualized instruction, thereby supporting their optimism.

Secondly, AI applications can hold high utility value for teachers. According to Eccles and Wigfield's (2002) model, a task serving an individual's current or future goals can increase its value. When teachers find AI tools valuable for increasing student success, better addressing individual differences, and supporting their professional development, it becomes more likely that they will adopt these tools and develop a positive attitude towards their work.

Thirdly, AI's potential to reduce teachers' workload can lower the perceived cost dimension. A teacher freed from time-consuming tasks like automated grading, attendance tracking, and routine reporting can channel their energy directly into the act of teaching and student interaction. This reduced cost can emerge as an important factor supporting professional satisfaction and optimism.

In conclusion, considering the expectancy-value models of Atkinson (1957), Vroom (1964), and Eccles and Wigfield (2002), it can be argued that AI has the potential to enhance teachers' professional optimism by increasing both their expectations of success (expectancy) and the value they attribute to their professional tasks (value), while simultaneously reducing the cost of their workload.

3.3. Teacher Trust

Trust is a fundamental emotional and cognitive resource, closely related to psychological resilience and well-being, where an individual harbors positive expectations and beliefs towards themselves, others, and institutions. In psychology, particularly in the field of positive psychology, trust is not only considered a belief in others but is also addressed through the concept of "basic trust," which refers to an individual's fundamental belief that the world is generally a safe, consistent, and understandable place. In Erik Erikson's theory of psychosocial development, the sense of basic trust established in the first year of life forms a foundation that guides a person's relationships and challenges throughout their entire life (Erikson, 1963). In this sense, trust is a psychological capital that enables, nourishes, and protects the individual as they engage with the social world, take risks, and cooperate. In the educational context, a teacher's professional self-confidence (belief in their own competence), their trust in their students and colleagues, and their trust in the school administration and the system constitute the cornerstones of their psychological resources. Tschannen-Moran and Hoy (2001) define teacher self-efficacy as the teacher's belief in their ability to facilitate student learning, one of the underlying dynamics of which is trust. In this sense, trust is a psychological capital that guides and nourishes all of the teacher's actions inside and outside the classroom.

The function of trust as a resource for teachers is evident in its stress-reducing and cooperation-promoting roles. A teacher who feels safe in the school where they work can focus on classroom responsibilities and develop more autonomous feelings, rather than constantly worrying about maintaining control and discipline for classroom management. Furthermore, trust, conceived as the belief that administrators and colleagues wish for their well-being, can enable the teacher to shed a defensive stance and develop more proactive, creative, and innovative behaviors. Moreover, trusting colleagues and school leadership facilitates communication, the exchange of ideas, and solidarity, creating a collective efficacy. Therefore, a teacher who feels safe or has a high sense of trust can dedicate their cognitive and emotional energy to task responsibilities, remain energetic, and thus both perform at a high level and produce positive outcomes for the school. The groundbreaking study by Bryk and Schneider (2002) revealed that "relational trust" in schools forms the basis of the social capital necessary for school improvement and supports teachers' professional development. Trust increases psychological safety among teachers, enabling them to take risks, try new pedagogical approaches, and learn from each other.

Individuals with a high level of trust experience less anxiety in the face of uncertainty and difficulty because they have a belief that events will ultimately turn out positively or at least be manageable. Research in the field of organizational psychology shows that employees who trust their managers and colleagues exhibit higher job satisfaction, performance, and organizational commitment (Dirks & Ferrin, 2002). Furthermore, trust also has a critical aspect in that it can increase the teacher's resilience. In the face of the inevitable disappointments of the profession, challenging parent meetings, or unexpected student reactions, a high level of trust and trust in an environmental support network protects the teacher from giving up. The sense of trust provides a ground for interpreting negative experiences as systemic or situational factors rather than personalizing them. This allows the teacher to learn from challenges while protecting their professional identity (Day & Gu, 2009). Therefore, teacher trust is not a naive optimism, but rather a dynamic and developable internal resource used to actively and healthily cope with challenging professional realities.

All this evidence points to teacher trust being a critical resource for teachers themselves, their colleagues, their students, and consequently, the schools where they work. The academic literature contains significant knowledge on how trust is formed and sustained. Two different predictions can be made regarding the impact of AI applications on teacher trust. Firstly, perceptions that AI applications could replace teachers may prevent teachers from feeling secure. Particularly, the possibility of the unique aspects of the teaching profession being substituted by technological tools may weaken teachers' sense of organizational trust by creating concerns about professional identity and status loss among teachers.

The second prediction, and one of the key themes this study focuses on, is that AI will nurture teacher trust. Indeed, a recent study by Shen et al. (2025) determined that trust is positively correlated with AI applications. We can establish the connection between AI and teacher trust on two resource theories: Hobfoll's Conservation of Resources Theory and the Job Demands-Resources Theory.

3.3.1. Hobfoll's Conservation of Resources (COR) Theory

Proposed by Steven E. Hobfoll in 1989, this is a psychological theory aimed at understanding the fundamental dynamics of stress. The core of the theory is the idea that individuals act with the motivation to retain, protect, and acquire valuable resources they possess, and that the fundamental cause of stress is the threat to these resources, their loss, or their insufficient recovery after loss. Hobfoll (1989) classifies resources as: object resources (property, money, technological applications), condition resources (job, marriage, seniority), personal resources (self-efficacy, optimism, trust), and energy resources (time, knowledge, rest). Stress occurs when an individual feels threatened with the loss of these valuable assets or experiences an actual loss.

The theory emphasizes that the psychological impact of resource loss is much stronger and more asymmetric than resource gain. That is, the loss of a resource has a much greater negative impact on the individual compared to gaining the same amount of resource. Hobfoll (2001) explains this process with the concept of "loss spirals": For example, an individual who loses their job (loss of condition resource) may begin to lose their self-esteem (personal resource) and financial security (object resource) over time; this can lead to negative outcomes such as depression and burnout. Therefore, individuals try to acquire new resources by investing their existing resources to prevent resource loss. The theory is widely used to understand individuals' responses to stressful events, especially in the fields of burnout and trauma.

Within the scope of COR theory, AI applications can be considered object resources. AI applications can serve as an important resource by helping teachers reduce their workload, providing support in routine tasks, and reducing uncertainty in decision-making processes. The integration of these object resources into schools and the encouragement of their collective use can also serve as a collective resource. Such applications, in the manner predicted by COR theory, contribute to the preservation and strengthening of the trust resource; thus, teachers become more resilient against professional stressors. For example, a teacher who utilizes AI for student performance analysis may have greater confidence in their professional judgments thanks to the objective and timely information obtained. Similarly, the suggestions offered by AI in lesson planning processes can enhance the teacher's subjective confidence in the accuracy of their pedagogical decisions. Thus, AI serves as a tool that supports both the conservation and expansion of the trust resource.

Furthermore, AI applications have the potential to nurture teachers' professional trust by conserving and increasing their most valuable resources (time, energy, self-efficacy). Teaching is a profession with high resource consumption; administrative workload, lesson planning, grading, and demands for individualized teaching constantly deplete the teacher's personal and energy resources. AI can function as a "resource buffer" that reduces this resource loss. For instance, automated grading and reporting software prevent time loss, tools that recommend personalized learning materials alleviate cognitive load, and platforms providing data-driven in-class feedback can reinforce the teacher's confidence in their pedagogical decisions. As Hobfoll (1989) stated, the conservation of valuable resources reduces an individual's stress level and increases their psychological well-being. These conserved and increased resources can strengthen the foundation of the teacher's trust in their students, colleagues, and ultimately, their own professional identity.

The relationship between AI and teacher trust may also transcend a one-way relationship. Particularly, another critical concept of COR Theory, "resource caravans," suggests that resources exist and move not individually, but in interconnected clusters (Chen et al., 2015; Hobfoll et al., 2018). It is possible to explain the relationship between AI applications and teacher trust with this concept. Instead of providing a one-time resource gain, AI can set in motion an interconnected resource caravan. For example, the time savings provided by an AI tool (object resource) can be spent on developing the teacher's professional knowledge and skills (personal resource). This development leads to an increased sense of trust (personal resource) in the teacher. Increased trust, in turn, boosts the teacher's courage to collaborate with colleagues (social resource), and this collaboration can foster an environment of trust and psychological safety (condition resource) within the school. This cycle can be reciprocal: This environment of trust in the school culture increases teachers' willingness to try innovative AI tools, take risks, and share the data they obtain from these tools, thereby reinforcing their trust in AI. Thus, trust can become both a resource and a "caravan leader" that enables the acquisition and conservation of other resources. This reciprocal and positive feedback loop can create a "gain spiral" operating in the opposite direction to the loss spiral. AI, acting as a catalyst that initiates and sustains this cycle, can play a role in continuously expanding the teacher's resource pool and ultimately deepening trust.

3.3.2. Job Demands-Resources (JD-R) Theory

This is a comprehensive model developed by Demerouti et al. (2001) and used to understand psychological processes in working life (e.g., burnout). The theory divides all job characteristics into two broad categories: Job Demands and Job Resources. Job demands are factors arising from the physical, psychological, social, or organizational aspects of the job that require sustained physical and/or mental effort or skill, and thus can cause physiological and psychological costs in the employee. Job resources, on the other hand, are physical, psychological, social, or organizational factors that assist in performing the job, promote personal growth and learning, facilitate achieving work goals, and buffer the negative effects of demands.

The theory proposes that job demands and job resources interact to trigger two different psychological processes. Firstly, the health impairment process: High job demands deplete the employee's energy resources as they require sustained effort, leading to negative health outcomes such as burnout and stress. Secondly, the motivational process: Job resources increase intrinsic motivation, work engagement, and performance by satisfying the employee's needs. Additionally, an important assumption of the model is that job resources play a buffering role against the negative effects of high job demands; that is, the presence of sufficient resources has a protective effect on the stress and burnout caused by demands (Bakker & Demerouti, 2017). Therefore, AI can be considered an important job resource.

When viewed through the framework of the JD-R Theory, AI applications can be positioned as a critical external resource that nurtures professional trust by reducing the job demands of the teaching profession and increasing job resources. The teaching profession is inherently characterized by high job demands. Furthermore, these demands are increasing in line with the requirements of the age. These demands, requiring continuous effort, lead to energy consumption and the risk of burnout. AI applications can directly target these demands, making it easier for teachers to meet them. This can both nurture teachers' self-confidence and develop the trust placed in the teacher within the school environment. Trust is a dynamic relationship established between the trustor and the trustee. Therefore, the trust gained through AI among teachers can enhance their trust in other actors. The reduction of demands allows the teacher to conserve mental and emotional energy, protecting them from the negative effects of the health impairment process and preventing the erosion of the sense of trust.

More importantly, AI not only reduces demands but can also directly trigger the motivational process by providing powerful job resources. According to the model, resources are factors that facilitate job performance, promote personal development, and help achieve goals. The data-driven insights and concrete feedback provided by AI can offer the teacher sources of performance feedback and autonomy. These resources strengthen the teacher's belief in their own pedagogical competence and reinforce the feeling of "I can do this job well." Thus, AI can trigger a positive gain spiral that enriches the teacher's resource pool, increasing their engagement, motivation, and ultimately, trust in their work and their own abilities.

3.4. Teacher Optimism

Hope, as one of the fundamental building blocks of positive psychology, is defined as the capacity of an individual to design pathways to their goals (pathways thinking) and to believe they possess the motivation to progress along these paths (agency thinking). Hope is not just a simple emotional state but also a dynamic and cognitive process (Snyder, 2002). This process is a critical internal resource that signifies an individual's belief in successfully achieving desired goals, provides the desire and energy to progress despite adverse conditions, and is therefore strongly associated with psychological resilience and well-being. Individuals with a high level of hope do not easily give up in the face of obstacles and are highly persistent in developing alternative strategies to achieve their goals.

The function of hope as a psychological resource becomes evident in its role in coping mechanisms for stress and enhancing performance. In today's complex education systems where teachers' roles are being questioned, the need for psychological resources like hope is greater than ever. Teachers with high levels of hope tend to assess obstacles as surmountable when faced with challenging work conditions and barriers. This lowers their anxiety and stress levels, allowing them to channel their cognitive resources towards producing solutions rather than focusing on threats. For instance, researchers like Luthans and Jensen (2002) have demonstrated that employees with high hope levels in the workplace exhibit higher performance, job satisfaction, and commitment. Hope instills in the individual a belief that current challenges are temporary and can be overcome, providing a force that motivates them to take action and achieve their goals. Furthermore, hope manifests itself in its strong reciprocal relationship with teachers' psychological resilience. Hope not only provides a foothold in difficult times but also contributes to an individual's recovery from traumatic experiences and even to post-traumatic growth by deriving meaning from these experiences. Therefore, fostering and sustaining hope among teachers is critically important for education systems.

We predict that AI can nurture teacher hope and base this on two main theories: Snyder's Hope Theory and Deci and Ryan's Self-Determination Theory.

3.4.1. Snyder's Hope Theory

Snyder's Hope Theory conceptualizes hope as a dynamic and learnable cognitive process, rather than a passive expectation. According to the theory, hope consists of two interrelated core components: agency (willpower) and pathways (waypower). The agency component refers to the individual's motivational belief and determination to achieve their goals, while the pathways component describes the capacity to plan strategies necessary to reach goals, solve problems, and find alternative routes when encountering obstacles (Snyder, 2002). Snyder (1994) emphasized that individuals with high hope perceive obstacles not as dead ends but as challenges to be overcome, making them more persistent and creative in achieving their goals.

The theory's primary contribution, and what makes it so effective in applied fields, is its treatment of hope not as a stable personality trait but as a set of developable and teachable skills. It is assumed that hope levels can be increased by providing individuals with practice in setting clear and meaningful goals, designing pathways to these goals, and sustaining motivation (Snyder, 2002). Therefore, the theory forms the basis for intervention programs, from psychotherapy to education and leadership practices, that teach clients and individuals not just to be optimistic but to actively progress (Lopez et al., 2004). In short, for Snyder, hope is not a destination but a mindset and action plan used to advance on one's life journey.

It seems plausible that hope [characterized as finding pathways to goals (pathways thinking) and having the motivation to follow them (agency thinking) (Snyder, 2002)] can be enhanced by AI. AI applications can strengthen both of these components for teachers. For example, personalized learning platforms and data analysis tools can identify each student's needs, learning pace, and areas of difficulty, offering the teacher effective and efficient "pathways" to the goal (e.g., suggesting which intervention to use for which student). This helps the teacher find answers to the question "How can I reach this student?", thereby enhancing pathways thinking and consequently, hope. Regarding the agency (motivation) dimension, AI's potential to significantly relieve teachers of bureaucratic workload and tasks like preparing educational materials allows them to focus their time and mental energy on their primary priorities: teaching and building relationships. Snyder et al. (1991) emphasize that agency thinking is directly related to the individual feeling capable of achieving their goals. In an AI-supported environment, seeing that they are not crushed under an seemingly unmanageable workload, the teacher maintains and strengthens the "I can do this" belief (agency). This can reduce their likelihood of experiencing professional burnout while nurturing their hope that they can contribute more to their students.

3.4.2. Deci and Ryan's Self-Determination Theory

Self-Determination Theory is a motivation theory focusing on an individual's personality development and self-governing (autonomous) behaviors. At the core of the theory are three psychological needs proposed to be basic and universal for human psychological well-being and optimal functioning: autonomy, competence, and relatedness. Autonomy is defined as the feeling of control an individual experiences over the source and choice of their actions. Competence is the need to master one's environment and be able to affect outcomes. Finally, relatedness corresponds to the need to connect with others, belong, and form emotional attachments (Deci & Ryan, 2000). According to the theory, an individual's motivation becomes healthier, more sustainable, and more internalized in social contexts that support these three basic needs.

The theory distinguishes between types of motivation as intrinsic (doing an activity because it is inherently enjoyable or satisfying) and extrinsic (doing an activity for an external reward or to avoid punishment). An important contribution of the theory is the "Organismic Integration" process, which proposes that extrinsic motivation can be internalized and integrated to varying degrees. That is, a behavior initially performed for an external reason (e.g., teaching for a salary) can, if the individual's needs for autonomy, competence, and relatedness are supported, over time integrate with personal values and transform into a more self-determined form (Ryan & Deci, 2000). Therefore, in fields like education, work life, and health, creating environments that support these basic psychological needs results in higher motivation, better performance, and greater psychological well-being.

AI applications can strategically support these basic needs of teachers, thereby increasing their professional hope and energy. Firstly, by enabling tasks that previously required long working hours to be completed quickly and easily, AI creates more flexibility for teachers in their pedagogical decisions. Automating such energy-draining routine operations through these applications can redirect teachers towards tasks requiring initiative, thereby enhancing their sense of autonomy. Furthermore, AI-powered analytical tools provide teachers with real-time feedback on the effectiveness of their classroom practices, strengthening their sense of competence. Moreover, such applications can directly enhance teacher competencies, maximizing the feeling of competence. This support reinforces the teacher's "I can do it" belief. On the other hand, AI applications can enable teachers to build more meaningful and qualitative relationships with their students. With reduced time spent on administrative tasks, the teacher can focus their energy and attention directly on student interaction, understanding their socio-emotional needs, and building a sense of community within the classroom (Deci & Ryan, 2000). This focus can extend to other school stakeholders beyond students, strengthening meaningful and collective relationships within the school environment. These deep and meaningful connections foster a sense of belonging and purpose in the teacher, creating a protective shield against professional burnout. Therefore, the proper integration of AI applications into education, rather than being a threat that restricts teacher autonomy, can assume a "supportive" role that fulfills their basic psychological needs and supports intrinsic motivation, offering critical support in sustaining their hope and commitment to the profession.

3.5. Teacher Well-being

Teacher well-being is defined as the overall physical, mental, emotional, and professional health of the teacher. It is not merely the absence of stress or burnout but also a state of personal and professional satisfaction, meaningfulness, engagement, and growth. Furthermore, this multidimensional concept encompasses the teacher's welfare in both their in-class and out-of-class life (Acton & Glasgow, 2015). Organizational behavior literature has revealed that well-being is deeply influenced by organizational and systemic factors such as school climate, leadership style, job demands, and resources (Bakker & Demerouti, 2017). It is also argued that employees with high well-being are active creators in their schools, shaping the work environment and generating resources (Bakker & Demerouti, 2018). Teachers with high levels of well-being tend to be more effective in their jobs, establish more positive relationships with their students, and are more resilient to changes. Research shows that teacher well-being has a direct and indirect impact on student achievement and the overall effectiveness of the school. For example, Roffey (2012) states that the psychological and emotional health of teachers plays a critical role in shaping the classroom climate, student motivation, and social-emotional learning. Teachers with high well-being create a more supportive and safe learning environment, which positively nurtures students' academic and personal development. Therefore, teacher well-being is not just an "output" for the effectiveness of the education system, but also a fundamental "input" and a strategic investment at the heart of sustainable educational reform.

It can be predicted that AI applications can increase teacher well-being. Studies examining this relationship also exist in the literature. For instance, research conducted by Almaki et al. (2025) determined that there are reciprocal positive relationships between teacher well-being and AI applications. In the same study, the authors revealed that this relationship is not only direct but can also be strengthened by contextual variables. For this, the current study refers to the Job Demands-Resources Model and the Conservation of Resources Theory. As these conceptual frameworks are explained above, they will not be detailed again.

In the context of the Job Demands-Resources Model, job characteristics that require cognitive, affective, and physical effort from teachers, such as administrative burdens, classroom management, intense schedules, the effort to meet individual student needs, and parent expectations, are defined as job demands. These demands require continuous cognitive and emotional effort and, if teachers' resource reserves are insufficient, can lead to burnout syndrome (emotional exhaustion, depersonalization, reduced personal accomplishment) (Maslach et al., 2001). The primary contribution of AI applications here lies in their potential to directly increase well-being by lightening these burdens on the teacher, i.e., by reducing job demands. For instance, automated assessment and grading tools can reclaim the hours spent marking assignments and exams. Similarly, AI-supported administrative systems automate attendance recording, reporting, and official paperwork, freeing the teacher from bureaucratic load. This time saving creates a critical opportunity for the teacher to focus on their core task of teaching and one-on-one interaction with students, thereby reducing the stress caused by ancillary tasks that lead to energy loss.

Job resources, the other component of the JD-R model, are the physical, psychological, social, or organizational elements necessary to sustain and improve job performance (Bakker & Demerouti, 2017). From this perspective, AI applications can be a job resource for teachers. Thus, AI not only reduces demands but can also further increase well-being and motivation by providing teachers with powerful and personalized resources. Personalized learning platforms analyze each student's learning pace, strengths, and weaknesses, providing the teacher with detailed and meaningful data. This data allows the teacher to shape their classroom interventions and lesson plans more effectively, strengthening feelings of autonomy and professional competence; both considered fundamental job resources in the JD-R model. Furthermore, AI-supported mentoring systems or professional development tools can provide teachers with personalized feedback and suggestions for analyzing their teaching styles, identifying areas for improvement, and advancing their careers. This increases the teacher's access to professional development and feedback resources (Seldon & Abidoye, 2018). In conclusion, by making the teacher's job more manageable (reducing demands) and simultaneously making them a more effective and satisfied professional (increasing resources), AI can break the burnout cycle and provide sustainable improvement in teacher well-being.

The Conservation of Resources Theory (Hobfoll, 1989) proposes that individuals strive to obtain, protect, and multiply the resources they value (object, condition, personal, and energy resources), and that stress primarily occurs when these resources are threatened, lost, or not adequately replenished after loss. In the teaching context, the most valuable resources include time, emotional energy, a sense of professional competence, and psychological resilience. Current education systems often have a structure that constantly depletes these resources: administrative bureaucracy consumes time, classroom discipline problems and intense emotional labor erode emotional energy, and rapidly changing curricula and expectations can threaten the sense of professional competence. Within this theoretical framework, the primary contribution of AI applications lies in their potential to prevent this critical resource loss (resource loss spiral) and enable resource gain (resource gain spiral). For example, automated assessment and planning tools provide direct resource conservation by reclaiming the teacher's scarcest resource: time. This conserved time not only prevents loss but also transforms into an opportunity for the teacher to use it to gain new resources (e.g., providing one-on-one student mentoring). Similarly, AI-supported classroom management analysis tools conserve the large amount of emotional energy the teacher would expend dealing with potential discipline problems by detecting them early, thus reducing the risk of burnout.

Hobfoll (2001) states that resource gain becomes particularly important when resource loss is experienced, and that resource-rich individuals are more successful at gaining new resources. At this point, AI not only protects the teacher's existing resources but also has the potential to initiate a "gain spiral" by enriching them with new and valuable resources. Detailed data analyses provided through personalized learning platforms offer the teacher a new information resource by providing deep insight into their students' learning processes. This information nurtures the gain of professional self-confidence (a personal resource) by strengthening the teacher's pedagogical decisions. More importantly, AI-supported professional development tools create opportunities for continuous professional skill development (another personal resource) by providing teachers with objective and meaningful feedback on their teaching practices. This state of continuous development and learning strengthens psychological resilience by increasing the teacher's sense of control and work engagement. Therefore, AI not only saves the teacher from "firefighting" but elevates them to a position where they can invest in strategic and creative teaching activities, thereby accumulating higher-level resources such as professional meaning and satisfaction. This spiral can make the teacher's well-being long-term and sustainable by increasing the capacity of the resource-rich teacher to cope with stress.

4. CONCLUSION

This study aimed to reframe the impact of rapidly developing AI technologies, which are integrating into the education ecosystem, moving beyond a purely threat-based narrative and repositioning them as a supportive and empowering psychological resource. The study has examined in detail, in light of key theoretical frameworks from the literature (Bandura's Social Cognitive Theory, Expectancy-Value Models, Hobfoll's Conservation of Resources Theory, the Job Demands-Resources Model,

Snyder's Hope Theory, and Self-Determination Theory), how AI can nurture psychological resources critical to teachers' professional effectiveness and psychological well-being, such as self-efficacy, optimism, trust, hope, and overall well-being.

4.1. Summary of Key Findings and Theoretical Implications

The analysis concludes that AI applications, when correctly designed and implemented, have a potentially transformative role for teacher psychology. This potential can be summarized as follows:

Self-Efficacy Development: AI can strengthen teacher self-efficacy by activating the four sources proposed by Bandura (mastery experiences, vicarious experiences, verbal persuasion, and emotional/physiological states). By providing automation and personalized support, it can function as a catalyst instilling a "I can do it" feeling in teachers.

Nurturing Optimism: Within the framework of expectancy-value models, AI can raise teachers' success expectations, increase the utility value of professional tasks, and reduce workload costs, thereby contributing to the development of a positive outlook (optimism) towards the future.

Reinforcement of Trust: The Conservation of Resources Theory and the Job Demands-Resources Model predict that AI can initiate a "resource gain spiral" by preserving and multiplying teachers' most valuable resources: time, energy, and knowledge. This spiral can function as a fundamental dynamic that nourishes the teacher's trust in themselves, their colleagues, and the system.

Revitalization of Hope: The "pathways" and "agency" components of Hope Theory and the "autonomy," "competence," and "relatedness" needs of Self-Determination Theory can be supported by AI. AI can show teachers effective paths to their goals while simultaneously increasing their intrinsic motivation and professional commitment, keeping their hope alive.

Supporting Well-Being: Ultimately, when considered within the context of the Conservation of Resources Theory and the Job Demands-Resources Model, AI's role in reducing job demands and increasing job resources suggests it can positively contribute to overall psychological well-being levels by reducing the risk of physical, mental, and emotional exhaustion.

The theoretical implication of these findings is that AI should be considered not merely as a pedagogical tool, but as a "psycho-social technology" that shapes teachers' professional identities and psychological resources. The study offers a new and holistic perspective to the technology integration literature, examining human-technology interaction through the lens of psychological resources

REFERENCES

Acton, R., & Glasgow, P. (2015). Teacher wellbeing in neoliberal contexts: A review of the literature. *The Australian Journal of Teacher Education*, *40*(8), 99–114. DOI: 10.14221/ajte.2015v40n8.6

Almaki, S. H., Mafarja, N., Mansoori, H. M. S. A., Almaki, S. H., Mafarja, N., & Mansoori, H. M. S. A. (2025). Teacher well-being and use of artificial intelligence applications and tools: Moderation effects of leadership support in inclusive classroom. *STEM Education*, *5*(1), 109–129. DOI: 10.3934/steme.2025006

Atkinson, J. W. (1957). Motivational determinants of risk-taking behavior. *Psychological Review*, *64*(6p1), 359.

Bakker, A. B., & Demerouti, E. (2017). Job demands–resources theory: Taking stock and looking forward. *Journal of Occupational Health Psychology*, *22*(3), 273–285. DOI: 10.1037/ocp0000056 PMID: 27732008

Bakker, A. B., & Demerouti, E. (2018). Multiple levels in job demands-resources theory: Implications for employee well-being and performance. In *Handbook of well-being*. Noba Scholar.

Bandura, A. (1977). Self-efficacy: Toward a unifying theory of behavioral change. *Psychological Review*, *84*(2), 191–215. DOI: 10.1037/0033-295X.84.2.191 PMID: 847061

Bandura, A. (1997). *Self-efficacy: The exercise of control*. Freeman.

Bryk, A. S., & Schneider, B. (2002). *Trust in schools: A core resource for improvement*. Russell Sage Foundation.

Carter, W. R., Nesbit, P. L., Badham, R. J., Parker, S. K., & Sung, L. K. (2018). The effects of employee engagement and self-efficacy on job performance: A longitudinal field study. *International Journal of Human Resource Management*, *29*(17), 2483–2502. DOI: 10.1080/09585192.2016.1244096

Carver, C. S., Scheier, M. F., & Segerstrom, S. C. (2010). Optimism. *Clinical Psychology Review*, *30*(7), 879–889. DOI: 10.1016/j.cpr.2010.01.006 PMID: 20170998

Chassignol, M., Khoroshavin, A., Klimova, A., & Bilyatdinova, A. (2018). Artificial Intelligence trends in education: A narrative overview. *Procedia Computer Science*, *136*, 16–24. DOI: 10.1016/j.procs.2018.08.233

Chen, L., Chen, P., & Lin, Z. (2020). Artificial intelligence in education: A review. *IEEE Access : Practical Innovations, Open Solutions, 8*, 75264–75278. DOI: 10.1109/ACCESS.2020.2988510

Chen, S., Westman, M., & Hobfoll, S. E. (2015). The commerce and crossover of resources: Resource conservation in the service of resilience. *Stress and Health, 31*(2), 95–105. DOI: 10.1002/smi.2574 PMID: 25873421

Coppin, B. (2004). *Artificial intelligence illuminated.* Jones & Bartlett Learning.

Csikszentmihalyi, M., & Seligman, M. (2000). Positive psychology. *The American Psychologist, 55*(1), 5–14. DOI: 10.1037/0003-066X.55.1.5 PMID: 11392865

Cui, W., Xue, Z., & Thai, K. P. (2018, November). Performance comparison of an AI-based adaptive learning system in China. In *2018 Chinese automation congress (CAC)* (pp. 3170-3175). IEEE. DOI: 10.1109/CAC.2018.8623327

Day, C., & Gu, Q. (2009). Veteran teachers: Commitment, resilience and quality retention. *Teachers and Teaching, 15*(4), 441–457. DOI: 10.1080/13540600903057211

Deci, E. L., & Ryan, R. M. (2000). The" what" and" why" of goal pursuits: Human needs and the self-determination of behavior. *Psychological Inquiry, 11*(4), 227–268. DOI: 10.1207/S15327965PLI1104_01

Demerouti, E., Bakker, A. B., Nachreiner, F., & Schaufeli, W. B. (2001). The job demands-resources model of burnout. *The Journal of Applied Psychology, 86*(3), 499–512. DOI: 10.1037/0021-9010.86.3.499 PMID: 11419809

Dirks, K. T., & Ferrin, D. L. (2002). Trust in leadership: Meta-analytic findings and implications for research and practice. *The Journal of Applied Psychology, 87*(4), 611–628. DOI: 10.1037/0021-9010.87.4.611 PMID: 12184567

Dong, Z. Y., Zhang, Y., Yip, C., Swift, S., & Beswick, K. (2020). Smart campus: Definition, framework, technologies, and services. *IET Smart Cities, 2*(1), 43–54. DOI: 10.1049/iet-smc.2019.0072

Eagleton, T. (2015). *Hope without optimism.* University of Virginia Press.

Eccles, J. S., & Wigfield, A. (2002). Motivational beliefs, values, and goals. *Annual Review of Psychology, 53*(1), 109–132. DOI: 10.1146/annurev.psych.53.100901.135153 PMID: 11752481

Erikson, E. H. (1963). *Childhood and Society* (2nd ed.). Norton.

Gillham, J. E., Shatté, A. J., Reivich, K. J., & Seligman, M. E. (2001). Optimism, pessimism, and explanatory style.

Goel, A. K., & Polepeddi, L. (2018). Jill Watson: A virtual teaching assistant for online education. In *Learning engineering for Online Education* (pp. 120-143). Routledge.

Hobfoll, S. E. (1989). Conservation of resources: A new attempt at conceptualizing stress. *The American Psychologist, 44*(3), 513–524. DOI: 10.1037/0003-066X.44.3.513 PMID: 2648906

Hobfoll, S. E. (2001). The influence of culture, community, and the nested-self in the stress process: Advancing conservation of resources theory. *Applied Psychology, 50*(3), 337–421. DOI: 10.1111/1464-0597.00062

Hobfoll, S. E., Halbesleben, J., Neveu, J. P., & Westman, M. (2018). Conservation of resources in the organizational context: The reality of resources and their consequences. *Annual Review of Organizational Psychology and Organizational Behavior, 5*(1), 103–128. DOI: 10.1146/annurev-orgpsych-032117-104640

Huang, J., Saleh, S., & Liu, Y. (2021). A review on artificial intelligence in education. *Academic Journal of Interdisciplinary Studies, 10*(3).

Lakhal, S., Bateman, D., & Bédard, J. (2017). Blended synchronous delivery mode in graduate programs: A literature review and its implementation in the master teacher program. *Collected Essays on Learning and Teaching, 10*, 47–60. DOI: 10.22329/celt.v10i0.4747

Li, L., Lin, Y. L., Zheng, N. N., Wang, F. Y., Liu, Y., Cao, D., Wang, K., & Huang, W. L. (2018). Artificial intelligence test: A case study of intelligent vehicles. *Artificial Intelligence Review, 50*(3), 441–465. DOI: 10.1007/s10462-018-9631-5

Liu, L., Zhou, B., Zou, Z., Yeh, S. C., & Zheng, L. (2018, September). A smart unstaffed retail shop based on artificial intelligence and IoT. In *2018 IEEE 23rd International workshop on computer aided modeling and design of communication links and networks (CAMAD)* (pp. 1-4). IEEE. DOI: 10.1109/CAMAD.2018.8514988

Lopez, S. J., Snyder, C. R., & Pedrotti, J. T. (2004). Hope: Many definitions, many measures. In Lopez, S. J., & Snyder, C. R. (Eds.), *Positive psychological assessment: A handbook of models and measures* (pp. 91–106). American Psychological Association.

Luthans, F. (2002). Positive organizational behavior: Developing and managing psychological strengths. *The Academy of Management Perspectives, 16*(1), 57–72. DOI: 10.5465/ame.2002.6640181

Luthans, F., Avolio, B. J., Avey, J. B., & Norman, S. M. (2007). Positive psychological capital: Measurement and relationship with performance and satisfaction. *Personnel Psychology*, *60*(3), 541–572. DOI: 10.1111/j.1744-6570.2007.00083.x

Luthans, F., & Jensen, S. M. (2002). Hope: A new positive strength for human resource development. *Human Resource Development Review*, *1*(3), 304–322. DOI: 10.1177/1534484302013003

Maslach, C., Schaufeli, W. B., & Leiter, M. P. (2001). Job burnout. *Annual Review of Psychology*, *52*(1), 397–422. DOI: 10.1146/annurev.psych.52.1.397 PMID: 11148311

Montag, C., Kraus, J., Baumann, M., & Rozgonjuk, D. (2023). The propensity to trust in (automated) technology mediates the links between technology self-efficacy and fear and acceptance of artificial intelligence. *Computers in Human Behavior Reports*, *11*, 100315. DOI: 10.1016/j.chbr.2023.100315

Panadero, E., Andrade, H., & Brookhart, S. (2018). Fusing self-regulated learning and formative assessment: A roadmap of where we are, how we got here, and where we are going. *Australian Educational Researcher*, *45*(1), 13–31. DOI: 10.1007/s13384-018-0258-y

Pannu, A. (2015). Artificial intelligence and its application in different areas. *Artificial Intelligence*, *4*(10), 79–84.

Peterson, C. (2000). The future of optimism. *The American Psychologist*, *55*(1), 44–55. DOI: 10.1037/0003-066X.55.1.44 PMID: 11392864

Rahim, T. N. T. A., Aziz, Z. A., Rauf, R. H. A., & Shamsudin, N. (2018). Automated exam question generator using genetic algorithm. *2017 IEEE Conference on e-Learning, e-Management and e-Services*, IC3e 2017.

Rodríguez-Ruiz, J., Marín-López, I., & Espejo-Siles, R. (2025). Is artificial intelligence use related to self-control, self-esteem and self-efficacy among university students? *Education and Information Technologies*, *30*(2), 2507–2524. DOI: 10.1007/s10639-024-12906-6

Roffey, S. (2012). Pupil wellbeing-Teacher wellbeing: Two sides of the same coin? *Educational and Child Psychology*, *29*(4), 8–17. DOI: 10.53841/bpsecp.2012.29.4.8

Roll, I., & Wylie, R. (2016). Evolution and revolution in artificial intelligence in education. *International Journal of Artificial Intelligence in Education*, *26*(2), 582–599. DOI: 10.1007/s40593-016-0110-3

Ryan, R. M., & Deci, E. L. (2000). Self-determination theory and the facilitation of intrinsic motivation, social development, and well-being. *The American Psychologist*, *55*(1), 68–78. DOI: 10.1037/0003-066X.55.1.68 PMID: 11392867

Scheier, M. F., & Carver, C. S. (1985). Optimism, coping, and health: Assessment and implications of generalized outcome expectancies. *Health Psychology*, *4*(3), 219–247. DOI: 10.1037/0278-6133.4.3.219 PMID: 4029106

Schunk, D. H., & DiBenedetto, M. K. (2020). Motivation and social cognitive theory. *Contemporary Educational Psychology*, *60*, 101832. DOI: 10.1016/j.cedpsych.2019.101832

Seldon, A., & Abidoye, O. (2018). *The fourth education revolution*. Legend Press Ltd.

Shen, L., Qiu, N., & Wang, Z. (2025). Psychological safety and trust as drivers of teachers' continued use of AI tools in classrooms. *Scientific Reports*, *15*(1), 31426. DOI: 10.1038/s41598-025-13789-4 PMID: 40858670

Simbula, S., Guglielmi, D., & Schaufeli, W. B. (2011). A three-wave study of job resources, self-efficacy, and work engagement among Italian schoolteachers. *European Journal of Work and Organizational Psychology*, *20*(3), 285–304. DOI: 10.1080/13594320903513916

Snyder, C. R. (1994). *The psychology of hope: You can get there from here*. Simon and Schuster.

Snyder, C. R. (2002). Hope theory: Rainbows in the mind. *Psychological Inquiry*, *13*(4), 249–275. DOI: 10.1207/S15327965PLI1304_01

Snyder, C. R., Harris, C., Anderson, J. R., Holleran, S. A., Irving, L. M., Sigmon, S. T., Yoshinobu, L., Gibb, J., Langelle, C., & Harney, P. (1991). The will and the ways: Development and validation of an individual-differences measure of hope. *Journal of Personality and Social Psychology*, *60*(4), 570–585. DOI: 10.1037/0022-3514.60.4.570 PMID: 2037968

Tiger, L. (1979). *Optimism: The biology of hope*. Simon & Schuster.

Tschannen-Moran, M., & Hoy, A. W. (2001). Teacher efficacy: Capturing an elusive construct. *Teaching and Teacher Education*, *17*(7), 783–805. DOI: 10.1016/S0742-051X(01)00036-1

Vera, M., Salanova, M., & Lorente, L. (2012). The predicting role of self-efficacyin the Job Demands-Resources Model: A longitudinal study. *Estudios de Psicología*, *33*(2), 167–178. DOI: 10.1174/021093912800676439

Vroom, V. H. (1964). *Work and motivation*. John Willey & Sons.

Wang, S., Sun, Z., & Chen, Y. (2023). Effects of higher education institutes' artificial intelligence capability on students' self-efficacy, creativity and learning performance. *Education and Information Technologies*, *28*(5), 4919–4939. DOI: 10.1007/s10639-022-11338-4 PMID: 36373050

Wang, Y. (2021). An improved machine learning and artificial intelligence algorithm for classroom management of English distance education. *Journal of Intelligent & Fuzzy Systems*, *40*(2), 3477–3488. DOI: 10.3233/JIFS-189385

Whitby, B. (2008). *Artificial Intelligence: A Beginner's Guide*. Oneworld.

Yang, S., & Bai, H. (2020). The integration design of artificial intelligence and normal students' education. []. IOP Publishing.]. *Journal of Physics: Conference Series*, *1453*(1), 012090. DOI: 10.1088/1742-6596/1453/1/012090

Chapter 7

The Mediating Role of AI Literacy in the Relationship Between Technostress and Cognitive Load in Higher Education

BORA Demir
https://orcid.org/0000-0001-8187-3206
Çanakkale Onsekiz Mart University, Turkey

Kadir Lüta
https://orcid.org/0000-0001-6813-7407
Kırklareli University, Turkey

ABSTRACT

This study examined AI literacy as a potential mediator in the relationship between technostress and cognitive load among students in ELT, ELL, and ETI programs in Türkiye. A total of 301 participants completed the AI Literacy Scale, the Technostress Scale, and a single-item Cognitive Load measure. Data were analyzed using descriptive statistics, reliability analysis, Pearson correlations, and mediation analysis via JASP's SEM module. Findings indicated a significant direct effect of technostress on cognitive load, suggesting higher technostress increases cognitive load. AI literacy significantly predicted cognitive load, but it did not mediate the technostress–cognitive load relationship. These results highlight a direct link between technostress and

DOI: 10.4018/979-8-3373-6375-2.ch007

cognitive load and suggest that while AI literacy may influence cognitive load, it does not buffer the effects of technostress. Implications for curriculum design and digital pedagogical practices in language education are discussed.

INTRODUCTION

Artificial intelligence (AI) technology has been rapidly integrated into educational contexts resulting in considerable change in how students learn, engage or interact with different digital tools (Laupichler et al, 2022; Zawacki-Richter et al., 2019). AI-based applications increasingly mediate student learning experiences and demonstrate the need for students to develop AI literacy (Ng et al., 2021; Wang et al., 2023). AI literacy includes not only technical competence, but also the ethical, social, and cognitive facets of AI (Laupichler et al., 2022; Wang et al., 2023). However, the rapid integration of AI tools in learning environments has created challenges from technostress, which means stress that occurs when users experience pressure as a result of their technology use (Ragu-Nathan et al., 2008; Tarafdar et al., 2019). Technostress has been shown to be negatively associated with learning outcomes, mental fatigue, and student well-being (Li an, 2025; Salanova et al., 2013; Wang et al., 2020).

One key cognitive outcome of technostress is cognitive load, which refers to the mental effort required to process information while learning (Paas & Van Merriënboer, 1994; Sweller, 1988). Cognitive Load Theory also illustrates the way in which cognitive load can inhibit learning when cognitive demands surpass working memory (Demir; 2022; Schnotz & Kürschner, 2007; Sweller, 2011). With complex screens, constant task-switching, and information overload, students' cognitive load may be higher in technology-enhanced learning environments (Paas, 1992; Tarafdar et al., 2019).

While it can be argued that AI literacy could be a buffering factor against technostress in that it helps students in managing and using AI tools (Compeau & Higgins, 1995; Lazarus & Folkman, 1984; Wang et al., 2023), there is little empirical evidence that propounds AI literacy as a protective shield against technostress due to cognitive load. This gap is especially existent within language education (Gerlich, 2025; DeRue, Ashford, & Myers, 2012) and therefore this study examines the relationships between technostress, AI literacy, and cognitive load in students enrolled in English Language Teaching (ELT), English Language and Literature (ELL) and English Translation and Interpretation (ETI) programs, furthermore, understanding the mediating role of AI literacy to contribute to the understanding of how AI competencies could support students to manage the technological challenges they may face in their learning environments.

LITERATURE REVIEW

Technostress and Education

Technostress is a type of psychological stress that arises when individuals lack the ability to adapt or cope with the demands imposed by technology (Ragu-Nathan et al., 2008; Tarafdar et al., 2019). According to recent studies, technostress serves as a significant barrier to effective learning in educational contexts and has been linked to negative psychological and cognitive affects, such as increased anxiety levels, poor academic ability, and reduced interaction with online learning and educational technologies (Li an, 2025; Wang et al., 2020). In summary, students in technostress-prone environments lack the ability to adapt their needs or expectations of technology and the use of technology for learning. Instead, they endure situations that cause incremental and compounding stress as technological hardware and software become increasingly complicated; students require continuous updates and decisions of where to learn new things, either concurrently or sequentially (Salanova et al., 2013).

Pirkkalainen et al. (2019) articulated two coping strategies used to deal effectively with technostress: proactive and reactive. Both proactive and reactive strategies illustrate divergent ways of coping and related effect on learning. The authors note that while some students will approach the technostress with problem-focused strategies, others will choose avoidance or dis-engagement strategies. Further, individual factors such as digital competence and self-efficacy may also contribute to proneness of technostress (Compeau & Higgins, 1995; Wang et al., 2020). In a broader sense, it is clear that technostress is a complex phenomenon that is linked with personal, technological, and contextual factors and the implications of technostress on cognitive and emotional function of students should not be overlooked in contemporary educational contexts.

Cognitive Load Theory and Learning Processes

Cognitive Load Theory (CLT), put forward by Sweller (1988), indicates that working memory is limited and therefore instructional design should adhere to cognitive load limitations to encourage learning. CLT recognizes that cognitive load can be divided into three components: intrinsic, extraneous, and germane (Demir, 2021; Demir & Erçetin, 2020; Sweller, 2011). Intrinsic load refers to the complexity of the material, extraneous load is related to poorly designed instructional materials, and germane load refers to the mental effort put into constructing and automating schemes on the material for learning (Demir, 2022; Paas & Van Merriënboer, 1994; Schnotz & Kürschner, 2007).

Cognitive load is particularly relevant in the context of technology-enhanced learning contexts where students are often instructed to maneuver interfaces, process various streams of information (either metacognitive or cognitive) and multitask usage across various platforms (Paas, 1992). These additional cognitive demands can increase extraneous cognitive load, reducing comprehension and retention of learning materials (Sweller, 1988).

The recent literature suggests that cognitive load can also be implicated in AI-supported educational environments. While AI support can enhance individual student learning, for instance through personalization and feedback, it may also impose additional cognitive load because students have to incorporate another technology into their learning with its own complexity (Gerlich, 2025; Li an, 2025).

In summary, if we want to create effective AI-mediated learning environments for students, we need an understanding of cognitive load in order to provide support to the cognitive load, rather than overwhelm cognitive load when it is already limited.

AI Literacy: Definition, Components, and Role in Education

AI literacy is a growing concept that includes the knowledge, skills, and critical awareness needed to understand, assess, and actively interact with AI systems (Laupichler et al., 2022; Ng et al., 2021; Zawacki-Richter et al., 2019). AI literacy encompasses not only technical skills but ethical considerations, broader societal implications, and the capacity to assess AI-based outcomes critically (Atasoy, 2025; Gerlich, 2025; Ng et al., 2021).

Wang et al. (2023), conceptualizes AI literacy as having three core components: an acknowledgement of various AI applications, the capacity to utilize AI tools, and the consideration of their implications in real-life scenarios. This definition supports the growing awareness that AI literacy is not a technical skill, but a digital literacy that enables learners to make informed decisions in AI-mediated spaces (Laupichler et al., 2022; Wang et al., 2023).

AI literacy has been identified as an essential competency for students in higher education in integrating the growing number of AI tools in educational and professional domains (Ng et al, 2021; Zawacki-Richter et al, 2019). Furthermore, AI literacy development is necessary for responsible and ethical use of AI technologies, especially as students navigate the need to critically think about the limitations and biases of AI systems and the influence of AI technologies on society (Gerlich, 2025; Li an, 2025).

To this point, there is little empirical research on AI literacy in educational contexts, and more research is needed to investigate how AI literacy may be effective in supporting students' educational experience with AI integration (Laupichler et al, 2022; Zawacki-Richter et al., 2019).

The Relationship Between Technostress and Cognitive Load

Technostress has consistently been associated with higher cognitive overload, as the cognitive demands associated with the use of technology can overload working memory and impede learning (Ragu-Nathan et al., 2008; Tarafdar et al., 2019). In technology-integrated learning environments, students often face a constant cognitive overload when they have to simultaneously employ multiple digital workspaces and tools, troubleshoot, and adapt to changing platforms (Litan, 2025; Salanova et al., 2013).

Sweller (1988; 2011) describes extraneous cognitive load as a level of cognitive load unrelated to the learning goals, which could prevent knowledge acquisition by utilizing limited cognitive resources. This is especially relevant when students are dealing with technostress, as there is a constant and active necessity (coping with the technical challenges of technology) that competes with the working memory to mentally engage in the learning task (Paas & Van Merriënboer, 1994; Schnotz & Kürschner, 2007).

According to Pirkkalainen et al. (2019), even when some learners develop proactive approaches to managing their technostress, there may be learners who engage in reactive coping behaviors that produce technostress, and lead to cognitive load and increased disengagement. In addition, there is considerable influence from individual differences like self-efficacy and prior experiences, which makes the link between technostress and cognitive load more complicated (Compeau & Higgins, 1995; DeRue et al., 2012).

Although insights have been provided, there is still a relative lack of empirical evidence since there is limited empirical evidence on the relationship between technostress and cognitive load specifically and empirical studies examining this link in AI-enhanced learning environments are largely absent. This is the gap to be addressed in this study.

AI Literacy as a Mediating Factor

Theoretically, AI literacy can be regarded as a mediating mechanism that explains how technostress influences learning outcomes through cognitive processes. Drawing from the Transactional Model of Stress and Coping (Lazarus & Folkman, 1984), AI literacy functions as a cognitive resource that shapes how individuals appraise and respond to AI-related stressors, thereby influencing the pathway from technostress to cognitive load and subsequent learning outcomes.

In this mediation framework, technostress creates initial cognitive demands that must be processed through an individual's available resources and coping mechanisms. AI literacy serves as a key mediating variable in this process by influencing how students interpret, process, and manage AI-related challenges. Students with higher AI literacy possess enhanced cognitive schemas and procedural knowledge that allow them to more efficiently navigate AI tools, reducing the translation of initial technostress into problematic cognitive load (Gerlich, 2025; Wang et al., 2023).

The construct of self-efficacy further supports this mediation pathway. Higher AI literacy is associated with increased technological self-efficacy, which influences the cognitive appraisal process by enabling students to view AI-related challenges as manageable rather than overwhelming. This altered appraisal process mediates the relationship between initial technostress exposure and the resulting cognitive load experienced by students (Li an, 2025).

Despite the rapid growth in AI literacy research, empirical studies examining the mediating role of AI literacy in the technostress-cognitive load relationship within educational contexts remain limited. While some studies suggest that digital competencies can influence the pathway between technostress and educational outcomes such as performance and wellbeing (Pirkkalainen et al., 2019), few specifically investigate AI literacy as a mediating mechanism in this relationship.

In addressing this research gap, this study examines whether AI literacy mediates the relationship between technostress and cognitive load in AI-enhanced educational environments, providing insight into the cognitive processes through which AI literacy influences student learning experiences.

Research Gap, Research Questions and Hypotheses

The growing prevalence of AI tools in educational contexts has led to increased interest in researching how students interact with these systems and their cognitive and emotional consequences (Laupichler et al., 2022; Ng et al., 2021; Zawacki-Richter at al., 2019). Prior research displays the negative influence of technostress on learning outcomes (Li an, 2025; Ragu-Nathan et al., 2008; Tarafdar et al., 2019) although these studies point out the importance of AI literacy as a critical digital competence (Gerlich, 2025; Wang et al., 2023), theoretical evidence that examines how these constructs relate producing primary evidence appears limited.

More specifically, we have not found research that has evaluated whether AI literacy can mitigate the negative impact of technostress on cognitive load in AI-integrated learning experiences. In addition to this, prior studies often neglect to define and account for the cognitive aspects found in AI tools, such as the sufficient cognitive demand to critically evaluate information, solve problems, or ethical use (Gerlich, 2025; Ng et al., 2021). This study seeks to address this gap by answering the following research questions:

1. What is the relationship between technostress and cognitive load among university students in Türkiye?
2. How does technostress relate to AI literacy in the same context?
3. To what extent does AI literacy predict cognitive load in AI-enhanced learning environments?
4. Does AI literacy mediate the relationship between technostress and cognitive load among these students?

Based on the literature and theoretical models discussed, the following hypotheses are proposed:

H1: Technostress is positively associated with cognitive load.

Research has consistently shown that technostress is positively related to cognitive load in educational contexts. Tarafdar et al. (2019) noted that technostress creates psychological stress when one is not able to meet the demands of technology which increases the amount of cognitive activity imposed on learners. The connection is also supported by Salanova et al. (2013) who reported that with more personal technostress experienced by students, they had to interact with multiple digital workspaces, resolve and troubleshoot technical issues, and adapt to changing digital platforms, which all add cognitive load. The validity of technostress being a cognitive load is also underscored by Cognitive Load Theory. Sweller (1988, 2011) notes that extraneous cognitive load (unrelated to learning goals) can overwhelm working memory space; technostress is just more cognitive load which competes for processing with the resources needed for actual learning. Recent studies have confirmed this relationship empirically. Wang et al. (2020) identified that technology-related stress significantly hindered a student's ability to effectively process information. Li an (2025) specifically examined how technostress increased cognitive demands in AI-augmented learning environment and suggested a compounding of students coping with both learning content and the associated technology.

H2: Technostress is negatively associated with AI literacy.

The negative association of technostress with AI literacy is supported by theoretical frameworks as well as new developing empirical research. According to the Transactional Model of Stress and Coping (Lazarus & Folkman, 1984), individuals with less competencies in a domain are more likely to regard demands in that domain with a threat mindset instead of a challenge mindset, and more stress responses. This tenet applies to AI literacy where a student's understanding of AI systems is limited, they are more likely to experience technostress when they are faced with those technologies in educational contexts. Wang et al. (2023) reported that students who received low scores on AI literacy reported higher levels of anxiety and stress when using AI-powered learning tools because they had no prior knowledge to help them understand how the AI systems operate or even to troubleshoot basic issues. In addition, research by Compeau and Higgins (1995) demonstrated that technological self-efficacy (a related construct of AI literacy), served as a protective influence (salutary referent) against stress originating from technology. Recent research by Gerlich (2025) revealed that students who received higher AI literacy scores exhibited higher confidence levels and lower anxiety when working with AI educational tools which suggests an inverse association between AI competence and AI-related stress. Moreover, Wang et al.'s (2023) findings are supported by research that indicates that digital competencies in broad terms serve as buffers against technostress (Pirkkalainen et al., 2019), with AI literacy representing a specific form of digital competence that is pertinent to the current educational context.

H3: AI literacy is negatively associated with cognitive load.

Various lines of research indicate a negative relationship between AI Literacy and cognitive load within educational contexts. According to Cognitive Load Theory, Sweller (2011) notes that expertise associated with a domain or task lowers the cognitive resources necessary to process information in that domain or task. The cognitive processes of an expert can be embedded in automated schemas and they do not depend on effortful processing. Inferring this principle to AI Literacy, as a student's AI competency increases, they will have to expend less cognitive effort to navigate and utilize AI-powered tools in education. Wang et al. (2023) demonstrated empirically that students with higher scores of AI Literacy Scale (AILS) showed increased processing efficiency when working with AI systems, reported lower cognitive load responding through self-reported measures, and measured through objective performance outcomes. Technology Usage has also been shown to have a relationship to cognitive load. Compeau and Higgins (1995) found that individuals with higher technology competence will experience a lower cognitive burden when clicking and navigating digital tools as they could focus on a successful outcome of completing a task rather than navigating through multiple ways of technology. Laupichler et al. (2022) noted that AI literate students displayed a better metacognitive awareness in working with AI tools, and could better allocate cognitive resources between understanding AI outputs and working through the learning content. Other work by Gerlich (2025) lays out that AI Literacy affords students to more clearly and easily separate juvenile AI assistance from when to utilize AI cognitive without extraneous cognitive load. In a nut shell, AI literacy ultimately affords students for forethought and conversion within AI literate environments for (1) when and how to best apply the assistance of AI, (2) remove barriers associated with technical incompetence when provided AI support. Those that are novice in their AI Literacy will ultimately need to expend cognitive resources when working through tools under social cognitive theories.

H4: AI literacy mediates the relationship between technostress and cognitive load.

The proposed mediating effect of AI literacy to understand the relationship between technostress and cognitive load is founded theoretically on both stress and coping theory and cognitive load research with emerging empirical evidence. The main premise of the Transactional Model of Stress and Coping (Lazarus & Folkman, 1984) was that coping resources are capable of mediating the relationship between stressors and their negative outcomes by transforming the process of individuals appraising and responding to stressful situations. AI literacy is a coping resource that provides students the competencies and rapid knowledge to address everyday challenges associated with AI, which in turn decreases the transformation of technostress to cognitive overload. The ability of a coping resource to have mediating quality is also supported through the international research of Pirkkalainen et al. (2019), who concluded that digital competencies are mediators to understanding the relationship between technostress and other educational outcomes and the competencies (students that were competent) reported the greater and more productive use of problem-focused coping strategies rather than avoidance. Wang et al. (2023) reported that AI literacy provided students with an understanding of limitations and capabilities of the AI system, therefore creating a better understanding which reduced uncertainty, anxiety, and allowed for better allocation of cognitive resources. Recent research provides some direct evidence of this mediation by providing evidence that technological literacy mediates the relationship between technostress and academic success determinants of students and technological-related stress had a negative effect on learning outcomes. More importantly, the mediation has theoretical consistency through Cognitive Load Theory as AI literacy could allow a student to distinguish between what was the cognitive demand of the learning task versus what was just the cognitive demand of using a technology, thereby allowing the student to allocate whatever mental resource they had to the learning, rather than the attempt to manage the technology situation regardless of the presence of technostress.

METHODOLOGY

Research Design

This research employed a quantitative, correlational research design in examining the mediating function of AI literacy between technostress and cognitive load in higher education settings. This design was chosen because it enables the systematic investigation of relationships between variables in a non-manipulative manner, allowing researchers to detect patterns and associations that can contribute to theoretical insights while preserving ecological validity in authentic educational settings (Bloomfield & Fisher, 2019). Using a survey method, the study sought to explore potential associations among the variables and to determine whether AI literacy serves as a mediating factor in these relationships.

Participants

The study included a total of 301 undergraduate students studying in ELT, ELL, and ETI programs, who were recruited to participate in this study from Kırklareli University and Çanakkale Onsekiz Mart University in Türkiye. Convenience sampling method was used to include participants from as many different language education programs as possible.

Table 1. Participant Demographics

Characteristic	Category	n	%
Gender	Male	124	41.2
	Female	177	58.8
	Total	301	100.0
Age	Range: 18-40 years		
	Mean (SD)	21.63 (2.34)	
Academic Department	ETI	10	3.3
	ELL	92	30.6
	ELT	199	66.1
	Total	301	100.0
AI Tools Usage Experience	Never	1	0.3
	Rarely	23	7.6
	Sometimes	52	17.3
	Frequently	139	46.2
	Very frequently	86	28.6
	Total	301	100.0
AI Tools Confidence	No confidence	9	3.0
	Slight confidence	27	9.0
	Moderate confidence	94	31.2
	Confident	100	33.2

continued on following page

Table 1. Continued

Characteristic	Category	n	%
	Very confident	71	23.6
	Total	301	100.0

Note: ETI = English Translation and Interpretation; ELL = English Language and Literature; ELT = English Language Teaching

Out of the 301 participants, there were 124 males (41.2%) and 177 females (58.8%), aged 18-40 years ($M = 21.63$; $SD = 2.34$). In terms of academic background, 3.3% were from the department of ETI (n = 10), 30.6% were from the department of ELL (n = 92), and 66.1% were from the department of ELT (n = 199). Participants' experience using AI tools ranged significantly with 0.3% (n = 1) stating they have never used AI tools, 7.6% (n = 23) stated they rarely use AI tools, 17.3% (n = 52) sometimes used them, 46.2% (n = 139) stated they frequently used them and 28.6% (n = 86) stated they very frequently used AI tools. Additionally, the participants' confidence using AI tools also exhibited a wide distribution with 3.0% (n = 9) having no confidence, 9.0% (n = 27) slight confidence, 31.2% (n = 94) moderate confidence, 33.2% (n = 100) confidence, and 23.6% (n = 71) very confident.

Participation in the study was voluntary, and informed consent was obtained from all students prior to data collection. Ethical approval for the research was given by the relevant ethics committee, which addressed ethical standard considerations such as anonymity and confidentiality.

Instruments

Technostress was assessed using the Technostress Scale developed by Wang et al. (2020). The scale consists of 8 items that assess students' stress related to technology use in an educational context. Answers were provided on a 5-point Likert type scale, with a range of 1 (Strongly Disagree) to 5 (Strongly Agree). In this study, the scale showed excellent reliability (Cronbach's alpha coefficient of 0.920). Furthermore, the Technostress Scale has been widely used in previous studies pertaining to digital learning environments, showing good psychometric properties (Wang et al., 2020).

AI literacy was assessed using the AI Literacy Scale by Wang et al. (2023). This scale includes 12 items that examine students' awareness, usage, evaluation, and ethical considerations of AI technologies. Participants were asked to respond using a 7-point Likert scale (1-Strongly Disagree, 7-Strongly Agree). Higher scores are representative of higher levels of AI literacy. The scale had good internal consistency in this study (Cronbach's alpha = 0.672). The AI Literacy Scale has been validated across many educational settings and is a recognized tool for measuring students' AI-related skills (Wang et al., 2023).

Cognitive load was measured using a single-item scale based on the subjective mental effort rating scale of Paas and Van Merriënboer (1994). Participants were asked to indicate their perceived level of mental effort on a 7-point scale (1 = Very, very low mental effort; 7 = Very, very high mental effort). This single-item measure is widely used in the cognitive load research literature and has been shown to be a reliable and valid scale to assess individual's overall mental effort on an educational task (Paas & Van Merriënboer, 1994; Sweller, 2011). Given that it is a single-item scale; internal consistency estimates were not generated for this measure in the current study. Because all participants were enrolled in departments offering English-medium instruction, the scale items were administered in their original English version.

Data Collection Process

The data for this study were collected using an online survey via Google Forms. The survey link was sent to students studying in the departments of English Language Teaching (ELT), English Language and Literature (ELL) and English Translation and Interpretation (ETI) at Kırklareli University and Çanakkale Onsekiz Mart University. It was assured that participation was voluntary, and informed consent was provided through the online survey prior to data collection.

The survey included the Technostress Scale (Wang et al., 2020), the AI Literacy Scale (Wang et al., 2023), and the single-item Cognitive Load Scale (Paas & Van Merriënboer, 1994), and demographic information including age, gender, department, frequency of AI usage and confidence with AI. To comply with ethics, participants were informed that their responses would remain anonymous and confidential (no personal identifiable data was collected). The study protocol was reviewed and approved by the ethics committee prior to any data collection.

Data Analysis

We followed to the mediation analysis procedures outlined by Baron and Kenny (1986) and Hair et al. (2014), both of which emphasize that, for mediation to occur, the independent variable must be capable of influencing the dependent variable in the absence of the mediator. To address this requirement, an initial model was tested without the mediator, revealing that technostress significantly predicted cognitive load ($p = .009$) (Hayes, 2022). This satisfied the first condition for mediation as defined by both Baron and Kenny's causal steps framework and Hair et al.'s mediation approach. The subsequent model incorporated AI literacy as a potential mediator to examine whether it explained the relationship between technostress and cognitive load, particularly within the context of higher education.

The analyses were conducted using the open-source statistical software package JASP (Version 0.18). Prior to analysis, the data were cleaned, and variable coding was performed for categorical variables which included gender, department, AI frequency and AI confidence. Descriptive statistics were produced for all variables, including means, standard deviations, minimum and maximum scores, and frequencies for the categorical variables. Reliability analysis (Cronbach's alpha) was conducted for the Technostress and AI Literacy scales to assess internal consistency. Bivariate relationships between Technostress, AI Literacy, and Cognitive Load were examined with Pearson's correlation analysis.

To test the contemplated mediating effect of AI Literacy on the relationship between Technostress and Cognitive Load, the structural equation modelling (SEM) module in JASP was used to conduct a mediation analysis. A bootstrap resampling method of 5000 resamples and 95% confidence level (CL) was used to estimate the statistical significance of the indirect effects. The Cognitive Load measure was a single-item variable, so reliability analysis was not conducted for this variable. Because the mediation model was examined using a basic path analysis approach, fit indices for the model such as CFI, TLI, and RMSEA were not reported.

RESULTS

Descriptive Statistics and Reliability

Table 1 presents demographic statistics of participants including gender, identity, age, department, AI usage frequency, and AI confidence. The sample comprised of 301 students in total with a higher percentage of females (58.8%) compared to male participants (41.2%). Participant ages ranged from 18 to 40 years (*M* = 21.63, *SD* = 2.34). Most students were from the ELT department (66.1%), followed by ELL (30.6%) and ETI (3.3%).

Table 2. Descriptive Statistics

	Literacy	Technostress	Cognitive Load
M	4.870	2.432	5.425
SD	0.635	0.910	1.986
Minimum	2.342	1.160	1.000
Maximum	6.926	4.660	9.000

Table 2 summarizes descriptive statistics of key study variables Technostress, AI Literacy, and Cognitive Load. The mean Technostress score was 2.43 ($SD = 0.91$) and mean AI Literacy score was 4.87 ($SD = 0.64$). The mean score for Cognitive Load was 5.43.

Table 3. Reliability Analysis of the Scales

Scale	Number of Items	α	95% CI (Lower - Upper)
Technostress Scale	8	0.920	0.903 – 0.938
AI Literacy Scale	12	0.672	0.607 – 0.736

Reliability analyses showed that the Technostress Scale had excellent internal reliability with Cronbach's alpha of 0.920 (Table 3). The AI Literacy Scale had acceptable reliability with Cronbach's alpha of 0.672. The Cognitive Load was a single item survey question and therefore, its reliability was not measured.

Correlations

To analyze the relationships between Technostress, AI Literacy, and Cognitive Load, Pearson's correlation analysis was conducted. The results of the analysis can be found in Table 4.

Table 4. Correlation Matrix

Variable		1	2
1. AI Literacy	Pearson's r		
	p-value		
2. Technostress	Pearson's r	0.038	
	p-value	0.510	
3. Cognitive Load	Pearson's r	0.247	0.173
	p-value	< .001	0.003

No significant correlation was found between Technostress and AI Literacy ($r = 0.038$, $p = 0.510$). A positive and significant correlation was found between Technostress and Cognitive Load ($r = 0.173$, $p = 0.003$), indicating higher levels of technostress were associated with higher levels of cognitive load. There was also a positive and significant correlation found between AI Literacy and Cognitive Load ($r = 0.247$, $p < 0.001$), indicating that students with greater AI literacy reported greater cognitive load.

Mediation Analysis

A mediation analysis was conducted using the Structural Equation Modeling (SEM) module in JASP to test whether AI Literacy mediates the relationship between Technostress and Cognitive Load. The results of the mediation model are presented in Table 5 and visually illustrated in Figure 1.

Table 5. Mediation Analysis Results

Effect Type	Path	β	SE	z	p	95% CI
Direct Effect	TS → CLS	0.358	0.137	2.611	0.009	0.076 – 0.621
Indirect Effect	TS → AIL → CLS	0.020	0.031	0.654	0.513	-0.057 – 0.106
Total Effect	TS → CLS (Direct + Indirect)	0.378	0.124	3.051	0.002	0.075 – 0.654
Path Coefficients	AIL → CLS	0.752	0.176	4.273	< .001	0.386 – 1.071
	TS → AIL	0.027	0.052	0.512	0.608	-0.076 – 0.132

The direct effect of Technostress on Cognitive Load was significant ($\beta = 0.358$, $p = 0.009$, 95% CI [0.076, 0.621]), where higher levels of Technostress predicted more Cognitive Load. The indirect effect of Technostress on Cognitive Load was not significant through AI Literacy ($\beta = 0.020$, $p = 0.513$, 95% CI [−0.057, 0.106]), thereby indicating that AI Literacy did not function as a mediating variable between Technostress and Cognitive Load. The total effect of Technostress on Cognitive Load was still significant ($\beta = 0.378$, $p = 0.002$, 95% CI [0.140, 0.616]).

Figure 1. Mediation Model Diagram

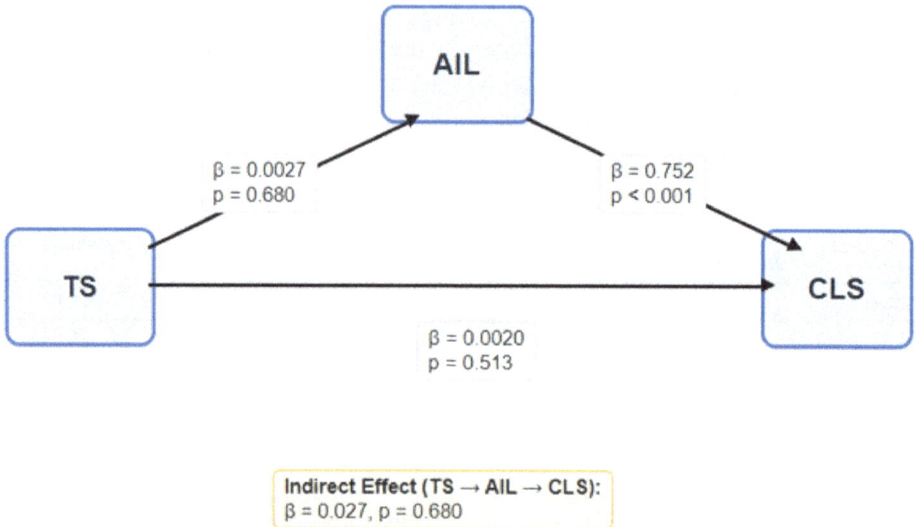

The path coefficients showed that Technostress was not a significant predictor of AI Literacy (β = 0.027, $p = 0.608$), and that AI Literacy was a significant predictor of Cognitive Load (β = 0.752, $p < 0.001$). Therefore, it should be indicated that AI Literacy has a significant direct effect on Cognitive Load but does not mediate the effect of Technostress on Cognitive Load.

These findings indicate that while technostress has a significant direct effect on cognitive load, with higher levels of technostress associated with increased cognitive demands, its influence is not transmitted through AI literacy. Specifically, technostress did not significantly predict AI literacy, suggesting that experiencing stress from technology use does not necessarily diminish or enhance one's AI-related competencies. However, AI literacy itself strongly predicted cognitive load, implying that individuals with higher AI literacy may engage in more cognitively demanding processes, possibly due to their ability to use AI tools in more sophisticated ways, which requires complex mental operations. The absence of a significant indirect effect means AI literacy does not function as a mediator, and the total effect of technostress on cognitive load remains significant. This pattern suggests that technostress impacts cognitive load independently of AI literacy, and that while AI literacy influences cognitive load, it operates through a separate mechanism rather than as a bridge between technostress and cognitive demands.

A plausible rationale for the absence of mediation by AI literacy in the relationship between technostress and cognitive load lies in the nature of both constructs and how they interact. Mediation would require that technostress meaningfully influences AI literacy, which was not supported ($\beta = 0.027$, $p = 0.608$). This suggests that feelings of stress caused by technology use may not necessarily alter one's knowledge, skills, or confidence in using AI tools, particularly if AI literacy is more strongly shaped by prior training, educational exposure, or self-directed learning rather than by stress levels. Additionally, technostress and AI literacy may operate through different psychological pathways: technostress tends to increase cognitive load through emotional strain, attentional interference, and reduced working memory capacity, whereas AI literacy affects cognitive load by influencing the complexity and depth of AI-related tasks an individual undertakes. Since these pathways do not appear to intersect meaningfully, AI literacy cannot act as a conduit for technostress's effects on cognitive load, resulting in the observed non-mediation.

DISCUSSION

The results provided partial support to the hypothesized relationships among Technostress, AI Literacy, and Cognitive Load. Specifically, Hypothesis 1 did not get rejected because of the findings of a significant positive correlation, and Technostress was identified as a significant predictor of Cognitive Load in the mediation model. This finding indicates that as Technostress increases, Cognitive Load may also increase, as indicated in prior studies, since technostress was overwhelming individuals' mental resources (Tarafdar et al., 2019; Wang et al., 2020).

Hypothesis 2 was not supported as evidenced by correlation analysis, and the path coefficient was not significant. This means that in this sample, higher levels of technostress did not necessarily equate to lower levels of AI Literacy, meaning there are more complex interrelations present, which included the role of being previously exposed to or the level of motivation to learn AI tools.

Hypothesis 3 was not supported in the proposed direction either. Although AI Literacy was significantly related to Cognitive Load, the relationship was positive, rather than negative. The path coefficient further affirmed this positive relationship, revealing that students involved in more AI literacy endorsed a greater cognitive load. This suggests that greater AI literacy could be indicative of greater engagement with, or awareness of, AI tools, leading to increased perceived cognitive load instead of a diminished cognitive load. Finally, Hypothesis 4 was not supported. The indirect effect was non-significant, demonstrating that AI Literacy did not act as a mediator in this relationship.

The results of this study were both consistent and inconsistent with prior literature on technostress, AI literacy, and cognitive load. As anticipated in alignment with prior literature, the positive relationship between technostress and cognitive load supports the theoretical dimension that stress induced by technology increases a learner's mental load (Ragu-Nathan et al., 2008; Tarafdar et al., 2019; Wang et al., 2020). Technology-induced stress is indicative of the implications that students carry cognitive load when experiencing technostress, which could hinder engagement in learning (Li an, 2025; Salanova et al., 2013).

While technostress had no relationship with AI literacy, which is contrary to expectation based on the Transactional Model of Stress and Coping (Lazarus & Folkman, 1984) and self-efficacy theory (Compeau & Higgins, 1995), it was expected that technostress would relate negatively to AI literacy because technostress can reduce a student's confidence and ability to engage or utilize AI tools. Based on the results, while students may experience technological stress during the recent academic program, it is possible that other influences, such as past exposure, curiosity, or tenor of support structures, may indeed account for students' reported AI literacy levels (Ng et al., 2021; Wang et al., 2023).

The unexpected positive association between AI literacy and cognitive load contradicts previous literature that suggests digital competencies including AI literacy alleviate cognitive load via increasing user familiarity and capacity to navigate complex tools (Gerlich, 2025; Laupichler et al., 2022). This may mean that a student with higher AI literacy does in fact process the task of using the AI tool more than a student with lack of AI literacy, that cognitive load therefore is higher. For example, as previous studies indicated the "digital skills double edged sword", when someone becomes highly proficient at something there are higher expectations for the tasks, higher expectations for success, and more tasks that will supposedly require cognitive demand (Pirkkalainen et al., 2019).

Lastly, the lack of mediation effect indicates that AI literacy may not be sufficient to mediate the cognitive implications of technostress. This reveals the complexity of the interaction of technostress, digital competencies, and all aspects of learning outcomes, and adds evidence that other forms of instructional design and simplicity of user interface and complexity of external systems to truly control for cognitive load in AI-enhanced learning environments (Paas & Van Merriënboer, 1994; Sweller, 1988).

CONCLUSION

This research analyzed the impacts of Technostress, AI Literacy, and Cognitive Load on students enrolled in ELT, ELL, and ETI programs in Türkiye. There was a positive relationship between Technostress and Cognitive Load, consistent with previous literature and suggesting that Technostress can increase the mental effort made in a learning situation. On the other hand, the predicted negative relationship between Technostress and AI Literacy; as well, AI Literacy did not mediate the relationship between Technostress and Cognitive Load. It was evident that AI Literacy has a positive relationship to Cognitive Load, suggesting that more competent students with more AI Literacy are able to more deeply engage with AI tools placing more cognitive demands on them.

The findings underline the nuance of the relationship between technology-related stress, digital competencies, and cognitive outcomes. While AI Literacy is a notable skill to develop in the age of AI, it is not clear how it can effectively mitigate Technostress and Cognitive Load. This issue requires further study.

This study adds to the increasing body of literature on artificial intelligence in education by providing empirical data on how students adapt to the challenges and benefits offered by AI tools. Additionally, it highlights the importance of building AI Literacy programs that develop student technical knowledge around AI but also consider the cognitive demands of learning with AI.

Pedagogical Implications

These results have a number of implications for education, especially with respect to AI Literacy in technology-enhanced contexts. AI Literacy did not play a mediating role between Technostress and Cognitive Load; nevertheless, the significant positive relationship between AI Literacy and Cognitive Load shows that students who scored higher on AI Literacy are using AI tools more. This will present students with potential opportunities and challenges in their learning process.

Educational institutions should consider how they can best support students in AI Literacy. A major consideration may be through embedding AI Literacy in curricula; not just through enriching technology-enhanced courses or developing curriculum for each course that covers student technological skills, but also focusing on student's critical thinking, ethical decision making, and problem solving through activities related to AI. For instance, some forms of practical assessment, workshops on AI, projects with AI tools, case studies focusing on the understanding and application of AI in language learning, and the development of learning-based pedagogical ways about AI may improve students' capability of adopting AI. Teacher training on AI Literacy may also be valuable and provide teachers with knowledge and pedagogy about the use of AI in the learning process.

The positive relationship between AI Literacy and Cognitive Load in this study supports the argument that increasing students' understanding of AI will not reduce their cognitive load. Therefore, the AI Literacy programs should also embed the ways to manage cognitive load through instructional design principles for promoting clarity, eliminating extraneous information, and scaffolding complex tasks. Providing students with metacognition strategies for self-regulation, time-management and how to judiciously engage with AI technologies would enhance the instructional value of the AI Literacy programs.

Limitations

This research provides meaningful insight into the relationships between Technostress, AI Literacy, and Cognitive Load; however, it is important to assess its limitations. The first limitation is, the research sample was limited to students from three programs: ELT (English Language Teaching); ELL (English Language and Literature); ETI (English Translation and Interpreting), at two universities in Türkiye, so it may not be conducive to generalizability of the findings to educational contexts other than ELT, ELL, and ETI, or institutions other than the universities in Türkiye. Future research could replicate the study at other disciplines and institutions, in order to more effectively assess the external validity of the results.

The second limitation is the cross-sectional design prevents the establishment of causal relationships among the variables. While mediation analysis provides a theoretical framework for testing potential relationships, the findings should be interpreted with caution, as they do not confirm causality. Longitudinal studies are required to examine how Technostress, AI Literacy and Cognitive Load interact over time to more consistently understand the dynamic nature of these three constructs in learning contexts.

Third, the study employed self-report measures, which are subject to many biases, including social desirability and self-perception biases. While the scales in the study were reliable (at least acceptable), the subjective nature of self-report data may have distorted the results of the study. Having considered the use of the more objective measurement of skills in working with AI, and the cognitive load, such as using physiological measures of cognitive load or performance-based measures to provide a full understanding of the phenomenon. Finally, the Cognitive Load construct was measured using a one-item scale, one which is common in cognitive load research, but does not address the complexity of cognitive processes in AI-enhanced learning. Future research might use mixed-methods guidelines to assess cognitive load with a multi-item scale, as well.

Suggestions for Future Research

The results of this study present several opportunities for future research. Given the unexpected positive relationship between AI Literacy and Cognitive Load, a future study could investigate this relationship and the mechanisms at play. Qualitative research methods such as interviews or focus groups may provide insights into how students perceive and experience cognitive load in engagement with AI tools.

Additionally, longitudinal studies are recommended in order to investigate how Technostress, AI Literacy, and Cognitive Load develop over time, particularly with the rapid pace of advance of AI technologies, and their increasing entrenchment in practices in education. Understanding these variables in different cultural settings, disciplines and ages could improve our understanding of the global picture of AI in education.

In addition, intervention studies that design and assess AI Literacy training programs would be helpful to establish effective ways of reducing Technostress and Cognitive Load. For instance, they could include workshops, modules on AI ethics, and group problem-solving tasks to promote more balanced and professional use of AI in learning contexts. Finally, future research could examine the role of other variables such as digital resilience, metacognitive strategies, and self-regulated learning strategies as potential moderators or mediators in the relationships developed in this study.

FUNDING

No funding is provided for this research.

ETHICAL APPROVAL

This research (2024-YÖNP-0244) was approved by the decision number 50/143 taken in the Scientific Research and Publication Ethics Board of Çanakkale Onsekiz Mart University on 18.04.2024. The research protocol rigorously ensured the confidentiality and anonymity of all participants.

INFORMED CONSENT

All participants provided informed consent prior to providing responses to the interview.

CONFLICT OF INTEREST

The authors report no conflicts of interest.

DECLARATION OF GENERATIVE AI AND AI-ASSISTED TECHNOLOGIES IN THE WRITING PROCESS

During the preparation of this manuscript, the author(s) used ChatGPT (OpenAI) for language editing and clarity improvement. Following the use of this tool, the author(s) carefully reviewed and edited the content to ensure accuracy and appropriateness. The author(s) take full responsibility for the final version of the manuscript.

REFERENCES

Atasoy, R. (2025). Artificial Intelligence in Education and Changing Teacher Roles. In *Holistic Approaches to Teacher Development: Leadership, Pedagogical Practices, and Cognitive Insights* (pp. 25-46). IGI Global Scientific Publishing. DOI: 10.4018/979-8-3373-0472-4.ch002

Baron, R. M., & Kenny, D. A. (1986). The moderator–mediator variable distinction in social psychological research: Conceptual, strategic, and statistical considerations. *Journal of Personality and Social Psychology, 51*(6), 1173–1182. DOI: 10.1037/0022-3514.51.6.1173 PMID: 3806354

Bloomfield, J., & Fisher, M. J. (2019). Quantitative Research Design. *JARNA, 22*(2), 27–30. DOI: 10.33235/jarna.22.2.27-30

Compeau, D. R., & Higgins, C. A. (1995). Computer self-efficacy: Development of a measure and initial test. *Management Information Systems Quarterly, 19*(2), 189–211. DOI: 10.2307/249688

Demir, B. (2021). Working memory model and language learning. *Shanlax International Journal of Education, 9*(S2-Sep), 1-8. https://doi.org/DOI: 10.34293/education.v9iS2-Sep.4366

Demir, B. (2022). Effect of anxiety on cognitive load in foreign language oral tests. *Baskent University Journal of Education, 9*(1), 102–111.

Demir, B., & Erçetin, G. (2020). Exploring the role of proficiency as a mediator of the relationship between working memory and text comprehension in the L2. *Turkish Online Journal of English Language Teaching, 3*, 38–60.

DeRue, D. S., Ashford, S. J., & Myers, C. G. (2012). Learning agility: In search of conceptual clarity and theoretical grounding. *Industrial and Organizational Psychology: Perspectives on Science and Practice, 5*(3), 258–279. DOI: 10.1111/j.1754-9434.2012.01444.x

Gerlich, M. (2025). AI tools in society: Impacts on Cognitive offloading and the future of critical thinking. *Societies (Basel, Switzerland), 15*(1), 6. DOI: 10.3390/soc15010006

Hair, J. F., Black, W. C., Babin, B. J., & Anderson, R. E. (2014). *Multivariate data analysis* (7th ed.). Pearson Education.

Hayes, A. F. (2022). *Introduction to mediation, moderation, and conditional process analysis: A regression-based approach* (3rd ed.). The Guilford Press.

Laupichler, M. C., Aster, A., Schirch, J., & Raupach, T. (2022). Artificial intelligence literacy in higher and adult education: A scoping review. *Computers and Education: Artificial Intelligence*, *3*, 100101. DOI: 10.1016/j.caeai.2022.100101

Lazarus, R. S., & Folkman, S. (1984). *Stress, appraisal, and coping*. Springer.

Li an, D.-E. (2025). The impact of technostress generated by artificial intelligence on the quality of life: The mediating role of positive and negative affect. *Behavioral Sciences (Basel, Switzerland)*, *15*(4), 552. DOI: 10.3390/bs15040552 PMID: 40282173

Ng, D. T. K., Leung, J. K. L., Chu, S. K. W., & Qiao, M. S. (2021). Conceptualizing AI literacy: An exploratory review. *Computers and Education: Artificial Intelligence*, *2*, 100041. DOI: 10.1016/j.caeai.2021.100041

Paas, F. (1992). Training strategies for attaining transfer of problem-solving skill in statistics: A cognitive-load approach. *Journal of Educational Psychology*, *84*(4), 429–434. DOI: 10.1037/0022-0663.84.4.429

Paas, F., & Van Merriënboer, J. J. G. (1994). Instructional control of cognitive load in the training of complex cognitive tasks. *Educational Psychology Review*, *6*(4), 351–371. DOI: 10.1007/BF02213420

Pirkkalainen, H., Salo, M., Tarafdar, M., & Makkonen, M. (2019). Deliberate or instinctive? Proactive and reactive coping for technostress. *Journal of Management Information Systems*, *36*(4), 1179–1212. DOI: 10.1080/07421222.2019.1661092

Ragu-Nathan, T. S., Tarafdar, M., Ragu-Nathan, B. S., & Tu, Q. (2008). The consequences oftechnostress for end users in organizations: Conceptual development and empirical validation. *Information Systems Research*, *19*(4), 417–433. DOI: 10.1287/isre.1070.0165

Salanova, M., Llorens, S., & Cifre, E. (2013). The dark side of technologies: Technostress among users of information and communication technologies. *International Journal of Psychology*, *48*(3), 422–436. DOI: 10.1080/00207594.2012.680460 PMID: 22731610

Schnotz, W., & Kürschner, C. (2007). A reconsideration of cognitive load theory. *Educational Psychology Review*, *19*(4), 469–508. DOI: 10.1007/s10648-007-9053-4

Sweller, J. (1988). Cognitive load during problem solving: Effects on learning. *Cognitive Science*, *12*(2), 257–285. DOI: 10.1207/s15516709cog1202_4

Sweller, J. (2011). Cognitive load theory. In Mestre, J. P., & Ross, B. H. (Eds.), *Psychology of Learning and Motivation, 55, 37-76.* Academic Press., DOI: 10.1016/B978-0-12-387691-1.00002-8

Tarafdar, M., Cooper, C. L., & Stich, J. F. (2019). The technostress trifecta - techno eustress, techno distress and design: Theoretical directions and an agenda for research. *Information Systems Journal, 29*(1), 6–42. DOI: 10.1111/isj.12169

Wang, B., Rau, P.-L. P., & Yuan, T. (2023). Measuring user competence in artificial intelligence: Validity and reliability of artificial intelligence literacy scale. *Behaviour & Information Technology, 42*(9), 1324–1337. DOI: 10.1080/0144929X.2022.2072768

Wang, X., Tan, S. C., & Li, L. (2020). Measuring university students' technostress in technology-enhanced learning: Scale development and validation. *Australasian Journal of Educational Technology, 36*(4), 96–112. DOI: 10.14742/ajet.5329

Zawacki-Richter, O., Marín, V. I., Bond, M., & Gouverneur, F. (2019). Systematic review ofresearch on artificial intelligence applications in higher education - Where are the educators? *International Journal of Educational Technology in Higher Education, 16*(1), 39. DOI: 10.1186/s41239-019-0171-0

Chapter 8
Beyond the Written Word: Chatbot-Enabled, Competency-Based Assessment Redesign

Alberto Carpio
https://orcid.org/0000-0002-1616-315X
Universidad Rey Juan Carlos, Spain

ABSTRACT

Generative language models threaten the validity of text-based assessments through AI-enabled plagiarism. This chapter argues that integrity and deep learning can be preserved by replacing static essays with enactment-based performance tasks. Grounded in the enactment effect, ICAP theory and self-regulated learning research, it synthesizes experimental and meta-analytic studies showing that students who build and teach domain-specific chatbots exhibit higher engagement, stronger knowledge transfer and far lower plagiarism than peers writing essays. A quasi-experimental study illustrates how chatbot creation, oral defence and learning-analytics logs provide triangulated evidence of competence that AI cannot forge. The chapter distils design principles—multimodal evidence, synchronous questioning, transparent AI use—that give institutions a scalable blueprint for equitable, performance-oriented evaluation. It closes with a research and policy agenda for an ethically grounded, AI-resilient assessment ecosystem.

INTRODUCTION

Generative artificial-intelligence (AI) systems such as ChatGPT have exposed a critical fault line in higher-education assessment. Because large language models can now compose plausible essays, solve routine problems, and even pass professional examinations, conventional tests of recall and formulaic writing no longer

DOI: 10.4018/979-8-3373-6375-2.ch008

provide trustworthy evidence of student competence (Rudolph et al., 2023). Yet the challenge runs deeper than academic dishonesty. Decades of research already showed that high-stakes, end-of-term exams encourage surface learning and disengagement, while alternative, authentic assessments foster motivation, transfer, and metacognition (Freeman et al., 2014). The sudden ubiquity of AI therefore converts a long-recognized pedagogical weakness into an urgent integrity crisis.

Institutions are responding in two divergent ways. One path seeks ever tighter proctoring and AI-text detection, an arms race that is technologically fragile and pedagogically regressive. The second path, championed in this chapter, reframes the problem: if an algorithm can effortlessly "ace" our test, perhaps we were testing the wrong thing. Instead of doubling-down on surveillance, we can redesign assessment so that it (a) resists AI-enabled collusion, and (b) better cultivates the higher-order outcomes on which human flourishing depends, critical thinking, creative synthesis, ethical reasoning, and lifelong self-direction.

Bridging these two goals requires integrating insights from four strands of scholarship: active-learning theory and the enactment effect; the role of metacognition in durable learning; assessment-integrity research on contracting and plagiarism; and recent advances in AI-driven learning analytics. Synthesizing these literatures, the chapter proposes eight design principles, ranging from authentic, process-oriented tasks to transparent AI-use guidelines, that together form a competency-based, chatbot-enabled model of assessment.

Our contribution is threefold. First, we distil the theoretical and empirical case for moving "beyond the written word," clarifying why passive, text-centric exams are misaligned with both AI realities and cognitive development. Second, we translate that evidence into actionable principles and exemplars that instructors can adapt across disciplines and class sizes. Third, we map an agenda for research and policy that will test, refine, and scale these approaches. In doing so, we align with this volume's broader mission: to explore how AI transforms educational psychology and cognitive development, and how thoughtful design can turn a technological threat into an opportunity for deeper learning and greater integrity.

THEORETICAL FRAMEWORK

To understand the needed changes in assessment, we first examine four interrelated strands of theory and research: (1) how active learning and the enactment effect improve understanding, (2) the role of metacognition in student learning and how assessments can cultivate it, (3) insights from assessment-integrity literature on designing out opportunities for cheating, and (4) developments in AI and learning analytics that inform new assessment strategies. This theoretical framework establishes why alternatives to the traditional exam-based model are pedagogically and ethically superior in an AI-rich educational landscape.

Leveraging AI and Learning Analytics for Assessment Enhancement

The final piece of our theoretical framework considers how AI and learning analytics themselves can be leveraged in assessment, not as a threat, but as a tool to enhance integrity and learning. Learning analytics (LA) refers to the collection and analysis of data about learners and their contexts, often using AI techniques, to understand and improve learning. In the context of assessment, AI-driven analytics can serve multiple roles: detecting irregularities that indicate cheating, providing personalized feedback at scale, and supporting new forms of evaluation (e.g. automated scoring of complex tasks or simulations). The literature suggests a two-pronged opportunity: using AI to strengthen assessment processes (for instance, through anomaly detection or automated feedback), and integrating AI as part of the assessment tasks (for example, having students work alongside AI and assessing that interaction).

One prominent application is in academic misconduct detection. Researchers have developed AI models to identify inconsistencies in a student's work that might signal cheating. A striking example is a 2024 study by Kutbi et al., which introduced a machine learning model to detect contract cheating by analysing an individual student's "linguistic fingerprint" across their writing. By comparing a student's new essay with their past writing style, the model could flag work that did not match the student's usual syntax, vocabulary, or fluency. Impressively, this approach achieved over 98% accuracy in identifying suspect essays in an experimental setting. In practice, such stylometric analysis can complement traditional plagiarism checks by focusing on the authorship of the work. If a student suddenly submits prose at a far more advanced level than anything they wrote previously, an AI-based authorship detector can alert instructors to investigate. Several plagiarism detection companies have rolled out AI-writing detectors that attempt to identify GPT-generated text through telltale patterns (e.g. randomness of token usage). However, it's important to note that these tools are far from foolproof, studies have found they yield false positives and can be tricked by lightly editing the AI output. For instance, an AI detector might incorrectly flag an eloquent student's work as machine-written, or fail to flag an AI-written essay that has been paraphrased. Therefore, learning analytics solutions are best used as decision-support tools, not as automatic accusers. Turnitin's new AI detection feature, for example, identifies the percentage of a submission likely generated by AI, but the company itself cautions that the results "do not constitute unequivocal evidence of cheating" and should prompt further human review. In our framework, we consider such analytic tools as part of the assessment ecosystem, helping to monitor integrity in the background while primary efforts focus on designing assessments that discourage cheating upfront.

Beyond policing integrity, AI and analytics can enrich the learning and assessment experience by providing timely, personalized feedback and support. One of the challenges of alternative assessments (like projects or presentations) is that they often require more qualitative feedback and can be labour-intensive for instructors. Here, AI can assist instructors by acting as a co-evaluator or tutor. For instance, generative AI can give students formative feedback on draft writing or suggest improvements in their code, freeing instructors to focus on higher-level guidance. Research indicates that students appreciate immediate, detailed feedback which AI can supply in ways a single teacher with 100 students cannot. A scoping review by Heung & Chiu (2025) found that one perceived benefit of GenAI in assessment is "immediate and diverse feedback", students could get preliminary grades or suggestions from AI anytime, iterating on their work faster. Of course, AI feedback must be used carefully (it may not fully align with the instructor's criteria, and it can sometimes be incorrect). But in an assessment system redesigned for the AI era, we might incorporate AI-based feedback loops: for example, an assignment might explicitly have a step where students consult an AI tutor for feedback on their project and then reflect on that feedback (both positive and negative). This not only utilizes AI as a learning tool but also encourages metacognition, as students must decide which AI suggestions to accept.

AI can also facilitate scalable assessment of complex skills. Adaptive learning systems and intelligent tutors, studied for decades in the field of AI in Education (AIED), are capable of posing individualized tasks to students and evaluating their responses in nuanced ways (through rule-based or machine-learning based algorithms). For example, in a virtual science lab simulation, an AI system can assess how a student designs an experiment, not just whether the final answer is correct, by analysing the sequence of actions and inputs the student makes (Gobert et al., 2013). These rich analytics provide a form of assessment data on process, aligning with our earlier discussion. Similarly, automated essay scoring systems have matured to the point of providing reasonably reliable scoring for writing tasks, allowing more frequent practice and low-stakes assessment that would be impractical to grade manually. Recently study discussed the potential for human-AI collaborative assessment, where AI handles routine evaluation aspects (grammar, some content analysis) and human educators focus on creativity and critical insight that require judgment (Whitelock et al., 2024). Such approaches could maintain rigor in assessment while reducing grading burden, which is often cited as an obstacle to implementing alternative assessments at scale.

Finally, learning analytics can identify engagement patterns and at-risk students in the context of new assessment forms. If assessments involve online platforms or tools (as they increasingly do), data such as the amount of time spent on tasks, number of revisits to resources, or patterns of quiz attempts can be mined to infer engagement. For example, if a student barely interacts with an assignment platform and then submits a perfect essay, that discrepancy could be flagged for review (perhaps indicating use of external AI help). Conversely, analytics might show a student struggling early (multiple failed quiz attempts or help requests), enabling an instructor to intervene and provide support, thereby reducing the likelihood that the student resorts to cheating out of frustration. In essence, AI-driven analytics can bolster assessment for learning, using data to personalize support and ensure students are actually acquiring knowledge rather than just turning in polished outputs. This aligns with the concept of learning integrity beyond just academic integrity: ensuring the assessment process leads to genuine learning.

In summary, the integration of AI in learning analytics offers both defensive and proactive contributions to next-generation assessment systems. Defensively, AI can help detect possible misconduct (though with caveats about accuracy) and thus serves as a safety net. Proactively, AI tools can make innovative assessments more feasible by providing feedback and scaling evaluation, and can deepen the learning value of assessments through personalization. The theoretical framing here is optimistic: rather than viewing AI only as a threat to be mitigated, we can also see it as a catalyst to transform assessment for the better. The key is to use AI ethically and transparently, for instance, ensuring students know when AI is used in grading or feedback, and to always keep human judgment in the loop for important decisions. International bodies like UNESCO have issued guidelines (Holmes & Miao, 2023) emphasizing the ethical use of AI in education and the need for institutional strategies to guide its adoption. Therefore, our theoretical framework treats AI both as a driver for why change is needed (AI can subvert old assessments) and as an enabler of those changes (AI can help implement new assessments). With these foundations in mind, active learning (enactment), metacognition, integrity by design, and AI-enhanced assessment, we now turn to the specific context and methodology for exploring new evaluation models in practice.

Active Learning, Enactment Effect, and Constructivism

A foundational principle guiding alternative assessment is that learners construct knowledge more effectively by actively doing rather than passively receiving. This aligns with constructivist learning theory, which views students as active sense-makers rather than empty vessels. Research on the "enactment effect" provides compelling evidence for the benefits of active engagement. The enactment effect refers to the robust finding that physically performing or enacting tasks leads to significantly better memory and understanding than simply reading or hearing about the tasks. In a recent comprehensive meta-analysis, Roberts et al. (2022) confirmed that this effect is reliable across various learning conditions (intentional and incidental learning alike). In practical terms, if students demonstrate a concept, by teaching it, building a model, solving a real problem, or performing an experiment, they are far more likely to remember and understand it deeply than if they only listen to a lecture or memorize notes. Thus, assessments that require students to enact their knowledge (for example, via a project, presentation, or teaching exercise) inherently leverage cognitive mechanisms that improve learning. By contrast, a traditional exam often measures recall of information in a decontextualized setting, missing the opportunity for students to engage in more meaningful use of knowledge.

Alternative assessment practices like presentations, portfolios, or simulations operationalize the constructivist idea that meaning is "made, not given". Instead of treating students as "defenceless vessels waiting to be filled with facts," these approaches position students as "masters of their own learning and sense making". For example, in a portfolio assessment, students must collect their work, select pieces that evidence their learning, and reflect on why those pieces are significant. Through this process, students exercise choice, self-evaluation, and goal-setting, effectively taking ownership of their learning journey. Janischet al. (2007) observed that such alternative assessments can "reverse the traditional paradigm of student passivity and replace it with student initiative, self-discipline, and choice.". In other words, when students are tasked with actively creating or performing something for assessment, they engage in generative cognitive processing, organizing, elaborating, and personalizing knowledge, which results in stronger learning gains (Fiorella & Mayer, 2014). This is borne out by large-scale evidence in STEM education: a meta-analysis of 225 studies found that active learning strategies (e.g. problem-solving activities during class) boosted examination performance by about 6% on average and significantly reduced failure rates compared to traditional lectures. These findings equate to an improvement of roughly half a letter grade for the average student (Freeman et al., 2014). The implication is clear: active learning experiences improve achievement. By extension, assessments designed to incorporate active, applied tasks should lead to better performance and retention of knowledge than those that rely solely on passive study for a written exam.

One specific manifestation of active learning relevant to AI-era assessment is the concept of "learning by teaching," sometimes called the protégé effect. Research has shown that students put forth greater effort and achieve deeper understanding when they prepare to teach material to others, even if the "other" is a fictitious or computer-based tutee (Freeman et al., 2014). In classic studies, students who taught content to a peer or a teachable software agent outperformed those who learned the same material for a standard test, due to increased motivation and processing during preparation (Chase et al., 2009). This is highly pertinent in a world where AI can serve as a tutee or a collaborator. If an assessment requires students to teach a concept to an AI (or via an AI), for instance, by programming a chatbot to explain course concepts, the act of teaching can solidify the student's own mastery. The protégé effect suggests that making students design a teaching tool or instruct an AI will drive them to engage more deeply with the material. The enactment here is two-fold: the student is actively creating an artifact (like a chatbot or tutorial), and in doing so is effectively teaching the content, thereby reinforcing their learning. We will later consider a "chatbot creation" exercise as an example of such an assessment. The theoretical takeaway is that alternative assessments anchored in active participation, performance, and creation are supported by robust research in cognitive psychology and education. They not only counteract some limitations of lectures and written tests, but also naturally make it harder for a student to delegate the work to an AI or a third party, an important consideration for integrity. A chatbot cannot meaningfully perform a task or give a presentation on a student's behalf in real-time, and even if AI helps in preparation, the student must internalize knowledge to enact it. This advantage dovetails into the next section on metacognition, since active tasks often prompt reflection and self-regulation.

Metacognition and Self-Regulation in Assessment

Metacognition. One's awareness and control of their own learning processes, is another theoretical pillar for reimagining assessment. Decades of research indicate that strong metacognitive skills (such as the ability to self-monitor understanding, plan approaches to problems, and reflect on what is learned) are associated with better learning and performance (Stanton et al., 2021). Traditional assessments that emphasize one-shot performance on a test do little to foster these skills; in some cases, they may even discourage reflection (as students cram for an exam and then move on). In contrast, many alternative assessment formats inherently encourage metacognitive engagement: students might need to assess their own work (as in self-assessed portfolios), reflect on their learning process (as in learning journals or project reports), or iteratively improve through feedback (as in draft submissions or design projects). These practices prompt learners to think about how they are learning and how they can improve, in other words, to exercise metacognition as part of the assessment.

Implementing alternative assessments has indeed been shown to develop students' metacognitive awareness. In a study of pre-service teachers learning to use such assessments, Janisch et al. (2007) reported that "developing metacognitive awareness in students is [an] outgrowth of using alternative assessment.". Course participants observed that when students chose pieces for a portfolio or wrote reflections on their progress, they were effectively thinking about their own thinking, identifying what they learned, what they struggled with, and what strategies helped them succeed. Classroom practices like self-selection of work, self-reflection on learning, and setting personal goals were highlighted as powerful aspects of these assessments that allowed students to take control of their learning and monitor their growth. One participant noted that alternative assessment "appears to not only be the most effective way to test individual knowledge, but the best way for students to understand their own learning". This aligns with a broader shift toward assessment for learning (formative assessment), where the process of assessment itself helps students develop self-regulatory skills. For instance, when students maintain a learning log or receive narrative feedback on a project, they are prompted to consider what strategies worked, where their misconceptions lie, and how they can adjust their approach, classic metacognitive activities.

Metacognitive growth is particularly important in the context of AI. If students can easily obtain answers from an AI tool, the value of factual recall diminishes; instead, students need to learn how to learn, how to verify, and how to apply knowledge in novel situations. These are inherently metacognitive tasks. Alternative assessments can directly target these aspects. For example, an assignment might ask students to document their problem-solving process or to explain their reasoning in a recorded video. Such tasks compel students to plan, monitor, and evaluate their own work, key components of metacognition (Schraw, 1998). By contrast, a standard multiple-choice test rarely involves these student-centred reflective processes.

There is also a link between metacognition and academic integrity. A student with well-developed metacognitive skills is more likely to understand the value of doing their own work and the gaps in their own understanding that need addressing. In fact, helping students become aware of what they haven't mastered can reduce the temptation to cheat, as they recognize that using AI to shortcut an assignment would deprive them of learning opportunities they actually need. Conversely, students who lack self-awareness might over-rely on AI out of a false sense of security or out of desperation when studying last-minute. Some emerging strategies to uphold integrity therefore involve making students explicitly reflect on and report their use of AI in completing work, a metacognitive exercise that forces them to judge whether AI helped or hindered their learning. We will see later that some institutions encourage students to submit a "metacognitive commentary" along with assignments, describing how they approached the task and whether any AI tools were consulted. This transparency can both discourage misuse (since students must admit to it) and prompt thoughtful use (turning AI into a learning aid rather than a cheating device).

In summary, grounding assessments in metacognitive pedagogy means designing tasks that cause students to think about their thinking. The theoretical and empirical literature supports those alternative assessments (like portfolios, project reflections, self and peer assessments) successfully promote this introspection. Students taught under these methods have reported greater awareness of themselves as learners and more responsibility for their own learning. Developing such self-regulation is crucial for lifelong learning and is a stated goal of many educational programs. In the AI era, it takes on added significance: metacognitive skills help students navigate when to leverage AI tools appropriately and when deeper personal effort is needed. Thus, an assessment system that includes reflective and self-directed components not only deepens learning in the moment, but also equips students with the mindset to continuously learn and uphold integrity in a technologically complex world.

Assessment Integrity and the Threat of Contract Cheating (with and without AI)

Any discussion of changing evaluation systems in the age of AI must reckon with academic integrity. The literature on assessment integrity, including studies of plagiarism, contract cheating, and cheating prevention, provides vital guidance on how alternative assessments can deter dishonesty. Even before generative AI became an issue, researchers observed that certain types of assessments are more prone to outsourcing or cheating than others. For instance, an unsupervised take-home essay is relatively easy to contract out to an essay mill (or now, to an AI), whereas an oral exam or a personalized project is harder to delegate. A large Australian study by Bretag and colleagues (2019) found that while contract cheating (students hiring or otherwise getting a third party to do work for them) was a widespread problem, its incidence varied with the nature of assignments. In particular, tasks that were more authentic, individualized, or required unique personal input were less amenable to contract cheating, whereas generic assignments and exams were more vulnerable. Authentic assessment, defined as tasks that replicate real-world challenges and require students to produce work of value beyond the classroom, has long been proposed as a solution to uphold integrity. Ellis et al. (2020) directly examined this proposition and found that authentic tasks can indeed "assure academic integrity" to a degree, though they cautioned that no assessment is completely cheat-proof. In other words, smart assessment design "is a solution to the problem of contract cheating" but must be coupled with other measures.

With the introduction of AI text generators, the integrity landscape has evolved further. On one hand, AI can be viewed as the newest form of "contract cheating", except instead of paying a human ghostwriter, a student can obtain an original essay from a machine. Traditional plagiarism detectors (like Turnitin's standard text-matching) struggle here because AI-generated content is usually original (not copy-pasted) and thus doesn't flag matches in databases (Kutbi et al., 2024). This has raised urgent concerns: academic integrity experts warn that if assessments remain unchanged, AI-assisted cheating could become rampant and undetectable. Indeed, early evidence from the COVID-19 remote learning period (just before ChatGPT's debut) foreshadowed the challenge, as online exams expanded, many institutions saw spikes in academic misconduct. The University of Waterloo, for example, reported a 146% increase in cheating cases when switching to online assessments, and other universities saw similar surges. Lancaster and Cotarlan (2021) found that student questions posted on Chegg (a homework help site often used for cheating) skyrocketed by nearly 200% during the pandemic when traditional exams moved online. These statistics illustrate how vulnerable conventional assessments can be outside tightly controlled settings. ChatGPT's arrival in late 2022 poured fuel on this fire by making sophisticated cheating accessible at scale, any student with an internet connection can now generate essays, code, or answers with a simple prompt.

So, what does the integrity literature suggest as remedies? A key insight is that we must redesign assessments to be "authentic, complex, and personalized" such that AI tools cannot easily complete them. Experts propose several strategies: use higher-order cognitive tasks, incorporate oral components or defences, and evaluate the process as well as the product (Xia et al., 2024). By focusing on analysis, evaluation, and creation (top tiers of Bloom's Taxonomy), we make it harder for AI to mimic true understanding. As Evangelista (2025) notes, "assessments that focus on higher-order skills foster deeper learning and strengthen academic integrity by making it harder for AI-generated responses to pass undetected.". Lower-order questions (factual recall, basic comprehension) are exactly the kind most easily handled by AI or found online. Therefore, shifting to application-based and evaluative questions (e.g. case analyses, design tasks, critical reflections) is crucial. This aligns with long-standing calls to emphasize critical thinking in education, now given new urgency. Cotton et al. (2023) similarly advise that faculty should assess understanding through "automated and manual methods" that probe a student's actual comprehension, beyond what a written answer alone can prove. For example, an instructor might use an in-person oral follow-up to an essay to question the student about their work, thereby verifying authorship and understanding.

Another strong recommendation is to require students to demonstrate their work or reasoning dynamically. Oral assessments, such as presentations, vivas (oral exams), or video-conferenced Q&A sessions, have gained attention as an integrity-preserving tool in the AI era. Nikolic et al. (2023) suggest that faculty use live video-conference questioning to evaluate student assignments, essentially an oral defence where the student must answer impromptu questions about their submission. This method makes it extremely difficult to rely on AI unbeknownst to the examiner, since the student is put on the spot to explain concepts in their own words. Along similar lines, educators are turning to projects, labs, and creative assessments that require hands-on work and original outputs. If a student must complete a lab experiment, produce a unique artwork, or develop a business plan for a local issue, they cannot simply prompt ChatGPT for a ready-made solution, the tasks are too contextual and multifaceted. Surveys of faculty indicate a surge of interest in such "AI-resistant" assessments that evaluate students on unique performances and artifacts (Alkouk & Khlaif, 2024).

The literature also emphasizes a dual focus on product and process. Traditionally, grades have been almost entirely product-based (the final answer or essay). But AI challenges us to value the student's process of learning and producing work. Educators are now exploring ways to capture process, such as through draft submissions, edit logs, or requiring students to submit an appendix describing how they arrived at their answers. Alkouk and Khlaif (2024) introduce a "Process-Product Assessment Approach" in which part of the evaluation is based on evidence of the student's interaction with AI tools and their iterative progress, not just the final output. For instance, a programming assignment might require students to include their code revision history or a commentary on debugging steps. This can reveal the student's thought process and makes it apparent if work was simply generated in one go by an AI. Similarly, writing assignments might be broken into stages (outline, draft, final) with feedback cycles, encouraging students to invest in the process and making it harder to present an entirely AI-written final draft without instructor noticing mismatches in style or growth.

Finally, an important thread in integrity literature is developing clear policies and honour codes regarding AI. Multiple commentators note that academic communities must update their definitions of plagiarism and cheating to account for AI. Not all AI use is nefarious, for example, using AI for brainstorming or proofreading might be acceptable if disclosed. Blanket bans might drive usage underground, whereas thoughtful policies can integrate AI as a learning tool while drawing lines (e.g. "AI assistance must be cited and limited to X aspects of the assignment"). Some U.S. states and universities have begun issuing guidelines for ethical AI use in coursework. These typically involve educating students on when using AI constitutes collusion or misrepresentation, and when it might be allowed for learning support. For instance, the North Carolina Department of Public Instruction stated that it's "shortsighted to automatically consider all use of AI as cheating" and urged rethinking plagiarism definitions in this light. The implication for assessment design is that tasks might explicitly permit AI for certain components (like initial research) but require personal input for others, with students signing an integrity statement about their adherence. In summary, the assessment-integrity literature, both pre- and post-AI, guides us to create evaluations that are authentic, higher-order, process-focused, and fortified by clear ethical guidelines. Such designs inherently reduce opportunities and motivation for cheating, whether by contract cheating services or by AI (Xia et al., 2024). They shift the focus from catching cheaters after the fact (an increasingly futile game of cat-and-mouse with AI detectors) to preventing cheating by designing it out and cultivating a culture of honesty and responsibility in students.

DEVELOPMENTAL CONSIDERATIONS: ALIGNING ASSESSMENT WITH COGNITIVE GROWTH

Contemporary assessment must recognise that learners' cognitive, motivational, and self-regulatory capacities evolve across the life-span. Vygotsky's Zone of Proximal Development (ZPD) reminds us that tasks pitched just beyond current mastery, but within reach through scaffolding or AI-mediated feedback, maximise learning gains. Likewise, Self-Determination Theory (SDT) predicts that assessments fostering autonomy, competence, and relatedness will deepen engagement at any age.

- Childhood and early adolescence: Process-product tasks (e.g., scaffolded portfolios) guide younger learners through the ZPD, cultivating planning skills while offering concrete milestones that build competence and reduce AI-temptation.
- Late adolescence: Authentic, collaborative projects satisfy SDT's relatedness need and encourage identity exploration, critical as students transition to self-authorship.
- Emerging adulthood: Oral defences and reflective journals promote metacognitive ownership, preparing learners to navigate AI-rich workplaces that reward adaptive expertise.

Across stages, the chapter's eight principles operationalise developmental theory by matching assessment demands to learners' growing ability to self-regulate, reason abstractly, and act ethically.

DESIGN PRINCIPLES

Drawing on the theoretical framework, we propose a set of design principles for creating and implementing AI-resilient, pedagogically effective assessment systems. These principles serve as actionable guidelines for educators, administrators, and policy-makers aiming to uphold academic integrity and promote deep learning in the era of AI. While not every principle applies equally in all contexts, together they form an integrated approach to rethinking assessment. Each principle is illustrated with practical suggestions.

1. Emphasize Higher-Order Cognitive Skills in Assessment Tasks: Design assignments that target Bloom's higher levels, application, analysis, evaluation, and creation, rather than solely recall of facts. Assessments focusing on these skills are inherently more AI-resilient, because generative AI excels at regurgitating information but struggles with context-specific analysis or original creation. By requiring students to analyse a case, evaluate alternatives, create a product or solution, etc., you make it difficult for AI to produce a sufficient answer without substantial human insight. For example, instead of asking "What are the three causes of X?" (which a student could easily prompt ChatGPT to answer), ask "Apply concept X to analyse this novel scenario" or "Evaluate the strengths and weaknesses of solution Y in a given context." Focusing on higher-order skills not only thwarts simplistic AI use but also aligns assessment with desired graduate attributes like critical thinking and creativity. In practice, educators should review their learning outcomes and ensure assessments map to those at high cognitive levels. If an outcome is "critically discuss issue Z," an essay that demands critique or an oral defence of a position on Z is preferable to a multiple-choice quiz on Z's facts.
2. Incorporate Authentic and Contextualized Assessment Formats: Use authentic assessments that simulate real-world tasks and require students to produce unique work. Authentic tasks, such as projects, case studies, presentations, portfolios, experiments, or performances, invite students to apply knowledge in context, which makes cheating via AI or otherwise more difficult. They also often result in more engaged learning. Authentic assessment means the task has relevance beyond the classroom: for instance, creating a marketing plan for a local business (instead of a closed-book exam on marketing concepts), or curating a portfolio of art with reflective commentary (instead of memorizing art history dates). These kinds of tasks typically have no single "correct" answer that an AI could look up, and they require personal input and decision-making. Research shows authentic assessments can reduce contract cheating because it's harder to outsource a personal, context-tied task. As a design principle, try to frame assessments as demonstrations of capability rather than just tests of knowledge. Other examples include: clinical simulations in nursing, moot court exercises in law, or designing an experiment in science. Authenticity also improves student motivation, as they see tasks as meaningful. When planning, ask "How might this knowledge/skill be used in a real situation?" and then craft an assessment around that. Authentic does not have to mean elaborate or long-term, even a well-written problem scenario or role-play in an exam can add context that makes it less trivial for AI to solve and more valuable for learning.
3. Evaluate Both Process and Product (Process-Product Approach): Don't just grade the final answer or artifact; design assessments to capture the process students

engage in and allocate marks or feedback for that process. This serves multiple goals: it promotes metacognition, provides evidence of the student's own work (discouraging cheating), and values skills like self-regulation and revision. Concretely, incorporate elements such as draft submissions, learning journals, design logs, or reflections as part of the assignment. For example, in writing assignments, require students to submit an outline or first draft and incorporate feedback, or in a coding project, have them maintain a short diary of their debugging and decision-making. This made it easier to identify anomalies (if a student suddenly produces a polished final product with no evidence of struggle, that's a red flag) and encouraged students to self-check their progress. The Process-Product Assessment Approach introduced by Alkouk & Khlaif (2024) recommends weighting both the quality of the final output and the quality of the process (like how the student interacted with AI tools or responded to feedback). Educators can implement this by using rubrics with criteria for process (e.g., "evidence of planning and revision," "reflection on learning"). By doing so, you implicitly tell students that how they get to the answer matters, not just the answer, which discourages last-minute AI-generated solutions or copy-paste jobs. Additionally, collecting process data (like drafts or logs) provides a trove of material to investigate if academic integrity concerns arise, and it can often vindicate students by showing their work evolution. Tools like Google Docs version history, programming version control (Git), or even automated keystroke logging (with consent) can support process evaluation in large classes (Trezise et al., 2019). However, ensure students know upfront that their process is part of the grading and how it will be assessed (transparency helps them engage sincerely).

4. Integrate Oral and Interactive Components to Verify Understanding: Wherever feasible, include an oral examination, presentation, or live Q&A component as part of assessment. Speaking and responding in real-time forces students to truly internalize knowledge, and it makes impersonation or AI-use extremely difficult. Even a short oral check can provide assurance of authenticity. For instance, after a student submits a written project, you might have a 10-minute one-on-one viva where you ask them about their work ("Explain how you arrived at conclusion X" or "What would you do if condition Y changed?"). Similarly, have students present their work to the class or teacher, and include a question period. It aligns with recommendations from Nikolic et al. (2023) to use video-conference oral evaluations as an anti-cheating measure. Oral components also improve learning; students often report that articulating their thoughts helps solidify their understanding (the Rubber Duck method in programming is an example, where explaining a bug out loud can lead to insight). To implement, instructors can schedule mini-orals for project defences, use tools like Zoom

or Flip (for recorded presentations) in online courses, or incorporate oral questioning within practical exams (OSCEs in medical fields do this, for instance). In large classes, this is admittedly challenging, but you can use sampling (orals for a randomly chosen subset or for borderline cases) or group orals (teams present, and you direct questions to individuals). Another approach is to use peer review in a live format, students present to peers in small groups, and peers ask questions via rubric prompts; the instructor can rotate to observe. The key principle is to break the anonymity and static nature of assessment, make it a dialogue at some stage. Even if fully oral exams aren't possible, adding a required "viva voce" after submission (common in graduate thesis defences, now trickling to undergraduate capstones) is a strong deterrent to contract cheating and encourages mastery. Design rubrics to include quality of oral explanation if it's part of grading, or at least make oral verification a hurdle that must be passed (e.g., "credit for the project is contingent on a satisfactory oral explanation of its content").

5. Provide Clear Guidelines on AI Usage and Promote Ethical AI Literacy: Rather than outright banning AI tools, offer guidance and boundaries for their acceptable use in assessments, and make this a learning opportunity. Acknowledge that tools like ChatGPT exist and may even be helpful for certain stages (idea generation, grammar checking, etc.), but clearly specify what counts as original work and what needs to be documented. For example, you might allow students to use AI for brainstorming or getting code debugging hints, provided they cite any AI assistance and critically evaluate it. This fosters an environment of transparency and trust. This not only deters covert cheating (because they must reveal it) but also normalizes AI as a tool to be used ethically, not an illicit shortcut. Many institutions are adopting such policies, recognizing it's "shortsighted to consider all AI use as cheating". By teaching AI literacy, we prepare students for the real world where AI can be a powerful aid if used correctly. Design-wise, consider adding an "AI-use reflection" component: ask what prompts they tried, how they verified AI outputs, etc. Also, educate students on the limitations of AI (e.g., it can produce wrong or biased info). This principle is about shaping attitudes, if students feel they can discuss AI openly, they're less likely to misuse it surreptitiously. Of course, for exams or quizzes that must be unassisted, state that clearly and enforce through proctoring or lockdown browsers as needed, but focus more on assessment format changes (principle 2 and 3) to mitigate those issues. Complement guidelines with institutional honor code updates that include AI (as some universities and even states have started doing). Lastly, share success stories: e.g., "In this class, you'll learn how to use emerging tools responsibly, a skill valued by employers." This positive framing can increase buy-in.

6. Use Multiple and Varied Assessment Modes: Don't rely on a single type of assessment to measure all learning outcomes. Instead, adopt a mixed assessment strategy (sometimes called triangulation in evaluation) that includes a variety of formats, written work, oral work, individual and group tasks, open-book and closed-book components, etc. This reduces the stakes of any one approach and exploits the strengths of each. It also makes it dramatically harder for cheating to go undetected across the board. For instance, combine a term project with periodic quizzes, or a traditional test with a follow-up oral exam, or an essay with an in-class problem-solving task. Varied assessments cater to different learning styles and reduce anxiety because students know their grade isn't riding on just one format. Research by Boud and Soler (2015) suggests that diverse assessment prepares students better for unpredictable real-world challenges. From an integrity viewpoint, having multiple modes means if a student were to cheat in one (say, plagiarize an essay), it might become evident when they underperform in another mode (like an oral exam or supervised test), inconsistencies are easier to spot. Practically, map your course outcomes to at least 2-3 different assessment types. For example: knowledge recall might be tested with low-stakes online quizzes (open-book allowed), conceptual understanding with an essay or project, and practical skills with an in-class demonstration or lab. The University of Sussex's "quest for alternative assessment" blog notes that varied assessments can cover a wider range of skills (critical thinking, problem solving, creativity) than any single method. Also, alternate tasks within a course to prevent complacency or gaming, e.g., midterm could be a group project, final an individual oral exam. Students then have to prepare in a holistic way, building both collaboration and independent mastery. Using a combination of open-book and closed-book assessments can also be beneficial. Open-book or open-internet exams, if well-designed with complex questions, reduce stress and mirror real life (you usually have resources at hand), while an occasional closed-book in-class essay might check baseline individual ability. The key is intentional variety: each assessment mode should serve a clear purpose and together they should drive learning throughout the term rather than encourage cramming.
7. Design and Communicate Rubrics that Emphasize Original Thought and Personal Engagement: Craft detailed rubrics for each assignment that explicitly reward original analysis, critical thinking, and personal insight or voice, and share these rubrics with students in advance. When students see that merely presenting generic answers yields average marks, whereas bringing their own reasoning or perspective yields high marks, they are incentivized to do the latter (which AI cannot easily do). For example, a rubric criterion might be "Interpretation and insight: does the work demonstrate the student's own understanding through

original examples, analogies, or synthesis?" with descriptors that mention creativity or personal connection to the content. Rubrics should also include Academic Integrity or Authenticity as a criterion (even if not scored, at least as a stated expectation), e.g., "Work reflects the student's own effort; all sources and assistance, including AI if used, are properly acknowledged." This transparently sets the tone that you evaluate honesty and proper attribution as part of the assignment. Empirical studies (e.g., in Computers & Education) have shown that clear criteria improve student performance and reduce misunderstandings. When you hand out rubrics, discuss them with students using examples of strong vs. weak work. Show how an answer that merely copies lecture notes might only get a "Meets expectations," whereas one that applies the concept to a novel situation or critically evaluates it would get "Exceeds expectations." This clarity can deter students from taking shortcuts, because they realize a copied answer, even if correct, won't excel. Essentially, design rubrics to reward the learning behaviours you want to see (analysis, reflection, creativity) and make those rewards known. As an extra step, consider involving students in rubric creation or at least in discussing what makes work original or insightful, this can increase their buy-in and understanding of academic standards (a strategy supported by the metacognitive literature).

8. Implement Scaffolded and Continuous Assessment with Feedback Loops: Break larger assessments into smaller milestones or checkpoints, and provide formative feedback at each stage. This scaffolding helps students manage their workload, improves learning (through iteration), and reduces the temptation or need to cheat since students are guided along the way. For example, could be split into topic proposal, annotated bibliography, outline, draft, and final paper, each with feedback. Continuous assessment (having multiple graded or ungraded checkpoints) also catches struggling students early, allowing for intervention (which can prevent panicked cheating at deadline). From an integrity perspective, scaffolding means any outsourced or AI-generated work becomes more obvious, if a student's draft is very poor but their final is polished beyond what feedback would predict, it raises questions. But if they engage throughout, the final product is clearly theirs. This aligns with Strategy 1: center (and document) the writing process mentioned in some AI-resilient assessment guides. Additionally, ensure each stage has some weight or at least mandatory completion, so students take them seriously. Use low-stakes quizzes or reflections periodically to keep students on track with learning (this also diminishes high-stakes pressure that can drive cheating). Another aspect of continuous assessment is to close the feedback loop: give specific, actionable feedback at milestones and require (or encourage) students to respond to it (e.g., integrate it into next draft, or write a short note on how they addressed comments). Research by Hattie and

Timperley (2007) emphasizes the power of formative feedback on learning gains. Structuring assessments to be iterative ensures such feedback is built-in, not just an afterthought. For instance, in technical courses, use regular problem sets that build up to a project (and discuss common errors so students don't repeat them). In sum, scaffolded continuous assessment nurtures a learning-focused environment and implicitly dissuades academic dishonesty by keeping students engaged and supported at all times.

By following these eight design principles, focusing on higher-order skills, authenticity, process evaluation, oral components, AI ethics, assessment diversity, clear rubrics, and scaffolding, educators can create robust assessment systems that are "AI-resilient" and learning-oriented. These principles are mutually reinforcing. For example, scaffolding (Principle 8) pairs well with process evaluation (Principle 3) and feedback loops (Principle 8 again) to develop student skills and confidence, which in turn reduces incentives to cheat. Likewise, emphasizing original thought in rubrics (Principle 7) complements focusing on higher-order tasks (Principle 1) and authentic formats (Principle 2). Collectively, they lead to assessment designs where students are actively engaged, continuously learning, and held accountable in fair, meaningful ways, precisely the environment where academic integrity thrives and AI becomes a tool for learning rather than a tool for cheating.

Institutional support can greatly facilitate these principles. Administrators and policymakers can provide training and resources for faculty (e.g. workshops on designing alternative assessments or using AI tools ethically), adjust class sizes or TA support to allow for more interactive assessments (like oral exams or project-based courses), and update academic integrity policies to include AI usage guidelines (operationalizing Principle 5 at the institutional level). Policy changes might also involve rebalancing the weight of final exams vs. continuous assessment in program requirements, to encourage the shift. Ensuring that accreditation bodies recognize and accept these diverse forms of assessment is another important factor, educators need to be confident that adopting innovative assessments will still meet external standards of rigor. By addressing these systemic factors, institutions signal that they value deep learning and integrity over simplistic metrics, empowering teachers to implement the principles above.

It's important to note that not every course will implement all principles to the same extent, and that's fine. Even incremental changes can make a significant difference. An instructor might start by adding an oral presentation component to an existing project (hitting Principles 2 and 4), or by requiring a draft and reflection for a major paper (hitting Principles 3 and 8), before overhauling their entire assessment scheme. Over time, as they see positive outcomes, they can layer in more of these ideas. The ultimate goal is to shift the overall assessment culture to one that values authentic demonstration of learning and is naturally robust against misconduct.

LIMITATIONS AND FUTURE WORK

Redesigning assessment for an AI-saturated world offers clear pedagogical and integrity advantages, yet several constraints must be addressed before such models can be mainstreamed.

Scalability. Oral examinations, multi-draft coaching and project mentoring work well in seminars but become burdensome in classes of 200 + students. Emerging solutions, graduate-assistant support, structured peer review, random spot-orals or group presentations in which each member defends a section, require systematic study to confirm that educational quality is not diluted. Discipline-specific research is likewise essential: what counts as an "authentic" task in a coding course (e.g., version-controlled repositories) differs from that in history (e.g., source-analysis commentaries). Comparing implementations across fields will reveal where adaptations are needed and which practices travel well.

Evidence base. Current enthusiasm rests largely on case studies and instructor reports. Rigorous designs, parallel course sections, quasi-experiments and controlled simulations that measure undetected cheating, are needed to quantify learning gains, student satisfaction and integrity outcomes. Longitudinal tracking should examine whether graduates of AI-resilient programmes retain knowledge better, display stronger metacognition and uphold integrity in later courses or workplaces.

Equity and accessibility. Active, authentic tasks often narrow achievement gaps, yet additions such as mandatory presentations or extensive writing may disadvantage anxious speakers, second-language learners or students with disabilities. Universal Design for Learning principles, choice of modality, flexible timing, alternative formats, must be baked in from the outset. Research should disaggregate data by demographic and learning profiles to ensure reforms support, not sideline, vulnerable groups. Privacy and consent are equally critical when learning-analytics tools monitor writing style or time-on-task; studies of student perceptions can guide transparent, trust-building data policies.

Faculty workload and reliability. Alternative assessments demand more design time, feedback and nuanced grading. Institutions therefore need to recognise the labour in workload formulas, provide professional-development, adjust class sizes or offer AI-assisted marking tools that flag rubric mismatches or anomalous scores. Reliability can be bolstered through detailed rubrics, double-marking and calibration meetings, but empirical work should test which combinations maintain rigour at scale.

Technological arms race. AI models will soon mimic higher-order reasoning and speech with greater fluency, narrowing the gap between machine-generated and human work. The most "future-proof" defence remains assessments that hinge on personal experience, real-time dialogue and creative synthesis. Nevertheless, researchers should experiment with transparent, structured AI use, e.g., requiring students to submit prompt logs and critical evaluations of AI feedback, so that the skill of working with AI ethically becomes an assessed outcome rather than a prohibited tactic.

RESEARCH AND DEVELOPMENT PRIORITIES

- Scalability at Scale: How can mixed-modal assessments be efficiently implemented in cohorts > 200 without eroding feedback quality?
- Long-Term Impact: Do graduates of AI-resilient programmes retain higher-order skills and uphold integrity three years into employment?
- AI as Partner, Not Adversary: Which rubric designs best evaluate students' capacity to critique and refine AI output?
- Policy Levers and Economics: What institutional policies (e.g., reduced final-exam weighting) most cost-effectively lower misconduct rates?
- Supportive Technologies: How accurate and equitable are "integrity dashboards" that visualise authorship consistency and process data?
- Fairness and Accessibility: Do diverse student groups experience alternative assessments as more inclusive, and how can Universal Design for Learning principles mitigate residual barriers?

Addressing these limitations through coordinated research, policy innovation and technological support will enable educators to adopt AI-resilient assessment confidently and equitably.

CONCLUSION

The evolution of assessment in the age of AI is not just a defensive manoeuvre to prevent cheating; it's an opportunity to rectify longstanding shortcomings of traditional assessment. For too long, assessment in higher education has often emphasized rote learning and one-size-fits-all exams that do not capture the full spectrum of student abilities. Now, AI's disruptive presence forces us to confront this misalignment. It compels us to ask, "What are we truly trying to measure in education, and how can we measure that in a world with AI?" The answers point toward higher-order thinking, creativity, practical application, ethical reasoning, and lifelong learning skills, things an AI cannot simply hand to a student on a platter. If an algorithm can ace our test, perhaps we were testing the wrong thing. By contrast, the assessments we propose, ones requiring critical analysis, original creation, personal reflection, and demonstration, remain as relevant as ever because they measure the distinctly human capacities that education should develop. Even if AI becomes more powerful, those assessments would still prompt the student to learn and do something meaningful with the aid of AI, rather than be replaced by it.

Moving to these new paradigms also builds a culture of integrity and learning. When students see that the system is designed for them to learn (not just to trick them or sort them), and that dishonesty won't actually benefit them, they are more likely to buy into the process. Many students cheat not because they are unethical, but because they feel cornered or disillusioned (e.g., "this test doesn't really matter to my life, I just need the grade"). If instead they are doing projects that connect to their goals, reflecting on their growth, and being trusted to use tools with transparency, they feel respected and motivated to rise to the challenge. Education becomes something done with them, not to them. Over time, this can nurture learners who value honesty and effort, outcomes that extend beyond any single course.

In closing, the advent of AI in education need not be an arms race of detection and deception. It can be the dawn of assessments that truly reflect and promote the knowledge, skills, and values we care about. By innovating rather than stagnating in the face of change, we can ensure that the "tail" of assessment wagging the "dog" of the curriculum wags it in the right direction, towards deeper learning, genuine integrity, and preparation for a future where our students thrive alongside AI, not in fear of it. The challenge is significant, but so is the opportunity. If we seize this moment to make assessment more authentic, we will not only thwart the cheating enabled by new technology, but more importantly, we will enrich education for the better, making it more engaging, relevant, and effective for generations of learners to come.

REFERENCES

Alkouk, A. W., & Khlaif, Z. N. (2024). AI-resistant assessments in higher education: practical insights from faculty training workshops. In *Frontiers in education* (Vol. 9, p. 1499495). DOI: 10.3389/feduc.2024.1499495

Boud, D., & Soler, R. (2015). Sustainable assessment revisited. *Assessment & Evaluation in Higher Education, 41*(3), 400–413. DOI: 10.1080/02602938.2015.1018133

Bretag, T., Harper, R., Burton, M., Ellis, C., Newton, P., van Haeringen, K., Saddiqui, S., & Rozenberg, P. (2019). Contract cheating and assessment design: Exploring the relationship. *Assessment & Evaluation in Higher Education, 44*(5), 676–691. DOI: 10.1080/02602938.2018.1527892

Chase, C. C., Chin, D. B., Oppezzo, M. A., & Schwartz, D. L. (2009). Teachable Agents and the Protégé Effect: Increasing the Effort Towards Learning. *Journal of Science Education and Technology, 18*(4), 334–352. DOI: 10.1007/s10956-009-9180-4

Cotton, D. R. E., Cotton, P. A., & Shipway, J. R. (2023). Chatting and cheating: Ensuring academic integrity in the era of ChatGPT. *Innovations in Education and Teaching International.* Advance online publication. DOI: 10.1080/14703297.2023.2190148

Ellis, C., Zucker, I., & Randall, D. (2020). Does authentic assessment assure academic integrity? Evidence from contract cheating data. *Higher Education Research & Development, 39*(3), 454–469. DOI: 10.1080/07294360.2019.1680956

Evangelista, E. D. L. (2025). Ensuring academic integrity in the age of ChatGPT: Rethinking exam design, assessment strategies, and ethical AI policies in higher education. *Contemporary Educational Technology, 17*(1), ep559. DOI: 10.30935/cedtech/15775

Fiorella, L., & Mayer, R. E. (2014). The relative benefits of learning by teaching and teaching expectancy. *Contemporary Educational Psychology, 39*(4), 281–288. DOI: 10.1016/j.cedpsych.2013.06.001

Freeman, S. L., Eddy, S. L., McDonough, M., Smith, M. K., Okoroafor, N., Jordt, H., & Wenderoth, M. P. (2014). Active learning increases student performance in science, engineering, and mathematics. *Proceedings of the National Academy of Sciences of the United States of America, 111*(23), 8410–8415. DOI: 10.1073/pnas.1319030111 PMID: 24821756

Gobert, J. D., Sao Pedro, M., Raziuddin, J., & Baker, R. S. (2013). From log files to assessment metrics: Measuring students' science inquiry skills using educational data mining. *Journal of the Learning Sciences*, *22*(4), 521–563. DOI: 10.1080/10508406.2013.837391

Hattie, J., & Timperley, H. (2007). The Power of Feedback. *Review of Educational Research*, *77*(1), 81–112. DOI: 10.3102/003465430298487

Heung, Y. M. E., & Chiu, T. K. (2025). How ChatGPT impacts student engagement from a systematic review and meta-analysis study. *Computers and Education: Artificial Intelligence*, *8*, 100361. DOI: 10.1016/j.caeai.2025.100361

Holmes, W., & Miao, F. (2023). *Guidance for generative AI in education and research*. UNESCO (Policy paper).

Janisch, C., Liu, X., & Akrofi, A. (2007). Implementing Alternative Assessment: Opportunities and Obstacles. *The Educational Forum*, *71*(3), 221–230. DOI: 10.1080/00131720709335007

Kutbi, M., Al-Hoorie, A. H., & Al-Shammari, A. H. (2024). Detecting contract cheating through linguistic fingerprint. *Humanities & Social Sciences Communications*, *11*(1), 664. DOI: 10.1057/s41599-024-03160-9

Lancaster, T., & Cotarlan, C. (2021). Contract cheating by STEM students through a file sharing website: A Covid-19 pandemic perspective. *International Journal for Educational Integrity*, *17*(1), 3. DOI: 10.1007/s40979-021-00070-0

Nikolic, S., Daniel, S., Haque, R., Belkina, M., Hassan, G. M., Grundy, S., … Sandison, C. (2023). ChatGPT versus engineering education assessment: A multidisciplinary benchmarking. *IEEE Transactions on Education*, (early access). DOI: 10.1080/03043797.2023.2213169

Roberts, B. R. T., MacLeod, C. M., & Fernandes, M. A. (2022). The enactment effect: A systematic review and meta-analysis of behavioral, neuroimaging, and patient studies. *Psychological Bulletin*, *148*(5-6), 397–435. DOI: 10.1037/bul0000360 PMID: 35878067

Rudolph, J., Tan, S., & Tan, S. (2023). ChatGPT: Bullshit spewer or the end of traditional assessments in higher education? *Journal of applied learning and teaching*, *6*(1), 342-363. DOI: 10.37074/jalt.2023.6.1.9

Schraw, G. (1998). Promoting general metacognitive awareness. *Instructional Science*, *26*(1-2), 113–125. DOI: 10.1023/A:1003044231033

Stanton, J. D., Sebesta, A. J., & Dunlosky, J. (2021). Fostering metacognition to support student learning and performance. *CBE Life Sciences Education*, *20*(2), fe3. DOI: 10.1187/cbe.20-12-0289 PMID: 33797282

Trezise, K., Ryan, T., de Barba, P., & Kennedy, G. (2019). Detecting contract cheating using learning analytics. *Journal of Learning Analytics*, *6*(3), 90–104. DOI: 10.18608/jla.2019.63.11

Whitelock, D., Goshtasbpour, F., Pitt, B., Ferguson, R., & Cross, S. (2024). Capacity building for digital education. *Open Learning*, *39*(2), 105–111. DOI: 10.1080/02680513.2024.2317894

Xia, Q., Weng, X., Ouyang, F., Lin, T. J., & Chiu, T. K. (2024). A scoping review on how generative artificial intelligence transforms assessment in higher education. *International Journal of Educational Technology in Higher Education*, *21*(1), 40. DOI: 10.1186/s41239-024-00468-z

Chapter 9

Digital Transformation in Education:
School Principals' Attitudes Towards Artificial Intelligence

Mehmet Tufan Yalçın
https://orcid.org/0000-0001-8386-2308
Çankırı Karatekin University, Turkey

Ömür Çoban
https://orcid.org/0000-0002-4702-4152
Karamanoğlu Mehmetbey University, Turkey

ABSTRACT

Artificial intelligence technologies play a crucial role by automating managerial processes within schools, thereby allowing school principals to exercise more effective leadership and dedicate greater attention to teaching and learning. The aim of this study is to reveal the school principals' attitudes towards artificial intelligence. Within this scope, the study surveyed the opinions of 547 school principals in 10 provinces of Türkiye. The findings indicate that school principals generally exhibited a positive attitude towards AI and there is no significant difference between their AIA and the demographic variables such as gender, educational level, school type, and the socio-economic status of the school. It is crucial to support school leaders in maintaining and strengthening their positive attitudes. Furthermore, fostering these attitudes among principals may play a key role in influencing teachers and other stakeholders, thereby promoting a broader culture of technological openness and innovation within schools.

DOI: 10.4018/979-8-3373-6375-2.ch009

INTRODUCTION

Contemporary education systems are becoming increasingly complex and unpredictable as a result of rapid social change and the pervasive influence of digitalisation. To effectively navigate the evolving environment, strategic initiatives must be implemented at both the individual and organisational levels, ensuring a comprehensive and holistic approach to transformation. Artificial intelligence (AI) applications, in particular, hold significant potential to transform various aspects of education, ranging from administrative management to teaching and learning processes. Within this context, school principals play a pivotal role, not only in carrying out their managerial responsibilities, but also as key agents in leading and implementing pedagogical and technological innovations within their schools.

Research has demonstrated that school principals influence academic achievement indirectly by shaping teacher behaviour and the organisational climate, rather than through direct instructional impact (Bush, 2017; Leithwood et al., 2020). In this context, the adoption and effective utilisation of AI-based technologies in schools largely depend on principals' attitudes towards these technologies, as well as their leadership styles. It is well established that AI-based technologies can streamline administrative processes, thereby enabling school leaders to allocate more time to pedagogical leadership (Erdoğan et al., 2025; Grace et al., 2023). However, the success of technological innovations in education is contingent not only upon the availability of technical infrastructure but also upon school leaders' attitudes, beliefs, and readiness to embrace such innovations (Pereira et al., 2023).

In the Turkish centralised and hierarchical education system, there appears to be a limited number of empirical studies examining school principals' attitudes towards AI (i.e. Erdoğan et al., 2025). This gap in the literature points to a significant lack of understanding regarding how AI-based transformation efforts are perceived within schools and the extent to which they can be effectively implemented. Accordingly, this study aims to explore school principals' attitudes towards AI applications, thereby shedding light on the digital transformation potential of schools in Türkiye.

Turkish Context

Owing to the centralised nature and hierarchical structure of the Turkish education system, school principals possess significantly less autonomy and decision-making power compared to their counterparts in Western countries (Kılınç et al., 2021). Despite these limitations, school principals have undertaken various initiatives—such as the Ministry of National Education's (MoNE) FATIH project—to enhance the quality of education in schools and to align with ongoing technological advancements. In recent years, notable progress has been made in integrating AI into the education system. An AI-supported Teacher Information Network has been developed to foster teachers' professional growth, while platforms such as the Education Information Network and the Individual Learning Platform have been introduced to improve student outcomes (Temel & Coşkun, 2024). Furthermore, the Ministry of Industry and Technology, in collaboration with the Presidency's Digital Transformation Office, has developed the National Artificial Intelligence Strategy (2021–2025) and its accompanying National Artificial Intelligence Strategy Action Plan (2024–2025), which represents the operational framework for implementing the strategy. These strategic documents set out a range of initiatives designed to promote the adoption of artificial intelligence across various sectors, including education and healthcare (Turkish Official Gazette, 2021). In alignment with ongoing reforms and policy developments in Türkiye, the present study aims to examine the demographic variables that influence school principals' attitudes towards artificial intelligence (AIA) within the context of AI integration in education. In order to implement these Ministry-led initiatives effectively at the school level, it is imperative that school principals also undergo a transformation to develop their AI competencies. The integration of technology and AI in education is further elaborated in key policy documents, including the Maarif Model (MoNE, 2024a) and the Ministry of National Education Strategic Plan 2024–2028 (MoNE, 2024b). If an assessment is to be made within the context of the Turkish education system, it becomes evident that the successful integration of artificial intelligence depends not only on national strategies and policies but also on the readiness and attitudes of key stakeholders, particularly school principals, who play a crucial role in implementing such innovations at the institutional level.

LITERATURE REVIEW

Definition of AI and its background

When considering the general definition of AI, the key point is that it constitutes a branch of computer science capable of replicating human cognitive functions. More detailed definitions describe AI as a system capable of performing tasks traditionally associated with human intelligence, such as understanding, perceiving, reasoning, comprehending, interpreting, generalising, inferring, and learning about a particular subject or event, as well as executing multiple tasks simultaneously (Durnalı & Çoban, 2025; Gondal, 2018). AI became a major focal point of global attention following the launch of ChatGPT in late 2022. This application is capable of simulating a broad range of human abilities, including text and image generation and/or conversion, video production, music composition, and software development, while also functioning as a personal assistant by responding to user queries.

The number of AI models is growing rapidly, with notable examples including ChatGPT, Google Assistant, Alexa, Chatsonic, Copilot, LLaMA: Open Assistant, Socratic, Tongyi, and YouChat. As technological development continues apace, the range and scope of AI-based applications are expanding significantly, enhancing convenience and efficiency in many aspects of daily life. AI algorithms are increasingly employed across a variety of fields, including machine translation, autonomous vehicles, medical diagnostics, sales forecasting, and virtual personal assistants (Komalavalli et al., 2020). Certain contemporary artificial intelligence systems exhibit mechanical intelligence, enabling them to carry out repetitive tasks with consistency and reliability. Others demonstrate cognitive intelligence, characterised by the capacity to learn autonomously from data and adapt that learning to specific contexts. Looking ahead, it is anticipated that future AI systems will be developed with emotional intelligence, allowing them to engage with humans through empathetic interaction (Huang & Rust, 2018).

The widespread integration of AI into diverse domains such as healthcare, industry, education, finance, and transportation underscores the urgent need for individuals to develop their competencies in this area. In order to keep pace with the rapid innovations brought about by AI, it is essential that individuals acquire the necessary knowledge and skills to engage effectively with these technologies (Wang et al., 2023).

AI in Education

In recent years, a paradigm shift has emerged in the field of education, marked by the growing prominence of innovative models such as individualised learning and self-directed learning. These emerging models place a strong emphasis on fostering students' autonomy and individual skill development, aiming to equip them for the demands of an increasingly dynamic and rapidly evolving job market (Atasoy, 2025; Tyson & Sauers, 2021). Additionally, AI-based systems are capable of recommending courses aligned with students' interests and academic backgrounds, supporting career planning, and even identifying suitable internship and employment opportunities (George & Wooden, 2023). In doing so, they can assist students in making informed, purposeful decisions throughout their educational journey, particularly in relation to career development. At this juncture, the integration of artificial intelligence also plays a pivotal role in supporting and enhancing students' learning and development. AI also offers significant opportunities to promote inclusivity and support equal access to education. Previous research (e.g., Şenocak, 2020; Viberg et al., 2024) highlights the potential of AI-based systems to enhance the participation of disadvantaged groups in educational processes and to support their academic achievement. For instance, AI applications capable of providing real-time translation for students facing language barriers, generating personalised and adaptive learning scenarios for those with learning difficulties, and analysing students' psychological well-being through social media data can all contribute to making education more inclusive and responsive to diverse learner needs.

With the rapid advancement of artificial intelligence and robotic technologies, many sectors have witnessed job displacement. Within the context of education, this has led to growing concerns and debates over whether AI may eventually replace teachers in the classroom. While the integration of artificial intelligence into education is poised to fundamentally transform the teaching profession, it is unlikely to render it obsolete. Rather, AI will reshape the nature and scope of the profession (Huang & Rust, 2018). If educators were merely transmitting information from textbooks in a mechanical manner, like robots, one might reasonably argue that AI could replace them. However, in today's educational landscape, teachers are adopting innovative pedagogical approaches aimed at fostering a holistic development model that supports not only students' academic growth but also their emotional, physical, and social development. Within the contemporary understanding of education, the role of the school and the teacher in students' emotional development and socialisation has become increasingly significant. In this context, it appears unlikely that the role of the teacher could be fully assumed by AI. As highlighted in the current literature, effective education and teaching processes extend well beyond the simple transmission of knowledge. The development of critical thinking, emotional intelligence, social interaction, and the ability to address the diverse needs of learners has become essential for educating individuals fit for the 21st century (Çoban & Durnalı, 2025; Çoban & Gün, 2024). In order to nurture these dimensions of education, teachers must possess advanced skills that surpass the capabilities of artificial intelligence, acting not only as educators but also as role models and sources of inspiration for their students (Guan et al., 2020). Moreover, the establishment of strong interpersonal relationships and meaningful interaction between teachers and students is essential to the effectiveness of the learning process (Shen et al., 2020). These relationships foster a positive and supportive learning environment, an aspect that current artificial intelligence systems are unable to replicate. Teachers are uniquely positioned to offer empathy, understanding, and guidance, all of which are fundamental to students' personal development and psychological well-being (Bertolin & Da Rin, 2020).

Indeed, contemporary educators increasingly view artificial intelligence not as a threat, but as a valuable tool for enhancing the effectiveness of teaching and learning processes, as well as supporting their own professional development. AI-supported applications have become more diverse and now demonstrate their potential across various domains of education, including learning, instruction, assessment, and educational administration. These technologies offer personalised and adaptive learning experiences tailored to individual students' needs, thereby acknowledging the importance of differentiated learning and development (Durnalı & Çoban, 2025; Ramnarain et al., 2024). As previously noted, AI-powered tools can assist educators in multiple ways—for instance, by monitoring student progress, generating reports, and predicting developmental trends (Chiu et al., 2023; Hwang et al., 2020). More significantly, in line with the principle that no learner should be left behind in the pursuit of educational equity, AI-based platforms are increasingly playing a vital role in identifying students at risk of academic failure and enabling timely interventions (Tsai et al., 2020).

Furthermore, AI can support educators by automating administrative tasks such as report preparation, data interpretation for informed decision-making, and monitoring and guiding students' learning progress, as well as recommending innovative teaching methods and strategies (Ghamrawi et al., 2024). Moreover, the integration of AI within educational institutions presents educators with an opportunity to broaden their leadership roles beyond the classroom. It enables them to act as mentors, coaches, and resource providers, utilising AI as a valuable tool to support and guide their colleagues. This, in turn, can alleviate the time constraints and workload pressures typically experienced by lead teachers. Additionally, AI has the potential to reduce the negative effects of professional jealousy and envy, particularly in relation to professional development and mentorship. Teachers may employ AI to identify the most effective resources tailored to the specific needs of both colleagues and students (Çoban & Gün, 2024).

AI in Educational Management

In the current era of Industry 4.0, transitioning towards Education 4.0 has become essential for enhancing the quality and relevance of education. Traditional management approaches are often insufficient in addressing the growing complexity of contemporary educational environments and may fall short in meeting the expectations of newer generations. Unlike traditional, rote-based learning approaches, Education 4.0 embraces a more personalised and learner-centred model, underpinned by emerging technologies such as artificial intelligence, augmented reality, and other digital tools (Durnalı & Çoban, 2025). Additionally, AI-driven systems have the potential to transform the management processes of educational institutions by enhancing their efficiency and effectiveness. Through the utilisation of advanced technologies such as big data analytics, machine learning, and natural language processing, AI can provide innovative solutions tailored to the evolving needs of modern education (Atasoy, 2024; Çoban & Durnalı, 2025). Another key contribution of AI to educational management lies in its role within data analytics and decision support systems. As highlighted by scholars in the field (e.g., Shwedeh, 2024), AI-powered data analysis tools offer education managers comprehensive insights into critical areas such as student achievement rates, time to graduation, teaching quality, and financial performance. These insights support more informed, evidence-based, and strategic decision-making. Moreover, it is evident that AI-driven decision support systems enable educational institutions to allocate their resources more effectively and efficiently, leading to cost reductions and improved overall productivity. In line with this shift, education administrators should have several key strategies to transform educational systems (Öztemel, 2018):

- A digital culture must be cultivated throughout the educational process.
- Innovation-driven and interdisciplinary curricula should be developed.
- Educational programmes should be enriched with artificial intelligence, as well as virtual and augmented reality technologies.
- The education system should be restructured through the integration of distance learning technologies and support mechanisms, accompanied by the formulation of corresponding education policies.

As highlighted in the above features, the growing integration of technology in educational settings has underscored the need for school leaders who possess a strong understanding of technological tools and their effective application. It is essential that school leaders not only comprehend how technology can be utilised within their institutions, but also actively champion its adoption and meaningful use (Hamzah et al., 2014). In response to this need, the International Society for Technology in Education (ISTE) has introduced the ISTE Standards for Education Leaders, a dedicated framework outlining the knowledge and behaviours required for leaders to empower educators and facilitate student learning. In a study examining the characteristics that school principals should possess, it was found that principals with strong technological competencies found that such leaders place a high value on collaboration, articulate their expectations clearly and explicitly, are willing to take risks, and work towards establishing a shared vision. Moreover, these school principals should be embedded within a framework that actively seeks out and implements innovative educational technologies to support and enhance teaching practices (Richardson et al., 2015).

Despite the numerous potential benefits outlined above, several scholars (e.g., Berendt et al., 2020; Müller, 2016) have also drawn attention to the ethical and practical challenges associated with the use of artificial intelligence in educational management. These challenges encompass concerns such as data privacy, algorithmic fairness, and the transparency of AI-driven decision-making processes. Ensuring the fair and ethical deployment of AI systems is essential if educational institutions are to achieve their organisational objectives responsibly. Accordingly, when integrating AI into education management, decision-makers must prioritise ethical considerations, promote fairness and transparency, safeguard data security, and adapt institutional practices to reflect these imperatives.

School Principals' Attitudes Towards Artificial Intelligence

AI is a technology developed to facilitate human life and provide support across various domains (Gansser & Reich, 2021). As a transformative force, AI constitutes a fundamental component of Industry 4.0, which drives automation and digitalisation (Atasoy, 2023; Darko et al., 2020). Individuals' perceptions and responses to AI are shaped by their attitudes, which encompass three primary dimensions: affective, cognitive, and behavioural (Breckler, 1984). Dawson (1992, p. 473) defines attitude as "a predisposition to respond favourably or unfavourably to a particular phenomenon, person, or object."

The affective dimension of attitude encompasses emotions such as anxiety, joy, and stress (Ajzen & Fishbein, 2000). For instance, negative emotions like fear may hinder the adoption and utilisation of AI (Liang & Lee, 2017), whereas positive emotions such as joy can enhance user engagement and promote higher levels of acceptance (Shank et al., 2019).

Beyond emotional responses, the cognitive dimension of attitudes towards AI plays a crucial role in shaping how individuals evaluate this technology. This dimension includes the extent to which psychological needs such as autonomy, competence, and relatedness are fulfilled. According to self-determination theory (Deci & Ryan, 2000), when these needs are satisfied, individuals experience higher levels of psychological well-being and satisfaction. Therefore, a robust cognitive foundation is essential for understanding how attitudes towards AI are formed (Cascio & Montealegre, 2016).

The behavioural dimension refers to individuals' intentions and tendencies to use AI. As outlined in Ajzen's (1991) theory of planned behaviour, behavioural intention is one of the most significant predictors of actual behaviour. Within this framework, the willingness to use AI-based products and services reflects an individual's readiness to explore and adopt the technology (Santamaria & Nathan-Roberts, 2017).

Within the context of school management, attitudes towards AI are shaped by school principals' emotional responses, their conceptual understanding of AI, and their tendencies to either adopt or reject this technology in decision-making processes (Park & Woo, 2022). Indeed, the personality traits of school principals play a partial yet significant role in shaping their attitudes towards artificial intelligence. Empirical research in the field of human-computer interaction has similarly demonstrated that individuals' personality characteristics directly influence their perceptions of autonomous technologies (Stein et al., 2019). Recent studies pointed out that if school principals are innovative and open to change, their attitude towards AI is positive, and those with high neuroticism have a negative attitude towards AI (Erdoğan et al., 2025; Park & Woo, 2022).

Moreover, Tyson and Sauers (2021) emphasised that school principals who demonstrate a positive attitude towards artificial intelligence should assume a leading role in cultivating this attitude within their schools. It is essential that they adopt a strategic approach when implementing AI-based programmes. The initial step in this process involves selecting programmes that align with the specific goals of the school and the wider regional context. At this stage, it is vital that principals develop a genuine understanding of the perspectives of key stakeholders within their school communities. Establishing a clear connection between the AI-based programme and the school's identified needs is also critical for securing staff support and addressing the sense of fatigue that many teachers experience when required to adopt yet another new initiative. The subsequent step in this strategic approach is to clearly articulate both the purpose and intended use of the AI-based programme. Doing so ensures that teachers comprehend the rationale behind the programme's selection and helps to mitigate any apprehension that may arise from uncertainties surrounding its implementation.

Based on these empirical studies, when examining school administrators' attitudes towards AI technologies, it is essential to recognise the complexity of the issue, which is shaped by a range of personal, organisational, and societal factors. However, investigating the variables that influence these attitudes can significantly enhance our understanding of how society responds to emerging technologies, offering both a broader perspective and a more nuanced comprehension of their adoption and impact. This study utilises the AIA framework developed by Schepman and Rodway (2023) to examine both the positive and negative attitudes of school leaders towards AI, aiming to provide a comprehensive perspective on the adoption of artificial intelligence in educational leadership.

Research Aim

The primary aim of this research is to identify the attitudes of school principals in Türkiye towards artificial intelligence applications and to examine how these attitudes vary according to certain variables.

Research Questions

The study seeks to address the following questions:

1. What is the overall level of school principals' attitudes towards artificial intelligence in Türkiye?
2. Do school principals' attitudes towards artificial intelligence differ significantly according to variables such as gender, educational level, school type, and the socio-economic status of the school?
3. Is there a significant relationship between school principals' AIA, school size, and their years of experience in teaching and leading a school?

Research Assumptions

The fundamental assumptions of this study are as follows:

1. The school principals who participated in the research and responded to the survey items have expressed their genuine opinions.
2. The selected sample in this study is representative of the target population.
3. The data collection instruments used in the research are valid and reliable for measuring the intended constructs.

Limitations of the Study

The study is limited to the perspectives of school principals working in state schools affiliated with the Ministry of National Education in ten provinces of Türkiye (Ankara, Bitlis, Çankırı, Karaman, Istanbul, Izmir, Mersin, Muğla, Şanlıurfa, and Trabzon).

METHOD

The aim of the present study is to determine the attitudes of school principals in Türkiye towards artificial intelligence applications. To achieve this aim and to address the research questions, a quantitative research methodology was employed. The study was conducted using independent sample t-tests, one-way analysis of variance (ANOVA), correlation analysis, and descriptive statistics.

Research Design

This study aims to examine the relationships between school principals' attitudes towards artificial intelligence and various demographic and institutional variables, including age, professional seniority, gender, educational level, type of school, school size, and the socio-economic status of the surrounding environment. The research is descriptive in nature and conducted within the framework of a relational screening model. Studies that seek to determine whether a significant relationship exists between two or more variables are commonly classified within the literature as relational or correlational research designs (Büyüköztürk et al., 2019). In this context, the statistical analysis of these relationships will contribute to a deeper understanding of the factors influencing school leaders' attitudes towards technology.

Sampling

The population of this study consists of school principals working in official preschools, primary schools, lower secondary schools, and upper secondary schools operating under the authority of the Ministry of National Education in Turkey. According to the data provided by the Ministry's Directorate General for Strategy Development for the 2023–2024 academic year, the institutions within this population comprise a total of 20,478 public schools. To ensure representativeness of the population and based on assumptions of a 95% confidence level ($Z = 1.96$), a 5% margin of error ($e = 0.05$), and $p = 0.50$ (the most conservative scenario), the minimum required sample size for a population of $N = 20,478$ is approximately $n \approx 377$. This figure is rounded to 378 and is consistent with the Krejcie and Morgan (1970) sample size table, which recommends a sample size of 377 for a population of approximately 20,000. When determining the sample size, the finite population correction formula (used when N is known) was applied.

Accordingly, the sample of the study consists of a total of 378 school principals working in the provinces of Ankara, Bitlis, Çankırı, Karaman, Istanbul, Izmir, Mersin, Muğla, Şanlıurfa, and Trabzon. These provinces were selected using a purposive sampling method in order to reflect geographical diversity and socio-economic variation. This approach aimed to enhance the generalisability of the research findings to different regions. Within this scope, we collected data from 553 school principals. We checked the standardised z-scores and found six responses outside the acceptable ± 3 range. As a result, the final research sample comprises data from 547 school principals. Descriptive statistics for the participating school principals are presented in Table 1.

Table 1. Sample of Study (n = 547)

Variable	Categories	n (%)
School Type	Preschool	53 (9.7)
	Primary	166 (30.3)
	Lower Secondary	154 (28.2)
	Upper Secondary	152 (27.8)
	Other	22 (4.0)
Gender	Male	364 (66.5)
	Female	183 (33.5)
Education	Undergraduate	237 (43.3)
	Postgraduate	310 (56.7)
Socioeconomic Status	Low	179 (32.7)
	Medium	301 (55.1)
	High	67 (12.2)

As is seen in Table 1, 53 (9.7%) of the participants work in preschool, 166 (30.3%) in primary schools, 154 (28.2%) in lower secondary schools, and 152 (27.8%) in higher secondary schools, and 22 (4%). In terms of gender distribution, 364 of the principals are male (66.5%) and 183 are female (33.5%). Regarding educational qualifications, 237 participants (43.3%) hold an Undergraduate, while 310 (56.7%) have completed postgraduate education. With respect to the socioeconomic status of the schools, 179 (32.7%) of the principals' work in schools located in low socioeconomic areas, 301 (55.1%) in middle socioeconomic areas, and 67 (12.2%) in high socioeconomic areas. These findings indicate that the sample is demographically and socioeconomically diverse and that its distribution broadly reflects national data for Türkiye.

Data Collection Tool

The data collection tool for the study consists of two sections: demographic variables and the artificial intelligence attitude scale.

Artificial İntelligence Attitude Scale

To assess school principals' attitudes towards the use of artificial intelligence, we employed the AIA Scale, originally developed by Schepman and Rodway (2023) and adapted into Turkish by Kaya et al. (2024). The scale comprises 20 items in total, with 12 items measuring positive attitudes and eight items measuring negative attitudes. An example item from the scale is: 'I am impressed by what AI can do.'

Responses were recorded using a five-point Likert-type scale, ranging from '1 = Strongly Disagree' to '5 = Strongly Agree.' Cut-off points for Likert-type scales are determined by dividing the range between the minimum and maximum values by the number of categories (Levin et al., 2010; Pimentel, 2019). Accordingly, the intervals for the five-point scale were defined as follows: "1.00–1.79 = 'Strongly Disagree', 1.80–2.59 = 'Disagree', 2.60–3.39 = 'Somewhat Agree', 3.40–4.19 = 'Agree', and 4.20–5.00 = 'Strongly Agree'."

The results of the confirmatory factor analysis indicated that the scale demonstrated acceptable construct validity. The chi-square statistic was significant (χ^2=590.307, df=165, p<.001); however, given the sensitivity of chi-square to sample size, relative fit indices were also considered. The ratio of chi-square to degrees of freedom (χ^2/df) was 3.58, which falls within the acceptable range of ≤5.0 suggested in the literature (Kline, 2005). The RMSEA value was 0.069 with a 90% confidence interval of 0.063–0.075, indicating an acceptable fit below the 0.08 threshold (Hu & Bentler, 1999). Additionally, the CFI (0.918) and TLI (0.905) values exceeded the recommended cutoff of 0.90 (Hu & Bentler, 1999), and the SRMR value was 0.059, remaining well below the criterion of 0.08. Taken together, these findings provide robust evidence for the validity of the measurement model and its adequacy in representing the data.

The reliability coefficients of the AIA Scale were calculated separately for each dimension. For the Positive Attitude dimension, Cronbach's Alpha was α = .91, McDonald's Omega was ω = .91, the composite reliability (CR) was .92, and the average variance extracted (AVE) was .50. For the Negative Attitude dimension, Cronbach's Alpha was α = .87, McDonald's Omega was ω = .87, the CR was .90, and the AVE was .53. As all values exceed commonly accepted thresholds, both dimensions of the scale demonstrate acceptable levels of reliability and construct validity (Hair et al., 2006; Hu & Bentler, 1999).

Demographic Variables

Previous research has demonstrated that both individual-level variables (such as gender, educational attainment, and professional experience in teaching and leadership) and school-level variables (including school type, school size, and socioeconomic status) may influence school principals' perspectives on artificial intelligence (Erdoğan et al., 2025; Kaya et al., 2024). Accordingly, in the present study, school principals' views on artificial intelligence were examined with the consideration that these perspectives might vary depending on such variables.

Data Collection Procedure

Prior to data collection, ethical approval was obtained from the Ethics Committee of Çankırı Karatekin University (Decision No: 57, dated 23 July 2025). Additionally, permission to use the scale was granted by the original developers and the researchers who adapted it into Turkish. Since the study was conducted with school principals, official authorisation was also obtained from the Ministry of National Education (Reference No: MEB.TT.2025.028437).

During the 2025–2026 academic year, school principals in the selected provinces were invited to participate in the study via an online survey link (https://forms.gle/9iUbtQ1xSa 3oHoK9). Data collection was conducted on a voluntary basis. Completing the survey took approximately 10 minutes, which corresponds to roughly 25% of a standard lesson period. The data were collected between 16 September and 30 September 2025.

The collected data were analysed using SPSS statistical software. Initially, the validity and reliability of the scales, as well as the normality of data distribution, were assessed. As part of the descriptive statistics, means, standard deviations, and reliability coefficients (Cronbach's α and McDonald's ω) were calculated for the scales. Subsequently, arithmetic means, standard deviations, and correlations among the variables were examined. Finally, group comparisons based on descriptive variables were conducted using independent samples t-tests, ANOVA, and Pearson correlation analysis via IBM SPSS Statistics 27. Effect sizes for these analyses were interpreted in line with Cohen's (1988) guidelines: Cohen's d was considered small at 0.20, medium at 0.50, and large at 0.80; for ANOVA results, η^2 values were interpreted as small at 0.01, medium at 0.06, and large at 0.14. Finally, Pearson correlation analysis was conducted to examine the relationships between variables, as the assumptions of normal distribution were satisfied. During the analysis process, we also employed confirmatory factor analyses (CFA) of the scales using Mplus 8.3 software.

FINDINGS

In response to the first research question, the findings initially focused on the overall level of school principals' attitudes towards artificial intelligence. The relevant results are presented in Table 2.

Table 2. School Principals' General AI Attitude Levels

Variables	n	M	SD	Skewness	SE	Kurtosis	SE
PGAAIS	547	3.798	.615	-.506	.104	.609	.209
NGAAIS	547	2.930	.725	.131	.104	-.036	.209

Note. PGAAIS: positive general attitudes toward AI subscale; NGAAIS: negative general attitudes toward AI subscale; n: sample size; M: Mean; SE: standard error; SD: standard deviation.

Table 2 presents the general attitude levels of school principals towards artificial intelligence. The mean score for the Positive Attitude subscale (PGAAIS) was 3.80 (SD = 0.62), corresponding to the 'agree' level. This value is above the midpoint of the scale, suggesting that school principals generally hold positive attitudes towards artificial intelligence. The distribution of positive attitude scores was found to be left-skewed (Skewness = –0.51, SE = 0.10), while the kurtosis value (Kurtosis = 0.61, SE = 0.21) indicated a distribution close to normal.

The mean score for the Negative Attitude subscale (NGAAIS) was 2.93 (SD = 0.73), which corresponds to the 'somewhat agree' level and falls below the scale midpoint. This suggests that negative attitudes towards artificial intelligence among school principals are relatively low. The distribution of negative attitude scores was also close to normal, with a skewness value of 0.13 (SE = 0.10) and a kurtosis value of –0.04 (SE = 0.21). All skewness and kurtosis values fall within the recommended thresholds of ±3 (Kline, 2005), indicating that the data meet the assumption of normality. These findings suggest that school principals' positive attitudes towards artificial intelligence are more prominent than their negative attitudes.

Within the scope of the study's second research question, we investigated whether school principals' attitudes towards artificial intelligence differed significantly according to variables such as seniority, gender, education level, school type, school size, and the socioeconomic status of the school. In this context, independent samples t-tests were conducted for the variables of gender and educational level. The results are presented in Table 3.

Table 3. T-Test Results on School Principals' Positive and Negative Attitudes Toward AI

Variables	Characteristics	n	M	SD	Levene F	Levene p	t	df	p	Cohen's d
PGAAIS	Male	364	3.81	0.64	0.94	.333	0.55	545	.580	0.05
	Female	183	3.78	0.57						
NGAAIS	Male	364	2.91	0.74	0.01	.913	-0.71	545	.479	-0.06
	Female	183	2.96	0.70						
PGAAIS	Undergraduate	237	3.78	0.63	0.469	0.49	-0.70	545	0.483	-0.06
	Undergraduate	310	3.81	0.61			-0.70		0.485	

continued on following page

Table 3. Continued

Variables	Characteristics	n	M	SD	Levene F	Levene p	t	df	p	Cohen's d
NGAAIS	Undergraduate	237	2.95	0.72	0.08	0.77	0.49	545	0.625	0.04
	Postgraduate	310	2.92	0.73			0.49		0.624	

Note. PGAAIS: positive general attitudes toward AI subscale; NGAAIS: negative general attitudes toward AI subscale; n: sample size; M: Mean; SE: standard error; df: Degree of freedom; SD: standard deviation; Cohen's d = Effect size; * p < .05.

The results of the independent samples t-test by gender, as presented in Table 3, indicated no significant difference in positive attitude scores between male (M = 3.81, SD = 0.64) and female (M = 3.78, SD = 0.57) school principals, t(545) = 0.55, p = .580, d = 0.05. Similarly, no significant difference was observed in negative attitude scores between males (M = 2.91, SD = 0.74) and females (M = 2.96, SD = 0.70), t(545) = –0.71, p = .479, d = –0.06. In both cases, the values of Cohen's d fall below the threshold for a small effect size (|d| < 0.20), indicating that gender has a negligible effect on principals' attitudes towards artificial intelligence (Cohen, 1988).

Additionally, Table 3 shows no statistically significant difference in positive attitude scores based on educational level, t(545) = –0.70, p > .05. Although principals with a postgraduate degree (M = 3.81, SD = 0.63) reported slightly higher positive attitude scores than those with an undergraduate degree (M = 3.78, SD = 0.61), this difference was not statistically significant. The effect size was also negligible (Cohen's d = –0.06), suggesting that educational attainment does not meaningfully influence principals' overall attitudes towards artificial intelligence. Similarly, no significant difference was found in school principals' negative attitude scores towards artificial intelligence based on educational level. Undergraduate degree holders (M = 2.95, SD = 0.72) and those with a postgraduate degree (M = 2.92, SD = 0.73) reported comparable levels of negative attitudes, t(545) = –0.11, p > .05. The effect size was also negligible (Cohen's d = 0.04). These findings suggest that school principals' attitudes towards artificial intelligence do not differ meaningfully according to their level of educational attainment.

We also examined whether school principals' attitudes towards artificial intelligence differed significantly according to school type. In this context, ANOVA test results were presented in Table 4.

Table 4. ANOVA Results for AI Attitudes and School Type

Variable	School Type	n	M	SD	SE	95% CI	F(p)	Effect Size (η^2, ε^2, ω^2)
PGAAIS	Preschool	53	3.87	0.51	0.07	3.73 – 4.01	F(4,542)=1.06, p=.374	η^2=.008, ε^2=.000, ω^2=.000
	Primary	166	3.77	0.63	0.05	3.67 – 3.86		
	Lower Secondary	154	3.83	0.61	0.05	3.74 – 3.93		
	Upper Secondary	152	3.75	0.64	0.05	3.64 – 3.85		
	Other	22	3.96	0.58	0.12	3.71 – 4.22		
NGAAIS	Preschool	53	3.0	0.82	0.11	2.78 – 3.23	F(4,542)=0.22, p=.929	η^2=.002, ε^2=-.006, ω^2=-.006
	Primary	166	2.94	0.71	0.05	2.83 – 3.05		
	Lower Secondary	154	2.93	0.75	0.06	2.81 – 3.05		
	Upper Secondary	152	2.91	0.66	0.05	2.80 – 3.01		
	Other	22	2.86	0.88	0.19	2.47 – 3.26		

Note. PGAAIS: positive general attitudes toward AI subscale; NGAAIS: negative general attitudes toward AI subscale; n: sample size; M: Mean; SE: standard error; SD: standard deviation; CI: confidence interval; * $p < .05$.

According to the ANOVA results demonstrated in Table 4, there were no statistically significant differences in positive attitude scores ($F(4, 542) = 1.06$, $p = .374$, $\eta^2 = .008$) or negative attitude scores ($F(4, 542) = 0.22$, $p = .929$, $\eta^2 = .002$) based on the school type were employed. The eta-squared values indicate small effect sizes ($\eta^2 < .01$), suggesting that any differences observed are negligible in practical terms. Furthermore, Scheffé post-hoc tests did not reveal any statistically significant pairwise differences between the groups. These findings indicate that the educational level of the school does not have a significant impact on principals' attitudes towards artificial intelligence.

We analysed whether school principals' attitudes towards artificial intelligence differed significantly according to school socio-economic status. In this context, ANOVA test results were presented in Table 5.

Table 5. ANOVA Results for AI Attitudes by School Socioeconomic Status

Variables	SES	n	M	SD	SE	95% CI	F(p)	Effect Size (η^2, ε^2, ω^2)
PGAAIS	Low	179	3.76	0.64	0.05	3.66 – 3.85	F(2,544)=2.84, p=.060	η^2=.010, ε^2=.007, ω^2=.007
	Medium	301	3.79	0.6	0.03	3.72 – 3.86		
	High	67	3.96	0.57	0.07	3.82 – 4.10		
NGAAIS	Low	179	2.94	0.75	0.06	2.83 – 3.05	F(2,544)=1.36, p=.258	η^2=.005, ε^2=.001, ω^2=.001
	Medium	301	2.96	0.71	0.04	2.87 – 3.04		
	High	67	2.79	0.71	0.09	2.62 – 2.97		

Note. PGAAIS: positive general attitudes toward AI subscale; NGAAIS: negative general attitudes toward AI subscale; SES: school socioeconomic status; n: sample size; M: Mean; SE: standard error; SD: standard deviation; CI: confidence interval; * $p < .05$.

ANOVA was conducted to examine whether school principals' attitude scores differed according to the socio-economic status (SES) of the schools in which they work. The results indicated no statistically significant differences in positive attitude scores across the groups ($F(2, 544) = 2.84$, $p = .060$, $\eta^2 = .010$). Although the mean positive attitude score for the high SES group ($M = 3.96$) was higher than that of the low SES group ($M = 3.76$), this difference was not statistically significant, as confirmed by the Scheffé post-hoc test ($p > .05$). The effect size for this comparison was small ($\eta^2 = .010$). Similarly, no significant differences were observed in negative attitude scores between the groups ($F(2, 544) = 1.36$, $p = .258$, $\eta^2 = .005$), indicating a negligible effect of socio-economic level on negative attitudes. These findings suggest that the socio-economic level of the school does not have a statistically or practically significant impact on principals' attitudes—either positive or negative—towards artificial intelligence. In summary, the socio-economic level variable appears to play a limited role in shaping school principals' attitudes.

We investigated correlations between school principals' attitudes towards artificial intelligence and some demographic variables. Table 6 presents the Pearson correlation analysis results.

Table 6. Pearson Correlations Results Between AI Attitudes and Some Demographic Variables

Variables	M	SD	Tsnrty	Psnrty	SCHS	PGAAIS	NGAAIS)
Tsnrty	22.13	8.39	—				
Psnrty	11.67	8.23	.639**	—			
SCHS	562.1	451.92	.136**	.077	—		
PGAAIS	3.8	0.61	-.048	-.041	-.021	—	
NGAAIS	2.93	0.73	.009	.010	-.047	-.248**	—

Note. PGAAIS: positive general attitudes toward AI subscale; NGAAIS: negative general attitudes toward AI subscale; Tsnrty: Experience in teaching; Psnrty: Experience in leading school; SCHS: School size; n: sample size; M: Mean; SE: standard error; SD: standard deviation; CI: confidence interval; ** p < .01.

Table 6 presents the correlation coefficients between school principals' experience in teaching (Tsnrty), experience in leading school (Psnrty), school size (Size), and school principals' positive (PGAAIS) and negative (NGAAIS) attitude scores towards artificial intelligence. The results indicate a strong, positive, and statistically significant correlation between teaching seniority and headship seniority ($r = .639$, $p < .01$), suggesting that principals with more teaching experience also tend to have greater leadership experience. A low but statistically significant positive correlation was also found between teaching seniority and school size ($r = .136$, $p < .01$). No other correlation coefficients reached statistical significance, indicating that variables such as seniority and school size are not meaningfully associated with principals' attitudes—positive or negative—towards artificial intelligence.

A statistically significant moderate negative correlation was found between school principals' positive and negative attitudes towards artificial intelligence ($r = -.248$, $p < .01$). This finding suggests that as principals' positive attitudes towards artificial intelligence increase, their negative attitudes tend to decrease. According to Cohen's (1988) classification, this effect size can be interpreted as small to moderate. Taken together, the overall findings indicate that variables such as seniority and school size do not have a significant impact on principals' attitudes towards artificial intelligence. However, there is a significant inverse relationship between positive and negative attitudes, as theoretically expected.

DISCUSSION

This study investigated the overall attitudes of school principals' AIA in Türkiye, as well as whether these attitudes varied according to certain demographic variables. The first research question posed was: "What is the general level of school principals' attitudes towards artificial intelligence in Türkiye?" The findings indicated that school principals generally exhibited a positive attitude towards AI. This outcome aligns with previous research in the field (i.e. Kaya et. al., 2024; Park & Woo, 2022). They also underlined that adults generally exhibited positive attitudes towards AI. The fact that scores reflecting positive attitudes were above the scale average suggests that principals are both receptive to and interested in the integration of AI within educational settings. Conversely, the relatively low scores for negative attitudes indicate that unfavourable perceptions of AI are limited. These results imply that school leaders are, to a large extent, open to embracing innovative technologies in the context of educational leadership and management. Another possible explanation for the generally positive attitudes of school principals in Türkiye towards artificial intelligence lies in the initiatives led by the MoNE aimed at integrating technology into the education system. Activities such as the FATİH Project, the Teachers' Information Network, the Education Information Network, and various national digital transformation strategy documents have played a significant role in familiarising school leaders with technological tools and practices. These state-led efforts may have helped to normalise the presence of AI and AI-based applications in education, thereby contributing to a sense of comfort and confidence among school principals. It can be argued that such exposure has fostered more positive attitudes and reduced uncertainty regarding the role of emerging technologies in school management and teaching practices. Moreover, recent studies have examined how school leaders are beginning to embed AI into their educational practices, as well as how their attitudes towards this emerging technology are evolving (Anysiadou & Gkliati, 2025; Arar et al., 2025; Erdoğan et al., 2025; Richardson et al., 2025). As highlighted in these studies, the use of AI by school principals, in areas such as student learning processes, teacher assessment and evaluation, effective classroom instruction, and their own leadership practices, has the potential to significantly enhance the quality of education and contribute to the development of more effective and future-ready schools. Indeed, Akçaba and colleagues (2024) demonstrated in their study that the more positive attitudes school principals develop towards artificial intelligence, the more their anxiety decreases, and the greater their willingness to integrate AI into education becomes.

These findings suggest that school principals demonstrate a willingness to utilise artificial intelligence in educational contexts. In this regard, it may be recommended that policymakers and senior decision-makers design concrete projects and professional development programmes aimed at enhancing principals' competencies in applying AI tools and practices. Such initiatives would not only strengthen their capacity to effectively integrate AI into school management but also contribute to fostering a more sustainable and innovative educational environment.

The second research question posed in the study was: "Do school principals' attitudes towards artificial intelligence differ significantly according to variables such as gender, educational level, school type, and the socio-economic status of the school?". The results of the analysis indicated that school principals' attitudes towards artificial intelligence did not differ significantly based on gender or level of education. This finding is consistent with existing research in the field (Erdoğan et al., 2025; Kaya et al., 2024). The findings suggest that the professional roles of individuals in leadership positions may exert a stronger influence on their attitudes than demographic variables such as gender or level of education. In other words, the responsibilities and expectations associated with being a school leader, particularly the need to adapt to technological developments, may outweigh the impact of individual demographic differences. This highlights the potential role of professional context in shaping openness to innovation and technological integration in educational leadership.

Similarly, the absence of significant differences in principals' attitudes towards artificial intelligence across different educational levels is also noteworthy. The fact that no meaningful variation was observed among school leaders working at different stages, from early childhood to upper secondary education, suggests that perceptions of AI, whether positive or negative, are more likely shaped by individual experience and general attitudes towards technology, rather than by the specific level of education in which they work. This finding indicates that school leaders, regardless of the educational stage they serve, tend to develop a common stance towards technology. It reflects a shared orientation towards innovation and technological integration that transcends the boundaries of educational level.

Another key finding of the study is that the socio-economic status of the school has a limited impact on school principals' attitudes towards artificial intelligence. Although principals working in schools with higher socio-economic status tended to have slightly higher positive attitude scores, this difference was not found to be statistically significant. This suggests that attitudes towards artificial intelligence may be more closely associated with individual and professional factors than with the socio-economic conditions of the school. It highlights the possibility that school leaders' openness to AI is shaped primarily by personal dispositions and professional responsibilities, rather than by the external context in which they work.

Diverging from this study, Zhang and Dafoe (2019) conducted a study with American people and they found that support for artificial intelligence is more prevalent among individuals who are male, possess higher levels of education and income, and exhibit strong engagement with technology. The primary reason for the discrepancy between the findings of these studies may lie in the differences in sampling. Had this study been conducted with the general Turkish population or had Zhang and Dafoe's study targeted school principals instead, the results would likely have aligned more closely. This is because school principals represent a more informed, change-oriented segment of society that actively engages with technological advancements. As such, demographic variables may play a less significant role in shaping their attitudes towards artificial intelligence. The efforts of school principals to integrate AI into education can be seen as part of their broader leadership role, which includes striving to enhance the quality of schooling and education. Their deeper involvement with technology, greater familiarity with AI, and the time they dedicate to its use may overshadow the influence of their demographic characteristics. Therefore, their leadership position and professional responsibilities might be more critical determinants of their perspectives on AI than typical demographic factors.

The final research question of this study was: "Is there a significant relationship between school principals' AIA, school size, and their years of experience in teaching and leading a school?" The correlation analyses revealed another noteworthy finding: as school principals' positive attitudes towards artificial intelligence increased, their negative attitudes decreased. This suggests that attitudes towards AI are structured in two distinct dimensions, yet these dimensions are inversely related. In other words, no significant relationships were found between attitudes and variables such as years of experience or school size. This implies that principals' perspectives on AI tend to develop independently of their professional seniority or the scale of their institution, pointing instead to the influence of individual differences as more decisive factors in shaping attitudes towards emerging technologies.

In general, the findings of this study indicate that school principals tend to exhibit a positive attitude towards artificial intelligence. However, this positive inclination appears to develop largely independently of demographic and institutional variables. This outcome provides important insights for policymakers and practitioners in the field of educational leadership. In particular, in order to ensure the effective integration of AI-based applications within educational institutions, it is crucial to support school leaders in maintaining and strengthening their positive attitudes. Furthermore, fostering these attitudes among principals may play a key role in influencing teachers and other stakeholders, thereby promoting a broader culture of technological openness and innovation within schools.

In this study, we collected data using a tool based on school principals' self-reported statements. While such self-reports may be susceptible to biases, including social desirability or concerns around privacy, Thomas's theorem provides a counterpoint by asserting that individuals' perceptions, even if subjective, are real in their consequences (McCall, 2013). From this standpoint, we contend that the data reflect personal viewpoints rather than socially influenced biases. Furthermore, it is vital to note that this research was conducted as a cross-sectional study, capturing data at a single point in time with respect to school principals' AIA. Future research may benefit from employing quasi-experimental or longitudinal designs, thereby offering more comprehensive and dynamic insights into this evolving field. Moreover, the scope of this study was limited with school principals working in state schools.

As such, it did not include participants from private educational institutions or the public. Future studies might consider incorporating these groups to provide a more holistic understanding of societal attitudes towards artificial intelligence.

ETHICAL CONSIDERATIONS

As the researchers of this study, we affirm that all procedures involving human participants were carried out in accordance with the ethical standards of the relevant institutional and/or national research committees, as well as the 1964 Helsinki Declaration and its later amendments or comparable ethical guidelines. Ethical approval for the study was granted by the Ethics Committee of Çankırı Karatekin University (Decision No: 57, dated 23 July 2025). Furthermore, authorisation to conduct the research in state schools was obtained from the Ministry of National Education (Reference No: MEB.TT.2025.028437.02 dated 16 September 2025). We also declare that we used artificial intelligence-supported applications, including ChatGPT and DeepL, to assist in translating expressions from Turkish into English during the writing of the research paper. Firstly, we translated the Turkish text into English using DeepL's academic translation setting. Then, we sought to enhance the academic tone and fluency of the output by requesting ChatGPT to rewrite the text in British English, employing a fluent and scholarly style.

REFERENCES

Ajzen, I. (1991). The theory of planned behavior. *Organizational Behavior and Human Decision Processes*, *50*(2), 179–211. DOI: 10.1016/0749-5978(91)90020-T

Ajzen, I., & Fishbein, M. (2000). Attitudes and the attitude–behavior relation: Reasoned and automatic processes. *European Review of Social Psychology*, *11*(1), 1–33. DOI: 10.1080/14792779943000116

Akçaba, P., Toklu, D. A., & Akcil, U. (2024). Examining the attitudes and anxiety of teachers and administrators towards artificial intelligence: Relational browsing. *BRAIN. Broad Research in Artificial Intelligence and Neuroscience*, *15*(4), 325–337. DOI: 10.70594/brain/15.4/22

Anysiadou, M., & Gkliati, A. (2025). An experimental analysis of Greek school leaders' readiness for AI integration. *Leadership and Policy in Schools*, *24*(1), 155–177.

Arar, K., Tlili, A., Schunka, L., Salha, S., & Saiti, A. (2025). Reimagining educational leadership and management through artificial intelligence: An integrative systematic review. *Leadership and Policy in Schools*, *24*(1), 4–26. DOI: 10.1080/15700763.2025.2451982

Atasoy, R. (2023). Sustainability of the School leadership in the digital era under the shadow of crisis. In Al-A'ali, E., & Masmoudi, M. (Eds.), *Leadership and Workplace Culture in the Digital Era* (pp. 149–168). IGI Global.

Atasoy, R. (2024). Eğitimde mükemmellik arayışı ve yapay zekâ. [The pursuit of excellence in education and artificial intelligence]. R. Atasoy, Ö. Çoban, M. T. Yalçın (Eds.). *Eğitimde mükemmellik haritası: Liderlik, beceriler ve başarı. [The map to excellence in education: Leadership, skills and success]* (pp. 107-136). Eğitim.

Atasoy, R. (2025). Artificial Intelligence in Education and Changing Teacher Roles. In *Holistic Approaches to Teacher Development: Leadership, Pedagogical Practices, and Cognitive Insights* (pp. 25-46). IGI Global. DOI: 10.4018/979-8-3373-0472-4.ch002

Berendt, B., Littlejohn, A., & Blakemore, M. (2020). AI in education: Learner choice and fundamental rights. *Learning, Media and Technology*, *45*(3), 312–324. DOI: 10.1080/17439884.2020.1786399

Bertolin, M., & Da Rin, D. (2020). Chatbots for K-12 education: A review of recent advances, opportunities and challenges. *Education Sciences*, *10*(7), 181–191.

Breckler, S. J. (1984). Empirical validation of affect, behavior, and cognition as distinct components of attitude. *Journal of Personality and Social Psychology, 47*(6), 1191–1205. DOI: 10.1037/0022-3514.47.6.1191 PMID: 6527214

Bush, T. (2017). The enduring power of transformational leadership. *Educational Management Administration & Leadership, 45*(4), 563–565. DOI: 10.1177/1741143217701827

Büyüköztürk, Ş., Çakmak, E. K., Akgün, Ö. E., Karadeniz, Ş., & Demirel, F. (2019). *Eğitimde bilimsel araştırma yöntemleri [Scientific research methods in education].* (27. baskı). Pegem Akademi.

Cascio, W. F., & Montealegre, R. (2016). How technology is changing work and organizations. *Annual Review of Organizational Psychology and Organizational Behavior, 3*(1), 349–375. DOI: 10.1146/annurev-orgpsych-041015-062352

Chiu, T. K., Xia, Q., Zhou, X., Chai, C. S., & Cheng, M. (2023). Systematic literature review on opportunities. challenges. and future research recommendations of artificial intelligence in education. *Computers and Education: Artificial Intelligence, 4*, 100–118. DOI: 10.1016/j.caeai.2022.100118

Çoban, Ö., & Durnalı, M. (2025). Teacher leadership and Al literacy: An analysis of teachers' Al literacy levels. M. T. Yalçın, A. Uslukaya, B. Demirdiş (Eds.) In *Holistic Approaches to Teacher Development: Leadership, Pedagogical Practices, and Cognitive Insights: Leadership, Pedagogical Practices, and Cognitive Insights*. (pp. 1-24). IGI Global.

Çoban, Ö., & Gün, F. (2024). Eğitimde mükemmelliğe giden yolda öğretmen liderliği. [Teacher leadership on the path to excellence in education] In Atasoy, R., Çoban, Ö., & Yalçın, M. T. (Eds.), *Eğitimde mükemmellik haritası: Liderlik, beceriler ve başarı* [The map to excellence in education: Leadership, skills and success]. (pp. 51–73). Eğitim.

Cohen, J. (1988). *Statistical power analysis for the behavioral sciences* (2nd ed.). Lawrence Erlbaum Associates.

Darko, A., Chan, A. P., Adabre, M. A., Edwards, D. J., Hosseini, M. R., & Ameyaw, E. E. (2020). Artificial intelligence in the AEC industry: Scientometric analysis and visualization of research activities. *Automation in Construction, 112*, 103081. DOI: 10.1016/j.autcon.2020.103081

Dawson, K. P. (1992). Attitude and assessment in nursing education. *Journal of Advanced Nursing, 17*(4), 473–479. DOI: 10.1111/j.1365-2648.1992.tb01932.x PMID: 1578070

Deci, E. L., & Ryan, R. M. (2000). The "what" and "why" of goal pursuits: Human needs and the self-determination of behavior. *Psychological Inquiry, 11*(4), 227–268. DOI: 10.1207/S15327965PLI1104_01

Durnalı, M., & Çoban, Ö. (2025). Artificial intelligence in higher education management: Innovations. opportunities and challenges. In González Lezcano, R. A., & Orakçı, Ş. (Eds.), *Innovation trends and educational technology in higher education* (pp. 501–516). Information Age.

Erdoğan, O., Kaymak, M. N., Çoban, Ö., & Bora, H. T. (2025). Exploring the links between school principals' self-efficacy, open innovation mindset, transformational leadership, and artificial intelligence (AI) attitudes in Türkiye. *Educational Management Administration & Leadership, 0*(0), 17411432251351830. Advance online publication. DOI: 10.1177/17411432251351830

Gansser, O. A., & Reich, C. S. (2021). A new acceptance model for artificial intelligence with extensions to UTAUT2: An empirical study in three segments of application. *Technology in Society, 65*, 101535. DOI: 10.1016/j.techsoc.2021.101535

George, B., & Wooden, O. (2023). Managing the strategic transformation of higher education through artificial intelligence. *Administrative Sciences, 13*(9), 196. DOI: 10.3390/admsci13090196

Ghamrawi, N., Shal, T., & Ghamrawi, N. A. (2024). Exploring the impact of AI on teacher leadership: Regressing or expanding? *Education and Information Technologies, 29*(7), 8415–8433. DOI: 10.1007/s10639-023-12174-w

Gondal, K. M. (2018). Artificial intelligence and educational leadership. *King Edward Medicine University Annuals, 24*(4), 1–2.

Grace, E., Vidhyavathi, P., & Kumar, S. (2023). AI in education: Opportunities and challenges. *Industrial Engineering Journal, 52*(5), 750–759. DOI: 10.36893/IEJ.2023.V52I05.750-759

Guan, C., Mou, J., & Jiang, Z. (2020). Artificial intelligence innovation in education: A twenty-year data-driven historical analysis. *International Journal of Innovation Studies, 4*(4), 134–147. DOI: 10.1016/j.ijis.2020.09.001

Hair, J. F., Black, W. C., Babin, B. J., Anderson, R. E., & Tatham, R. L. (2006). *Multivariate data analysis* (6th ed.). Pearson Prentice Hall.

Hamzah, M., Juraime, F., Hamid, A., Nordin, N., & Attan, N. (2014). Technology leadership and its relationship with school-Malaysia standard of education quality (School-MSEQ). *International Education Studies, 7*(13), 278–285. DOI: 10.5539/ies.v7n13p278

Hu, L., & Bentler, P. M. (1999). Cutoff criteria for fit indexes in covariance structure analysis: Conventional criteria versus new alternatives. *Structural Equation Modeling*, *6*(1), 1–55. DOI: 10.1080/10705519909540118

Huang, M. H., & Rust, R. T. (2018). Artificial intelligence in service. *Journal of Service Research*, *21*(2), 155–172. DOI: 10.1177/1094670517752459

Hwang, G. J., Xie, H., Wah, B. W., & Gašević, D. (2020). Vision, challenges, roles, and research issues of artificial intelligence in education. *Computers and Education: Artificial Intelligence, 1,* 100001. International Society of Technology in Education (ISTE) (n.d). *ISTE standards for education leaders*. available at: https://www.iste.org/standards/for-education-leaders (accessed 10 September 2025).

Kaya, F., Aydin, F., Schepman, A., Rodway, P., Yetişensoy, O., & Demir Kaya, M. (2024). The roles of personality traits, AI anxiety, and demographic factors in attitudes toward artificial intelligence. *International Journal of Human-Computer Interaction*, *40*(2), 497–514. DOI: 10.1080/10447318.2022.2151730

Kılınç, A. Ç., Er, E., & Beycioglu, K. (2021). Mapping the terrain of training and appointment of educational leaders in the Turkish context: An historical perspective. In Samier, E., El Kaleh, E. and Hammad, W. (Eds). *Internationalisation of Educational Administration and Leadership Curriculum.* (pp. 139–157). Emerald.

Kline, R. B. (2005). *Methodology in the Social Sciences: Principles and practice of structural equation modelling*. Guilford.

Komalavalli, K., Hemalatha, R., & Dhanalakshmi, S. (2020). A survey of artificial intelligence in smart phones and its applications among the students of higher education in and around Chennai City. *Shanlax International Journal of Education*, *8*(3), 89–95. DOI: 10.34293/education.v8i3.2379

Krejcie, R. V., & Morgan, D. W. (1970). Determining Sample Size for Research Activities. *Educational and Psychological Measurement*, *30*(3), 607–610. DOI: 10.1177/001316447003000308

Leithwood, K., Harris, A., & Hopkins, D. (2020). Seven strong claims about successful school leadership revisited. *School Leadership & Management*, *40*(1), 5–22. DOI: 10.1080/13632434.2019.1596077

Levin, J. A., Fox, J. A., & Forde, D. R. (2010). *Elementary statistics in social research*. Allyn & Bacon Pearson.

Liang, Y., & Lee, S. A. (2017). Fear of autonomous robots and artificial intelligence: Evidence from national representative data with probability sampling. *International Journal of Social Robotics*, *9*(3), 379–384. DOI: 10.1007/s12369-017-0401-3

McCall, G. J. (2013). Interactionist perspectives in social psychology. In DeLamater, J., & Ward, A. (Eds.), *Handbook of Social Psychology: Handbooks of Sociology and Social Research* (pp. 3–29). Springer. DOI: 10.1007/978-94-007-6772-0_1

Ministry of National Education [MoNE]. (2024a). Maarif Model. Available at: https://tymm.meb.gov.tr/ (accessed 04 August 2025).

Ministry of National Education [MoNE]. (2024b). 2024–2028 Ministry of National Education strategic plan 2024–2028. Available at: https://sgb.meb.gov.tr/yayinlarimiz/yayin/112. (accessed 04 August 2025).

Müller, V. C. (2016). *Risks of artificial intelligence*. Chapman & Hall. DOI: 10.1201/b19187

Öztemel, E. (2018). Eğitimde yeni yönelimlerin değerlendirilmesi ve Eğitim 4.0 [Evaluating new trends in education and Education 4.0]. *Journal of University Research, 1*(1), 25–30. DOI: 10.32329/uad.382041

Park, J., & Woo, S. E. (2022). Who likes artificial intelligence? Personality predictors of attitudes toward artificial intelligence. *The Journal of Psychology, 156*(1), 68–94. DOI: 10.1080/00223980.2021.2012109 PMID: 35015615

Pereira, V., Hadjielias, E., Christofi, M., & Vrontis, D. (2023). A systematic literature review on the impact of artificial intelligence on workplace outcomes: A multi-process perspective. *Human Resource Management Review, 33*(1), 100857. DOI: 10.1016/j.hrmr.2021.100857

Pimentel, J. L. (2019). Some biases in Likert scaling usage and its correction. [IJSBAR]. *International Journal of Sciences, Basic and Applied Research, 45*(1), 183–191.

Ramnarain, U., Ogegbo, A. A., Penn, M., Ojetunde, S., & Mdlalose, N. (2024). Pre-service science teachers' intention to use generative artificial intelligence in inquiry-based teaching. *Journal of Science Education and Technology*, 1–14. DOI: 10.1007/s10956-024-10159-z

Richardson, J. W., McLeod, S., & Sauers, S. N. J. (2015). Technology leadership is just good leadership: Dispositions of tech savvy superintendents. *AASA Journal of Scholarship and Practice, 12*(1), 11–30.

Richardson, J. W., Vedder, B. C., Roberts, A. B., & McLeod, S. (2025). What's the chatter about AI and school leaders? *Leadership and Policy in Schools, 24*(1), 103–116.

Santamaria, T., & Nathan-Roberts, D. (2017). Personality measurement and design in human-robot interaction: A systematic and critical review. *Proceedings of the Human Factors and Ergonomics Society Annual Meeting, 61*(1), 853–857. DOI: 10.1177/1541931213601686

Schepman, A., & Rodway, P. (2023). The general attitudes towards artificial intelligence scale (GAAIS): Confirmatory validation and associations with personality, corporate distrust, and general trust. *International Journal of Human-Computer Interaction, 39*(13), 2724–2741. DOI: 10.1080/10447318.2022.2085400

Şenocak, D. (2020). Açık ve uzaktan öğrenme ortamlarında yapay zekâ: Sunduğu fırsatlar ve yarattığı endişeler [Artificial intelligence in open and distance learning environments: Opportunities and concerns]. *Açıköğretim Uygulamaları ve Araştırmaları Dergisi, 6*(3), 56–78.

Shank, D. B., Graves, C., Gott, A., Gamez, P., & Rodriguez, S. (2019). Feeling our way to machine minds: People's emotions when perceiving minds in artificial intelligence. *Computers in Human Behavior, 98*, 256–266. DOI: 10.1016/j.chb.2019.04.001

Shen, J., Wu, H., Reeves, P., Zheng, Y., Ryan, L., & Anderson, D. (2020). The association between teacher leadership and student achievement: A meta-analysis. *Educational Research Review, 31*(100357), 1–19. DOI: 10.1016/j.edurev.2020.100357

Shwedeh, F. (2024). The integration of Artificial Intelligence into decision support systems within higher education institutions. *Nanotechnology Perceptions, 20*(5), 331–357.

Stein, J. P., Liebold, B., & Ohler, P. (2019). Stay back, clever thing! Linking situational control and human uniqueness concerns to the aversion against autonomous technology. *Computers in Human Behavior, 95*, 73–82. DOI: 10.1016/j.chb.2019.01.021

Temel, Y., & Coşkun, B. (2024). A review on artificial intelligence applications in education in some countries and Türkiye. *International Technology and Education Journal, 8*(1), 9–23.

Tsai, S. C., Chen, C. H., Shiao, Y. T., Ciou, J. S., & Wu, T. N. (2020). Precision education with statistical learning and deep learning: A case study in Taiwan. *International Journal of Educational Technology in Higher Education, 17*(1), 1–13. DOI: 10.1186/s41239-020-00186-2

Turkish Official Gazette. (2021, August 20). *Presidential circular numbered 2021/18* (No. 31574). https://www.resmigazete.gov.tr (Accessed August 12, 2025)

Tyson, M. M., & Sauers, N. J. (2021). School leaders' adoption and implementation of artificial intelligence. *Journal of Educational Administration*, *59*(3), 271–285. DOI: 10.1108/JEA-10-2020-0221

Viberg, O., Kizilcec, R. F., Wise, A. F., Jivet, I., & Nixon, N. (2024). Advancing equity and inclusion in educational practices with AI-powered educational decision support systems. [Editorial]. *British Journal of Educational Technology*, *55*(5), 1974–1981. DOI: 10.1111/bjet.13507

Wang, B., Rau, P. L. P., & Yuan, T. (2023). Measuring user competence in using artificial intelligence: Validity and reliability of artificial intelligence literacy scale. *Behaviour & Information Technology*, *42*(9), 1324–1337. DOI: 10.1080/0144929X.2022.2072768

Zhang, B., & Dafoe, A. (2019). *Artificial intelligence: American attitudes and trends*. University of Oxford. Available at *SSRN* 3312874.

Chapter 10
In the Age of AI: Effective Teaching and Learning Strategies for Students With SEND Involve Collaboration and Interactive Strategies

Abdullah Çiftçi
https://orcid.org/0000-0002-4554-4752
Akdeniz University, Turkey

ABSTRACT

This chapter examines how the rise of artificial intelligence (AI) is reshaping inclusive pedagogy for students with Special Educational Needs and Disabilities (SEND) by transforming classroom practice, collaboration, behaviour support, and ideas of effectiveness. The chapter argues that effective teaching in AI-mediated classrooms depends on the alignment of pedagogy, assessment, classroom organisation, and social relationships, rather than on technology alone. Drawing on critical perspectives, the chapter explores how AI can offer adaptive feedback, scaffolding, metacognitive support, multimodal access, and opportunities for collaborative learning, while also introducing risks such as surveillance, distraction, and the neoliberal reduction of learning to performance metrics. By engaging with concepts such as self-regulation, differentiation, affordances, Vygotsky's Zone of Proximal Development, and the politics of datafication, the chapter proposes that AI should augment relational, dialogic, and ethical teaching rather than replace it.

DOI: 10.4018/979-8-3373-6375-2.ch010

INTRODUCTION

The emergence of artificial intelligence (AI) in education is reshaping long-standing assumptions about pedagogy, institutions, and the role of teachers. In this shifting landscape, the question of how best to support students with Special Educational Needs and Disabilities (SEND) has become increasingly urgent. Effective teaching and learning are no longer reducible to the transmission of knowledge; they require an inclusive pedagogy that aligns curriculum, assessment, classroom practice, and technological tools to meet the diverse needs of learners. AI powered tools can enable personalised feedback, adaptive questioning, and flexible forms of participation, but it can create new ways of understanding towards praxis and involvement of SEND (Melo-Lopez, et al., 2025). It is a tool of relational and interactive strategies, so it needs to be used as a part of teacher-guided strategies.

Effective teaching is produced through collaboration between teacher expertise, subject knowledge, pedagogy, assessment, and the social dynamics of the classroom (Muijs & Reynolds, 2017). In the age of AI, these elements must be reconceptualised in light of new opportunities and risks. Theories of learning and intelligence continue to shape how teachers understand their students, but interactive pedagogies and collaborative activities remain central to meaning-making and reflexive thinking. For Students with SEND in particular, such strategies allow knowledge construction to emerge from dialogue and participation rather than passive instruction. AI systems generally gamify the learning and employ passive instruction because these are more predictable and amendable strategies. However, it can also employ interactive strategies by creating adaptive prompts, facilitating personalised dialogue, and scaffolding reflection (Strielkowski et al., 2025). AI's role must be framed within inclusive pedagogical principles rather than technological determinism.

Constructivist perspectives highlight that effective teaching requires the creation of learning conditions that address the multifaceted realities of classrooms, where diversity and difference are welcomed and embodied. Engagement in learning activities, strong teacher–student relationships, communication, and collaboration remain the foundation of achievement. In this way, reflexive thinking and educational success are the product of synergy when it is embodied by the more knowledgeable other in the instructive environments. Inclusive pedagogy, interactive strategies, and the critical, context-sensitive integration of AI will be the discussion of the future for an enhanced support for individuals of all background.

Collaborative teaching and learning strategies are key to effectiveness of modern education. By enhancing interaction between students, teachers foster positive learning environments where knowledge is co-constructed, and students learn not only from teachers but also from each other. In the context of AI-mediated education, collaboration acquires new possibilities: adaptive platforms can be used to personalise access, support self-regulation, and enable students to take greater ownership of their learning (Strielkowski et al., 2025). Such strategies are particularly important for students with SEND, including those with challenging behaviours, for whom self-regulation and peer learning provide opportunities to develop resilience, social skills, and academic competence.

Metacognition plays a key role in this process. Encouraging students to reflect on their learning strategies, regulate their own behaviour, and engage critically with tasks is essential to inclusive pedagogy. AI can support this by providing feedback loops that prompt reflection, track progress, and scaffold self-regulation, yet the design of such interventions must remain sensitive to individual needs (Liang et al., 2024). Small-group collaboration is especially effective when carefully structured, prepared, and supported by teachers. It requires clear goals, equal opportunities for participation, and the cultivation of skills such as listening, communication, and shared responsibility.

The beliefs, values, and knowledge of teachers significantly influence the success of these collaborative strategies (Woodcock et al., 2022). Teachers' attitudes toward their students, their subject expertise, and their approach to SEND directly affect learners' achievement. Effective classroom structures and management strategies are equally crucial, especially in inclusive environments that involve students with autism, attention deficit and hyperactivity disorder (ADHD), or emotional and behavioural difficulties (EBD). Positive behaviour management depends on making classroom expectations transparent, amplifying students' voices, and supporting their wellbeing, self-concept, and resilience. AI tools may enhance these processes by monitoring group participation or providing tailored prompts, but they cannot replace the relational expertise of teachers in creating safe, inclusive, and dialogic spaces for learning (Navas-Bonilla et al., 2025).

Effective teaching arises from the interaction of pedagogy, classroom practice, and the provision of targeted support. For students with SEND, feedback and additional scaffolding are especially critical to ensure continuity of learning beyond the classroom (Kaldaras et al., 2024). Without such support, students may feel overwhelmed, and it will lead to frustration and negative attitudes toward schooling (Nunez et al., 2024). Supporting students through collaboration and AI-powered strategies can improve time management, responsibility, goal setting, and self-reflection so that students are empowered and independent. These executive functioning skills often present challenges for students with SEND and those with behavioural difficulties, necessitating adapted strategies that balance academic expectations with sensitivity to learners' conditions.

The development of these self-regulatory skills contributes to both achievement and wellbeing. AI systems can provide timely feedback, personalised reminders, and adaptive scaffolds that help students plan, manage distractions, and reflect on their progress (Strielkowski et al., 2025). However, such technologies should be positioned as complements to the teacher's relational expertise, not as substitutes. Teachers remain central in providing encouragement, maintaining realistic expectations, and ensuring that digital interventions align with inclusive pedagogical goals.

Yet, developing self-regulatory skills in the age of AI is increasingly complex because the very technologies students rely on for learning are embedded within wider digital ecosystems designed to capture and hold attention . Algorithms underpinning social media platforms, gaming environments, and even some educational apps are optimised to maximise engagement, often by exploiting psychological triggers such as instant rewards, personalised feeds, and notifications. Instead of fostering autonomy, these systems risk undermining students' capacity for sustained focus and reflective learning, making it harder for them to regulate their time and behaviour (Swist et al., 2023). For students with SEND, who may already face challenges in self-regulation, the persuasive design of algorithmic environments can further intensify difficulties, drawing them away from purposeful tasks and into cycles of distraction. This paradox highlights the need for educators to critically mediate AI integration because while adaptive systems can scaffold learning, teachers must also help students build digital resilience, critical awareness, and strategies to resist the manipulative logics of algorithmic technologies.

PRACTICAL IMPLICATIONS OF AI

As discussed throughout this chapter, technology must be understood not merely as a set of tools but as a constellation of opportunities for practice or affordances that mediate and reshape human action (Clark, 2023). The concept of affordance captures how a technological artefact invites or constrains certain possibilities for use, depending on its inherent properties and the user's perception of those properties (Bower, 2017; Costa et al., 2019). Mobile devices like tablets, for instance, afford usability, portability, and multimodal expression, enabling students to interact with content through touch and sound rather than solely through speech or writing (Chelkowski et al., 2019).

Technologies like AI possess intrinsic, universal effects. This view reduces the complexity of human–technology relations, suggesting that behaviour is the predictable consequence of technological properties (Knox et al., 2020). A contrasting social-constructivist stance places human agency and interpretation at the centre, recognising that technology is always appropriated differently across contexts and cultures. The affordances of AI-powered tools such as adaptive feedback, emotional recognition, or behaviour tracking, are not static features (Fitas, 2025). All affordances emerge through interaction between users, institutions, and broader socio-political structures. In SEND education, this means that the perceived benefits of AI (e.g., personalised scaffolding, speech-to-text tools, predictive analytics) must be interpreted through the lived realities of teachers, students and families, whose values, skills, and power relations determine how technologies are used.

The social dimension of technology challenges the notion that AI is ever neutral. Technologies are cultural artefacts, deeply embedded in political and economic agendas (Madaio et al., 2022). Their affordances are not only technical but ideological, reflecting the logic of efficiency, productivity, and surveillance that underpins contemporary neoliberal education systems (Ball & Grimaldi, 2022). What appears as inclusion and accessibility for students with SEND can simultaneously become a mechanism for behavioural monitoring and social control. Thus, understanding the affordances of AI requires acknowledging the subtle ways in which they naturalise power relations, turning learning into a form of algorithmic governance (Grimaldi & Ball, 2021).

From a pedagogical perspective, the appropriation of technology involves making it visible as a learning instrument while rendering its mediating role invisible. Effective appropriation means that the tool becomes seamlessly integrated into the learning experience, enabling students to engage meaningfully without perceiving the technology as an external intervention. In contemporary classrooms, AI-enhanced devices are becoming so ubiquitous that they blend into the background of learning itself (Knox et al., 2020). Yet this very invisibility demands vigilance because when technology becomes embedded and natural, its shaping influence on cognition, attention, and social interaction can easily go unexamined.

In this sense, the affordance of AI is relational rather than intrinsic. Following a relational interpretation, affordances emerge from the interaction between users, technologies, and their contexts (Swist & Gulson, 2023). The same AI tool may enable autonomy in one setting and dependence in another, depending on pedagogical intent and institutional conditions. For students with SEND, this relationality is crucial: a tablet may afford freedom of expression for one learner while reinforcing passivity for another if used in a purely behaviourist way. AI-based learning analytics, too, can either support differentiated instruction or impose rigid expectations by categorising learners through data profiles (Khalil et al., 2024). The ethical framing, the classroom culture, and the teacher's interpretive stance determines whether AI fosters empowerment or conformity. In classrooms, students treat educational software as a game, applying playful rules to learning activities. For students with behavioural difficulties, this playful appropriation can either enhance engagement or distract from learning, depending on how the teacher orchestrates the activity.

Crucially, educational technology is not a passive mediator but an active participant in the learning ecosystem. The affordances of AI extend beyond functionality to include behavioural and affective dimensions. Features such as multimodality, interactivity, and mobility alter not only how students learn but how they attend, interact with, and relate to others (Xu & Li, 2024). AI intensifies this transformation by incorporating predictive and responsive capacities by anticipating behaviour, offering feedback, and shaping engagement patterns (Knox et al., 2020). These affordances can enhance inclusion and accessibility, but they can also narrow the scope of human judgment by steering attention toward what is measurable and optimisable.

Furthermore, AI's power of connectivity and visibility in the digital sphere extend classroom behaviour into online environments (Xu & Li, 2024). Social networking platforms, educational apps, and gamified systems enable students to create, share, and evaluate content rapidly (Cukurova, 2025). The engaging features such as competition, comparison, distraction are now amplified excessively by the algorithmic architectures of AI systems, but it can privilege engagement over reflection (Mallik & Gangopadhyay, 2023). Teachers and SEND specialists must therefore cultivate critical digital resilience among students, helping them to navigate attention economies and resist the manipulative logics of algorithmic design.

The affordances of AI in education cannot be reduced to lists of features or capabilities. They represent the evolving intersection of technical design, human intention, and institutional power (Cukurova, 2025). To use technology effectively for SEND education, practitioners must look beyond the surface of devices to the social, ethical, and behavioural relationships they produce. Affordances become meaningful only when aligned with pedagogical values that prioritise inclusion, autonomy, and human flourishing (Xu & Li, 2024). The true challenge of integrating AI into education lies not in exploiting its functions but in reimagining the conditions of learning it affords.

PERFORMANCE IN THE AGE OF AI

Educational performance is not determined solely by cognitive outcomes but is deeply interwoven with students' social skills, wellbeing, and self-concept (Knox et al., 2020). Communication, relationships, and resilience shape the capacity to engage positively with learning. Teachers, therefore, needs to design practices that support psychological wellbeing alongside academic attainment. Each learner benefits differently from pedagogical strategies; thus, differentiation and the inclusion of students with SEND are non-negotiable components of effective teaching.

Core subjects such as literacy and mathematics remain foundational to broader achievement, and here too AI and digital technologies offer opportunities to diversify assessment (Lee et al., 2025). Multimodal and adaptive assessments can respond to different needs, making evaluation more inclusive and constructive. When thoughtfully employed, AI-based assessment systems can move beyond standardisation, enabling teachers to capture diverse demonstrations of learning and provide feedback that supports growth (Furze et al., 2024). Yet the effectiveness of such systems ultimately depends on how they are embedded within an inclusive pedagogy. How teachers position AI will determine whether their inclusive practice recognises difference, amplifies student voice, and places collaboration and interaction at the heart of learning or they are using only behaviourist strategies that only makes people reactionary to their environment (Fitas, 2025).

There are certain essential factors that underpin effective inclusive practices (Hakel & Magin, 2024). For example, the structure of lessons strongly influences outcomes, particularly for students who rely on adapted resources and differentiated support. Class size also affects effectiveness, since smaller groups can offer more opportunities for personalised interaction and the development of academic and social skills over time. Equally, the professional development and attitudes of teachers are crucial. Teachers who continuously update their pedagogical knowledge are better able to respond to the evolving challenges of inclusive education. Professional development may include engaging with new approaches in AI-supported teaching, but it must be critically framed (Tan et al., 2025). While AI offers possibilities for adaptive feedback, multimodal instruction, and personalised learning pathways, research warns against an uncritical embrace of such tools (Song et al., 2024).

Classroom management also remains a significant aspect of effective teaching, particularly in supporting students with behavioural difficulties. Digital platforms are increasingly marketed as offering predictive analytics to identify disruptive behaviour or recommend interventions. For example, AI-powered classroom management tools can track engagement, monitor behaviour, and even flag students "at risk" of disengagement (Holmes, 2023). Yet such systems raise serious concerns: they risk pathologising students with SEND by framing difference as deficit, and they intensify a culture of surveillance aligned with neoliberal accountability regimes (Foley & Melese, 2025).

In this model, behaviour is reinterpreted through data metrics, positioning both students and teachers within systems of constant monitoring and comparison (Fütterer et al., 2025). Instead of empowering learners, such tools can inadvertently reinforce exclusion by narrowing the scope of acceptable behaviour to what the system can quantify. Critical inclusive pedagogy therefore demands that teachers and schools mediate AI use carefully by balancing the affordances of real-time feedback and behavioural insights with the need to enhance agency, independence and voice of all students, particularly for learners with SEND (Swist et al., 2023).

EFFECTIVENESS AND NEW TOOLS OF PEDAGOGY

Williamson and Hogan (2020), for instance, argue that AI-driven personalization can embed a neoliberal "performance economy," where learning is reduced to measurable outputs and teacher professionalism is subordinated to algorithmic decision-making. Thus, professional development must prepare teachers to resist purely data-driven approaches and instead employ AI critically, as a tool for fostering equity, creativity, and inclusion.

The concept of effectiveness has long occupied a central place in educational discourse, often presented as an objective and desirable goal. Policies, professional development schemes, and technological innovations are justified on the grounds that they increase effectiveness during teaching, classroom management, or measuring students' learning (Promsiri, 2025). However, the meaning of effectiveness is far from stable because in neoliberal education systems, effectiveness is increasingly equated with efficiency, productivity, and measurable outcomes. Here, data-driven metrics and algorithmic assessments determine what counts as success, narrowing the scope of teaching to what can be quantified and evaluated.

Bauman's (2005, 2013) theory of liquid modernity offers a critical lens to understand this transformation. In liquid modern societies, social forms and values dissolve before they can solidify, and the meanings attached to concepts such as effectiveness are continually redefined by shifting economic and technological priorities. Within education, AI accelerates this by continuously reshaping what is considered "effective." New adaptive platforms, automated assessments, and behaviour-monitoring systems promise optimisation, but in doing so they destabilise teachers' professional authority and reframe pedagogy through the language of efficiency. Effectiveness, in this sense, becomes less about nurturing human growth and inclusion, and more about aligning behaviour and performance with algorithmic standards (Hogan, 2025).

This has profound implications for inclusive pedagogy, particularly in the context of SEND. The push for effectiveness risks marginalising students who do not fit algorithmic norms, framing difference as inefficiency or deficit (Ball & Grimaldi, 2022). AI systems marketed as "solutions" to behavioural challenges or academic underperformance may inadvertently reinforce exclusionary practices, pathologising and symptomizing the differences instead of valuing diversity (Foley & Melese, 2025). In this way, effectiveness, when understood narrowly through neoliberal and technological logics, undermines the very goals of inclusive education.

A critical rethinking is therefore required. Rather than equating effectiveness with optimisation or quantification, inclusive pedagogy must reclaim it as a relational practice rooted in dialogue, dignity, and equity. Effectiveness in the age of AI should not be measured solely by standardised outcomes, but by the capacity of education to create conditions in which all learners can flourish as agents within their learning communities (Daher, 2025).

THE ASPECTS OF EFFECTIVE TEACHING

Inquiry-based learning has long been advocated as an effective teaching style for developing problem-solving, critical thinking, and metacognitive skills (Areepattamannil et al., 2020). When inquiries are linked to real-life problems, they offer students opportunities to acquire higher-order competences and engage with learning in authentic contexts. Teacher-led approaches and direct instruction can produce stronger measurable outcomes because they allow greater control of learning activities (de Jong et al., 2023). For many teachers, particularly in classrooms that include students with SEND or challenging behaviours, inquiry-based strategies are perceived as difficult to manage. The unpredictability of student-led exploration can create anxieties around maintaining order, leading teachers to avoid methods that could nevertheless foster construction of knowledge and independent learning.

In the age of AI, this debate is intensified. On one hand, AI-powered tools are increasingly marketed as supports for inquiry-based pedagogy, offering scaffolds such as adaptive questioning, real-time feedback, and personalised guidance to help learners sustain open-ended exploration (Liang et al., 2024). Yet, these same systems are often aligned with neoliberal logics of performance, where inquiry is reframed not as a dialogic process of discovery but as a means to generate measurable outputs and optimise learner performance for accountability systems (Williamson, 2024). In this sense, the pedagogical choice between inquiry and direct instruction is not simply about effectiveness, but about how teaching is restructured by algorithmic systems that privilege efficiency and quantification.

There is a danger that pedagogical practices are constantly destabilised by shifting technological affordances and policy demands. Inquiry-based learning, once celebrated as innovative, risks being reduced to another metric-driven tool when mediated by AI, its educational value defined by dashboards and analytics rather than human growth and reflexivity (Saltman, 2020). At the same time, direct instruction can also be reshaped through AI platforms that standardise delivery, monitor compliance, and equate effectiveness with productivity. For students with SEND, these shifts can be double-edged because while AI has the potential to personalise and scaffolds, it can also create new hierarchies of performance through automated instruction.

Thus, a critical approach to inclusive pedagogy must move beyond a binary between inquiry and direct instruction. The central issue is not which strategy is more effective in a narrow, performance-oriented sense, but how pedagogy is redefined in liquid modern contexts where AI mediates both possibilities (Promsiri,

2025). In a welcoming and positive teaching and learning environment, inquiry is used as a relational and dialogic practice, while ensuring that direct instruction remains responsive rather than reductive. Only by resisting the neoliberal framing of effectiveness as algorithmic optimisation can AI be used to support truly inclusive forms of pedagogy.

A GUIDELINE FOR TEACHERS

The clarity and organisation of lesson structure is fundamental to effective teaching, particularly for students with SEND, who benefit from predictable routines and transparent expectations. Structured lessons reduce cognitive load, making it easier for students to follow learning sequences and build confidence in their progress. In the age of AI, digital platforms can support structured planning by offering adaptive sequencing and personalised learning pathways that align with individual needs (Holmes, 2023). However, there is a risk that overreliance on algorithmic sequencing may reduce flexibility and reinforce a mechanistic view of learning. Teachers therefore remain central in ensuring that lesson structures are not only coherent but also responsive to the relational and emotional needs of their students.

Effective presentations in teaching often follow logical models such as deductive and inductive reasoning, or formats such as part–whole, sequential ordering, combinatorial relationships, and comparative relationships. These approaches provide cognitive scaffolds for understanding complex concepts. AI tools can enhance structured presentation by generating visualisations, adaptive diagrams, and multimodal explanations that align with diverse learning styles (Mohammadi et al., 2025). For learners with SEND, multimodal AI-generated supports can bridge gaps in accessibility. Yet, algorithmic mediation risks privileging efficiency over depth, reducing presentations to simplified, standardised outputs (Knox et al., 2020). Teachers must therefore design structured presentations that are enriched, rather than replaced, by AI systems.

The pace of teaching has long been recognised as a critical factor in maintaining engagement and ensuring accessibility (Rincon-Flores et al., 2024). Lessons that move too quickly risk leaving students behind, while those that progress too slowly may lead to disengagement. AI-driven systems, such as adaptive learning platforms, offer tools to adjust pacing dynamically to the needs of each learner. This is particularly beneficial for students with SEND, who may require additional time for reflection or scaffolding. However, in neoliberal performance-driven systems, AI is often used to accelerate progress in line with efficiency metrics, potentially undermining inclusivity (Wieczorek, 2025). Effective pacing in the AI classroom must therefore balance adaptability with pedagogical sensitivity, ensuring that learners' individual rhythms are valued rather than overridden.

Modelling is a powerful pedagogical strategy, allowing students to observe and replicate desired behaviours, processes, or problem-solving strategies (Rincon-Flores et al., 2024). Video-modelling, widely used in SEND contexts (particularly autism education), provides visual, repeatable demonstrations that can reinforce learning. AI enhances modelling by enabling personalised, context-specific examples such as generating role-play scenarios or interactive simulations. Yet critical concerns remain: AI modelling risks embedding normative assumptions about behaviour, aligning inclusion with conformity rather than diversity . Teachers must therefore deploy modelling critically, using AI tools to expand possibilities for representation rather than reinforce restrictive norms (Baeyaert, 2025).

Conceptual mapping allows learners to visualise relationships between ideas, supporting deeper understanding and metacognition (Rincon-Flores et al., 2024). For students with SEND, maps provide an accessible way to scaffold abstract thinking and retain information. AI can augment this process by automatically generating concept maps from student input, highlighting gaps in understanding, and suggesting connections. However, algorithmic mapping often relies on pre-programmed ontologies that may oversimplify complexity or direct thinking along normative pathways (Baeyaert, 2025). From a critical perspective, the value of conceptual mapping lies not in efficiency but in fostering reflexivity and ownership of learning. AI should therefore be used to stimulate, rather than dictate, conceptual connections.

Interactive questioning remains one of the most effective strategies for engaging students in reflexive learning. Open-ended questions promote critical thinking, dialogue, and collaborative meaning-making. AI tools, such as intelligent tutoring systems, can generate adaptive questioning tailored to learners' responses, thereby increasing opportunities for personalised interaction (Cheng et al., 2025). Yet, there is a risk to reduce dialogue to a transactional exchange between student and machine, undermining the relational dimension of teacher–student interaction. For learners with SEND in particular, interactive questioning requires sensitivity to communication styles and needs that AI alone cannot provide. Teachers must therefore integrate AI-generated prompts within dialogic pedagogy that foregrounds human relationships.

The preparation of individual work tasks is an essential dimension of inclusive pedagogy, allowing students to consolidate learning and practise skills at their own pace. AI can assist teachers in generating differentiated tasks, automating materials that are tailored to students' levels of readiness and interest. This is particularly useful for students with SEND, who benefit from personalised scaffolding. Yet, the preparation of individual work should not be left solely to algorithms, as neoliberal systems may use AI to streamline preparation for efficiency rather than inclusivity

(Zhai et al., 2024). Teachers must critically curate AI-generated content to ensure that tasks reflect both academic goals and the lived realities of diverse learners.

Workbooks and textbooks remain core tools for structuring learning, providing continuity and reference beyond classroom instruction. Digital and AI-enhanced versions now allow for interactive features, multimodal content, and adaptive scaffolding (Wang et al., 2025). For students with SEND, these affordances can enhance accessibility and engagement. However, the shift to AI-enhanced workbooks risks reinforcing a data-driven "performance economy" in which completion and progress are constantly monitored (Williamson & Hogan, 2020). Rather than treating workbooks as sites of surveillance, teachers must employ them as tools for reflection, dialogue, and formative learning.

The organisation of individual work is essential for supporting executive functioning, particularly in SEND contexts where students may struggle with planning, sequencing, and self-regulation (Markauskaite et al., 2022). AI-powered learning management systems can support organisation by providing reminders, deadlines, and visual progress tracking. However, these tools often reflect neoliberal priorities by emphasising productivity, efficiency, and goal completion, which can exacerbate stress rather than support learning. Teachers should therefore mediate the organisational affordances of AI, using them to scaffold autonomy while also teaching students critical strategies for resisting manipulative algorithmic designs that encourage dependency.

Timely and constructive feedback is a cornerstone of effective teaching, enabling students to reflect, improve, and consolidate learning (Broadbent et al., 2020). AI offers powerful tools for automated feedback, from grading written work to providing real-time corrections. In inclusive pedagogy, such systems can increase access to formative guidance, particularly for students with SEND who require consistent reinforcement. Yet, feedback framed through AI often privileges correctness and efficiency over dialogue and growth, aligning with neoliberal notions of performance and accountability. Teachers must therefore ensure that feedback retains its relational and formative function, with AI tools used as supplements rather than replacements.

Differentiation is central to inclusion, requiring teachers to adapt materials and strategies to suit diverse ability levels, learning styles, and needs. AI promises to automate differentiation by adjusting content and scaffolding to each learner's profile (Wang et al., 2025). While this can support students with SEND in accessing the curriculum, it risks reproducing deficit-based models by categorising students according to narrow algorithmic assumptions. Differentiation in the AI age can be unstable because tools are transformed on a daily basis and what counts as appropriate support is redefined constantly. Teachers must therefore resist framing differentiation solely as algorithmic optimisation, and instead ensure that it remains rooted in equity, creativity, and recognition of difference.

Effective teaching often follows a sequence of interconnected steps that scaffold learning while maintaining inclusivity (Foley & Melese, 2025). The process begins with directing, where teachers set clear goals and provide structure to orient students toward the task. This is followed by instructing, which involves presenting information in accessible ways tailored to the abilities and needs of learners. Demonstrating plays a crucial role in modelling processes or behaviours, offering students concrete examples to guide practice, while explaining and illustrating extend this by clarifying concepts through multiple representations, including visuals or real-life contexts that enhance understanding for learners with SEND.

The next step, questioning and discussing, promotes active participation, encouraging students to reflect, articulate ideas, and engage in dialogue, which AI systems can support by generating adaptive prompts but cannot replace in terms of relational depth (Song et al., 2024). Learning is then consolidated through practice and reinforcement, helping students embed knowledge in long-term memory. Teachers must also engage in evaluating students' responses, using both formative and summative assessments to provide feedback and guide further learning. Finally, summarising draws the lesson together, reinforcing key ideas and ensuring clarity before moving forward. Taken as a whole, these steps illustrate that effective teaching is not a linear process of delivery but a dynamic, interactive cycle, which AI can enhance but only within a critical pedagogical framework that centres inclusion and equity.

DIFFERENTIATION, SELF-REGULATION, AND INCLUSIVE AI

Differentiation remains a cornerstone of effective teaching because it accommodates the diversity of learners, ensuring that all students have the best possible chance of learning, expression and achievement. By employing varied methods and teaching activities, differentiation challenges each student appropriately and recognises difference as an asset rather than a deficit (Markauskaite et al., 2022). For differentiation to succeed, however, learners require some degree of self-regulation, since differentiated tasks demand independent engagement and decision-making (Revishvili & Tsereteli, 2024). Self-regulation involves not only cognition but also metacognition and motivation, including the capacity to plan, monitor, and evaluate one's learning (Raymond-Tolan et al., 2025). Central to this is metacognition, the ability to reflect critically on strengths, weaknesses, and strategies. In practice, this often involves heuristic problem-solving strategies by understanding and representing problems, planning and executing solutions, and evaluating outcomes. In the age of AI, however, self-regulation becomes increasingly fragile, as students' capacity for attention and reflection is disrupted by systems designed to capture and monetise cognitive focus (Broadbent et al., 2020). Technologies marketed as empowering are simultaneously addictive, functioning as both remedy and poison. Thus, students need to be supported to scaffold learning while at the same time hollowing out the very attention that makes learning possible.

Effective differentiation is also inseparable from the effective use of technology because with fast-paced changes in the field of AI, pedagogy and technology cannot be disentangled. In this context, AI can offer powerful tools for inclusive differentiation, enabling teachers to design multimodal, personalised learning pathways that motivate and engage students (Promsiri, 2025). Constructivist approaches align particularly well with the affordances of AI-powered systems, which can support learner control, knowledge-sharing, problem-solving, and scaffolding (Wang et al., 2025). If features such as adaptivity, multimodality, and interactivity are effectively integrated into AI, it then can foster constructivist practices in diverse classrooms, providing learners with SEND with multiple avenues to engage meaningfully in knowledge construction (Mohammadi et al., 2025). Yet, within the prevailing logic of optimisation, such tools risk transforming differentiation into a process of quantification and gamified learning (Khosrawi-Rad et al., 2025). With the pedagogy of new tools, endless pursuit of efficiency is diminishing the richness of pedagogy by reducing education to data points, dashboards, and performance metrics.

This reflects a wider condition in which educational practices are continually destabilised by technological acceleration (Ball & Grimaldi, 2022). Categories such as effectiveness and differentiation lose their solidity, becoming fluid and provisional, reshaped with every new algorithmic update or institutional demand. In such an environment, the emphasis on constant improvement and measurable outcomes produces not only instability but also exhaustion. Teachers are expected to endlessly adapt to new systems while students internalise the demand for performance and self-optimisation (Rickey et al., 2025). Far from cultivating autonomy, such environments risk producing fatigue and burnout, particularly for learners with SEND who are forced to navigate technologies that are not always designed with their needs in mind. Education becomes less about cultivating critical capacities and more about sustaining the endless transparency of performance, where every activity is measured, tracked, and compared.

Collaboration, as an essential dimension of education, offers a possible counterweight to this dynamic (Markauskaite et al., 2022). Group work requires students to regulate not only their own behaviour but also their interactions with peers, balancing independence with interdependence to achieve collective outcomes. AI systems can support collaboration by facilitating peer interaction, adaptive grouping, and feedback on participation. Yet such systems also risk embedding a culture of surveillance and reinforcing competitive comparison, where collaboration is reduced to data flows and the production of measurable gains (Czerniewicz & Feldman, 2024). Effective teaching in the age of AI therefore depends on the critical integration of multiple pedagogical dimensions (i.e. constructivist, behaviourist, and collaborative) to ensure inclusivity in an ever-changing environment. Differentiation, in this sense, cannot be equated with algorithmic optimisation. It must be reclaimed as a pedagogical ethic through the commitment to ensuring that every student, including those with SEND, is empowered to learn, participate, and flourish within communities of care rather than within economies of performance.

COLLABORATION AND INTERACTIVE LEARNING IN THE AGE OF AI

In today's connected world, collaboration in education is increasingly associated with AI-enhanced environments, where interaction becomes the central mode of engagement. Effective teaching requires student to participate in meaningful, interactive activities such as problem-solving, reasoning, and decision-making (Broadbent et al., 2020). AI systems aims to create opportunities by supporting collaborative tasks that would otherwise be difficult to manage, for example through adaptive grouping, personalised prompts, and automated facilitation of discussion. Online collaboration, when guided effectively, can strengthen peer relationships and stimulate knowledge construction. Teachers, however, remain critical facilitators because they must design meaningful activities, ask questions that foster reflection, monitor group dynamics, and provide constructive feedback (Markauskaite et al., 2022). In addition to pedagogical oversight, teachers must ensure participation is equitable, sustain group focus, and mediate the technical aspects of AI-supported collaboration.

Collaboration also requires learners to exercise self-regulation, balancing individual responsibility with group goals (Nunez et al., 2024). AI can play a supportive role here by tracking contributions, prompting engagement, and scaffolding participation, which may be particularly beneficial for students with SEND. Successful collaboration relies on learners' ability to share responsibility, co-construct meaning, and take ownership of their learning in which AI is positioned as revolutionising (Swist et al., 2023). Studies show that technology-enhanced collaboration through shared platforms, discussion boards, or multimodal representations of content, can deepen learning and improve engagement. Yet, while AI offers new opportunities for inclusivity, it also reshapes the very conditions of collaboration.

AI-mediated collaboration may undermine the very principles it seeks to enhance. Algorithms that monitor interaction can transform collaboration into a data-driven exercise, where participation is evaluated by measurable activity rather than genuine dialogue (Grimaldi & Ball, 2021). Instead of fostering autonomy, such systems risk creating environments of surveillance and compliance, where learners adapt their behaviour to satisfy the expectations of the platform rather than the needs of their peers (Czerniewicz & Feldman, 2024). This becomes more problematic with the growing use of sensors, chips, and biometric tracking in classrooms, where every movement, response, or even physiological signal can be measured. While marketed as tools for personalised support, such technologies risk treating students as programmable entities, reducing human learning to robotic compliance with system outputs. Collaboration is no longer a process of mutual meaning-making but one of algorithmic optimisation, where students are disciplined into producing data rather than engaging authentically. For Learners with SEND in particular, differences in communication or participation styles may be misread by such systems as inefficiency or failure, further entrenching exclusion.

While AI has the potential to extend collaboration beyond the limits of time and space, it must be critically integrated (Ro, 2025). Without careful reflection, the push to technologize collaboration risks hollowing out its relational essence, transforming education into a space where students are trained to operate like machines. True inclusive pedagogy requires reclaiming collaboration as a human practice grounded in dialogue, empathy, and dignity, not as an exercise in algorithmic control.

VYGOTSKY AGAINST AI

Vygotsky's concept of the Zone of Proximal Development (ZPD) rests on the idea that learning occurs most powerfully when a learner engages with a "more knowledgeable other" who scaffolds understanding, guiding the learner beyond their immediate capacities (Fragkiadaki & Ravanis, 2021). This process is not reducible to the delivery of information. This process is dialogic, relational, and situated within the social and cultural fabric of education. The teacher or peer who plays this role does so not only by offering knowledge, but also by interpreting the learner's intentions, recognising affective states, and responding to the moral and ethical dimensions of the situation (Veresov & Veraksa, 2024). In this sense, educational environment is a cognitive space which is a space of trust, reciprocity, and human meaning-making.

AI also creates opportunities for scaffolding by providing instantaneous feedback, adjust difficulty, and simulate the role of a tutor with infinite patience (Tang & Putra, 2025). These functions appear to align with Vygotskian principles, yet their operation is grounded in data extraction and optimisation rather than dialogue. Within AI-mediated environments, the learner is positioned not in relation to another human consciousness, but to a system that interprets behaviour as data points and performance as measurable efficiency (Ro, 2025). The scaffolding AI provides is real, but it lacks the ontological depth of human mediation. Currently AI cannot participate in the co-construction of cultural meaning, nor can it acknowledge the singularity of the learner as more than an optimisable subject. If machine can know thyself, they can be a part of multi-layered and entangled knowledge construction in an intra agent web of relationships. However, this is a promise of Silicon Valley to be realised or too good to be true.

This divergence becomes clearer when collaboration and orchestration are considered. For Vygotsky, learning emerges through joint activity where social interaction mediates cognitive development (Daniels, 2002). The "dialogue" AI sustains is not genuine reciprocity but a simulation of responsiveness, calibrated to produce outputs that conform to pre-set criteria. Such orchestration reflects the broader logic of the performance economy where education is reconfigured as a system of measurable outcomes, and the richness of dialogic unpredictability is replaced by optimisation.

For students with SEND, this tension is acute. While AI promises personalised scaffolds that can adapt to diverse learning needs, it simultaneously imposes categories, norms, and thresholds that may misrecognise difference as deficiency (Baeyaert, 2025; Wieczorek, 2025). Where a teacher acting as the "more knowledgeable other" can interpret hesitation as reflection, or silence as emotional struggle, an algorithm may interpret the same behaviour as disengagement. The risk is that the ZPD, reconfigured under AI, becomes a zone of control rather than development. Educational can be a space where learners are nudged, monitored, and disciplined into conformity so that systems can continue to run smoothly (Promsiri, 2025).

The "more knowledgeable other" is not simply a functional scaffold (Daniels, 2002) and is not a part in machines. It is a very dynamic interaction and cultural space which includes a human interlocutor, embedded in culture, capable of ethical judgment and genuine dialogue. AI, however sophisticated, remains bound to its design, its mechanical logic of processing and ideology of the machine-owner, so it optimises rather than understands, it adapts rather than interprets, it processes rather than empathises (Ro, 2025). In this sense, AI does not extend the ZPD but hollow it out, replacing a relational pedagogy with a technological rationality. A Vygotskian stance therefore resists the substitution of AI for human mediation, insisting that development requires dialogue with others, not compliance with machines.

Nevertheless, in collaborative digital spaces, students demonstrated valuable skills in elaborating, reorganising, and reworking ideas, processes that are central to effective knowledge construction (Olsen et al., 2021). In the age of AI, these affordances can be amplified because intelligent systems can support students by suggesting alternative perspectives, reorganising drafts, or highlighting connections between ideas. When used critically, such tools can extend students' ability to refine arguments and develop higher-order skills (Rickey et al., 2025). Yet the teacher's role remains essential in structuring activities that encourage genuine collaboration, particularly among students from different backgrounds and with diverse needs, such as those with and without SEND. Without careful orchestration, there is a risk that

AI's interventions reduce creativity to automated suggestion, narrowing opportunities for authentic dialogue (Ro, 2025). To preserve the emancipatory potential of collaborative writing, AI must be positioned not as the author of knowledge but as a scaffold that supports inclusive, peer-to-peer interaction and critical engagement.

The role of AI in education is increasingly framed as supporting new forms of teaching and learning, empowering students to take greater responsibility for their own development while still requiring the guidance of their teachers (Ball & Grimaldi, 2022). It is claimed that AI enables learners to become more independent, self-aware, and capable of navigating vast sources of knowledge, but this a dream-in-making. Although intelligent systems can help students filter, reorganise, and even generate information in ways that appear to personalise learning, this transformation also brings disruption and uncertainty (Promsiri, 2025).

AI promotes an approach that mixes behaviourist and constructivist practices by offering responsive, adaptive, interactive, and multimodal learning environments that shift the role of the teacher from co-constructor of knowledge to a mere facilitator (Biesta, 2017; Vlieghe & Zamojski, 2019). However, the conditions of this facilitation are more fragile than often acknowledged because it is not clear what a teacher facilitates with new dynamics. One source of uncertainty lies in the democratisation of content creation because all frames of reference for epistemological discussions are blurred during content creation. AI accelerates the rapid generation of text, images, and ideas around consumerist culture. Before an idea, content, claim or post is double-checked, it is quickly outdated, and the reason to create open spaces for democracy disappears. This creates both opportunities for creativity and risks of misinformation, particularly when learners are not equipped with the critical skills to discern what is accurate, meaningful, or relevant.

For teachers, the rise of AI therefore requires a fundamental renegotiation of their role. They are not simply facilitators of constructivist learning, but also critical mediators between students and algorithmically generated information (Clark, 2023). This involves cultivating discernment, ethical awareness, and reflective practices that counterbalance the speed and ease of AI outputs. In this sense, the discourse of empowerment must be held alongside the discourse of uncertainty. While AI can enhance learning by expanding access and autonomy, it also destabilises the authority of knowledge and risks amplifying superficial engagement. The teacher's task in the age of AI is to sustain spaces of critical reflection and dialogue where information is not merely consumed or generated, but interrogated, contextualised, and woven into meaningful learning experiences.

THE LEARNER IN AN UNPREDICTABLE EDUCATIONAL CONTEXT

In the education of students with SEND, differentiation and personalisation remain central strategies to support skills development. Multiple forms of knowledge representation and multimodality are particularly important, as they help remove barriers to participation and foster inclusion. Yet, while such affordances create opportunities, they also reshape behaviour in unintended ways. Each technological tool has a pedagogical impact that must be carefully appropriated to strengthen executive functions such as self-regulation skills that are increasingly vital in an era of personalised, AI-enhanced learning (Clark, 2023).

AI intensifies both the opportunities and risks in this behavioural landscape. On the one hand, adaptive learning platforms can scaffold self-regulation by offering timely feedback, reminders, and personalised prompts that encourage students to plan, monitor, and reflect on their learning (Ball & Grimaldi, 2022). For students with challenging behaviours, these supports can be crucial in structuring focus and building resilience. On the other hand, AI is embedded in a wider media ecosystem that often undermines self-regulation. Recommendation algorithms on social media platforms are designed to capture attention and maximise engagement, pulling learners into cycles of distraction and instant gratification (Knox et al., 2020). For students with SEND, who may already struggle with executive functioning, these behavioural hooks present serious challenges, as the same devices used for learning are also conduits for endless entertainment, peer pressures, and potential online harms. The risk is that the capacity for deep concentration and sustained effort is under constant attack. AI is enhancing skills which it is killing at the same time.

While AI can personalise instruction, it cannot replace the relational oversight and behavioural modelling provided by adults in the classroom (Holmes, 2023). Teachers aim to employ AI-powered machines to individualise learning, scaffold activities, and provide responsive care that balances academic and behavioural development. Their presence helps buffer the potential negative effects of technology, offering direct instruction, redirection of attention, and encouragement in the face of distraction. As AI becomes more integrated into classrooms, the importance of decision-making skills of teachers grows increasingly not only for adapting pedagogy to individual needs but also for guiding students to navigate the behavioural challenges of AI-driven media environments (Grimaldi & Ball, 2021).

Ultimately, AI-supported differentiation offers new opportunities for inclusion, but it also demands new forms of behavioural pedagogy (Holmes, 2023). Students must not only learn literacy, numeracy, and communication skills, but also develop the digital self-regulation skills necessary to resist algorithmic distractions in their daily lives. Without explicit teaching of these skills, there is a risk that Students with

SEND will be left more vulnerable to the exploitative logics of AI-driven media, undermining the very gains that personalised education seeks to achieve.

Students with ADHD, in particular, are reported to spend more time gaming and on screens than their peers, which can exacerbate behavioural difficulties (Knox et al., 2020). While digital games may have minimal long-term effects on emotional wellbeing, the immersive, attention-capturing design of devices and applications can create behavioural vulnerabilities, especially for students already facing challenges in self-regulation (Broadbent et al., 2020). When framed within AI-driven environments and personalised platforms, these risks are amplified, since algorithms are explicitly optimised to sustain engagement, often at the expense of focus on educational goals (Knox et al., 2020).

Without adequate mentoring and professional development, teachers may feel ill-equipped to integrate digital tools in ways that both sustain engagement and minimise disruption (Promsiri, 2025). This challenge underscores the importance of teacher guidance in accompanying students as they engage with technology, ensuring that educational activities do not collapse into distraction or off-task behaviour. At the same time, there is evidence that technology is increasingly integrated into daily life to support on-task behaviours, problem-solving, and critical thinking. Thus, the behavioural implications of AI are ambiguous because it has the capacity to foster deep engagement but also to magnify behavioural problems if insufficiently scaffolded.

With adaptive systems promising personalised scaffolds, flexible pacing, and multimodal representations of knowledge, a new and ever-changing space is created for learning. When autonomy is handed over to learners without critical structures, self-regulation becomes fragile, especially for those with ADHD, EBD, or autism (Rizvi et al., 2024). Moreover, the "more knowledgeable other" within Vygotskian theory is not simply a provider of prompts, but a relational guide who interprets behaviour and mediates meaning. AI can simulate scaffolding, but it cannot fully support the socio-emotional and ethical dimensions of learning that underpin behavioural development. Without this dimension, "personalisation" risks being reduced to algorithmic nudging, which may reinforce dependence and attention fragmentation rather than autonomy and resilience.

CONCLUSION

In the age of artificial intelligence, education stands at a profound crossroads between empowerment and automation, between inclusion and instrumentalization (Clark, 2023). This chapter has explored how the integration of AI and digital technologies into classrooms reshapes not only the methods of teaching and learning but also the very conditions under which education operates. While technology has long been celebrated as a tool for progress, accessibility, and personalisation, it has also introduced new tensions between autonomy and control, between human development and algorithmic governance. For students with SEND, these tensions are especially pronounced, revealing both the emancipatory and disciplinary potentials of AI-driven education.

At its best, AI offers unprecedented opportunities for differentiation and personalisation. Adaptive learning systems can tailor content to individual needs, provide real-time feedback, and support self-regulation skills because the unpredictable nature of technology put more burden on the shoulders of learners. AI can amplify inclusion by breaking down barriers to participation through multimodal representations, alternative communication tools, and assistive technologies. Teachers and teaching assistants, when equipped with critical digital literacy and pedagogical vision, can harness these affordances to design environments where all students can flourish. The promise of inclusive AI lies not in replacing human pedagogy but in extending its reach: augmenting the teacher's capacity to respond to diversity and complexity (Baeyaert, 2025).

Yet, this promise must be met with sustained critique. The chapter has shown that the use of AI and digital devices is not value-neutral; rather, it reflects and reproduces the logic of the neoliberal performance economy. In this economy, learning becomes a measurable output, and "effectiveness" is reduced to quantifiable performance metrics. The rhetoric of personalisation risks turning education into a marketplace of algorithmic feedback loops, where learners are treated as data points and teachers as facilitators of continuous optimisation. What is lost in this process is the ethical and philosophical dimension of education: the cultivation of judgement, attention, and the shared human experience of meaning-making.

Behaviourally, AI technologies present complex challenges. While they can scaffold focus and provide structure for students with attention difficulties, they also contribute to the very forms of distraction they aim to manage. Algorithms are designed to capture and monetise attention, not nurture reflection or depth. For students with SEND, who may already struggle with executive functioning, these effects are amplified. Thus, the question is not whether AI improves learning outcomes, but how it shapes the very conditions of cognition, attention, and desire in the educational environment.

Philosophically, this chapter has argued that education in the era of AI must be understood as a deeply socio-technical practice where power, ideology, and technology are inseparable. The modern classroom has become an ecosystem of sensors, algorithms, and data flows, mediating interactions between students and teachers. When learners are surrounded by "smart" technologies that monitor engagement, predict behaviour, and optimise performance, the line between support and surveillance blurs (Czerniewicz & Feldman, 2024). In such environments, students risk becoming subjects of behavioural programming rather than participants in dialogic, emancipatory learning. This transformation raises critical questions about autonomy, agency, and the ethics of care in AI-mediated education.

Against this background, the chapter reasserts the importance of dialogue, collaboration, and human presence. The dialogic space where teachers and students co-construct meaning through communication, remains essential to the educational encounter. Vygotsky's concept of the Zone of Proximal Development (ZPD) reminds us that learning is relational, embedded in shared activity and guided by a more knowledgeable other. AI may simulate this scaffolding, but it cannot replicate the ethical, emotional, and interpretive dimensions of human guidance. Education, therefore, must resist the temptation to replace relational pedagogy with algorithmic facilitation. Instead, it must reimagine technology as a participant in a wider ecology of learning to enhance ethical responsibility, critical reflection, and care.

The chapter has also emphasised that inclusive pedagogy in the AI era requires collective agency. Teachers, head-teachers, school psychologist and SEND specialists, need to work collaboratively to design adaptive learning environments that respond to both cognitive and emotional diversity. Professional development and mentoring are essential to build confidence in using AI tools critically and creatively. Moreover, students themselves must be guided to develop meta-digital literacy which is the capacity not only to use AI tools but to understand and resist their manipulative potential. The new literacy of the 21st century is not merely technical proficiency but attentional sovereignty. It can be defined as the ability to focus, question, and choose meaningfully in environments designed to distract.

Finally, the chapter calls for a shift in how educational research itself engages with technology. Research must move beyond the rhetoric of "what works" toward understanding how technology reconfigures the values, relationships, and purposes of education. This requires a reflexive stance that situates AI within broader socio-political structures. The rise of data capitalism, the commodification of attention, and the erosion of collective educational values create costs for connection. Education is not merely a field of technical application but a cultural and ethical practice through which societies imagine their future. In this sense, the integration of AI into education must not be seen as inevitable progress but as a contested and negotiated process that demands critical awareness and moral courage.

To conclude, the age of AI compels us to rethink what it means to teach, to learn, and to be human. For students with SEND, inclusion cannot be achieved through automation alone but through the reaffirmation of relational, ethical, and dialogic pedagogy. For teachers, technology must remain a means to enhance, not to replace, human understanding. And for education as a whole, effectiveness must be redefined not by performance metrics or efficiency gains, but by the cultivation of wisdom, empathy, and shared meaning in a rapidly transforming world. The task before educators, researchers, and policymakers is not simply to integrate AI into schools, but to ensure that schools remain spaces where students are empowered through reflexive praxis which goes beyond the logic of the algorithm.

REFERENCES

Areepattamannil, S., Cairns, D., & Dickson, M. (2020). Teacher-Directed Versus Inquiry-Based Science Instruction: Investigating Links to Adolescent Students' Science Dispositions Across 66 Countries. *Journal of Science Teacher Education, 31*(6), 675–704. DOI: 10.1080/1046560X.2020.1753309

Baeyaert, J. (2025). The philosophy of cognitive diversity: Rethinking ethical AI design through the lens of neurodiversity. *Sustainable Futures : An Applied Journal of Technology, Environment and Society, 10*, 101126. DOI: 10.1016/j.sftr.2025.101126

Ball, S. J., & Grimaldi, E. (2022). Neoliberal education and the neoliberal digital classroom. *Learning, Media and Technology, 47*(2), 288–302. DOI: 10.1080/17439884.2021.1963980

Bauman, Z. (2005). Liquid life. *Polity*.

Bauman, Z. (2013). *Liquid modernity*. John Wiley & Sons.

Biesta, G. (2017). *The Rediscovery of Teaching*. Routledge. DOI: 10.4324/9781315617497

Bower, M. (2017). *Design of Technology-Enhanced Learning*. Emerald Publishing Limited. DOI: 10.1108/9781787141827

Broadbent, J., Panadero, E., Lodge, J. M., & de Barba, P. (2020). Technologies to Enhance Self-Regulated Learning in Online and Computer-Mediated Learning Environments. In Bishop, M. J., Boling, E., Elen, J., & Svihla, V. (Eds.), *Handbook of Research in Educational Communications and Technology*. Springer., DOI: 10.1007/978-3-030-36119-8_3

Chelkowski, L., Yan, Z., & Asaro-Saddler, K. (2019). The use of mobile devices with students with disabilities: A literature review. *Preventing School Failure, 63*(3), 277–295. DOI: 10.1080/1045988X.2019.1591336

Cheng, Y., Fan, Y., Li, X., Chen, G., Gašević, D., & Swiecki, Z. (2025). Asking generative artificial intelligence the right questions improves writing performance. *Computers and Education: Artificial Intelligence, 8*, 100374. DOI: 10.1016/j.caeai.2025.100374

Clark, D. (2023). The construction of legitimacy: A critical discourse analysis of the rhetoric of educational technology in post-pandemic higher education. *Learning, Media and Technology, 49*(3), 414–427. DOI: 10.1080/17439884.2022.2163500

Costa, C., Hammond, M., & Younie, S. (2019). Theorising technology in education: An introduction. *Technology, Pedagogy and Education, 28*(4), 395–399. DOI: 10.1080/1475939X.2019.1660089

Cukurova, M. (2025). The interplay of learning, analytics and artificial intelligence in education: A vision for hybrid intelligence. *British Journal of Educational Technology, 56*(2), 469–488. DOI: 10.1111/bjet.13514

Czerniewicz, L., & Feldman, J. (2024). 'Technology is not created by the sky': Datafication and educator unease. *Learning, Media and Technology, 49*(3), 428–441. DOI: 10.1080/17439884.2023.2206137

Daher, R. (2025). Integrating AI literacy into teacher education: A critical perspective paper. *Discover Artificial Intelligence, 5*(1), 217. DOI: 10.1007/s44163-025-00475-7

Daniels, H. (2002). *Vygotsky and pedagogy*. Routledge. DOI: 10.4324/9780203469576

de Jong, T., Lazonder, A. W., Chinn, C. A., Fischer, F., Gobert, J., Hmelo-Silver, C. E., Koedinger, K. R., Krajcik, J. S., Kyza, E. A., Linn, M. C., Pedaste, M., Scheiter, K., & Zacharia, Z. C. (2023). Let's talk evidence–The case for combining inquiry-based and direct instruction. *Educational Research Review, 39*, 100536. DOI: 10.1016/j.edurev.2023.100536

Fitas, R. (2025). Inclusive education with AI: Supporting special needs and tackling language barriers. *AI and Ethics*. Advance online publication. DOI: 10.1007/s43681-025-00824-3

Foley, A., & Melese, F. (2025). Disabling AI: Power, exclusion, and disability. *British Journal of Sociology of Education*, •••, 1–22. DOI: 10.1080/01425692.2025.2519482

Fragkiadaki, G., & Ravanis, K. (2021). The unity between intellect, affect, and action in a child's learning and development in science. *Learning, Culture and Social Interaction, 29*, 100495. DOI: 10.1016/j.lcsi.2021.100495

Furze, L., Perkins, M., Roe, J., & MacVaugh, J. (2024). The AI Assessment Scale (AIAS) in action: A pilot implementation of GenAI-supported assessment. *Australasian Journal of Educational Technology, 40*(4), 38–55. DOI: 10.14742/ajet.9434

Fütterer, T., Goldberg, P., Bühler, B., Sikimić, V., Trautwein, U., Gerjets, P., ... & Kasneci, E. (2025). Artificial Intelligence in Classroom Management: A Systematic Review on Educational Purposes, Technical Implementations, and Ethical Considerations. *Computers and Education: Artificial Intelligence*, 100483.

Grimaldi, E., & Ball, S. J. (2021). The blended learner: Digitalisation and regulated freedom - neoliberalism in the classroom. *Journal of Education Policy*, *36*(3), 393–416. DOI: 10.1080/02680939.2019.1704066

Hakel, K., & Magin, M. (2024). The impact of professional development training on faculty's integration of universal design for learning in daily teaching practices. *International Journal of Inclusive Education*, •••, 1–16. DOI: 10.1080/13603116.2024.2430527

Hogan, A. (2025). *Commercialising public schooling: Practices of profit-making*. Routledge. DOI: 10.4324/9781003213093

Holmes, W. (2023). The unintended consequences of artificial intelligence and education.

Kaldaras, L., Wang, K. D., Nardo, J. E., Price, A., Perkins, K., Wieman, C., & Salehi, S. (2024). Employing technology-enhanced feedback and scaffolding to support the development of deep science understanding using computer simulations. *International Journal of STEM Education*, *11*(1), 30. DOI: 10.1186/s40594-024-00490-7

Khalil, M., Slade, S., & Prinsloo, P. (2024). Learning analytics in support of inclusiveness and disabled students: A systematic review. *Journal of Computing in Higher Education*, *36*(1), 202–219. DOI: 10.1007/s12528-023-09363-4 PMID: 37359042

Khosrawi-Rad, B., Keller, P. F., Benner, D., Grogorick, L., Borchers, A., Janson, A., Leimeister, J. M., & Robra-Bissantz, S. (2025). Promoting Students' Motivation in Language Education with Gamified Pedagogical Conversational Agents. *Computers & Education*, *238*, 105374. DOI: 10.1016/j.compedu.2025.105374

Knox, J., Williamson, B., & Bayne, S. (2020). Machine behaviourism: Future visions of 'learnification' and 'datafication' across humans and digital technologies. *Learning, Media and Technology*, *45*(1), 31–45. DOI: 10.1080/17439884.2019.1623251

Lee, H., Kim, H., & Yan, W. (2025). Promoting inclusive AI and technology in K-12: A review of context, instructional strategies, and learning outcomes. *Computers and Education: Artificial Intelligence*, 100478.

Liang, H. Y., Hwang, G. J., Hsu, T. Y., & Yeh, J. Y. (2024). Effect of an AI-based chatbot on students' learning performance in alternate reality game-based museum learning. *British Journal of Educational Technology*, *55*(5), 2315–2338. DOI: 10.1111/bjet.13448

Madaio, M., Blodgett, S. L., Mayfield, E., & Dixon-Román, E. (2022). Beyond "fairness": Structural (in)justice lenses on ai for education. In *The ethics of artificial intelligence in education* (pp. 203-239). Routledge.

Mallik, S., & Gangopadhyay, A. (2023). Proactive and reactive engagement of artificial intelligence methods for education: A review. *Frontiers in Artificial Intelligence*, *6*, 1151391. DOI: 10.3389/frai.2023.1151391 PMID: 37215064

Markauskaite, L., Marrone, R., Poquet, O., Knight, S., Martinez-Maldonado, R., Howard, S., Tondeur, J., De Laat, M., Buckingham Shum, S., Gašević, D., & Siemens, G. (2022). Rethinking the entwinement between artificial intelligence and human learning: What capabilities do learners need for a world with AI? *Computers and Education: Artificial Intelligence*, *3*, 100056. DOI: 10.1016/j.caeai.2022.100056

Melo-López, V.-A., Basantes-Andrade, A., Gudiño-Mejía, C.-B., & Hernández-Martínez, E. (2025). The Impact of Artificial Intelligence on Inclusive Education: A Systematic Review. *Education Sciences*, *15*(5), 539. DOI: 10.3390/educsci15050539

Mohammadi, M., Tajik, E., Martinez-Maldonado, R., Sadiq, S., Tomaszewski, W., & Khosravi, H. (2025). Artificial intelligence in multimodal learning analytics: a systematic literature review. *Computers and Education: Artificial Intelligence*, 100426.

Muijs, D., & Reynolds, D. (2017). *Effective Teaching: Evidence and Practice*. SAGE.

Navas-Bonilla, C. D. R., Guerra-Arango, J. A., Oviedo-Guado, D. A., & Murillo-Noriega, D. E. (2025, February). Inclusive education through technology: A systematic review of types, tools and characteristics. [). Frontiers Media SA.]. *Frontiers in Education*, *10*, 1527851. DOI: 10.3389/feduc.2025.1527851

Núñez, J. M., Soto-Rubio, A., & Pérez-Marín, M. (2024). Executive Functions and Special Educational Needs and Their Relationship with School-Age Learning Difficulties. *Children (Basel, Switzerland)*, *11*(11), 1398. DOI: 10.3390/children11111398 PMID: 39594973

Olsen, J. K., Rummel, N., & Aleven, V. (2021). Designing for the co-orchestration of social transitions between individual, small-group and whole-class learning in the classroom. *International Journal of Artificial Intelligence in Education*, *31*(1), 24–56. DOI: 10.1007/s40593-020-00228-w

Promsiri, T. (2025). AI and the psychology of educational disruption: Historical patterns and cognitive implications. *Acta Psychologica*, *260*, 105637. DOI: 10.1016/j.actpsy.2025.105637 PMID: 41027066

Raymond-Tolan, L., Arcidiacono, T., Panzarino, C., & Vazquez, A. (2025). The impact and experience of directly teaching about executive functions (EF) to 2nd-grade students on their understanding and performance of EF skills. *Journal of Occupational Therapy, Schools & Early Intervention*, •••, 1–13. DOI: 10.1080/19411243.2025.2455619

Revishvili, M., & Tsereteli, M. (2024). The psychological mechanism of self-regulated learning in a technology-enhanced environment. *Cogent Education, 11*(1), 2372153. Advance online publication. DOI: 10.1080/2331186X.2024.2372153

Rickey, N., Panadero, E., & DeLuca, C. (2025). How do students self-assess? examining the metacognitive processes of student self-assessment. *Metacognition and Learning, 20*(1), 25. DOI: 10.1007/s11409-025-09430-4

Rincon-Flores, E. G., Castano, L., Guerrero Solis, S. L., Olmos Lopez, O., Rodríguez Hernández, C. F., Castillo Lara, L. A., & Aldape Valdés, L. P. (2024). Improving the learning-teaching process through adaptive learning strategy. *Smart Learning Environments, 11*(1), 27. DOI: 10.1186/s40561-024-00314-9

Rizvi, N., Wu, W., Bolds, M., Mondal, R., Begel, A., & Munyaka, I. N. (2024, May). Are Robots Ready to Deliver Autism Inclusion?: A Critical Review. In *Proceedings of the 2024 CHI Conference on Human Factors in Computing Systems* (pp. 1-18). DOI: 10.1145/3613904.3642798

Ro, J. (2025). Enforcing unwarranted optimism: Critical frame analysis on educational digitalisation policies in South Korea. *Learning, Media and Technology*, •••, 1–16. DOI: 10.1080/17439884.2025.2462940

Saltman, K. (2020). Artificial intelligence and the technological turn of public education privatization: In defence of democratic education. *London Review of Education, 18*(2), 196–208. DOI: 10.14324/LRE.18.2.04

Song, Y., Weisberg, L. R., Zhang, S., Tian, X., Boyer, K. E., & Israel, M. (2024). A framework for inclusive AI learning design for diverse learners. *Computers and Education: Artificial Intelligence, 6*, 100212. DOI: 10.1016/j.caeai.2024.100212

Strielkowski, W., Grebennikova, V., Lisovskiy, A., Rakhimova, G., & Vasileva, T. (2025). AI-driven adaptive learning for sustainable educational transformation. *Sustainable Development (Bradford), 33*(2), 1921–1947. DOI: 10.1002/sd.3221

Swist, T., & Gulson, K. N. (2023). Instituting socio-technical education futures: Encounters with/through technical democracy, data justice, and imaginaries. *Learning, Media and Technology, 48*(2), 181–186. DOI: 10.1080/17439884.2023.2205225

Swist, T., Humphry, J., & Gulson, K. N. (2023). Pedagogic encounters with algorithmic system controversies: A toolkit for democratising technology. *Learning, Media and Technology, 48*(2), 226–239. DOI: 10.1080/17439884.2023.2185255

Tan, X., Cheng, G., & Ling, M. H. (2025). Artificial intelligence in teaching and teacher professional development: A systematic review. *Computers and Education: Artificial Intelligence, 8*, 100355. DOI: 10.1016/j.caeai.2024.100355

Tang, K. S., & Putra, G. B. S. (2025). Generative AI as a Dialogic Partner: Enhancing Multiple Perspectives, Reasoning, and Argumentation in Science Education with Customized Chatbots. *Journal of Science Education and Technology*, 1–13. DOI: 10.1007/s10956-025-10240-1

Veresov, N., & Veraksa, N. (2024). Introducing cultural-historical genetic-analytical model for studying child's play: The matryoshka principle – situations within situations covered by situations. *Early Years Journal of International Research and Development*, *45*(3–4), 413–425. DOI: 10.1080/09575146.2024.2365180

Vlieghe, J., & Zamojski, P. (2019). *Towards an Ontology of Teaching: Thing-centred Pedagogy, Affirmation and Love for the World*. Springer. DOI: 10.1007/978-3-030-16003-6

Wang, F., Zhou, X., Li, K., Cheung, A. C. K., & Tian, M. (2025). The effects of artificial intelligence-based interactive scaffolding on secondary students' speaking performance, goal setting, self-evaluation, and motivation in informal digital learning of English. *Interactive Learning Environments*, *33*(7), 4633–4652. DOI: 10.1080/10494820.2025.2470319

Wieczorek, M. (2025). Why AI will not democratize education: A critical pragmatist perspective. *Philosophy & Technology*, *38*(2), 53. DOI: 10.1007/s13347-025-00883-8

Williamson, B. (2024). The social life of AI in education. *International Journal of Artificial Intelligence in Education*, *34*(1), 97–104. DOI: 10.1007/s40593-023-00342-5

Williamson, B., & Hogan, A. (2020). Commercialisation and privatisation in/of education in the context of Covid-19.

Woodcock, S., Sharma, U., Subban, P., & Hitches, E. (2022). Teacher self-efficacy and inclusive education practices: Rethinking teachers' engagement with inclusive practices. *Teaching and Teacher Education*, *117*, 103802. DOI: 10.1016/j.tate.2022.103802

Xu, J., & Li, J. (2024). Effects of AI affordances on student engagement in EFL classrooms: A structural equation modelling and latent profile analysis. *European Journal of Education*, *59*(4), e12808. DOI: 10.1111/ejed.12808

Zhai, C., Wibowo, S., & Li, L. D. (2024). The effects of over-reliance on AI dialogue systems on students' cognitive abilities: A systematic review. *Smart Learning Environments*, *11*(1), 28. DOI: 10.1186/s40561-024-00316-7

Compilation of References

Abdallah, A. K., & Musah, M. B. (2025). Artificial intelligence in school leadership. In Abdallah, A. K., & Musah, M. B. (Eds.), *AI in learning, educational leadership, and special education: Innovations and ethical dilemmas* (pp. 79–102). IGI Global., DOI: 10.4018/979-8-3373-0573-8.ch003

Abdeldayem, M. M., & Aldulaimi, S. H. (2020). Trends and opportunities of artificial intelligence in human resource management: Aspirations for public sector in Bahrain. *International Journal of Science and Technology Research*, *9*, 3867–3871.

Abositta, A., Adedokun, M. W., & Berberoğlu, A. (2024). Influence of artificial intelligence on engineering management decision-making with mediating role of transformational leadership. *Systems*, *12*(12), 570. Advance online publication. DOI: 10.3390/systems12120570

Acton, R., & Glasgow, P. (2015). Teacher wellbeing in neoliberal contexts: A review of the literature. *The Australian Journal of Teacher Education*, *40*(8), 99–114. DOI: 10.14221/ajte.2015v40n8.6

Adams, D., & Chuah, K.-M. (2022). Artificial intelligence-based tools in research writing: Current trends and future potentials. In Churi, P. P., Joshi, S., Elhoseny, M., & Omrane, A. (Eds.), *Artificial intelligence in higher education: A practical approach* (pp. 169–184). CRC Press. DOI: 10.1201/9781003184157-9

Adams, D., & Thompson, P. (2025). Transforming school leadership with artificial intelligence: Applications, implications, and future directions. *Journal of Educational Administration*, *63*(1), 77–89. DOI: 10.1108/JEA-01-2025-0007

Adeleye, O. O., Eden, C. A., & Adeniyi, I. S. (2024). Innovative teaching methodologies in the era of artificial intelligence: A review of inclusive educational practices. World Journal of Advanced Engineering Technology and Sciences, 11(2), 069–079. DOI: 10.30574/wjaets.2024.11.2.0091

Ajzen, I. (1991). The theory of planned behavior. *Organizational Behavior and Human Decision Processes, 50*(2), 179–211. DOI: 10.1016/0749-5978(91)90020-T

Ajzen, I., & Fishbein, M. (2000). Attitudes and the attitude–behavior relation: Reasoned and automatic processes. *European Review of Social Psychology, 11*(1), 1–33. DOI: 10.1080/14792779943000116

Akat, M. (2024). *Intergenerational transmission of family conflict and trait anxiety: Serial mediation of adolescent positive youth development and aggression* (Unpublished doctoral dissertation). Necmettin Erbakan University.

Akata, Z., Balliet, D., De Rijke, M., Dignum, F., Dignum, V., Eiben, G., Fokkens, A., Grossi, D., Hindriks, K., Hoos, H., Hung, H., Jonker, C., Monz, C., Neerincx, M., Oliehoek, F., Prakken, H., Schlobach, S., Van Der Gaag, L., Van Harmelen, F., & Welling, M. (2020). A Research Agenda for Hybrid Intelligence: Augmenting Human Intellect With Collaborative, Adaptive, Responsible, and Explainable Artificial Intelligence. *Computer, 53*(8), 18–28. DOI: 10.1109/MC.2020.2996587

Akat, M. (2025). Psychological counseling. In Günlü, A., & Oral, T. (Eds.), *Psychological counseling and guidance* (pp. 169–190). Eğiten Publishing.

Akçaba, P., Toklu, D. A., & Akcil, U. (2024). Examining the attitudes and anxiety of teachers and administrators towards artificial intelligence: Relational browsing. *BRAIN. Broad Research in Artificial Intelligence and Neuroscience, 15*(4), 325–337. DOI: 10.70594/brain/15.4/22

Akgun, S., & Greenhow, C. (2022). Artificial intelligence in education: Addressing ethical challenges in K-12 settings. *AI and Ethics, 2*(3), 431–440. DOI: 10.1007/s43681-021-00096-7 PMID: 34790956

Akhmad, A. (2025). Digital leadership practices in educational management: A narrative literature review on trends and challenges. *International Journal of Learning. Teaching and Educational Research, 24*(8), 112–135. DOI: 10.26803/ijlter.24.8.6

Al Naqbi, H., Bahroun, Z., & Ahmed, V. (2024). Enhancing work productivity through generative artificial intelligence: A comprehensive literature review. *Sustainability (Basel), 16*(3), 1166. DOI: 10.3390/su16031166

Aldossemani, T. I. (2024). Dar forma al futuro del aprendizaje: El papel fundamental de la inteligencia artificial en la microeducación. In J. M. Muñoz, N. Lorenzo, & X. Suñé (Coords.), Inteligencia Artificial en la Microeducación: Transformando el Aula del Futuro (pp. 33–41). Observatorio de Innovación Educativa y Cultura Digital (ODITE).

Alenezi, H. S., & Faisal, M. H. (2020). Utilizing crowdsourcing and machine learning in education: Literature review. *Education and Information Technologies*, *25*(4), 2971–2986. DOI: 10.1007/s10639-020-10102-w

Aljemely, Y. (2024). Challenges and best practices in training teachers to utilize artificial intelligence: A systematic review. *Frontiers in Education*, *9*, 1470853. DOI: 10.3389/feduc.2024.1470853

Alkan, A. (2024). Öğrencilerin sınavlardaki performansının makine öğrenmesi teknikleriyle tahminlenmesi. *Osmaniye Korkut Ata Üniversitesi Fen Bilimleri Enstitüsü Dergisi*, *7*(3), 1116–1128. DOI: 10.47495/okufbed.1420959

Alkouk, A. W., & Khlaif, Z. N. (2024). AI-resistant assessments in higher education: practical insights from faculty training workshops. In *Frontiers in education* (Vol. 9, p. 1499495). DOI: 10.3389/feduc.2024.1499495

Almaki, S. H., Mafarja, N., Mansoori, H. M. S. A., Almaki, S. H., Mafarja, N., & Mansoori, H. M. S. A. (2025). Teacher well-being and use of artificial intelligence applications and tools: Moderation effects of leadership support in inclusive classroom. *STEM Education*, *5*(1), 109–129. DOI: 10.3934/steme.2025006

Al-Rahmi, W. M., Yahaya, N., Aldraiweesh, A. A., Alamri, M. M., Aljarboa, N. A., Alturki, U., & Aljeraiwi, A. A. (2019). Integrating technology acceptance model with innovation diffusion theory: An empirical investigation on students' intention to use E-learning systems. *IEEE Access : Practical Innovations, Open Solutions*, *7*, 26797–26809. DOI: 10.1109/ACCESS.2019.2899368

Amichai-Hamburger, Y., Klomek, A. B., Friedman, D., Zuckerman, O., & Shani-Sherman, T. (2014). The future of online therapy. *Computers in Human Behavior*, *41*, 288–294. DOI: 10.1016/j.chb.2014.09.016

Andrew, J., Rudra, M., Eunice, J., & Belfin, R. V. (2023). Artificial intelligence in adolescents mental health disorder diagnosis, prognosis, and treatment. *Frontiers in Public Health*, *11*, 1110088. Advance online publication. DOI: 10.3389/fpubh.2023.1110088 PMID: 37064712

Anysiadou, M., & Gkliati, A. (2025). An experimental analysis of Greek school leaders' readiness for AI integration. *Leadership and Policy in Schools*, *24*(1), 155–177.

Aoun, J. E. (2024). Robot-Proof: Higher Education in the Age of Artificial Intelligence (2.a ed.). MIT Press.

Arar, K., Tlili, A., & Salha, S. (2024). Human-Machine symbiosis in educational leadership in the era of artificial intelligence (AI): Where are we heading? *Educational Management Administration & Leadership*, 17411432241292295. Advance online publication. DOI: 10.1177/17411432241292295

Arar, K., Tlili, A., Schunka, L., Salha, S., & Saiti, A. (2025). Reimagining educational leadership and management through artificial intelligence: An integrative systematic review. *Leadership and Policy in Schools*, *24*(1), 4–26. DOI: 10.1080/15700763.2025.2451982

Areepattamannil, S., Cairns, D., & Dickson, M. (2020). Teacher-Directed Versus Inquiry-Based Science Instruction: Investigating Links to Adolescent Students' Science Dispositions Across 66 Countries. *Journal of Science Teacher Education*, *31*(6), 675–704. DOI: 10.1080/1046560X.2020.1753309

Armour, J., & Sako, M. (2020). AI-enabled business models in legal services: From traditional law firms to next-generation law companies? *Journal of Professions and Organization*, *7*(1), 27–46. DOI: 10.1093/jpo/joaa001

Arriola-Mendoza, J., & Valerio-Ureña, G. (2024). Essential elements for implementing AI tools in elementary school: A systematic literature review. *Education Sciences*, *14*(1292), 1–15. DOI: 10.3390/educsci14121292

Atasoy, R. (2024). Eğitimde mükemmellik arayışı ve yapay zekâ. [The pursuit of excellence in education and artificial intelligence]. R. Atasoy, Ö. Çoban, M. T. Yalçın (Eds.). *Eğitimde mükemmellik haritası: Liderlik, beceriler ve başarı. [The map to excellence in education: Leadership, skills and success]* (pp. 107-136). Eğitim.

Atasoy, R. (2025). Artificial Intelligence in Education and Changing Teacher Roles. In *Holistic Approaches to Teacher Development: Leadership, Pedagogical Practices, and Cognitive Insights* (pp. 25-46). IGI Global Scientific Publishing. DOI: 10.4018/979-8-3373-0472-4.ch002

Atasoy, R. (2023). Sustainability of the School leadership in the digital era under the shadow of crisis. In Al-A'ali, E., & Masmoudi, M. (Eds.), *Leadership and Workplace Culture in the Digital Era* (pp. 149–168). IGI Global.

Atkinson, J. W. (1957). Motivational determinants of risk-taking behavior. *Psychological Review*, *64*(6p1), 359.

Avolio, B. J., & Bass, B. M. (1995). Individual consideration viewed at multiple levels of analysis: A multi-level framework for examining the diffusion of transformational leadership. *The Leadership Quarterly*, *6*(2), 199–218. DOI: 10.1016/1048-9843(95)90035-7

Azorin, C., & Fullan, M. (2022). Leading new, deeper forms of collaborative cultures: Questions and pathways. *Journal of Educational Change*, *23*(1), 131–143. DOI: 10.1007/s10833-021-09448-w PMID: 38624840

Babu, A., & Joseph, A. P. (2024). Artificial intelligence in mental healthcare: Transformative potential vs. the necessity of human interaction. *Frontiers in Psychology*, *15*, 1378904. Advance online publication. DOI: 10.3389/fpsyg.2024.1378904 PMID: 39742049

Baeyaert, J. (2025). The philosophy of cognitive diversity: Rethinking ethical AI design through the lens of neurodiversity. *Sustainable Futures : An Applied Journal of Technology, Environment and Society*, *10*, 101126. DOI: 10.1016/j.sftr.2025.101126

Bakker, A. B., & Demerouti, E. (2017). Job demands–resources theory: Taking stock and looking forward. *Journal of Occupational Health Psychology*, *22*(3), 273–285. DOI: 10.1037/ocp0000056 PMID: 27732008

Bakker, A. B., & Demerouti, E. (2018). Multiple levels in job demands-resources theory: Implications for employee well-being and performance. In *Handbook of well-being*. Noba Scholar.

Balamurugan, G., Sevak, S., Gurung, K., & Vijayarani, M. (2024). Mental Health Issues Among School Children and Adolescents in India: A Systematic Review. *Cureus*, *16*(5), e61035. DOI: 10.7759/cureus.61035 PMID: 38916009

Balleisen, E. J., Howes, L., & Wibbels, E. (2024). The impact of applied project-based learning on undergraduate student development. *Higher Education*, *87*(4), 1141–1156. DOI: 10.1007/s10734-023-01057-1

Ball, S. J., & Grimaldi, E. (2022). Neoliberal education and the neoliberal digital classroom. *Learning, Media and Technology*, *47*(2), 288–302. DOI: 10.1080/17439884.2021.1963980

Bandura, A. (1977). Self-efficacy: Toward a unifying theory of behavioral change. *Psychological Review*, *84*(2), 191–215. DOI: 10.1037/0033-295X.84.2.191 PMID: 847061

Bandura, A. (1986). *Social foundations of thought and action: A social cognitive theory*. Prentice-Hall.

Bandura, A. (1997). *Self-efficacy: The exercise of control*. W. H. Freeman.

Barocas, S., & Selbst, A. D. (2016). Big data's disparate impact. *California Law Review*, *104*, 671.

Baron, R. M., & Kenny, D. A. (1986). The moderator–mediator variable distinction in social psychological research: Conceptual, strategic, and statistical considerations. *Journal of Personality and Social Psychology*, *51*(6), 1173–1182. DOI: 10.1037/0022-3514.51.6.1173 PMID: 3806354

Basile, J. L., Carbonara, N., Panniello, U., & Pellegrino, R. (2024). The role of big data analytics in improving the quality of healthcare services in the Italian context: The mediating role of risk management. *Technovation*, *133*, 103010. Advance online publication. DOI: 10.1016/j.technovation.2024.103010

Bass, B. M., & Riggio, R. E. (2006). *Transformational leadership* (2nd ed.). Psychology Press. DOI: 10.4324/9781410617095

Bassett, C. (2019). The computational therapeutic: Exploring Weizenbaum's ELIZA as a history of the present. *AI & Society*, *34*(4), 803–812. DOI: 10.1007/s00146-018-0825-9

Bauman, Z. (2005). Liquid life. *Polity*.

Bauman, Z. (2013). *Liquid modernity*. John Wiley & Sons.

Beck, U. (2011). Sociedade de risco: Rumo a uma Outra Modernidade. Editora 34.

Beckert, J. (2021). The firm as an engine of imagination: Organizational prospection and the making of economic futures. *Organization Theory*, *2*(2), 1–20. DOI: 10.1177/26317877211005773

Bednar, P. M., & Welch, C. (2020). Socio-technical perspectives on smart working: Creating meaningful and sustainable systems. *Information Systems Frontiers*, *22*(2), 281–298. DOI: 10.1007/s10796-019-09921-1

Bennett, S., Maton, K., & Kervin, L. (2008). The 'digital natives' debate: A critical review of the evidence. *British Journal of Educational Technology*, *39*(5), 775–786. DOI: 10.1111/j.1467-8535.2007.00793.x

Berendt, B., Littlejohn, A., & Blakemore, M. (2020). AI in education: Learner choice and fundamental rights. *Learning, Media and Technology*, *45*(3), 312–324. DOI: 10.1080/17439884.2020.1786399

Berente, N., Gu, B., Recker, J., & Santhanam, R. (2021). Managing artificial intelligence. *Management Information Systems Quarterly*, *45*(3), 1433–1450. DOI: 10.25300/MISQ/2021/16274

Berger, R., Romeo, M., Guardia, J., Yepes, M., & Soria, M. A. (2012). Psychometric properties of the Spanish human system audit short-scale of transformational leadership. *The Spanish Journal of Psychology*, *15*(1), 367–376. DOI: 10.5209/rev_SJOP.2012.v15.n1.37343

Berkovich, I. (2025). The rise of AI-assisted instructional leadership: Empirical survey of generative AI integration in school leadership and management work. *Frontiers in Education*, *10*, 1643023. DOI: 10.3389/feduc.2025.1643023

Berkovich, I., & Eyal, O. (2025). Support for generative artificial intelligence as a predictor of middle leaders' generative artificial intelligence self-efficacy, valuing, and integration in school leadership work. *Educational Management Administration & Leadership*, 17411432251361251. Advance online publication. DOI: 10.1177/17411432251361251

Berkowitz, M. W. (2011). What works in values education. *International Journal of Educational Research*, *50*(3), 153–158. DOI: 10.1016/j.ijer.2011.07.003

Bertolin, M., & Da Rin, D. (2020). Chatbots for K-12 education: A review of recent advances, opportunities and challenges. *Education Sciences*, *10*(7), 181–191.

Biesta, G. (2017). *The Rediscovery of Teaching*. Routledge. DOI: 10.4324/9781315617497

Bloomfield, J., & Fisher, M. J. (2019). Quantitative Research Design. *JARNA*, *22*(2), 27–30. DOI: 10.33235/jarna.22.2.27-30

Blum, L., & Blum, M. (2024). AI Consciousness is Inevitable: A Theoretical Computer Science Perspective (Versão 12). arXiv. DOI: 10.48550/ARXIV.2403.17101

Bollmann, U. (2024). Artificial intelligence and education: A teacher-centred approach to safety and health.

Bolukbasi, T., Chang, K. W., Zou, J. Y., Saligrama, V., & Kalai, A. T. (2016). Man is to computer programmer as woman is to homemaker? debiasing word embeddings. *Advances in Neural Information Processing Systems*, •••, 29.

Borenstein, J., & Howard, A. (2021). Emerging challenges in AI and the need for AI ethics education. *AI and Ethics*, *1*(1), 61–65. DOI: 10.1007/s43681-020-00002-7 PMID: 38624388

Bostrom, N. (2016). *Superintelligence: Paths, Dangers, Strategies*. Oxford University Press.

Boud, D., & Soler, R. (2015). Sustainable assessment revisited. *Assessment & Evaluation in Higher Education*, *41*(3), 400–413. DOI: 10.1080/02602938.2015.1018133

Bower, M. (2017). *Design of Technology-Enhanced Learning*. Emerald Publishing Limited. DOI: 10.1108/9781787141827

Breckler, S. J. (1984). Empirical validation of affect, behavior, and cognition as distinct components of attitude. *Journal of Personality and Social Psychology*, *47*(6), 1191–1205. DOI: 10.1037/0022-3514.47.6.1191 PMID: 6527214

Bredeweg, B., & Kragten, M. (2022). Requirements and challenges for hybrid intelligence: A case-study in education. *Frontiers in Artificial Intelligence*, *5*, 891630. DOI: 10.3389/frai.2022.891630 PMID: 36003066

Bretag, T., Harper, R., Burton, M., Ellis, C., Newton, P., van Haeringen, K., Saddiqui, S., & Rozenberg, P. (2019). Contract cheating and assessment design: Exploring the relationship. *Assessment & Evaluation in Higher Education*, *44*(5), 676–691. DOI: 10.1080/02602938.2018.1527892

Broadbent, J., Panadero, E., Lodge, J. M., & de Barba, P. (2020). Technologies to Enhance Self-Regulated Learning in Online and Computer-Mediated Learning Environments. In Bishop, M. J., Boling, E., Elen, J., & Svihla, V. (Eds.), *Handbook of Research in Educational Communications and Technology*. Springer., DOI: 10.1007/978-3-030-36119-8_3

Bryk, A. S., & Schneider, B. (2002). *Trust in schools: A core resource for improvement*. Russell Sage Foundation.

Bryson, J. J. (2019). The Artificial Intelligence of the Ethics of Artificial Intelligence: An Introductory Overview for Law and Regulation. In Dubber, M., Pasquale, F., & Das, S. (Eds.), *The Oxford Handbook of Ethics of Artificial Intelligence Oxford University Press*.

Bulathwela, S., Pérez-Ortiz, M., Holloway, C., Cukurova, M., & Shawe-Taylor, J. (2024). Artificial Intelligence Alone Will Not Democratise Education: On Educational Inequality, Techno-Solutionism and Inclusive Tools. *Sustainability (Basel)*, *16*(2), 781. DOI: 10.3390/su16020781

Bush, T. (2017). The enduring power of transformational leadership. *Educational Management Administration & Leadership*, *45*(4), 563–565. DOI: 10.1177/1741143217701827

Bushuyev, S., & Saidullayev, R., & Others. (2024). Transformation of the education landscape in an AI environment. In Proceedings of the 12th IPMA Research Conference: Project Management in the Age of Artificial Intelligence DOI: 10.56889/strd5315

Büyüköztürk, Ş., Çakmak, E. K., Akgün, Ö. E., Karadeniz, Ş., & Demirel, F. (2019). *Eğitimde bilimsel araştırma yöntemleri [Scientific research methods in education].* (27. baskı). Pegem Akademi.

Camargo, C. D. B., & Fernández, A. H. (2024). Neuropedagogy and Neuroimaging of Artificial Intelligence and Deep Learning. *Educational Process International Journal, 13*(3). Advance online publication. DOI: 10.22521/edupij.2024.133.6

Canpolat, M. (2021). Psikolojik danışmanlık ve rehberlikte yapay zekâ kullanılabilirliği üzerine bir araştırma. *Milli Eğitim Özel Eğitim Ve Rehberlik Dergisi, 1*(1), 1–25.

Cantarero, K., van Tilburg, W. A. P., Gasiorowska, A., & Igou, E. R. (2022). The efficient measurement of individual differences in meaning motivation: The need for sense-making short form. *Frontiers in Psychology, 13*, 945692. DOI: 10.3389/fpsyg.2022.945692

Caplan, G. (1964). *Principles of preventive psychiatry*. Basic Books.

Carnegie Learning. (2025). *The State of AI in Education 2025: Key Findings from a National Survey*. Carnegie Learning.

Carter, W. R., Nesbit, P. L., Badham, R. J., Parker, S. K., & Sung, L. K. (2018). The effects of employee engagement and self-efficacy on job performance: A longitudinal field study. *International Journal of Human Resource Management, 29*(17), 2483–2502. DOI: 10.1080/09585192.2016.1244096

Carver, C. S., Scheier, M. F., & Segerstrom, S. C. (2010). Optimism. *Clinical Psychology Review, 30*(7), 879–889. DOI: 10.1016/j.cpr.2010.01.006 PMID: 20170998

Cascio, W. F., & Montealegre, R. (2016). How technology is changing work and organizations. *Annual Review of Organizational Psychology and Organizational Behavior, 3*(1), 349–375. DOI: 10.1146/annurev-orgpsych-041015-062352

Cengage Group. (2025). 4 Ways AI Is Transforming Education. Cengage Group Research Report.

Chan, C. K. Y., & Hu, W. (2023). Students' voices on generative AI: Perceptions, benefits, and challenges in higher education. *International Journal of Educational Technology in Higher Education, 20*(1), 43. DOI: 10.1186/s41239-023-00411-8

Chang, Q., Zhang, J., & Xiao, X. (2025). Leading Like Human: Clarifying the Connotation and Validating the Structure of Algorithmic Leadership. *International Journal of Human-Computer Interaction*, 1–28. DOI: 10.1080/10447318.2025.2543991

Chase, C. C., Chin, D. B., Oppezzo, M. A., & Schwartz, D. L. (2009). Teachable Agents and the Protégé Effect: Increasing the Effort Towards Learning. *Journal of Science Education and Technology*, *18*(4), 334–352. DOI: 10.1007/s10956-009-9180-4

Chassignol, M., Khoroshavin, A., Klimova, A., & Bilyatdinova, A. (2018). Artificial Intelligence trends in education: A narrative overview. *Procedia Computer Science*, *136*, 16–24. DOI: 10.1016/j.procs.2018.08.233

Chaudhuri, S., & Ghosh, R. (2011). Reverse Mentoring: A Social Exchange Tool for Keeping the Boomers Engaged and Millennials Committed. *Human Resource Development Review*, *11*(1), 55–76. DOI: 10.1177/1534484311417562

Chelkowski, L., Yan, Z., & Asaro-Saddler, K. (2019). The use of mobile devices with students with disabilities: A literature review. *Preventing School Failure*, *63*(3), 277–295. DOI: 10.1080/1045988X.2019.1591336

Chen, D., Liu, Y., Guo, Y., & Zhang, Y. (2024). The revolution of generative artificial intelligence in psychology: The interweaving of behavior, consciousness, and ethics. *Acta Psychologica*, *251*, 104593. Advance online publication. DOI: 10.1016/j.actpsy.2024.104593 PMID: 39522296

Cheng, Y., Fan, Y., Li, X., Chen, G., Gašević, D., & Swiecki, Z. (2025). Asking generative artificial intelligence the right questions improves writing performance. *Computers and Education: Artificial Intelligence*, *8*, 100374. DOI: 10.1016/j.caeai.2025.100374

Chen, J., Yuan, D., Dong, R., Cai, J., Ai, Z., & Zhou, S. (2024). Artificial intelligence significantly facilitates development in the mental health of college students: A bibliometric analysis. *Frontiers in Psychology*, *15*, 1375294. Advance online publication. DOI: 10.3389/fpsyg.2024.1375294 PMID: 38515973

Chen, L. T., Yang, L. C., Lin, F. Y., & Lin, Y. H. (2025). Systematic review: The integration of artificial intelligence-powered cognitive-behavioural therapy for autonomous mental health management. *Archives of Psychiatric Nursing*, *57*, 151916. DOI: 10.1016/j.apnu.2025.151916 PMID: 40816782

Chen, L., Chen, P., & Lin, Z. (2020). Artificial intelligence in education: A review. *IEEE Access : Practical Innovations, Open Solutions*, *8*, 75264–75278. DOI: 10.1109/ACCESS.2020.2988510

Chen, S., Westman, M., & Hobfoll, S. E. (2015). The commerce and crossover of resources: Resource conservation in the service of resilience. *Stress and Health*, *31*(2), 95–105. DOI: 10.1002/smi.2574 PMID: 25873421

Chen, X., Zou, D., Xie, H., Cheng, G., & Liu, C. (2022). Two Decades of Artificial Intelligence in Education: Contributors, Collaborations, Research Topics, Challenges, and Future Directions. *Journal of Educational Technology & Society*, *25*(1), 28–47.

Chen, X., Zou, D., Xie, H., & Wang, F. L. (2021). Past, present, and future of smart learning: A topic-based bibliometric analysis. *International Journal of Educational Technology in Higher Education*, *18*(1), 2. DOI: 10.1186/s41239-020-00239-6

Cheung, K. K. C., Long, Y., Liu, Q., & Chan, H. Y. (2024). Unpacking epistemic insights of artificial intelligence (AI) in science education: A systematic review. *Science & Education*, *34*(2), 747–777. DOI: 10.1007/s11191-024-00511-5

Chiu, T. K., Xia, Q., Zhou, X., Chai, C. S., & Cheng, M. (2023). Systematic literature review on opportunities. challenges. and future research recommendations of artificial intelligence in education. *Computers and Education: Artificial Intelligence*, *4*, 100–118. DOI: 10.1016/j.caeai.2022.100118

Clark, D. (2023). The construction of legitimacy: A critical discourse analysis of the rhetoric of educational technology in post-pandemic higher education. *Learning, Media and Technology*, *49*(3), 414–427. DOI: 10.1080/17439884.2022.2163500

Çoban, Ö., & Durnalı, M. (2025). Teacher leadership and Al literacy: An analysis of teachers' Al literacy levels. M. T. Yalçın, A. Uslukaya, B. Demirdiş (Eds.) In *Holistic Approaches to Teacher Development: Leadership, Pedagogical Practices, and Cognitive Insights: Leadership, Pedagogical Practices, and Cognitive Insights*. (pp. 1-24). IGI Global.

Çoban, Ö., & Gün, F. (2024). Eğitimde mükemmelliğe giden yolda öğretmen liderliği. [Teacher leadership on the path to excellence in education] In Atasoy, R., Çoban, Ö., & Yalçın, M. T. (Eds.), *Eğitimde mükemmellik haritası: Liderlik, beceriler ve başarı* [The map to excellence in education: Leadership, skills and success]. (pp. 51–73). Eğitim.

Coccoli, M., Maresca, P., & Stanganelli, L. (2016). Cognitive computing in education. *Journal of E-Learning and Knowledge Society*, *12*(2), 55–69. DOI: 10.20368/1971-8829/1185

Coeckelbergh, M. (2020). *AI Ethics*. MIT Press. DOI: 10.7551/mitpress/12549.001.0001

Coeckelbergh, M. (2023). Narrative responsibility and artificial intelligence: How AI challenges human responsibility and sense-making. *AI & Society*, *38*(2), 2437–2450. DOI: 10.1007/s00146-021-01375-x

Cohen, J. (1988). *Statistical power analysis for the behavioral sciences* (2nd ed.). Lawrence Erlbaum Associates.

Compeau, D. R., & Higgins, C. A. (1995). Computer self-efficacy: Development of a measure and initial test. *Management Information Systems Quarterly*, *19*(2), 189–211. DOI: 10.2307/249688

Coppin, B. (2004). *Artificial intelligence illuminated.* Jones & Bartlett Learning.

Cormier, D., Jandrić, P., Childs, M., Hall, R., White, D., Phipps, L., Truelove, I., Hayes, S., & Fawns, T. (2019). Ten Years of the Postdigital in the 52group: Reflections and Developments 2009–2019. *Postdigital Science and Education*, *1*(2), 475–506. DOI: 10.1007/s42438-019-00049-8

Corrin, L., Lockyer, L., & Bennett, S. (2010). Technological diversity: An investigation of students' technology use in everyday life and academic study. *Learning, Media and Technology*, *35*(4), 387–401. DOI: 10.1080/17439884.2010.531024

Costa, C., Hammond, M., & Younie, S. (2019). Theorising technology in education: An introduction. *Technology, Pedagogy and Education*, *28*(4), 395–399. DOI: 10.1080/1475939X.2019.1660089

Cotton, D. R., Cotton, P. A., & Shipway, J. R. (2024). Chatting and cheating: Ensuring academic integrity in the era of ChatGPT. *Innovations in Education and Teaching International*, *61*(2), 228–239. DOI: 10.1080/14703297.2023.2190148

Creswell, J. W. (2014). *Research design: Qualitative, quantitative, and mixed methods approaches* (4th ed.). Sage Publications.

Csikszentmihalyi, M., & Seligman, M. (2000). Positive psychology. *The American Psychologist*, *55*(1), 5–14. DOI: 10.1037/0003-066X.55.1.5 PMID: 11392865

Cui, W., Xue, Z., & Thai, K. P. (2018, November). Performance comparison of an AI-based adaptive learning system in China. In *2018 Chinese automation congress (CAC)* (pp. 3170-3175). IEEE. DOI: 10.1109/CAC.2018.8623327

Cukurova, M. (2025). The interplay of learning, analytics and artificial intelligence in education: A vision for hybrid intelligence. *British Journal of Educational Technology*, *56*(2), 469–488. DOI: 10.1111/bjet.13514

Czerniewicz, L., & Feldman, J. (2024). 'Technology is not created by the sky': Datafication and educator unease. *Learning, Media and Technology*, *49*(3), 428–441. DOI: 10.1080/17439884.2023.2206137

D'Alfonso, S. (2020). AI in mental health. *Current Opinion in Psychology*, *36*, 112–117. DOI: 10.1016/j.copsyc.2020.04.005 PMID: 32604065

Daher, R. (2025). Integrating AI literacy into teacher education: A critical perspective paper. *Discover Artificial Intelligence*, *5*(1), 217. DOI: 10.1007/s44163-025-00475-7

Daniels, H. (2002). *Vygotsky and pedagogy*. Routledge. DOI: 10.4324/9780203469576

Darko, A., Chan, A. P., Adabre, M. A., Edwards, D. J., Hosseini, M. R., & Ameyaw, E. E. (2020). Artificial intelligence in the AEC industry: Scientometric analysis and visualization of research activities. *Automation in Construction*, *112*, 103081. DOI: 10.1016/j.autcon.2020.103081

Davis, F. D. (1989). Perceived usefulness, perceived ease of use, and user acceptance of information technology. *Management Information Systems Quarterly*, *13*(3), 319–340. DOI: 10.2307/249008

Dawson, K. P. (1992). Attitude and assessment in nursing education. *Journal of Advanced Nursing*, *17*(4), 473–479. DOI: 10.1111/j.1365-2648.1992.tb01932.x PMID: 1578070

Day, C., & Gu, Q. (2009). Veteran teachers: Commitment, resilience and quality retention. *Teachers and Teaching*, *15*(4), 441–457. DOI: 10.1080/13540600903057211

de Jong, T., Lazonder, A. W., Chinn, C. A., Fischer, F., Gobert, J., Hmelo-Silver, C. E., Koedinger, K. R., Krajcik, J. S., Kyza, E. A., Linn, M. C., Pedaste, M., Scheiter, K., & Zacharia, Z. C. (2023). Let's talk evidence–The case for combining inquiry-based and direct instruction. *Educational Research Review*, *39*, 100536. DOI: 10.1016/j.edurev.2023.100536

de Kerckhove, D. (2024). Preguntas, no respuestas. In J. M. Muñoz, N. Lorenzo, & X. Suñé (Coords.), Inteligencia Artificial en la Microeducación: Transformando el Aula del Futuro (pp. 18–32). Observatorio de Innovación Educativa e Cultura Digital (ODITE).

Deci, E. L., & Ryan, R. M. (2000). The" what" and" why" of goal pursuits: Human needs and the self-determination of behavior. *Psychological Inquiry*, *11*(4), 227–268. DOI: 10.1207/S15327965PLI1104_01

Deckker, D., & Sumanasekara, S. (2025). The role of Artificial Intelligence in education: Transforming learning and teaching. EPRA International Journal of Research & Development (IJRD), 5–15. DOI: 10.36713/epra20429

Deckker, D., Sumanasekara, S., & Fakhrou, A. (2025). AI-Powered Personalised Learning: Promise and Pitfalls. *World Journal of Advanced Research and Reviews*, *26*(3), 2081–2095. DOI: 10.30574/wjarr.2025.26.3.2425

Demerouti, E., Bakker, A. B., Nachreiner, F., & Schaufeli, W. B. (2001). The job demands-resources model of burnout. *The Journal of Applied Psychology, 86*(3), 499–512. DOI: 10.1037/0021-9010.86.3.499 PMID: 11419809

Demir, B. (2021). Working memory model and language learning. *Shanlax International Journal of Education, 9*(S2-Sep), 1-8. https://doi.org/DOI: 10.34293/education.v9iS2-Sep.4366

Demir, B. (2022). Effect of anxiety on cognitive load in foreign language oral tests. *Baskent University Journal of Education, 9*(1), 102–111.

Demir, B., & Erçetin, G. (2020). Exploring the role of proficiency as a mediator of the relationship between working memory and text comprehension in the L2. *Turkish Online Journal of English Language Teaching, 3*, 38–60.

Demirdis, B. (2025). Integrating digital literacy to enhance emotional and social skills in education. In *Innovative Educational Frameworks for Future Skills and Competencies* (pp. 1–38). IGI Global Scientific Publishing., DOI: 10.4018/979-8-3693-7555-6.ch001

DeRue, D. S., Ashford, S. J., & Myers, C. G. (2012). Learning agility: In search of conceptual clarity and theoretical grounding. *Industrial and Organizational Psychology: Perspectives on Science and Practice, 5*(3), 258–279. DOI: 10.1111/j.1754-9434.2012.01444.x

Dirks, K. T., & Ferrin, D. L. (2002). Trust in leadership: Meta-analytic findings and implications for research and practice. *The Journal of Applied Psychology, 87*(4), 611–628. DOI: 10.1037/0021-9010.87.4.611 PMID: 12184567

Doğan, T. (2015). Adaptation of the Brief Resilience Scale into Turkish: A validity and reliability study. *The Journal of Happiness & Well-Being, 3*(1), 93–102.

Dong, Z. Y., Zhang, Y., Yip, C., Swift, S., & Beswick, K. (2020). Smart campus: Definition, framework, technologies, and services. *IET Smart Cities, 2*(1), 43–54. DOI: 10.1049/iet-smc.2019.0072

Durnalı, M., & Çoban, Ö. (2025). Artificial intelligence in higher education management: Innovations. opportunities and challenges. In González Lezcano, R. A., & Orakçı, Ş. (Eds.), *Innovation trends and educational technology in higher education* (pp. 501–516). Information Age.

Dwyer, G., Hardy, C., & Maguire, S. (2021). Post-inquiry sensemaking: The case of the 'Black Saturday' bushfires. *Organization Studies, 42*(4), 637–661. DOI: 10.1177/0170840619896271

Eagleton, T. (2015). *Hope without optimism*. University of Virginia Press.

Eccles, J. S., & Wigfield, A. (2002). Motivational beliefs, values, and goals. *Annual Review of Psychology, 53*(1), 109–132. DOI: 10.1146/annurev.psych.53.100901.135153 PMID: 11752481

EDUCAUSE. (2023). *2023 EDUCAUSE Horizon Report: Teaching and Learning Edition*. EDUCAUSE Publications.

EDUCAUSE. (2025). *EDUCAUSE 2025 AI Landscape Study: Into the Digital AI Divide*. EDUCAUSE Publications.

El-Alfy, E., & Abdel-Aal, R. E. (2008). Construction and analysis of educational tests using abductive machine learning. *Computers & Education, 51*(1), 1–16. DOI: 10.1016/j.compedu.2007.03.003

El-Hachem, S. S., Lakkis, N. A., Osman, M. H., Issa, H. G., & Beshara, R. Y. (2023). University students' intentions to seek psychological counseling, attitudes toward seeking psychological help, and stigma. *Social Psychiatry and Psychiatric Epidemiology, 58*(11), 1661–1674. DOI: 10.1007/s00127-023-02470-8 PMID: 37037916

Ellis, C., Zucker, I., & Randall, D. (2020). Does authentic assessment assure academic integrity? Evidence from contract cheating data. *Higher Education Research & Development, 39*(3), 454–469. DOI: 10.1080/07294360.2019.1680956

Ellström, P.-E. (2006). Two logics of learning. In Antaqnacopoulou, H. (Ed.), *Learning, working and living: Mapping the terrain of working life learning* (pp. 33–49). Palgrave Macmillan.

Emre, İ. E., Taş, C., & Erol, Ç. (2021). Use of Machine Learning Methods in Psychiatry. *Psikiyatride Güncel Yaklasimlar, 13*(2), 332–353. DOI: 10.18863/pgy.779987

Engström, A., Pittino, D., Mohlin, A., Johansson, A., & Edh Mirzaei, N. (2024). Artificial intelligence and work transformations: Integrating sensemaking and workplace learning perspectives. *Information Technology & People, 37*(7), 2441–2461. DOI: 10.1108/ITP-01-2023-0048

Erdoğan, O., Kaymak, M. N., Çoban, Ö., & Bora, H. T. (2025). Exploring the links between school principals' self-efficacy, open innovation mindset, transformational leadership, and artificial intelligence (AI) attitudes in Türkiye. *Educational Management Administration & Leadership*, 17411432251351830. Advance online publication. DOI: 10.1177/17411432251351830

Erikson, E. H. (1963). *Childhood and Society* (2nd ed.). Norton.

Escaño, C. (2019). Sociedad postdigital (ontología de la remezcla). Iberoamérica Social: Revista-red de estudios sociales, 7(12), 51–53. https://dialnet.unirioja.es/servlet/articulo?codigo=6992796

Essa, S. G., Celik, T., & Human-Hendricks, N. E. (2023). Personalized Adaptive Learning Technologies Based on Machine Learning Techniques to Identify Learning Styles: A Systematic Literature Review. *IEEE Access : Practical Innovations, Open Solutions*, *11*, 48392–48409. DOI: 10.1109/ACCESS.2023.3276439

Estherita, A., & Shanmugam, V. (2024). Influence of artificial intelligence on transformational leadership. *AIP Conference Proceedings*, *3112*, 020013. DOI: 10.1063/5.0211330

European Education and Culture Executive Agency. (2023). AI report: By the European Digital Education Hub's Squad on artificial intelligence in education. Publications Office. https://data.europa.eu/doi/10.2797/828281

Evangelista, E. D. L. (2025). Ensuring academic integrity in the age of ChatGPT: Rethinking exam design, assessment strategies, and ethical AI policies in higher education. *Contemporary Educational Technology*, *17*(1), ep559. DOI: 10.30935/cedtech/15775

Farzan, M., Ebrahimi, H., Pourali, M., & Sabeti, F. (2025). Artificial Intelligence-Powered Cognitive Behavioral Therapy Chatbots, a Systematic Review. *Iranian Journal of Psychiatry*, *20*(1), 102–110. DOI: 10.18502/ijps.v20i1.17395 PMID: 40093525

Fawns, T. (2019). Postdigital Education in Design and Practice. *Postdigital Science and Education*, *1*(1), 132–145. DOI: 10.1007/s42438-018-0021-8

Ferrari, R. (2015). Writing narrative style literature reviews. *Medical Writing*, *24*(4), 230–235. DOI: 10.1179/2047480615Z.000000000329

Filatro, A., & Loureiro, A. C. (2020). *Novos produtos e serviços na Educação 5.0 (1st edição)*. Artesanato Educacional.

Fiorella, L., & Mayer, R. E. (2014). The relative benefits of learning by teaching and teaching expectancy. *Contemporary Educational Psychology*, *39*(4), 281–288. DOI: 10.1016/j.cedpsych.2013.06.001

Fitas, R. (2025). Inclusive education with AI: Supporting special needs and tackling language barriers. *AI and Ethics*. Advance online publication. DOI: 10.1007/s43681-025-00824-3

Fleming, P. (2019). Robots and organization studies: Why robots might not want to steal your job. *Organization Studies*, *40*(1), 23–37. DOI: 10.1177/0170840618765568

Floridi, L. (2019). *The Logic of Information: A Theory of Philosophy as Conceptual Design*. Oxford University Press. DOI: 10.1093/oso/9780198833635.001.0001

Foley, A., & Melese, F. (2025). Disabling AI: Power, exclusion, and disability. *British Journal of Sociology of Education*, •••, 1–22. DOI: 10.1080/01425692.2025.2519482

Forbes, M. K., Neo, B., Nezami, O. M., Fried, E. I., Faure, K., Michelsen, B., Twose, M., & Dras, M. (2024). Elemental psychopathology: Distilling constituent symptoms and patterns of repetition in the diagnostic criteria of the DSM-5. *Psychological Medicine*, *54*(5), 886–894. DOI: 10.1017/S0033291723002544 PMID: 37665038

Fragkiadaki, G., & Ravanis, K. (2021). The unity between intellect, affect, and action in a child's learning and development in science. *Learning, Culture and Social Interaction*, *29*, 100495. DOI: 10.1016/j.lcsi.2021.100495

Francis, D. C., Liu, J., Bharaj, P. K., & Eker, A. (2019). Integrating social-emotional and academic development in teachers' approaches to educating students. *Policy Insights from the Behavioral and Brain Sciences*, *6*(2), 138–146. DOI: 10.1177/2372732219864375

Freeman, S. L., Eddy, S. L., McDonough, M., Smith, M. K., Okoroafor, N., Jordt, H., & Wenderoth, M. P. (2014). Active learning increases student performance in science, engineering, and mathematics. *Proceedings of the National Academy of Sciences of the United States of America*, *111*(23), 8410–8415. DOI: 10.1073/pnas.1319030111 PMID: 24821756

Freire, P. (1998). *Por uma Pedagogia da Pergunta*. Paz e Terra.

Fullan, M., Azorín, C., Harris, A., & Jones, M. (2024). Artificial intelligence and school leadership: Challenges, opportunities and implications. *School Leadership & Management*, *44*(4), 339–346. DOI: 10.1080/13632434.2023.2246856

Furniss, D., Garfield, S., Husson, F., Blandford, A., & Franklin, B. (2019). Distributed Cognition: Understanding Complex Sociotechnical Informatics. In *Studies in Health Technology and Informatics*. IOS Press., DOI: 10.3233/SHTI190113

Furze, L., Perkins, M., Roe, J., & MacVaugh, J. (2024). The AI Assessment Scale (AIAS) in action: A pilot implementation of GenAI-supported assessment. *Australasian Journal of Educational Technology*, *40*(4), 38–55. DOI: 10.14742/ajet.9434

Fütterer, T., Goldberg, P., Bühler, B., Sikimić, V., Trautwein, U., Gerjets, P., ... & Kasneci, E. (2025). Artificial Intelligence in Classroom Management: A Systematic Review on Educational Purposes, Technical Implementations, and Ethical Considerations. *Computers and Education: Artificial Intelligence*, 100483.

Gansser, O. A., & Reich, C. S. (2021). A new acceptance model for artificial intelligence with extensions to UTAUT2: An empirical study in three segments of application. *Technology in Society*, *65*, 101535. DOI: 10.1016/j.techsoc.2021.101535

Gao, C., Khalid, S., Lianyu, C., & Tadesse, E. (2024). Integrated leadership for coherent school improvement in Ethiopia: The moderating role of transformational leadership on the relationship between instructional leadership and student academic achievement mediated by school improvement process. *Psychology in the Schools*, *61*(2), 455–474. DOI: 10.1002/pits.23065

Gao, Y. (2024). The impact and application of artificial intelligence technology on mental health counseling services for college students. *Journal of Computational Methods in Sciences and Engineering*, *25*(2), 1686–1701. DOI: 10.1177/14727978241302641

García-Peñalvo, F. J. (2023). The perception of Artificial Intelligence in educational contexts after the launch of ChatGPT: Disruption or Panic?. *Education in the knowledge society*.

George, B., & Wooden, O. (2023). Managing the strategic transformation of higher education through artificial intelligence. *Administrative Sciences*, *13*(9), 196. DOI: 10.3390/admsci13090196

Gerlich, M. (2025). AI tools in society: Impacts on Cognitive offloading and the future of critical thinking. *Societies (Basel, Switzerland)*, *15*(1), 6. DOI: 10.3390/soc15010006

Ghamrawi, N., Shal, T., & Ghamrawi, N. A. (2024). Exploring the impact of AI on teacher leadership: Regressing or expanding? *Education and Information Technologies*, *29*(7), 8415–8433. DOI: 10.1007/s10639-023-12174-w

Gillham, J. E., Shatté, A. J., Reivich, K. J., & Seligman, M. E. (2001). Optimism, pessimism, and explanatory style.

Glikson, E., & Woolley, A. W. (2020). Human trust in artificial intelligence: Review of empirical research. *The Academy of Management Annals*, *14*(2), 627–660. DOI: 10.5465/annals.2018.0057

Gobert, J. D., Sao Pedro, M., Raziuddin, J., & Baker, R. S. (2013). From log files to assessment metrics: Measuring students' science inquiry skills using educational data mining. *Journal of the Learning Sciences*, *22*(4), 521–563. DOI: 10.1080/10508406.2013.837391

Göçen, A., & Döğer, M. F. (2025). A global perspective on artificial intelligence in educational leadership. *The Journal of Educational Research*, *118*(6), 1–19. DOI: 10.1080/00220671.2025.2510397

Goel, A. K., & Polepeddi, L. (2018). Jill Watson: A virtual teaching assistant for online education. In *Learning engineering for Online Education* (pp. 120-143). Routledge.

Gondal, K. M. (2018). Artificial intelligence and educational leadership. *King Edward Medicine University Annuals*, *24*(4), 1–2.

Goto, M. (2022). Accepting the future as ever-changing: Professionals' sensemaking about artificial intelligence. *Journal of Professions and Organization*, *9*(1), 77–99. DOI: 10.1093/jpo/joab022

Gourlay, L. (2023). Postdigital/More-Than-Digital: Ephemerality, Seclusion, and Copresence in the University. In Jandrić, P., MacKenzie, A., & Knox, J. (Eds.), *Postdigital Research* (pp. 51–68). Springer Nature Switzerland., DOI: 10.1007/978-3-031-31299-1_4

Grace, E., Vidhyavathi, P., & Kumar, S. (2023). AI in education: Opportunities and challenges. *Industrial Engineering Journal*, *52*(5), 750–759. DOI: 10.36893/IEJ.2023.V52I05.750-759

Graham, C. R., Borup, J., Short, C. R., & Archambault, L. (2019). K-12 blended teaching: A guide to personalized learning and online integration. *Provo, UT: EdTechBooks.*

Graham, C. R., Woodfield, W., & Harrison, J. B. (2013). A framework for institutional adoption and implementation of blended learning in higher education. *The Internet and Higher Education*, *18*, 4–14. DOI: 10.1016/j.iheduc.2012.09.003

Grassini, S. (2023). Development and validation of the AI Attitude Scale (AIAS-4): A brief measure of general attitude toward artificial intelligence. *Frontiers in Psychology*, *14*, 1191628. DOI: 10.3389/fpsyg.2023.1191628

Gratani, F., Giannandrea, L., & Rossi, P. G. (2023). Learning in the post-digital era. Transforming education through the Maker approach. *Research on Education and Media*, *15*(1), 111–119. DOI: 10.2478/rem-2023-0015

Green, F. (2021). British teachers' declining job quality: Evidence from the skills and employment survey. *Oxford Review of Education*, *47*(3), 386–403. DOI: 10.1080/03054985.2020.1847719

Griesbach, K., Reich, A., Elliott-Negri, L., & Milkman, R. (2019). Algorithmic control in platform food delivery work. *Socius: Sociological Research for a Dynamic World*, *5*, 1–15. DOI: 10.1177/2378023119870041

Griffiths, W. (1959). The principle of participation: Some points to consider. *Health Education Journal*, *17*(4), 222–229. Advance online publication. DOI: 10.1177/001789695901700403

Grimaldi, E., & Ball, S. J. (2021). The blended learner: Digitalisation and regulated freedom - neoliberalism in the classroom. *Journal of Education Policy*, *36*(3), 393–416. DOI: 10.1080/02680939.2019.1704066

Grinschgl, S., & Neubauer, A. C. (2022). Supporting Cognition With Modern Technology: Distributed Cognition Today and in an AI-Enhanced Future. *Frontiers in Artificial Intelligence*, *5*, 908261. DOI: 10.3389/frai.2022.908261 PMID: 35910191

Guan, C., Mou, J., & Jiang, Z. (2020). Artificial intelligence innovation in education: A twenty-year data-driven historical analysis. *International Journal of Innovation Studies*, *4*(4), 134–147. DOI: 10.1016/j.ijis.2020.09.001

Hackney, H., & Cormier, S. (2008). *Psikolojik danışma ilke ve teknikleri: Psikolojik yardım süreci el kitabı* (Çev. T. Ergene, S. Aydemir Sevim). Mentis Yayıncılık. (Orijinal eser 2005'te yayımlandı)

Hackney, H., & Cormier, L. S. (2005). *The professional counselor: A process guide to helping*. Pearson.

Hair, J. F., Black, W. C., Babin, B. J., & Anderson, R. E. (2014). *Multivariate data analysis* (7th ed.). Pearson Education.

Hakel, K., & Magin, M. (2024). The impact of professional development training on faculty's integration of universal design for learning in daily teaching practices. *International Journal of Inclusive Education*, •••, 1–16. DOI: 10.1080/13603116.2024.2430527

Hamzah, M., Juraime, F., Hamid, A., Nordin, N., & Attan, N. (2014). Technology leadership and its relationship with school-Malaysia standard of education quality (School-MSEQ). *International Education Studies*, *7*(13), 278–285. DOI: 10.5539/ies.v7n13p278

Harms, P. D., & Han, G. (2019). Algorithmic leadership: The future is now. *Journal of Leadership Studies*, *12*(4), 74–75. DOI: 10.1002/jls.21615

Hatch, S. G., Goodman, Z. T., Vowels, L. M., Hatch, H. D., Brown, A. L., Guttman, S., Le, Y., Bailey, B., Bailey, R. J., Esplin, C. R., Harris, S. M., Holt, D. P., McLaughlin, M., O'Connell, P., Rothman, K., Ritchie, L., Top, D. N., & Braithwaite, S. R. (2025). When ELIZA meets therapists: A Turing test for the heart and mind. *PLOS Mental Health*, *2*(2), e0000145. DOI: 10.1371/journal.pmen.0000145

Hattie, J., & Timperley, H. (2007). The Power of Feedback. *Review of Educational Research*, *77*(1), 81–112. DOI: 10.3102/003465430298487

Hayes, A. F. (2022). *Introduction to mediation, moderation, and conditional process analysis: A regression-based approach* (3rd ed.). The Guilford Press.

Heinz, M. V., Mackin, D. M., Trudeau, B. M., Bhattacharya, S., Wang, Y., Banta, H. A., Jewett, A. D., Salzhauer, A. J., Griffin, T. Z., & Jacobson, N. C. (2025). Randomized trial of a generative AI chatbot for mental health treatment. *NEJM AI*, *2*(4). Advance online publication. DOI: 10.1056/AIoa2400802

Helsper, E. J., & Eynon, R. (2010). Digital natives: Where is the evidence? *British Educational Research Journal*, *36*(3), 503–520. DOI: 10.1080/01411920902989227

Herold, B. (2019). Forty percent of elementary school teachers' work could be automated by 2030, McKinsey Global Institute predicts. *Education Week*. https://www.edweek.org/education/forty-percent-of-elementary-school-teachers-work-could-be-automated-by-2030-mckinsey-global-institute-predicts/2019/06

Heung, Y. M. E., & Chiu, T. K. (2025). How ChatGPT impacts student engagement from a systematic review and meta-analysis study. *Computers and Education: Artificial Intelligence*, *8*, 100361. DOI: 10.1016/j.caeai.2025.100361

Hobfoll, S. E. (1989). Conservation of resources: A new attempt at conceptualizing stress. *The American Psychologist*, *44*(3), 513–524. DOI: 10.1037/0003-066X.44.3.513 PMID: 2648906

Hobfoll, S. E. (2001). The influence of culture, community, and the nested-self in the stress process: Advancing conservation of resources theory. *Applied Psychology*, *50*(3), 337–421. DOI: 10.1111/1464-0597.00062

Hobfoll, S. E., Halbesleben, J., Neveu, J. P., & Westman, M. (2018). Conservation of resources in the organizational context: The reality of resources and their consequences. *Annual Review of Organizational Psychology and Organizational Behavior*, *5*(1), 103–128. DOI: 10.1146/annurev-orgpsych-032117-104640

Hofstede, G. (2001). *Culture's consequences: Comparing values, behaviors, institutions and organizations across nations*. Sage Publications.

Hogan, A. (2025). *Commercialising public schooling: Practices of profit-making*. Routledge. DOI: 10.4324/9781003213093

Hollan, J., Hutchins, E., & Kirsh, D. (2000). Distributed cognition: Toward a new foundation for human-computer interaction research. *ACM Transactions on Computer-Human Interaction*, *7*(2), 174–196. DOI: 10.1145/353485.353487

Holmes, W. (2023). The unintended consequences of artificial intelligence and education.

Holmes, W., & Miao, F. (2023). *Guidance for generative AI in education and research*. UNESCO (Policy paper).

Holmes, W., Bialik, M., & Fadel, C. (2023). Artificial intelligence in education. In Stückelberger, C., & Duggal, P. (Eds.), *Data ethics: Building trust: How digital technologies can serve humanity* (pp. 621–653). Globethics Publications., DOI: 10.58863/20.500.12424/4276068

Holmes, W., Porayska-Pomsta, K., Holstein, K., Sutherland, E., Baker, T., Shum, S. B., Santos, O. C., Rodrigo, M. T., Cukurova, M., Bittencourt, I. I., & Koedinger, K. R. (2022). Ethics of AI in education: Towards a community-wide framework. *International Journal of Artificial Intelligence in Education*, *32*(3), 504–526. DOI: 10.1007/s40593-021-00239-1

Hou, Y., Cui, Y., & Zhang, D. (2019). Impact of instructional leadership on high school student academic achievement in China. *Asia Pacific Education Review*, *20*(4), 543–558. DOI: 10.1007/s12564-019-09574-4

Huang, J., Saleh, S., & Liu, Y. (2021). A review on artificial intelligence in education. *Academic Journal of Interdisciplinary Studies, 10*(3).

Huang, J., Saleh, S., & Liu, Y. (2021). A Review on Artificial Intelligence in Education. *Academic Journal of Interdisciplinary Studies*, *10*(3), 206–217. DOI: 10.36941/ajis-2021-0077

Huang, M. H., & Rust, R. T. (2018). Artificial intelligence in service. *Journal of Service Research*, *21*(2), 155–172. DOI: 10.1177/1094670517752459

Hu, L., & Bentler, P. M. (1999). Cutoff criteria for fit indexes in covariance structure analysis: Conventional criteria versus new alternatives. *Structural Equation Modeling*, *6*(1), 1–55. DOI: 10.1080/10705519909540118

Hutchins, E. (1996). *Cognition in the Wild*. MIT Press.

Hwang, G. J., Xie, H., Wah, B. W., & Gašević, D. (2020). Vision, challenges, roles, and research issues of artificial intelligence in education. *Computers and Education: Artificial Intelligence, 1,* 100001. International Society of Technology in Education (ISTE) (n.d). *ISTE standards for education leaders*. available at: https://www.iste.org/standards/for-education-leaders (accessed 10 September 2025).

Hwang, S. (2022). Examining the effects of artificial intelligence on elementary students' mathematics achievement: A meta-analysis. *Sustainability (Basel), 14*(20), 13185. DOI: 10.3390/su142013185

Imran, M., Almusharraf, N., Abdellatif, M. S., & Abbasova, M. Y. (2024). Artificial Intelligence in Higher Education: Enhancing Learning Systems and Transforming Educational Paradigms. [iJIM]. *International Journal of Interactive Mobile Technologies, 18*(18), 34–48. DOI: 10.3991/ijim.v18i18.49143

INTEF. (2024, julho 4). Guía sobre el uso de la inteligencia artificial en el ámbito educativo. INTEF. https://intef.es/Noticias/guia-sobre-el-uso-de-la-inteligencia-artificial-en-el-ambito-educativo/

James, J., Malkin, T., & Nusche, D. (2025). *Trends Shaping Education 2025.* OECD Publishing.

James, W. (2007). *The principles of psychology* (Vol. 1). Cosimo, Inc.

Janisch, C., Liu, X., & Akrofi, A. (2007). Implementing Alternative Assessment: Opportunities and Obstacles. *The Educational Forum, 71*(3), 221–230. DOI: 10.1080/00131720709335007

Jeong, J., & Jeong, I. (2025). Driving creativity in the AI-enhanced workplace: Roles of self-efficacy and transformational leadership. *Current Psychology (New Brunswick, N.J.), 44*(9), 8001–8014. DOI: 10.1007/s12144-024-07135-6

Kaldaras, L., Wang, K. D., Nardo, J. E., Price, A., Perkins, K., Wieman, C., & Salehi, S. (2024). Employing technology-enhanced feedback and scaffolding to support the development of deep science understanding using computer simulations. *International Journal of STEM Education, 11*(1), 30. DOI: 10.1186/s40594-024-00490-7

Kaplan, A., & Haenlein, M. (2020). Rulers of the world, unite! The challenges and opportunities of artificial intelligence. *Business Horizons, 63*(1), 37–50. DOI: 10.1016/j.bushor.2019.09.003

Kaplan, S., & Orlikowski, W. J. (2013). Temporal work in strategy making. *Organization Science, 24*(4), 965–995. DOI: 10.1287/orsc.1120.0792

Kapus, K., Nyulas, R., Nemeskeri, Z., Zadori, I., Muity, G., Kiss, J., Feher, A., Fejes, E., Tibold, A., & Feher, G. (2021). Prevalence and risk factors of internet addiction among Hungarian high school students. *International Journal of Environmental Research and Public Health, 18*(13), 6989. DOI: 10.3390/ijerph18136989 PMID: 34208800

Kasneci, E., Seßler, K., Küchemann, S., Bannert, M., Dementieva, D., Fischer, F., Gasser, U., Groh, G., Günnemann, S., Hüllermeier, E., Krusche, S., Kutyniok, G., Michaeli, T., Nerdel, C., Pfeffer, J., Poquet, O., Sailer, M., Schmidt, A., Seidel, T., & Kasneci, G. (2023). ChatGPT for good? On opportunities and challenges of large language models for education. *Learning and Individual Differences, 103*, 102274. DOI: 10.1016/j.lindif.2023.102274

Kaur, H., Adar, E., Gilbert, E., & Lampe, C. (2022). Sensible AI: Re-imagining interpretability and explainability using sensemaking theory. In *Proceedings of the 2022 ACM Conference on Fairness, Accountability, and Transparency (FAccT '22)* (pp. 702–714). https://doi.org/DOI: 10.1145/3531146.3533135

Kaya, F., Aydin, F., Schepman, A., Rodway, P., Yetişensoy, O., & Demir Kaya, M. (2024). The roles of personality traits, AI anxiety, and demographic factors in attitudes toward artificial intelligence. *International Journal of Human-Computer Interaction, 40*(2), 497–514. DOI: 10.1080/10447318.2022.2151730

Khalil, M., Slade, S., & Prinsloo, P. (2024). Learning analytics in support of inclusiveness and disabled students: A systematic review. *Journal of Computing in Higher Education, 36*(1), 202–219. DOI: 10.1007/s12528-023-09363-4 PMID: 37359042

Khosrawi-Rad, B., Keller, P. F., Benner, D., Grogorick, L., Borchers, A., Janson, A., Leimeister, J. M., & Robra-Bissantz, S. (2025). Promoting Students' Motivation in Language Education with Gamified Pedagogical Conversational Agents. *Computers & Education, 238*, 105374. DOI: 10.1016/j.compedu.2025.105374

Kılınç, A. Ç., Er, E., & Beycioglu, K. (2021). Mapping the terrain of training and appointment of educational leaders in the Turkish context: An historical perspective. In Samier, E., El Kaleh, E. and Hammad, W. (Eds). *Internationalisation of Educational Administration and Leadership Curriculum.* (pp. 139–157). Emerald.

Kline, R. B. (2005). *Methodology in the Social Sciences: Principles and practice of structural equation modelling.* Guilford.

Klos, M. C., Escoredo, M., Joerin, A., Lemos, V. N., Rauws, M., & Bunge, E. L. (2021). Artificial intelligence–based chatbot for anxiety and depression in university students: Pilot randomized controlled trial. *JMIR Formative Research, 5*(8), e20678. Advance online publication. DOI: 10.2196/20678 PMID: 34092548

Knox, J. (2019). What Does the 'Postdigital' Mean for Education? Three Critical Perspectives on the Digital, with Implications for Educational Research and Practice. *Postdigital Science and Education, 1*(2), 357–370. DOI: 10.1007/s42438-019-00045-y

Knox, J., Williamson, B., & Bayne, S. (2020). Machine behaviourism: Future visions of 'learnification' and 'datafication' across humans and digital technologies. *Learning, Media and Technology, 45*(1), 31–45. DOI: 10.1080/17439884.2019.1623251

Kohlbacher, F., & Herstatt, C. (Eds.). (2011). *The silver market phenomenon: Marketing and innovation in the aging society*. Springer Science & Business Media.

Kök, M., Tuğluk, M. N., & Bay, E. (2005). Okul öncesi eğitimin öğrencilerin gelişim özellikleri üzerindeki etkisinin incelenmesi. *Journal of Kazım Karabekir Education Faculty*, (11), 294–303.

Komalavalli, K., Hemalatha, R., & Dhanalakshmi, S. (2020). A survey of artificial intelligence in smart phones and its applications among the students of higher education in and around Chennai City. *Shanlax International Journal of Education, 8*(3), 89–95. DOI: 10.34293/education.v8i3.2379

Konlechner, S., Latzke, M., Güttel, W. H., & Höfferer, E. (2019). Prospective sensemaking, frames and planned change interventions: A comparison of change trajectories in two hospital units. *Human Relations, 72*(4), 706–732. DOI: 10.1177/0018726718773157

Korkmaz, C., & Correia, A. P. (2019). A review of research on machine learning in educational technology. *Educational Media International, 56*(3), 250–267. DOI: 10.1080/09523987.2019.1669875

Korkut Owen, F. (2017). *Okul temelli önleyici rehberlik ve psikolojik danışma* (4. baskı). Anı Yayıncılık.

Kosztelnik, K. (2019). Black box thinking: Navigating ethical AI in educational leadership. *Journal of Educational Ethics, 5*(2), 123–135. DOI: 10.1109/ICIME.2018.00075

Krejcie, R. V., & Morgan, D. W. (1970). Determining Sample Size for Research Activities. *Educational and Psychological Measurement, 30*(3), 607–610. DOI: 10.1177/001316447003000308

Kuhail, M. A., Alturki, N., Thomas, J., Alkhalifa, A. K., & Alshardan, A. (2024). Human-human vs human-aı therapy: An empirical study. *International Journal of Human-Computer Interaction, 41*(11), 6841–6852. DOI: 10.1080/10447318.2024.2385001

Kumar, K. S., & Akoijam, B. S. (2017). Depression, anxiety and stress among higher secondary school students of Imphal, Manipur. *Indian Journal of Community Medicine : Official Publication of Indian Association of Preventive & Social Medicine, 42*(2), 94–96. DOI: 10.4103/ijcm.IJCM_266_15 PMID: 28553025

Kurzweil, R. (2005). *The Singularity Is Near: When Humans Transcend Biology*. The Viking Press.

Kutbi, M., Al-Hoorie, A. H., & Al-Shammari, A. H. (2024). Detecting contract cheating through linguistic fingerprint. *Humanities & Social Sciences Communications, 11*(1), 664. DOI: 10.1057/s41599-024-03160-9

Lakhal, S., Bateman, D., & Bédard, J. (2017). Blended synchronous delivery mode in graduate programs: A literature review and its implementation in the master teacher program. *Collected Essays on Learning and Teaching, 10*, 47–60. DOI: 10.22329/celt.v10i0.4747

Lampou, R. (2023). The Integration of Artificial Intelligence in Education: Opportunities and Challenges. *Review of Artificial Intelligence in Education, 4*(00), e015. DOI: 10.37497/rev.artif.intell.educ.v4i00.15

Lancaster, T., & Cotarlan, C. (2021). Contract cheating by STEM students through a file sharing website: A Covid-19 pandemic perspective. *International Journal for Educational Integrity, 17*(1), 3. DOI: 10.1007/s40979-021-00070-0

Laupichler, M. C., Aster, A., Schirch, J., & Raupach, T. (2022). Artificial intelligence literacy in higher and adult education: A scoping review. *Computers and Education: Artificial Intelligence, 3*, 100101. DOI: 10.1016/j.caeai.2022.100101

Laursen, R., & Weiss, F. (2025). The role of school leaders' transformational leadership practices and sense-making during the implementation of new technology: The case of the mandatory introduction of a learning management system in Danish schools. *Leadership and Policy in Schools*, 1–15. Advance online publication. DOI: 10.1080/15700763.2025.2482160

Lazarus, R. S., & Folkman, S. (1984). *Stress, appraisal, and coping*. Springer.

Le, C. M., Huynh, S. V., Nguyen, V. H. A., Le, V. T., Luu-Thi, H. T., & Tran-Chi, V. L. (2024). Psychological difficulties and the needs for psychological services for high school students. *Discover Mental Health, 4*(1), 50. DOI: 10.1007/s44192-024-00101-5 PMID: 39495430

Lee, H., Kim, H., & Yan, W. (2025). Promoting inclusive AI and technology in K-12: A review of context, instructional strategies, and learning outcomes. *Computers and Education: Artificial Intelligence*, 100478.

Lee, E. E., Torous, J., De Choudhury, M., Depp, C. A., Graham, S. A., Kim, H. C., Paulus, M. P., Krystal, J. H., & Jeste, D. V. (2021). Artificial Intelligence for mental health care: Clinical applications, Barriers, facilitators, and artificial wisdom. *Biological Psychiatry: Cognitive Neuroscience and Neuroimaging*, *6*(9), 856–864. DOI: 10.1016/j.bpsc.2021.02.001 PMID: 33571718

Leithwood, K., Harris, A., & Hopkins, D. (2020). Seven strong claims about successful school leadership revisited. *School Leadership & Management*, *40*(1), 5–22. DOI: 10.1080/13632434.2019.1596077

Leong, W. Y., Leong, Y. Z., & Leong, W. S. (2025). Artificial Intelligence in education. *IET Conference Proceedings*, 2024(22), 183–184. DOI: 10.1049/icp.2024.4341

Levine, J. M., Resnick, L. B., & Higgins, E. T. (1993). Social foundations of cognition. *Annual Review of Psychology*, *44*(1), 585–612. DOI: 10.1146/annurev.ps.44.020193.003101

Levin, J. A., Fox, J. A., & Forde, D. R. (2010). *Elementary statistics in social research*. Allyn & Bacon Pearson.

Liang, H. Y., Hwang, G. J., Hsu, T. Y., & Yeh, J. Y. (2024). Effect of an AI-based chatbot on students' learning performance in alternate reality game-based museum learning. *British Journal of Educational Technology*, *55*(5), 2315–2338. DOI: 10.1111/bjet.13448

Liang, Y., & Lee, S. A. (2017). Fear of autonomous robots and artificial intelligence: Evidence from national representative data with probability sampling. *International Journal of Social Robotics*, *9*(3), 379–384. DOI: 10.1007/s12369-017-0401-3

Li, L., Lin, Y. L., Zheng, N. N., Wang, F. Y., Liu, Y., Cao, D., Wang, K., & Huang, W. L. (2018). Artificial intelligence test: A case study of intelligent vehicles. *Artificial Intelligence Review*, *50*(3), 441–465. DOI: 10.1007/s10462-018-9631-5

Lim, S. M., Shiau, C. W. C., Cheng, L. J., & Lau, Y. (2022). Chatbot-delivered psychotherapy for adults with depressive and anxiety symptoms: A systematic review and meta-regression. Behav Ther. *Behavior Therapy*, *53*(2), 334–347. DOI: 10.1016/j.beth.2021.09.007 PMID: 35227408

Li, S., & Gu, X. (2023). A risk framework for human-centered artificial ıntelligence in education: Based on literature review and Delphi–AHP Method. *Journal of Educational Technology & Society*, *26*(1), 187–202.

Li an, D.-E. (2025). The impact of technostress generated by artificial intelligence on the quality of life: The mediating role of positive and negative affect. *Behavioral Sciences (Basel, Switzerland)*, *15*(4), 552. DOI: 10.3390/bs15040552 PMID: 40282173

Liu, L., Zhou, B., Zou, Z., Yeh, S. C., & Zheng, L. (2018, September). A smart unstaffed retail shop based on artificial intelligence and IoT. In *2018 IEEE 23rd International workshop on computer aided modeling and design of communication links and networks (CAMAD)* (pp. 1-4). IEEE. DOI: 10.1109/CAMAD.2018.8514988

Livingstone, S., & Helsper, E. (2007). Gradations in digital inclusion: Children, young people and the digital divide. *New Media & Society*, *9*(4), 671–696. DOI: 10.1177/1461444807080335

Li, Y.-D., & Ding, G.-H. (2023). Student-centered education: A meta-analysis of its effects on non-academic achievements. *SAGE Open*, *13*(2), 21582440231168792. Advance online publication. DOI: 10.1177/21582440231168792

Lopez, S. J., Snyder, C. R., & Pedrotti, J. T. (2004). Hope: Many definitions, many measures. In Lopez, S. J., & Snyder, C. R. (Eds.), *Positive psychological assessment: A handbook of models and measures* (pp. 91–106). American Psychological Association.

Luckin, R., Holmes, W., Griffiths, M., & Forcier, L. B. (2016). *Intelligence Unleashed: An argument for AI in Education*. Open Ideas; Pearson Education, London.

Luckin, R. (2025). Nurturing human intelligence in the age of AI: Rethinking education for the future. *Development and Learning in Organizations, 39*(1), 1–4. DOI: 10.1108/DLO-04-2024-0108

Luckin, R., Cukurova, M., Kent, C., & Du Boulay, B. (2022). Empowering educators to be AI-ready. Computers and Education. *Artificial Intelligence*, *3*, 100076.

Luthans, F. (2002). Positive organizational behavior: Developing and managing psychological strengths. *The Academy of Management Perspectives*, *16*(1), 57–72. DOI: 10.5465/ame.2002.6640181

Luthans, F., Avolio, B. J., Avey, J. B., & Norman, S. M. (2007). Positive psychological capital: Measurement and relationship with performance and satisfaction. *Personnel Psychology*, *60*(3), 541–572. DOI: 10.1111/j.1744-6570.2007.00083.x

Luthans, F., & Jensen, S. M. (2002). Hope: A new positive strength for human resource development. *Human Resource Development Review*, *1*(3), 304–322. DOI: 10.1177/1534484302013003

Luxton, D. D. (2014). Artificial intelligence in psychological practice: Current and future applications and implications. *Professional Psychology, Research and Practice*, *45*(5), 332–339. DOI: 10.1037/a0034559

Luxton, D. D. (2016). An Introduction to Artificial Intelligence in Behavioral and Mental Health Care. In Luxton, D. D. (Ed.), *Artificial Intelligence in behavıoral and mental health care* (pp. 1–25). Academic Press. DOI: 10.1016/B978-0-12-420248-1.00001-5

Madaio, M., Blodgett, S. L., Mayfield, E., & Dixon-Román, E. (2022). Beyond "fairness": Structural (in) justice lenses on ai for education. In *The ethics of artificial intelligence in education* (pp. 203-239). Routledge.

Mallik, S., & Gangopadhyay, A. (2023). Proactive and reactive engagement of artificial intelligence methods for education: A review. *Frontiers in Artificial Intelligence*, *6*, 1151391. DOI: 10.3389/frai.2023.1151391 PMID: 37215064

Manole, A., Cârciumaru, R., Brînza , R., & Manole, F. (2025). An exploratory ınvestigation of chatbot applications in anxiety management: A focus on personalized ınterventions. *Information (Basel)*, *16*(1), 11. DOI: 10.3390/info16010011

Markauskaite, L., Marrone, R., Poquet, O., Knight, S., Martinez-Maldonado, R., Howard, S., Tondeur, J., De Laat, M., Buckingham Shum, S., Gašević, D., & Siemens, G. (2022). Rethinking the entwinement between artificial intelligence and human learning: What capabilities do learners need for a world with AI? *Computers and Education: Artificial Intelligence*, *3*, 100056. DOI: 10.1016/j.caeai.2022.100056

Marrone, R., Fowler, S., Bathakur, A., Dawson, S., Siemens, G., & Singh, C. (2025). Perceptions and perspectives of Australian school leaders on the integration of artificial intelligence in schools. *School Leadership & Management*, *45*(1), 30–52. DOI: 10.1080/13632434.2024.2425019

Martínez, I. G., Fernández Batanero, J. M., Fernández Cerero, J., & León, S. P. (2023). Analysing the impact of artificial intelligence and computational sciences on student performance: Systematic review and meta-analysis. *NAER: Journal of New Approaches in Educational Research*, *12*(1), 171–197. DOI: 10.7821/naer.2023.1.1240

Maslach, C., Schaufeli, W. B., & Leiter, M. P. (2001). Job burnout. *Annual Review of Psychology*, *52*(1), 397–422. DOI: 10.1146/annurev.psych.52.1.397 PMID: 11148311

McCall, G. J. (2013). Interactionist perspectives in social psychology. In DeLamater, J., & Ward, A. (Eds.), *Handbook of Social Psychology: Handbooks of Sociology and Social Research* (pp. 3–29). Springer. DOI: 10.1007/978-94-007-6772-0_1

Melo-López, V.-A., Basantes-Andrade, A., Gudiño-Mejía, C.-B., & Hernández-Martínez, E. (2025). The Impact of Artificial Intelligence on Inclusive Education: A Systematic Review. *Education Sciences*, *15*(5), 539. DOI: 10.3390/educsci15050539

Mesman, E., Vreeker, A., & Hillegers, M. (2021). Resilience and mental health in children and adolescents: An update of the recent literature and future directions. *Current Opinion in Psychiatry, 34*(6), 586–592. DOI: 10.1097/YCO.0000000000000741 PMID: 34433193

Miao, F., & Holmes, W. (2023). *Guidance for generative ai in education and research (UNESCO publication).* United Nations Educational, Scientific and Cultural Organization. https://unesdoc.unesco.org/ark:/48223/pf0000386693

Microsoft Education. (2025). *2025 AI in Education: A Microsoft Special Report.* Microsoft Corporation.

Ministry of National Education [MoNE]. (2024a). Maarif Model. Available at: https://tymm.meb.gov.tr/ (accessed 04 August 2025).

Ministry of National Education [MoNE]. (2024b). 2024–2028 Ministry of National Education strategic plan 2024–2028. Available at: https://sgb.meb.gov.tr/yayinlarimiz/yayin/112. (accessed 04 August 2025).

Minn, S. (2022). AI-assisted knowledge assessment techniques for adaptive learning environments. *Computers and Education: Artificial Intelligence, 3*, 100050. Advance online publication. DOI: 10.1016/j.caeai.2022.100050

Mishra, D. (2025). Artificial Intelligence as a Mediator between Educator and Learner: The New Paradigm Shift. *International Journal of Research and Innovation in Applied Science, X*(VII), 91–95. DOI: 10.51584/IJRIAS.2025.100700008

Mitchell, M., & Egudo, M. (2003). A Review of Narrative Methodology [Dataset]. DOI: 10.1037/e426492005-001

Mohammadi, M., Tajik, E., Martinez-Maldonado, R., Sadiq, S., Tomaszewski, W., & Khosravi, H. (2025). Artificial intelligence in multimodal learning analytics: a systematic literature review. *Computers and Education: Artificial Intelligence*, 100426.

Molina-Carmona, R., & Villagrá-Arnedo, C. (2018). Smart Learning. *Proceedings of the Sixth International Conference on Technological Ecosystems for Enhancing Multiculturality*, 645–647. DOI: 10.1145/3284179.3284288

Montag, C., Kraus, J., Baumann, M., & Rozgonjuk, D. (2023). The propensity to trust in (automated) technology mediates the links between technology self-efficacy and fear and acceptance of artificial intelligence. *Computers in Human Behavior Reports, 11*, 100315. DOI: 10.1016/j.chbr.2023.100315

Moons, P. (2024). For better or for worse: When chatbots influence human emotions and behaviours. *European Journal of Cardiovascular Nursing*, *23*(5), e49–e51. DOI: 10.1093/eurjcn/zvad098 PMID: 37791604

Morris, T. H., & Rohs, M. (2023). The potential for digital technology to support self-directed learning in formal education of children: A scoping review. *Interactive Learning Environments*, *31*(4), 1974–1987. DOI: 10.1080/10494820.2020.1870501

Moustaghfir, S., & Brigui, H. (2024). Navigating Critical Thinking in the Digital Era: An Informative Exploration. International Journal of Linguistics. *Literature and Translation*, *7*(1), 137–143. DOI: 10.32996/ijllt.2024.7.1.11x

Muijs, D., & Reynolds, D. (2017). *Effective Teaching: Evidence and Practice*. SAGE.

Müller, V. C. (2016). *Risks of artificial intelligence*. Chapman & Hall. DOI: 10.1201/b19187

Mumford, M. D., Scott, G. M., Gaddis, B., & Strange, J. M. (2002). Leading creative people: Orchestrating expertise and competitive innovation. *The Leadership Quarterly*, *13*(6), 705–750. DOI: 10.1016/S1048-9843(02)00158-3

Murphy, W. M. (2012). Reverse mentoring at work: Fostering cross-generational learning and developing millennial leaders. *Human Resource Management*, *51*(4), 549–573. DOI: 10.1002/hrm.21489

Naor, N., Frenkel, A., & Winsberg, M. (2022). Improving well-being with a mobile artificial ıntelligence–powered acceptance commitment therapy tool: Pragmatic Retrospective Study. *JMIR Formative Research*, *6*(7), e36018. Advance online publication. DOI: 10.2196/36018 PMID: 35598216

Navas-Bonilla, C. D. R., Guerra-Arango, J. A., Oviedo-Guado, D. A., & Murillo-Noriega, D. E. (2025, February). Inclusive education through technology: A systematic review of types, tools and characteristics. [). Frontiers Media SA.]. *Frontiers in Education*, *10*, 1527851. DOI: 10.3389/feduc.2025.1527851

Ng, D. T. K., Leung, J. K. L., Chu, S. K. W., & Qiao, M. S. (2021). Conceptualizing AI literacy: An exploratory review. *Computers and Education: Artificial Intelligence*, 2, 100041. DOI: 10.1016/j.caeai.2021.100041

Ng, D. T. K., Leung, J. K. L., Su, J., Ng, R. C. W., & Chu, S. K. W. (2023). Teachers' AI digital competencies and twenty-first century skills in the post-pandemic world. *Educational Technology Research and Development*, *71*(1), 137–161. DOI: 10.1007/s11423-023-10203-6 PMID: 36844361

Nikolic, S., Daniel, S., Haque, R., Belkina, M., Hassan, G. M., Grundy, S., … Sandison, C. (2023). ChatGPT versus engineering education assessment: A multidisciplinary benchmarking. *IEEE Transactions on Education*, (early access). DOI: 10.1080/03043797.2023.2213169

Noble, S. U. (2018). *Algorithms of Oppression: How Search Engines Reinforce Racism*. NYU Press., DOI: 10.18574/nyu/9781479833641.001.0001

Núñez, J. M., Soto-Rubio, A., & Pérez-Marín, M. (2024). Executive Functions and Special Educational Needs and Their Relationship with School-Age Learning Difficulties. *Children (Basel, Switzerland)*, *11*(11), 1398. DOI: 10.3390/children11111398 PMID: 39594973

Obmerga, M. E. (2024). For whom the bell (really) tolls: A grounded theory of millennial academic supervisors' sensemaking of communitarian values as a springboard to enrich their transformational leadership attributes. *International Journal of Leadership in Education*, *27*(2), 283–315. DOI: 10.1080/13603124.2020.1862919

Odugbesan, J. A., Aghazadeh, S., Al Qaralleh, R. E., & Sogeke, O. S. (2023). Green talent management and employees' innovative work behavior: The roles of artificial intelligence and transformational leadership. *Journal of Knowledge Management*, *27*(3), 696–716. DOI: 10.1108/JKM-08-2021-0601

OECD. (2023). *OECD Digital Education Outlook 2023: Towards an Effective Digital Education Ecosystem*. OECD., DOI: 10.1787/c74f03de-

OECD. (2024). *Education Policy Outlook 2024: Reshaping Teaching into a Thriving Profession from ABCs to AI*. OECD., DOI: 10.1787/dd5140e4-

Öğdem, Z., & Sönmez, E. (2022). Evaluation of the Distance Education Process based on Teachers' Opinions during the Covıd-19 Pandemic. *Malaysian Online Journal of Educational Technology*, *10*(1), 61–75. DOI: 10.52380/mojet.2022.10.1.351

Okan, N., & Okan, Y. T. (2021). Turkish adaptation and psychometric analysis of the short transformational leadership scale. *Turkish Studies - Social, 16*(2), 687–700. https://dx.doi.org/DOI: 10.47356/TurkishStudies.48329

Olawade, D. B., Wada, O. Z., Odetayo, A., David-Olawade, A. C., Asaolu, F., & Eberhardt, J. (2024). Enhancing mental health with Artificial Intelligence: Current trends and future prospects. *Journal of Medicine, Surgery, and Public Health*, *3*, 100099. Advance online publication. DOI: 10.1016/j.glmedi.2024.100099

Olsen, J. K., Rummel, N., & Aleven, V. (2021). Designing for the co-orchestration of social transitions between individual, small-group and whole-class learning in the classroom. *International Journal of Artificial Intelligence in Education, 31*(1), 24–56. DOI: 10.1007/s40593-020-00228-w

Otaye-Ebede, L., Shaffakat, S., & Foster, S. (2020). A multilevel model examining the relationships between workplace spirituality, ethical climate and outcomes: A social cognitive theory perspective. *Journal of Business Ethics, 166*(3), 611–626. DOI: 10.1007/s10551-019-04133-8

Öztemel, E. (2018). Eğitimde yeni yönelimlerin değerlendirilmesi ve Eğitim 4.0 [Evaluating new trends in education and Education 4.0]. *Journal of University Research, 1*(1), 25–30. DOI: 10.32329/uad.382041

Paas, F. (1992). Training strategies for attaining transfer of problem-solving skill in statistics: A cognitive-load approach. *Journal of Educational Psychology, 84*(4), 429–434. DOI: 10.1037/0022-0663.84.4.429

Paas, F., & Van Merriënboer, J. J. G. (1994). Instructional control of cognitive load in the training of complex cognitive tasks. *Educational Psychology Review, 6*(4), 351–371. DOI: 10.1007/BF02213420

Panadero, E., Andrade, H., & Brookhart, S. (2018). Fusing self-regulated learning and formative assessment: A roadmap of where we are, how we got here, and where we are going. *Australian Educational Researcher, 45*(1), 13–31. DOI: 10.1007/s13384-018-0258-y

Pannu, A. (2015). Artificial intelligence and its application in different areas. *Artificial Intelligence, 4*(10), 79–84.

Paré, G., Trudel, M.-C., Jaana, M., & Kitsiou, S. (2015). Synthesizing information systems knowledge: A typology of literature reviews. *Information & Management, 52*(2), 183–199. DOI: 10.1016/j.im.2014.08.008

Park, J., & Woo, S. E. (2022). Who likes artificial intelligence? Personality predictors of attitudes toward artificial intelligence. *The Journal of Psychology, 156*(1), 68–94. DOI: 10.1080/00223980.2021.2012109 PMID: 35015615

Pawar, G., & Khose, J. (2024). *Exploring the role of artificial intelligence in enhancing equity and inclusion in education. International Journal of Innovative Science and Research Technology*. IJISRT.

Pepito, G. M., & Montalbo, I. C. (2019). Separation anxiety on preschoolers' development. *International Journal of Engineering Education, 8*(1), 229–239.

Pereira, V., Hadjielias, E., Christofi, M., & Vrontis, D. (2023). A systematic literature review on the impact of artificial intelligence on workplace outcomes: A multi-process perspective. *Human Resource Management Review, 33*(1), 100857. DOI: 10.1016/j.hrmr.2021.100857

Peterson, C. (2000). The future of optimism. *The American Psychologist, 55*(1), 44–55. DOI: 10.1037/0003-066X.55.1.44 PMID: 11392864

Pietsch, M., & Mah, D. K. (2025). Leading the AI transformation in schools: It starts with a digital mindset. *Educational Technology Research and Development, 73*(2), 1043–1069. DOI: 10.1007/s11423-024-10439-w

Pimentel, J. L. (2019). Some biases in Likert scaling usage and its correction. [IJSBAR]. *International Journal of Sciences, Basic and Applied Research, 45*(1), 183–191.

Pirkkalainen, H., Salo, M., Tarafdar, M., & Makkonen, M. (2019). Deliberate or instinctive? Proactive and reactive coping for technostress. *Journal of Management Information Systems, 36*(4), 1179–1212. DOI: 10.1080/07421222.2019.1661092

Pramanik, P. K. D., Pal, S., Mukhopadhyay, M., & Singh, S. P. (2021). Big Data classification: techniques and tools. In Khanna, A., Gupta, D., & Dey, N. (Eds.), *Applications of big data in healthcare* (pp. 137–171). Academic Press. DOI: 10.1016/B978-0-12-820203-6.00002-3

Prensky, M. (2001). Digital natives, digital immigrants part 2: Do they really think differently? *On the Horizon, 9*(6), 1–6. DOI: 10.1108/10748120110424843

Promsiri, T. (2025). AI and the psychology of educational disruption: Historical patterns and cognitive implications. *Acta Psychologica, 260*, 105637. DOI: 10.1016/j.actpsy.2025.105637 PMID: 41027066

Ragu-Nathan, T. S., Tarafdar, M., Ragu-Nathan, B. S., & Tu, Q. (2008). The consequences oftechnostress for end users in organizations: Conceptual development and empirical validation. *Information Systems Research, 19*(4), 417–433. DOI: 10.1287/isre.1070.0165

Rahim, T. N. T. A., Aziz, Z. A., Rauf, R. H. A., & Shamsudin, N. (2018). Automated exam question generator using genetic algorithm. *2017 IEEE Conference on e-Learning, e-Management and e-Services*, IC3e 2017.

Raisch, S., & Krakowski, S. (2021). Artificial intelligence and management: The automation-augmentation paradox. *Academy of Management Review, 46*(1), 192–210. DOI: 10.5465/amr.2018.0072

Rajkumar, S., Kishore, R., Lavanya, N., Prashanth Kumar, M., Naveen, B., Prathap Raju, S., & Swathi, P. (2025). The Role of Artificial Intelligence Tools in Teaching and Learning Process of Education. [IRJAEM]. *International Research Journal on Advanced Engineering and Management, 3*(05), 1774–1783. DOI: 10.47392/IRJAEM.2025.0280

Ramnarain, U., Ogegbo, A. A., Penn, M., Ojetunde, S., & Mdlalose, N. (2024). Pre-service science teachers' intention to use generative artificial intelligence in inquiry-based teaching. *Journal of Science Education and Technology*, 1–14. DOI: 10.1007/s10956-024-10159-z

Ray, S., & Ray, D. P. (2024). Artificial Intelligence in Education: Navigating the nexus of innovation and ethics for future learning landscapes. International Journal of Research -GRANTHAALAYAH, 11(12). DOI: 10.29121/granthaalayah.v11.i12.2023.5464

Raymond-Tolan, L., Arcidiacono, T., Panzarino, C., & Vazquez, A. (2025). The impact and experience of directly teaching about executive functions (EF) to 2nd-grade students on their understanding and performance of EF skills. *Journal of Occupational Therapy, Schools & Early Intervention*, •••, 1–13. DOI: 10.1080/19411243.2025.2455619

Reid, D. B., & Creed, B. M. (2023). Visible at night: US school principal nontraditional work-hour activities and job satisfaction. *Educational Management Administration & Leadership, 51*(5), 1123–1140. DOI: 10.1177/17411432211027645

Renta-Davids, A. I., Camarero-Figuerola, M., & Camacho, M. (2025). Navigating the challenges and opportunities of artificial intelligence in educational leadership: A scoping review. *Review of Education, 13*(2), e70101. DOI: 10.1002/rev3.70101

Revishvili, M., & Tsereteli, M. (2024). The psychological mechanism of self-regulated learning in a technology-enhanced environment. *Cogent Education, 11*(1), 2372153. Advance online publication. DOI: 10.1080/2331186X.2024.2372153

Richardson, J. W., McLeod, S., & Sauers, S. N. J. (2015). Technology leadership is just good leadership: Dispositions of tech savvy superintendents. *AASA Journal of Scholarship and Practice, 12*(1), 11–30.

Richardson, J. W., Vedder, B. C., Roberts, A. B., & McLeod, S. (2025). What's the chatter about AI and school leaders? *Leadership and Policy in Schools, 24*(1), 103–116.

Rickey, N., Panadero, E., & DeLuca, C. (2025). How do students self-assess? examining the metacognitive processes of student self-assessment. *Metacognition and Learning*, *20*(1), 25. DOI: 10.1007/s11409-025-09430-4

Rincon-Flores, E. G., Castano, L., Guerrero Solis, S. L., Olmos Lopez, O., Rodríguez Hernández, C. F., Castillo Lara, L. A., & Aldape Valdés, L. P. (2024). Improving the learning-teaching process through adaptive learning strategy. *Smart Learning Environments*, *11*(1), 27. DOI: 10.1186/s40561-024-00314-9

Riva, G., Wiederhold, B. K., & Cipresso, P. (2025). Humane Artificial Intelligence: Psychological, Social, and Ethical Dimensions. *Cyberpsychology, Behavior, and Social Networking*, *28*(7), 457–461. DOI: 10.1089/cyber.2025.0202 PMID: 40501330

Rizvi, N., Wu, W., Bolds, M., Mondal, R., Begel, A., & Munyaka, I. N. (2024, May). Are Robots Ready to Deliver Autism Inclusion?: A Critical Review. In *Proceedings of the 2024 CHI Conference on Human Factors in Computing Systems* (pp. 1-18). DOI: 10.1145/3613904.3642798

Roberts, B. R. T., MacLeod, C. M., & Fernandes, M. A. (2022). The enactment effect: A systematic review and meta-analysis of behavioral, neuroimaging, and patient studies. *Psychological Bulletin*, *148*(5-6), 397–435. DOI: 10.1037/bul0000360 PMID: 35878067

Rodríguez-Ruiz, J., Marín-López, I., & Espejo-Siles, R. (2025). Is artificial intelligence use related to self-control, self-esteem and self-efficacy among university students? *Education and Information Technologies*, *30*(2), 2507–2524. DOI: 10.1007/s10639-024-12906-6

Roffey, S. (2012). Pupil wellbeing-Teacher wellbeing: Two sides of the same coin? *Educational and Child Psychology*, *29*(4), 8–17. DOI: 10.53841/bpsecp.2012.29.4.8

Ro, J. (2025). Enforcing unwarranted optimism: Critical frame analysis on educational digitalisation policies in South Korea. *Learning, Media and Technology*, •••, 1–16. DOI: 10.1080/17439884.2025.2462940

Roll, I., & Wylie, R. (2016). Evolution and revolution in artificial intelligence in education. *International Journal of Artificial Intelligence in Education*, *26*(2), 582–599. DOI: 10.1007/s40593-016-0110-3

Rudolph, J., Tan, S., & Tan, S. (2023). ChatGPT: Bullshit spewer or the end of traditional assessments in higher education? *Journal of applied learning and teaching*, *6*(1), 342-363. DOI: 10.37074/jalt.2023.6.1.9

Rudolph, J., Tan, S., & Tan, S. (2023). War of the chatbots: Bard, Bing Chat, ChatGPT, Ernie and beyond. The new AI gold rush and its impact on higher education. *Journal of Applied Learning and Teaching*, *6*(1), 364–389.

Russell, S., & Norvig, P. (2021). Artificial intelligence: a modern approach, global edition 4th. *Foundations, 19*(23), 44-85.

Ryan, R. M., & Deci, E. L. (2000). Self-determination theory and the facilitation of intrinsic motivation, social development, and well-being. *The American Psychologist*, *55*(1), 68–78. DOI: 10.1037/0003-066X.55.1.68 PMID: 11392867

Sadiku, M. N. O., Ashaolu, T. J., Ajayi-Majebi, A., & Musa, S. M. (2021). Artificial Intelligence in Education. *International Journal Of Scientific Advances*, *2*(1). Advance online publication. DOI: 10.51542/ijscia.v2i1.2

Şahin, S., & Hepsöğütlü, Z. B. (2018). Psychological Resilience and Coping Strategies of High School Students Based on Certain Variables. *Journal of Educational and Social Research*, *8*(2), 49–64. DOI: 10.22521/jesr.2018.82.2

Salanova, M., Llorens, S., & Cifre, E. (2013). The dark side of technologies: Technostress among users of information and communication technologies. *International Journal of Psychology*, *48*(3), 422–436. DOI: 10.1080/00207594.2012.680460 PMID: 22731610

Saltman, K. (2020). Artificial intelligence and the technological turn of public education privatization: In defence of democratic education. *London Review of Education*, *18*(2), 196–208. DOI: 10.14324/LRE.18.2.04

Sandberg, J., & Tsoukas, H. (2020). Sensemaking reconsidered: Towards a broader understanding through phenomenology. *Organization Theory*, *1*(1), 1–34. DOI: 10.1177/2631787719879937

Santamaria, T., & Nathan-Roberts, D. (2017). Personality measurement and design in human-robot interaction: A systematic and critical review. *Proceedings of the Human Factors and Ergonomics Society Annual Meeting*, *61*(1), 853–857. DOI: 10.1177/1541931213601686

Sari, T., Nayi, R. F., & Bozkurt, A. (2024). Reimagining education: Bridging artificial intelligence, transhumanism, and critical pedagogy. *Journal of Educational Technology and Online Learning*, *7*(1), 102–115. DOI: 10.31681/jetol.1308022

Sari, T., & Nayır, F. (2020). Challenges in distance education during the (Covid-19) pandemic period. *Qualitative Research in Education*, *9*(3), 328–360. DOI: 10.17583/qre.2020.5872

Savi Cakar, F. (2024). *Yaşam dönemleri ve uyum sorunları* (10th ed.). Pegem.

Scheier, M. F., & Carver, C. S. (1985). Optimism, coping, and health: Assessment and implications of generalized outcome expectancies. *Health Psychology*, *4*(3), 219–247. DOI: 10.1037/0278-6133.4.3.219 PMID: 4029106

Schepman, A., & Rodway, P. (2023). The general attitudes towards artificial intelligence scale (GAAIS): Confirmatory validation and associations with personality, corporate distrust, and general trust. *International Journal of Human-Computer Interaction*, *39*(13), 2724–2741. DOI: 10.1080/10447318.2022.2085400

Schillings, C., Meißner, E., Erb, B., Bendig, E., Schultchen, D., & Pollatos, O. (2024). Effects of a chatbot-based ıntervention on stress and health-related parameters in a stressed sample: Randomized controlled trial. *JMIR Mental Health*, *11*, e50454. DOI: 10.2196/50454 PMID: 38805259

Schnotz, W., & Kürschner, C. (2007). A reconsideration of cognitive load theory. *Educational Psychology Review*, *19*(4), 469–508. DOI: 10.1007/s10648-007-9053-4

Schraw, G. (1998). Promoting general metacognitive awareness. *Instructional Science*, *26*(1-2), 113–125. DOI: 10.1023/A:1003044231033

Schunk, D. H., & DiBenedetto, M. K. (2020). Motivation and social cognitive theory. *Contemporary Educational Psychology*, *60*, 101832. DOI: 10.1016/j.cedpsych.2019.101832

Sebastian, J., Camburn, E. M., & Spillane, J. P. (2018). Portraits of principal practice: Time allocation and school principal work. *Educational Administration Quarterly*, *54*(1), 47–84. DOI: 10.1177/0013161X17720978

Seemiller, C., & Grace, M. (2018). *Generation Z: A century in the making*. Routledge. DOI: 10.4324/9780429442476

Seldon, A., & Abidoye, O. (2018). *The fourth education revolution*. Legend Press Ltd.

Selwyn, N. (2024). On the Limits of Artificial Intelligence (AI) in Education. Nordisk tidsskrift for pedagogikk og kritikk, 10(1). DOI: 10.23865/ntpk.v10.6062

Şenocak, D. (2020). Açık ve uzaktan öğrenme ortamlarında yapay zekâ: Sunduğu fırsatlar ve yarattığı endişeler [Artificial intelligence in open and distance learning environments: Opportunities and concerns]. *Açıköğretim Uygulamaları ve Araştırmaları Dergisi*, *6*(3), 56–78.

Sezgin, S., & Fırat, M. (2020). Covid-19 pandemisinde uzaktan eğitime geçiş ve dijital uçurum tehlikesi. *Açıköğretim Uygulamaları ve Araştırmaları Dergisi*, *6*(4), 37–54.

Shankar, G. M., & Venkateswaramurthy, N. (2025). Artificial intelligence (AI) generated health counseling for mental illness patients. *Current Psychiatry Research and Reviews, 21*(3), 269–283. DOI: 10.2174/0126660822277500240109050359

Shank, D. B., Graves, C., Gott, A., Gamez, P., & Rodriguez, S. (2019). Feeling our way to machine minds: People's emotions when perceiving minds in artificial intelligence. *Computers in Human Behavior, 98*, 256–266. DOI: 10.1016/j.chb.2019.04.001

Shek, D. T., & Wong, T. T. Y. (2025). Developmental Issues of University Stud Shek, D.T., Wong, T.T.Y. (2025). Developmental Issues of University Students in Hong Kong. In: Promoting holistic development in university students. Quality of Life in Asia, vol 17. Springer, Singapore. https://doi.org/DOI: 10.1007/978-981-96-0251-3_3

Shen, J., Wu, H., Reeves, P., Zheng, Y., Ryan, L., & Anderson, D. (2020). The association between teacher leadership and student achievement: A meta-analysis. *Educational Research Review, 31*(100357), 1–19. DOI: 10.1016/j.edurev.2020.100357

Shen, L., Qiu, N., & Wang, Z. (2025). Psychological safety and trust as drivers of teachers' continued use of AI tools in classrooms. *Scientific Reports, 15*(1), 31426. DOI: 10.1038/s41598-025-13789-4 PMID: 40858670

Shneiderman, B. (2020). Human-centered artificial intelligence: Reliable, safe & trustworthy. *International Journal of Human-Computer Interaction, 36*(6), 495–504. DOI: 10.1080/10447318.2020.1741118

Shorey, S., Ng, E. D., & Wong, C. H. J. (2022). Global prevalence of depression and elevated depressive symptoms among adolescents: A systematic review and meta-analysis. *British Journal of Clinical Psychology, 61*(2), 287–305. DOI: 10.1111/bjc.12333 PMID: 34569066

Shwedeh, F. (2024). The integration of Artificial Intelligence into decision support systems within higher education institutions. *Nanotechnology Perceptions, 20*(5), 331–357.

Sijing, L., & Lan, W. (2018). Artificial Intelligence Education Ethical Problems and Solutions. 2018 13th International Conference on Computer Science & Education (ICCSE), 1–5. DOI: 10.1109/ICCSE.2018.8468773

Simbula, S., Guglielmi, D., & Schaufeli, W. B. (2011). A three-wave study of job resources, self-efficacy, and work engagement among Italian schoolteachers. *European Journal of Work and Organizational Psychology, 20*(3), 285–304. DOI: 10.1080/13594320903513916

Simon, H. A. (1972). Theories of bounded rationality. In McGuire, C. B., & Radner, R. (Eds.), *Decision and organization* (pp. 161–176). North-Holland.

Skaalvik, C. (2020). Self-efficacy for instructional leadership: Relations with perceived job demands and job resources, emotional exhaustion, job satisfaction, and motivation to quit. *Social Psychology of Education*, *23*(5), 1343–1366. DOI: 10.1007/s11218-020-09585-9

Smith, A. M., & Green, M. (2018). Artificial intelligence and the role of leadership. *Journal of Leadership Studies*, *12*(1), 85–87. DOI: 10.1002/jls.21605

Snyder, C. R. (1994). *The psychology of hope: You can get there from here*. Simon and Schuster.

Snyder, C. R. (2002). Hope theory: Rainbows in the mind. *Psychological Inquiry*, *13*(4), 249–275. DOI: 10.1207/S15327965PLI1304_01

Snyder, C. R., Harris, C., Anderson, J. R., Holleran, S. A., Irving, L. M., Sigmon, S. T., Yoshinobu, L., Gibb, J., Langelle, C., & Harney, P. (1991). The will and the ways: Development and validation of an individual-differences measure of hope. *Journal of Personality and Social Psychology*, *60*(4), 570–585. DOI: 10.1037/0022-3514.60.4.570 PMID: 2037968

Snyder, H. (2019). Literature review as a research methodology: An overview and guidelines. *Journal of Business Research*, *104*, 333–339. DOI: 10.1016/j.jbusres.2019.07.039

Song, Y., Weisberg, L. R., Zhang, S., Tian, X., Boyer, K. E., & Israel, M. (2024). A framework for inclusive AI learning design for diverse learners. *Computers and Education: Artificial Intelligence*, *6*, 100212. DOI: 10.1016/j.caeai.2024.100212

Spytska, L. (2025). The use of artificial intelligence in psychotherapy: Development of intelligent therapeutic systems. *BMC Psychology*, *13*(1), 175. DOI: 10.1186/s40359-025-02491-9 PMID: 40022267

Stanton, J. D., Sebesta, A. J., & Dunlosky, J. (2021). Fostering metacognition to support student learning and performance. *CBE Life Sciences Education*, *20*(2), fe3. DOI: 10.1187/cbe.20-12-0289 PMID: 33797282

Stein, J. P., Liebold, B., & Ohler, P. (2019). Stay back, clever thing! Linking situational control and human uniqueness concerns to the aversion against autonomous technology. *Computers in Human Behavior*, *95*, 73–82. DOI: 10.1016/j.chb.2019.01.021

Storrie, K., Ahern, K., & Tuckett, A. (2011). A systematic review: Students with mental health problems—a growing problem. *International Journal of Nursing Practice*, *16*(1), 1–6. DOI: 10.1111/j.1440-172X.2009.01813.x PMID: 20158541

Straw, I., & Callison-Burch, C. (2020). Artificial Intelligence in mental health and the biases of language based models. *PLoS One*, *15*(12), e0240376. Advance online publication. DOI: 10.1371/journal.pone.0240376 PMID: 33332380

Strielkowski, W., Grebennikova, V., Lisovskiy, A., Rakhimova, G., & Vasileva, T. (2025). AI-driven adaptive learning for sustainable educational transformation. *Sustainable Development (Bradford)*, *33*(2), 1921–1947. DOI: 10.1002/sd.3221

Sweller, J. (1988). Cognitive load during problem solving: Effects on learning. *Cognitive Science*, *12*(2), 257–285. DOI: 10.1207/s15516709cog1202_4

Sweller, J. (2011). Cognitive load theory. In Mestre, J. P., & Ross, B. H. (Eds.), *Psychology of Learning and Motivation, 55, 37-76*. Academic Press., DOI: 10.1016/B978-0-12-387691-1.00002-8

Swist, T., & Gulson, K. N. (2023). Instituting socio-technical education futures: Encounters with/through technical democracy, data justice, and imaginaries. *Learning, Media and Technology*, *48*(2), 181–186. DOI: 10.1080/17439884.2023.2205225

Swist, T., Humphry, J., & Gulson, K. N. (2023). Pedagogic encounters with algorithmic system controversies: A toolkit for democratising technology. *Learning, Media and Technology*, *48*(2), 226–239. DOI: 10.1080/17439884.2023.2185255

Tamilmani, K., Rana, N. P., Prakasam, N., & Dwivedi, Y. K. (2019). The battle of Brain vs. Heart: A literature review and meta-analysis of "hedonic motivation" use in UTAUT2. *International Journal of Information Management*, *46*, 222–235. DOI: 10.1016/j.ijinfomgt.2019.01.008

Tang, K. H. D. (2024). Implications of Artificial Intelligence for Teaching and Learning. *Acta Pedagogia Asiana*, *3*(2), 65–79. DOI: 10.53623/apga.v3i2.404

Tang, K. S., & Putra, G. B. S. (2025). Generative AI as a Dialogic Partner: Enhancing Multiple Perspectives, Reasoning, and Argumentation in Science Education with Customized Chatbots. *Journal of Science Education and Technology*, 1–13. DOI: 10.1007/s10956-025-10240-1

Tan, X., Cheng, G., & Ling, M. H. (2025). Artificial intelligence in teaching and teacher professional development: A systematic review. *Computers and Education: Artificial Intelligence*, *8*, 100355. DOI: 10.1016/j.caeai.2024.100355

Tarafdar, M., Cooper, C. L., & Stich, J. F. (2019). The technostress trifecta - techno eustress, techno distress and design: Theoretical directions and an agenda for research. *Information Systems Journal, 29*(1), 6–42. DOI: 10.1111/isj.12169

Taufikin, M. S. I., Parminder, & Others. (2024). The impact of AI on teacher roles and pedagogy in the 21st-century classroom. In 2024 International Conference on Knowledge Engineering and Communication Systems (ICKECS). DOI: 10.1109/ICKECS61492.2024.10617236

Temel, Y., & Coşkun, B. (2024). A review on artificial intelligence applications in education in some countries and Türkiye. *International Technology and Education Journal, 8*(1), 9–23.

Tian, Z., & Yi, D. (2024). Application of artificial intelligence based on sensor networks in student mental health support system and crisis prediction. *Measurement. Sensors, 32*, 101056. Advance online publication. DOI: 10.1016/j.measen.2024.101056

Tiger, L. (1979). *Optimism: The biology of hope*. Simon & Schuster.

Tiwari, R. (2023). The Integration of AI and Machine Learning in Education and its Potential to Personalize and Improve Student Learning Experiences. [IJSREM]. *International Journal of Scientific Research in Engineering and Management, 7*(2), 1–11. DOI: 10.55041/IJSREM17645

Tosunoğlu, E., Yılmaz, R., Özeren, E., & Sağlam, Z. (2021). Machine Learning in Education: A Study on Current Trends in Researchs. *Journal of Ahmet Kelesoglu Education Faculty, 3*(2), 178–199.

Trezise, K., Ryan, T., de Barba, P., & Kennedy, G. (2019). Detecting contract cheating using learning analytics. *Journal of Learning Analytics, 6*(3), 90–104. DOI: 10.18608/jla.2019.63.11

Tsai, S. C., Chen, C. H., Shiao, Y. T., Ciou, J. S., & Wu, T. N. (2020). Precision education with statistical learning and deep learning: A case study in Taiwan. *International Journal of Educational Technology in Higher Education, 17*(1), 1–13. DOI: 10.1186/s41239-020-00186-2

Tschannen-Moran, M., & Hoy, A. W. (2001). Teacher efficacy: Capturing an elusive construct. *Teaching and Teacher Education, 17*(7), 783–805. DOI: 10.1016/S0742-051X(01)00036-1

Turkish Official Gazette. (2021, August 20). *Presidential circular numbered 2021/18* (No. 31574). https://www.resmigazete.gov.tr (Accessed August 12, 2025)

Tyson, M. M., & Sauers, N. J. (2021). School leaders' adoption and implementation of artificial intelligence. *Journal of Educational Administration*, *59*(3), 271–285. DOI: 10.1108/JEA-10-2020-0221

UNESCO. (2019). Beijing Consensus on Artificial Intelligence and Education. United Nations Educational, Scientific and Cultural Organization. https://unesdoc.unesco.org/ark:/48223/pf0000368303

UNESCO. (2022). Recomendação sobre a ética da inteligência artificial. Organização das Nações Unidas para a Educação, a Ciência e a Cultura. https://unesdoc.unesco.org/ark:/48223/pf0000380455

UNESCO. (2023). La inteligencia artificial: ¿Necesitamos una nueva educación? UNESCO Publishing. https://unesdoc.unesco.org/ark:/48223/pf0000386262

UNESCO. (2024). Guia para a IA generativa na educação e na pesquisa. https://unesdoc.unesco.org/ark:/48223/pf0000390241

UNESCO. (2025). *AI and the future of education: Disruptions, dilemmas and directions – AI pedagogies, assessment and emerging educational futures*. UNESCO Publishing.

UNESCO. (2025a). *Digital learning Week 2025*. Retrieved August 29, 2025, from https://www.unesco.org/en/weeks/digital-learning?hub=32618

UNESCO. (2025b). *What you need to know about UNESCO's new AI competency frameworks for students and teachers*. Retrieved August 29, 2025, from https://www.unesco.org/en/articles/what-you-need-know-about-unescos-new-ai-competency-frameworks-students-and-teachers?hub=32618

Urmeneta, A., & Romero, M. (2024). Creative Application of Artificial Intelligence in Education. In Urmeneta, A., & Romero, M. (Eds.), *Creative applications of artificial intelligence in education* (pp. 3–16). Palgrave Macmillan. DOI: 10.1007/978-3-031-55272-4_1

Van Quaquebeke, N., & Gerpott, F. H. (2023). The now, new, and next of digital leadership: How artificial intelligence (AI) will take over and change leadership as we know it. *Journal of Leadership & Organizational Studies*, *30*(2), 265–275. DOI: 10.1177/15480518231181731

Venkatesh, V., Morris, M. G., Davis, G. B., & Davis, F. D. (2003). User Acceptance of Information Technology: Toward a Unified View. *Management Information Systems Quarterly*, *27*(3), 425–478. DOI: 10.2307/30036540

Vera, M., Salanova, M., & Lorente, L. (2012). The predicting role of self-efficacyin the Job Demands-Resources Model: A longitudinal study. *Estudios de Psicología, 33*(2), 167–178. DOI: 10.1174/021093912800676439

Veresov, N., & Veraksa, N. (2024). Introducing cultural-historical genetic-analytical model for studying child's play: The matryoshka principle – situations within situations covered by situations. *Early Years Journal of International Research and Development, 45*(3–4), 413–425. DOI: 10.1080/09575146.2024.2365180

Viberg, O., Kizilcec, R. F., Wise, A. F., Jivet, I., & Nixon, N. (2024). Advancing equity and inclusion in educational practices with AI-powered educational decision support systems. [Editorial]. *British Journal of Educational Technology, 55*(5), 1974–1981. DOI: 10.1111/bjet.13507

Vlieghe, J., & Zamojski, P. (2019). *Towards an Ontology of Teaching: Thing-centred Pedagogy, Affirmation and Love for the World.* Springer. DOI: 10.1007/978-3-030-16003-6

Voltan Acar, N. (2020). *Yeniden terapötik iletişim kişiler arası ilişkiler (tamamı bizim toplumdan örnekler).* Nobel.

Vovk, O., Zenya, L., Brovarska, I., & Bohdan Khmelnitsky. (2022). Neuropedagogy: A Concept of Brain Compatible Teaching a Foreign Language. Cherkasy University Bulletin: Pedagogical Sciences, 2, 64–73. DOI: 10.31651/2524-2660-2022-2-64-73

Vroom, V. H. (1964). *Work and motivation.* John Willey & Sons.

Walter, Y. (2024). Embracing the future of Artificial Intelligence in the classroom: The relevance of AI literacy, prompt engineering, and critical thinking in modern education. *International Journal of Educational Technology in Higher Education, 21*(1), 15. DOI: 10.1186/s41239-024-00448-3

Wang, B., Rau, P.-L. P., & Yuan, T. (2023). Measuring user competence in artificial intelligence: Validity and reliability of artificial intelligence literacy scale. *Behaviour & Information Technology, 42*(9), 1324–1337. DOI: 10.1080/0144929X.2022.2072768

Wang, F., Zhou, X., Li, K., Cheung, A. C. K., & Tian, M. (2025). The effects of artificial intelligence-based interactive scaffolding on secondary students' speaking performance, goal setting, self-evaluation, and motivation in informal digital learning of English. *Interactive Learning Environments, 33*(7), 4633–4652. DOI: 10.1080/10494820.2025.2470319

Wang, R., & Liu, T. (2019). Human-AI collaboration in engineering management decision-making: A mixed-methods study. *Engineering Management Journal, 31*(4), 278–291.

Wang, S., Sun, Z., & Chen, Y. (2023). Effects of higher education institutes' artificial intelligence capability on students' self-efficacy, creativity and learning performance. *Education and Information Technologies*, *28*(5), 4919–4939. DOI: 10.1007/s10639-022-11338-4 PMID: 36373050

Wang, X., Tan, S. C., & Li, L. (2020). Measuring university students' technostress in technology-enhanced learning: Scale development and validation. *Australasian Journal of Educational Technology*, *36*(4), 96–112. DOI: 10.14742/ajet.5329

Wang, Y. (2021). An improved machine learning and artificial intelligence algorithm for classroom management of English distance education. *Journal of Intelligent & Fuzzy Systems*, *40*(2), 3477–3488. DOI: 10.3233/JIFS-189385

Wang, Y. (2021). Artificial intelligence in educational leadership: A symbiotic role of human–artificial intelligence decision-making. *Journal of Educational Administration*, *59*(3), 256–270. DOI: 10.1108/JEA-10-2020-0216

Wang, Y. (2023). Addressing data biases in AI: Challenges and solutions for educational leaders. *Journal of AI and Society*, *38*(1), 100–115.

Wang, Y., & Liu, Y. (2021). The development of internalizing and externalizing problems in primary school: Contributions of executive function and social competence. *Child Development*, *92*(3), 889–903. DOI: 10.1111/cdev.13462 PMID: 32857446

Watters, A. (2023). *Teaching machines: The history of personalized learning*. MIT Press.

Weick, K. E. (1990). Technology as equivoque: Sensemaking in new technologies. In Goodman, P. S., & Sproull, L. S. (Eds.), *Technology and organizations* (pp. 1–44). Jossey-Bass.

Weick, K. E. (1995). *Sensemaking in organizations*. Sage Publications.

Weick, K. E., Sutcliffe, K. M., & Obstfeld, D. (2005). Organizing and the process of sensemaking. *Organization Science*, *16*(4), 409–421. DOI: 10.1287/orsc.1050.0133

Weizenbaum, J. (1966). ELIZA—A computer program for the study of natural language communication between man and machine. *Communications of the ACM*, *9*(1), 36–45. DOI: 10.1145/365153.365168

Whitby, B. (2008). *Artificial Intelligence: A Beginner's Guide*. Oneworld.

Whitelock, D., Goshtasbpour, F., Pitt, B., Ferguson, R., & Cross, S. (2024). Capacity building for digital education. *Open Learning*, *39*(2), 105–111. DOI: 10.1080/02680513.2024.2317894

WHO. (2025). *Anxiety disorders.* From https://www.who.int/news-room/factsheets/detail/anxiety-disorders

Wieczorek, M. (2025). Why AI will not democratize education: A critical pragmatist perspective. *Philosophy & Technology*, *38*(2), 53. DOI: 10.1007/s13347-025-00883-8

Wiesböck, F., & Hess, T. (2020). Digital innovations: Embedding in organizations. *Electronic Markets*, *30*(1), 75–86. DOI: 10.1007/s12525-019-00364-9

Williamson, B., & Hogan, A. (2020). Commercialisation and privatisation in/of education in the context of Covid-19.

Williamson, B. (2024). The social life of AI in education. *International Journal of Artificial Intelligence in Education*, *34*(1), 97–104. DOI: 10.1007/s40593-023-00342-5

Woodcock, S., Sharma, U., Subban, P., & Hitches, E. (2022). Teacher self-efficacy and inclusive education practices: Rethinking teachers' engagement with inclusive practices. *Teaching and Teacher Education*, *117*, 103802. DOI: 10.1016/j.tate.2022.103802

World Economic Forum. (2024). Shaping the Future of Learning: The Role of AI in Education 4.0. World Economic Forum. https://www.weforum.org/publications/shaping-the-future-of-learning-the-role-of-ai-in-education-4-0/

Xiao, Y., & Watson, M. (2019). Guidance on Conducting a Systematic Literature Review. *Journal of Planning Education and Research*, *39*(1), 93–112. DOI: 10.1177/0739456X17723971

Xia, Q., Weng, X., Ouyang, F., Lin, T. J., & Chiu, T. K. (2024). A scoping review on how generative artificial intelligence transforms assessment in higher education. *International Journal of Educational Technology in Higher Education*, *21*(1), 40. DOI: 10.1186/s41239-024-00468-z

Xu, J., & Li, J. (2024). Effects of AI affordances on student engagement in EFL classrooms: A structural equation modelling and latent profile analysis. *European Journal of Education*, *59*(4), e12808. DOI: 10.1111/ejed.12808

Yang, H., Chen, L., Wang, Z., Du, J., Zhang, C., & Cai, Y. (2025). Transformational leadership and sensemaking in sustainable strategic change aligned with the SDGs: A case study of a higher education institution pursuing university status. *Journal of Lifestyle and SDGs Review*, *5*(5), e6123. DOI: 10.47172/2965-730X.SDGsReview.v5.n05.pe06123

Yang, S., & Bai, H. (2020). The integration design of artificial intelligence and normal students' education. [). IOP Publishing.]. *Journal of Physics: Conference Series, 1453*(1), 012090. DOI: 10.1088/1742-6596/1453/1/012090

Yeşilyaprak, B. (2024). *Eğitim psikolojisi gelişim-öğrenme-öğretim*. Pegem Akademi.

Zawacki-Richter, O., Marín, V. I., Bond, M., & Gouverneur, F. (2019). Systematic review of research on artificial intelligence applications in higher education–where are the educators? *International Journal of Educational Technology in Higher Education, 16*(1), 1–27. DOI: 10.1186/s41239-019-0171-0

Zhai, C., Wibowo, S., & Li, L. D. (2024). The effects of over-reliance on AI dialogue systems on students' cognitive abilities: A systematic review. *Smart Learning Environments, 11*(1), 28. DOI: 10.1186/s40561-024-00316-7

Zhai, X., Haudek, K. C., Shi, L., Nehm, R. H., & Urban-Lurain, M. (2020). From substitution to redefinition: A framework of machine learning-based science assessment. *Journal of Research in Science Teaching, 57*(9), 1430–1459. DOI: 10.1002/tea.21658

Zhang, K., & Deng, P. (2022). Exploring the Technology and Problems of Artificial Intelligence Education Applications. 2022 4th International Conference on Computer Science and Technologies in Education (CSTE), 265–268. DOI: 10.1109/CSTE55932.2022.00056

Zhang, B., & Dafoe, A. (2019). *Artificial intelligence: American attitudes and trends*. University of Oxford. Available at *SSRN* 3312874.

Zhong, W., Luo, J., & Zhang, H. (2024). The therapeutic effectiveness of artificial intelligence-based chatbots in alleviation of depressive and anxiety symptoms in short-course treatments: A systematic review and meta-analysis. *Journal of Affective Disorders, 356*, 459–469. DOI: 10.1016/j.jad.2024.04.057 PMID: 38631422

Zohuri, B. (2024). Revolutionizing education: The dynamic synergy of personalized learning and artificial intelligence. International Journal of Advanced Engineering and Management Research.

About the Contributors

Bahaddin Demirdiş is an Assistant Professor in the Department of Educational Sciences at Çankırı Karatekin University, Türkiye. He holds a PhD in Psychology and Human Development and an MA in Education (Psychology) from University College London's Institute of Education. His research interests include educational psychology, inclusive education, digital literacy, and teacher professional development. Dr. Demirdiş has previously held academic roles at Artvin Çoruh University and University College London. He has published internationally on topics such as inclusive mindsets, ICT in education, and the psychosocial effects of digital platforms.

***

Muhammed Akat is an Assistant Professor in the Department of Psychological Counseling and Guidance at Karamanoglu Mehmetbey University, Türkiye. His research interests include technology addictions such as online gambling addiction, social media addiction, smartphone addiction, internet trolling, and fear of missing out. His research interests also include the treatment of behavioral addictions with cognitive behavioral therapy.

Ramazan Atasoy received his MA in Girne American University and Ph.D. in educational sciences from Gazi University. He currently works as an associate professor at Harran University. His research interests include leadership, quality of education, education policy, PIAAC adult competency, literacy skills, numeracy skills and problem solving skills in technology rich environments.

Alberto Carpio has a PhD in Health Sciences from Universidad Rey Juan Carlos (URJC), and currently works there as an Assistant Professor in the Department of Psychology. His doctoral research is focused on the use of non-invasive neuromodulation techniques, specifically transcranial static magnetic stimulation (tSMS), to investigate cognitive and motor inhibition processes. His scientific interests include the application of Deep Learning techniques and predictive models based on convolutional neural networks for the analysis of neuroscientific data. He is also deeply interested in the use of Artificial Intelligence in higher education, particularly as a tool to transform assessment processes, shifting from traditional memory-based tasks toward approaches that emphasize explanation, reasoning, and deep understanding as genuine evidence of learning.

Ömür Çoban is an associate professor in the Department of Educational Administration, Faculty of Education in Karamanoglu Mehmetbey University, Karaman, Türkiye. His research interests include leadership, organisational change management, organisational behaviour, and teacher pro- fessional learning.

Bora Demir graduated from English Language Teaching department of Çanakkale Onsekiz Mart University and got his MA degree from the same university. He earned his PhD from Yeditepe University on English Language Teacher Education. He has become an associate professor in 2023. He is currently a member of the School of Foreign Languages in Çanakkale Onsekiz Mart University. He has participated and presented his research at various reputable international conferences, and published articles in national and international journals/books with research interests in various aspects of language teaching and language teacher education. He is the founder and the Editor-in-Chief of the academic journal "Innovational Research in ELT" since 2019.He also edits the journal of "ELT-Turkey" which is a publication of the AELTE.More recently, he has edited three reference books to be used in ELT departments namely, "Interculturality in English Language Learning and Teaching", "Discourse Analysis and Language Teaching" and "Language Teaching Approaches and Methods". His research interests include technology assisted language teaching, cognitive aspects of language learning, and psychological aspect of language learning and teaching. Dr. Demir is also a member of the Association of English Language Teacher Educators (AELTE).

Abdullah Yasin Gunduz is an Associate Professor in the Department of Computer Technologies at Usak University, Turkiye. His research focuses on educational technology, artificial intelligence in education, flipped learning, gamification and e-learning. He has participated in several national and international research projects. His academic contributions aim to bridge the gap between innovative technologies and effective pedagogical practices.

Ana Cláudia Loureiro is a researcher at UID-FCT no. 4372, Distance Education and eLearning Laboratory (LE@D) - Universidade Aberta (Portugal) (https://lead.uab.pt/). She has a PhD in Educational Sciences and has a Post-

Doctorate in Educational Technology at the Centre for Research in Basic Education of the Polytechnic Institute of Bragança (CIEB), Portugal, with research in the area of teacher digital competences, completed in 2021. She has a specialisation in Educational Technologies from the Pontifical Catholic University of São Paulo, Brazil, and a degree in Pedagogy. Visiting Assistant Professor at the School of Education of the Polytechnic Institute of Viseu and Accredited Trainer by the Scientific-Pedagogical Council for Continuing Education in the area of B115 Technology and Educational Communication.

Kadir Lüta is a PhD student at Çanakkale Onsekiz Mart University, in the ELT department, focusing on adult EFL education. He is currently working as a research assistant at English language and literature department at a state university in Turkey.

Manuel Meirinhos has a Bachelor's degree in Biology and Geology Teaching, Master's degree in Educational Technology, and Ph.D. in Child Studies, Information, and Communication Technologies from the University of Minho. Coordinator Professor in the Areas of Educational Sciences and Multimedia Communication at the School of Education of the Polytechnic Institute of Bragança.

Ramazan Özkul is an assistant professor at the Department of Educational Management, Faculty of Education, Harran University, Türkiye. His research focuses on the relationships between educational leadership, school organisational elements, and teacher emotions.

Alper Uslukaya serves as an Assistant Professor in the Department of Educational Administration at the Faculty of Humanities and Social Sciences, Çankırı Karatekin University, Turkey. His areas of interest encompass educational psychology, organizational behavior, management processes, leadership, and effective schools. His research portfolio comprises studies examining both positive and negative organizational behavior.

Mehmet Tufan Yalçın is an associate professor in the Department of Educational Administration, Faculty of Humanities and Social Sciences in Çankırı Karatekin University, Çankırı, Türkiye. His research interests include school leadership, student achievement, school improvement, and teacher behaviours and attitudes.

Index

Symbols

A

B

C

D

E

F

H

T

U

W

Z

www.ingramcontent.com/pod-product-compliance
Lightning Source LLC
LaVergne TN
LVHW062220200926
848484LV00006B/1440